When the Rain Comes

When the Rain Comes

Comfort for Troubled Hearts

by
Frank R. Shivers

LIGHTNING SOURCE
1246 Heil Quaker Blvd.
La Vergne, TN

Unless otherwise noted, Scripture quotations are from
The Holy Bible *King James Version*

Library of Congress Cataloging-in-Publication Data

Shivers, Frank R., 1949-
When the Rain Comes / Frank Shivers
ISBN 978-1-878127-44-0

Library of Congress Control Number:
2020910121

Cover design by
Tim King

For Information:
Frank Shivers Evangelistic Association
P. O. Box 9991
Columbia, South Carolina 29290
www.frankshivers.com

This book is compassionately given to minister the riches of Christ's grace, peace, comfort, and hope.

To

_____

By

_____

Date

_____

"Many a sufferer, in the lone watches of the night, has felt God's presence. Oh, the comfort and the strength to know that He is our Friend and our Shepherd and our Savior! He is our fellow pilgrim, and He is with us in strength forever."[1] ~ W. A. Criswell

To

Timothy Faulk

A reliable, supportive and trusted friend (rain or shine) that I first met while a student-pastor at South Flomaton Baptist Church, Century, Florida while a student at New Orleans Baptist Theological Seminary (1972)

Begone, unbelief; my Savior is near
And for my relief will surely appear.
By prayer let me wrestle and He will perform;
With Christ in the vessel I smile at the storm.[2]
John Newton (1725–1807)

How firm a foundation, you saints of the Lord,
Is laid for your faith in His excellent Word!
What more can He say than to you He has said,
To you who for refuge to Jesus have fled?

"Fear not; I am with you. Oh, be not dismayed,
For I am your God and will still give you aid.
I'll strengthen you, help you, and cause you to stand,
Upheld by My righteous, omnipotent hand.

"When through the deep waters I call you to go,
The rivers of sorrow shall not overflow;
For I will be with you, your troubles to bless
And sanctify to you your deepest distress.

"When through fiery trials your pathway shall lie,
My grace, all-sufficient, shall be your supply.
The flame shall not hurt you; I only design
Your dross to consume and your gold to refine.

"E'en down to old age all my people shall prove
My sovereign, eternal, unchangeable love;
And when hoary hairs shall their temples adorn,
Like lambs they shall still in my bosom be borne.

"The soul that on Jesus has leaned for repose
I will not, I will not desert to his foes.
That soul, though all Hell should endeavor to shake,
I'll never, no never, no never forsake." ~ attributed to George Keith (1787)

Contents

Preface

"A saved soul," writes J. C. Ryle, "has many sorrows. He has a body like other men—weak and frail. He has a heart like other men—and often a more sensitive one too. He has trials and losses to bear like others—and often more. He has his share of bereavements, deaths, disappointments, crosses. He has the world to oppose, a place in life to fill blamelessly, unconverted relatives to bear with patiently, persecutions to endure, and a death to die. And who is sufficient for these things? What shall enable a believer to bear all this? Nothing but 'the consolation there is in Christ' (Philippians 2:1)."[3] Apart from Christ there is no comfort or hope in the troubles of life or the face of death. Billy Graham comments, "Humanity wants comfort in its sorrow, light in its darkness, peace in its turmoil, rest in its weariness, and healing in its sickness and diseases. The Gospel gives all of this to us."[4]

In this writing, the precious and powerful "consolation in Christ" (Philippians 2:1) is provided (Isaiah 61:1 and Psalm 147:3) to strengthen and sustain the saint *When the Rain Comes* through bereavement, trouble, sickness and suffering. Additionally, uplifting and calming meditations are included for saints preparing for their heavenly transition.

Now in my seventies, the awareness, acknowledgement and anticipation of my exodus to Heaven grows ever brighter. Death, the conveyance by which I will make that trip, perhaps already has saddled its horse and is en route. So the meditations on dying are as much for me as they are for anyone else.

Concisely put, *When the Rain Comes* is *a biblical help manual for the troubles of life and the confrontation with death.* Earnest effort was made to weave throughout the book coping, soothing, encouraging and healing medicine (hymns, poems, Bible promises, inspirational biblical insights and ministering quotes from great saints) for every discomfort and affliction of the soul.

It's not if but when the rain will fall upon our life. So if it's not raining presently, keep this book handy like an umbrella for when it does fall. For the reader now in the rain, my sincerest prayer is that the Holy Spirit will use the meditations (healing salve) in this volume to lessen or altogether alleviate the pain and hardship. "He healeth the broken in heart, and bindeth up their wounds" (Psalm 147:3). C. H. Spurgeon, the great London pastor of the nineteenth century, said, "The road of sorrow is the road to Heaven, but there are wells of refreshing water all along the route."[5] Within the coming pages are a myriad of wells filled with "waters" of healing, hope and comfort awaiting the bucket of the hurting and troubled to bountifully fill. 'Come, everyone who is thirsty'; here is *healing* water! (Isaiah 55:1 GNB).

Will your anchor hold in the storms of life,
When the clouds unfold their wings of strife?
When the strong tides lift and the cables strain,
Will your anchor drift or firm remain?

We have an anchor that keeps the soul
Steadfast and sure while the billows roll,
Fastened to the Rock which cannot move,
Grounded firm and deep in the Savior's love.

It is safely moored; 'twill the storm withstand,
For 'tis well secured by the Savior's hand;
And the cables passed from His heart to mine
Can defy the blast, through strength divine.

It will firmly hold in the straits of fear,
When the breakers have told the reef is near;
Though the tempest rave and the wild winds blow,
Not an angry wave shall our bark o'erflow.

It will surely hold in the floods of death,
When the waters cold chill our latest breath;
On the rising tide it can never fail,
While our hopes abide within the veil. ~ Priscilla Jane Owens (1829–1907)

"Blessed be the God and Father of our Lord Jesus Christ, the Father of mercies and God of all comfort, *who comforts us in all our affliction*, so that we may be able to comfort those who are in any affliction, with the comfort with which we ourselves are comforted by God. For as we share abundantly in Christ's sufferings, so through Christ *we share abundantly in comfort too*" (2 Corinthians 1:3–5 ESV).

How to Use This Book

Use *When the Rain Comes* to bolster faith, hope, peace, and comfort to your soul and that of others in times of sickness, suffering and sorrow. Its "medicine" is just what the doctor ordered. Use it in the home, church, assisted living facility, hospital, and with hospice. Water it with prayers that it will flourish to the consolation and uplifting of its recipient(s) to the glory of God.

1
Cure for the Troubled Heart

Among the biblical passages it would be well to memorize or at least to become thoroughly familiar with is John 14:1–6, for it provides an antidote to the troubled heart. It is a medicine bottle to be kept on the nightstand for ready use in difficult and challenging days. Without exception, all will need it sooner or later.

The world offers various "cures" for the feeling of hopelessness, sorrow, despair, suffering, and fear.

There is the cure of **suicide.** In Job's hour of horrendous sorrow and pain—loss of property, children, health, and friends—his wife encouraged him to "curse God, and die."[6] But suicide is not the answer to the troubled heart. The path which you now walk, others have trod victoriously by looking beyond the moment to the future, holding onto the promise of God that He will neither forsake nor fail them (Hebrews 13:5).

A second cure the world provides the troubled heart is that of **denial.**[7] It advocates that the answer to a broken or anxious heart is denying its existence; refuse to acknowledge or accept the troublesomeness. Pretending that the facts are untrue simply cannot heal the afflicted heart. Pretend as you may, the pain remains.

Intoxication with pleasure or pain killers or alcohol is another proposal the world gives to resolve inner turmoil and restlessness of soul. The absorption of mind-altering substances and the full gamut of unrestricted pleasure simply dulls the heartache temporally; it fails to grant healing.

Yet the world gives another answer to the troubled heart—**ignore** it. Somehow it will miraculously disappear. But how can ignoring the present sorrow, suffering, sickness and/or impending death dismiss its solemn reality and thus grant relief?

But what does Jesus say is the *only cure* for the troubled heart. He says, "Let not your heart be troubled: ye believe in God, believe also in me. In my Father's house are many mansions: if it were not so, I would have told you. I go to prepare a place for you. And if I go and prepare a place for you, I will come again, and receive you unto myself; that where I am, there ye may be also" (John 14:1–3). In Luke 4:18 He says, "He [God] hath sent me to heal the brokenhearted." In Matthew 11:28 He says, "Come unto me, all ye that labor and are heavy laden, and I will give you rest." The psalmist instructs, "Cast thy burden upon the LORD, and he shall sustain thee" (Psalm 55:22).

In Christ an anchor is found that holds despite the fierceness of the storm, an antidote (certainty of His abiding presence and Heaven that gives a peace that passes all understanding) that relieves the heavily burdened heart vexed and confused by its circumstances, and true and tried promises that will sustain. They are each awesome wind and sails to the troubled heart.

C. H. Spurgeon says, "You are his [God's] peculiar care, His regal treasure which He guards as the apple of His eye, His vineyard over which He watches day and night. 'The very hairs of your head are all numbered.'…'I will never leave thee, nor forsake thee.' God says that as much to you as to any saint of old. 'Fear not,…I am thy shield, and thy exceeding great reward.' We lose much consolation by the habit of reading His promises for the whole church instead of taking them directly home to ourselves. Believer, grasp the divine word with a personal, appropriating faith. Think that you hear Jesus say, 'I have prayed for thee, that thy faith fail not.' Think you see Him walking on the waters of thy trouble, for He is there, and He is saying, 'Fear not,' 'it is I; be not afraid.' Oh, those sweet words of Christ! May the Holy Ghost *make you feel them as spoken to you*; forget others for a while—accept the voice of Jesus as addressed to you and say, 'Jesus whispers consolation; I cannot refuse it; I will sit under His shadow with great delight.'"[8]

A former world chess champion visited a famous art gallery to view a picture of a chess match. The artist depicted a young man seated despairingly at a chessboard in a match against the Devil whose face glowed with a look of malicious triumph. The painting was simply entitled "Checkmated." The former champion looked intently upon the picture studying the position of the chess pieces. Suddenly with a loud voice that rung through the art gallery he said, "Bring me a chessboard. I can save him yet." The mastermind chess champion had discovered the way out of the Devil's supposed checkmate.

It may appear the Devil has you checkmated with no way out of the uncertainty, fear, pain, and despair now experienced. But Jesus shouts to the heart, "Let not your heart be troubled: ye believe in God, believe also in me." With Jesus, there's a tolerable solution for every intolerable problem faced. He promises to walk through the "valley of darkness" hand in hand with you; to still the boisterous winds and waves beating upon the vessel of your life, saying, "Peace, be still." Don't panic. Wait on Him. Trust in Him. Cling to Him. He cannot and will not abandon you.

Soon the raging sea will become as a sheet of glass and tranquility will reign supreme. Soon you shall sit in His presence wardrobed with a new body, in Heaven's new Home, to enjoy eternal happiness and health with family and friends. Stay the mind upon these eternal realities and be comforted and strengthened.

Samuel Rutherford said, "The hope of Heaven under troubles is like the wind and sails to the soul."[9] The psalmist says, "In his favor is life: weeping may endure for a night, but joy cometh in the morning" (Psalm 30:5).

Sometimes this world brings troubles
     That I find so hard to bear;
I know I could not make it
     Without Jesus being there.
It's so encouraging to know,
     However deep we're in despair
That Jesus never fails.

Jesus never fails;
Jesus never fails;
Jesus never fails.
You might as well get thee behind me Satan;
You cannot prevail,
Because Jesus never fails. ~ Arthur A. Luther (1927)

2

Confidence at the End of the Road

Billy Graham often declared, "For the Christian, the grave is not the end; nor is death a calamity, for he has a glorious hope—the hope of Heaven."[10] That same hope is expressed by Paul: "Therefore, we are always confident" (2 Corinthians 5:6). Paul confidently, therefore courageously and fearlessly, viewed death and that which lies beyond it. The *confidence* was not based on theories or opinions of man but the inerrant Word of God that teaches:

(1. The acquisition of a glorified body ("house") at death for the believer (2 Corinthians 5:1)

(2. That the new house, unlike the present one of flesh and blood, is eternal, permanent (2 Corinthians 5:1b)

(3. The guarantee of the new house and that mortality will be swallowed up by immortality; a transformation awaits at death (2 Corinthians 5:3–4)

(4. The abiding presence and work of the Holy Spirit—God's pledge (down payment) insuring "the final installment" is coming, that all God's promises regarding future life will be fulfilled (2 Corinthians 5:5; 2 Corinthians 1:22)

(5. That the Holy Spirit places in man's heart a groaning to see God and be in Heaven; not only does the Holy Spirit confirm salvation in the inner heart (Romans 8:16) but also the reality of Heaven (2 Corinthians 5:2)

(6. The soul's immediate presence with the Lord at death—no soul sleep in the grave awaiting the rapture of the church (2 Corinthians 5:8); Jesus told the penitent thief upon the cross, "To day shalt thou be with me in paradise" (Luke 23:43)

When the Rain Comes

(7. The promise of a Heavenly Home, "an house not made with hands, eternal in the heavens" (2 Corinthians 5:1b; John 14:1–3)

Further, Paul states that we find grounds for unshakable faith in the believer's transformation from slaves to sin to sons of God (Galatians 4:7). Alan Redpath says, "He (Paul) knew God so intimately, not as a stranger but as a Father, because he believed in Christ. He was a member of God's great family, and he knew that the Father one day would welcome him home. You see, this man was sure, and he had grounds for his confidence because Father, Son and Holy Spirit witnessed to him of the absolute assurance that one day he would be with Jesus."[11]

With these assurances for the future life, Paul said, "For in this we groan, earnestly desiring to be clothed upon with our house which is from heaven" (2 Corinthians 5:2). The present "house" is loaded with hardships (horrendous and devastating diseases, disabilities, despair) caused by the curse of sin; therefore, we groan earnestly for the day when it will be supernaturally replaced.

Paul's confidence in eternal realities is underscored by its reiteration in 2 Corinthians 5:8. Warren Wiersbe says, "Because he had this kind of confidence, Paul was not afraid of suffering and trials, or even of dangers. He walked by faith and not by sight. He looked at the eternal unseen, not the temporal seen (2 Corinthians 4:18). Heaven was not simply a destination for Paul; it was a motivation."[12] Another writer comments, "It filled him with fortitude to endure, with boldness and strength to do."[13] George Wright said, "Confidence in eternal things gives courage in earthly things."[14] Though the outward man is "perishing" or wasting away (2 Corinthians 4:16), the assuring confidence of eternal life in Heaven with God (based upon the eternal verities of God and His Holy Word, not "blind faith") instills boldness, inspiration and motivation. The believer can without doubt say, "I know whom I have believed, and am persuaded that he is able to keep that which I have committed unto him against that day" (2 Timothy 1:12).

I know not what of good or ill
    May be reserved for me,
Of weary ways or golden days
    Before his face I see.

I know not when my Lord may come,
    At night or noonday fair,
Nor if I'll walk the vale with him
    Or meet him in the air.

But "I know whom I have believed,
    And am persuaded that he is able
To keep that which I've committed
    Unto him against that day." ~ D. W. Whittle (1883)

3

The Secret of Contentment in Difficult Times

"For I have learned, in whatsoever state I am, therewith to be content" (Philippians 4:11).

Contentment's implication. It says that it is possible to attain a state of mind of satisfaction despite bad circumstances of life, insufficient funds or affliction of body. Often the tranquility (rest, peace, comfort) of contentment is misinterpreted by observers as apathy (indifference) or lunacy toward life's hardships and troubles on the part of the one who has it. It's a peace that surpasses all their understanding (Philippians 4:7).

Contentment's foundation. Contentment with "godliness" is great gain (1 Timothy 6:6). True contentment is founded upon a personal intimate love relationship with Jesus Christ. To seek it elsewhere is to seek in vain.

Contentment's acquisition. Contentment is not found in change of place and circumstance, exchange of position, or gain of treasures (some of the wealthiest are the most discontent).

Paul states contentment was something that he learned ("I have learned"). Based upon the tense of "have," this learning was continual over a period of time, being initiated at his conversion.[15]

(1. He learned to be content by the enablement of Christ's power. Paul said, "I have learned to be content, whatever the circumstances may be. I know now how to live when things are difficult and I know how to live when things are prosperous. In general and in particular I have learned the secret of facing either poverty or plenty. I am ready for anything through the strength of the one who lives within me." (Philippians 4:12–13 PHILLIPS). Continuously abiding in Christ and relying upon His power to meet every adverse circumstance of life victoriously is the secret of true contentment. See John 15:5; 11.

(2. He learned to be content by exhibiting trust in God's plan. Whatever befalls believers is orchestrated or allowed by sovereign God for their best and His glory. Jeremiah testifies to that truth: "'For I know the plans I have for you,' declares the Lord, 'plans to prosper you and not to harm you, plans to give you hope and a future'" (Jeremiah 29:11 NIV). "Contentedness requires that we should believe our condition, whatever it may be, to be determined by God, or at least that He permits

5

it according to His pleasure."[16] To trust God implicitly brings contentment inexplicable.

> To trust God implicitly brings contentment inexplicable.

Joseph Parker said, "'Abraham believed God' (Romans 4:3) and said to his eyes, 'Stand back!' and to the laws of nature, 'Hold your peace!' and to an unbelieving heart, 'Silence, you lying tempter!' He simply 'believed God.'"[17]

(3. He learned to be content through hope that was infused into his soul from the Holy Scriptures. Apart from hope, there can be no true contentment. Contentment comes along with hope for healing, deliverance, relief and rescue, either in the present life or in the world to come. The psalmist said, "I wait for the LORD, my soul doth wait, and in his word do I hope" (Psalm 130:5). See Psalm 102:28. The hope of Heaven, a glorified body free from sickness and sorrow, reunion with the saints, eternity in a domain free from sin and evil, and continuous fellowship with the Lord all infuse hope that yields peace, calm and contentment in life's struggles.

(4. He learned to be content through the hardships of life. Paul gained invaluable lessons from times of pain (a hard schoolhouse) that made each successive hardship more serene and easier to bear. See 2 Corinthians 11:24–27. A. W. Pink wrote, "Instead of complaining at his lot, a contented man is thankful that his condition and circumstances are no worse than they are. Instead of greedily desiring something more than the supply of his present need, he rejoices that God still cares for him. Such an one is 'content' with such as he has."[18]

The exercise of faith and its proven effectualness produce greater faith in facing future hardships or calamity. The Bible says, "And not only this, but [with joy] let us exult in our sufferings and rejoice in our hardships, knowing that hardship (distress, pressure, trouble) produces patient endurance; and endurance, proven character (spiritual maturity); and proven character, hope and confident assurance [of eternal salvation]. Such hope [in God's promises] never disappoints us, because God's love has been abundantly poured out within our hearts through the Holy Spirit who was given to us" (Romans 5:3–5 AMP).

(5. Doubtlessly, Paul also learned how to be content through the observation of saints that in the fire of affliction and trouble stood immovable, always abounding in the Lord with all eagerness and gladness. All of Paul's "teachers" taught him that God was dependable to take care of him despite the storm that may assail. Therefore, he could be at rest, peace and calm (not anxious or fretting). And this, he said, was exactly the case. Paul's contentment may be experienced by all believers, provided they are willing to *learn* from the same five able instructors.

Comfort for Troubled Hearts

Contentment's manifestation. It replaces the "gloom and doom" of life with an optimistic and satisfying disposition. It changes the "woe is me" to the "great is He," enabling a 'peace that passes all understanding.' It sweetens that which is sour. It overrides the voice of pain, discomfort, anxiety and fear with that of Christ, who says, "When thou passest through the waters, I will be with thee; and through the rivers, they shall not overflow thee: when thou walkest through the fire, thou shalt not be burned; neither shall the flame kindle upon thee" (Isaiah 43:2), and, "I will never leave thee, nor forsake thee" (Hebrews 13:5).

The contented are not complainers about their burdens but applauders of God's sufficiency to sustain them in their burdens. The contented are cheerful and happy, knowing this present suffering is nothing compared to the glory He will reveal to them later (Romans 8:18) and that all things work together for their good (verse 28). The contented express gratitude to God in their hardship (for enabling grace to endure, in realization it could be worse, and in knowing it fulfills God's purpose). See 1 Thessalonians 5:18.

Contentment puts a positive spin on the negative. "How dismal you look," said a water bucket to his companion as they were going to the well.

"Ah!" replied the other, "I was reflecting on the uselessness of our being filled; for, let us go away ever so full, we always come back empty."

"Dear me! how strange to look at it in this way," said the bucket. "Now I enjoy the thought that however empty we come, we always go back full. Only look at it in that light, and you will be as cheerful as I am."[19]

Contentment's continuation. Paul remained "content" until his death (Philippians 1:23–25). Contentment will remain and reign supreme in the believer's heart in proportion to the faith exhibited in Christ. For the devoted believer it is, therefore, habitual.

I am happy, oh, so happy
   At God's side;
I am walking in His presence,
   Satisfied.
Hallelujah, hallelujah,
I am walking in His presence,
   Satisfied.

I am drinking at the fountain
   Of sweet peace,
While the blessings from my Father
   Never cease.
Hallelujah, hallelujah,
Blessings from my heav'nly Father
   Never cease. ~ William J. Kirkpatrick (1899)

Warren Wiersbe summarizes how to gain contentment, saying, "Real contentment must come from within. You and I cannot change or control the world around us, but we can change and control the world within us. It has often been said that what life does *to* us depends on what life finds *within* us. This explains Paul's great testimony, 'For I have learned, in whatsoever state I am, therewith to be content.'"[20] Helen Keller wrote, "Everything has its wonders, even darkness and silence, and I learn, whatever state I may be in, therein to be content."[21]

4

An Overcoming Faith

Some have found the readiness of their faith to easily accept and handle courageously, calmly and triumphantly whatever happens while soaring on the mountaintop, dissipate (not dissolve) in the valley of deepest woe and suffering. For such, the real depth and measure of their faith was miscalculated. It is when faith is put into the furnace, with naught else or anyone else to cling to, that the depth of faith we possess is revealed and manifested.

> Faith exhibits a firm grasp on unseen fact.

Faith is the act of believing, a firm and confident expectation that what God has promised will be done. The Bible says, "Now faith is being sure we will get what we hope for. It is being sure of what we cannot see" (Hebrews 11:1 NLV). Faith exhibits a firm grasp on unseen fact.[22] It is not based on "empirical evidence, but divine assurance."[23]

Martin Luther stated, "Faith is a living and unshakable confidence, a belief in God so assured that a man would die a thousand deaths for its sake." Biblical hope is based on faith. Faith says it will happen; hope anticipates its happening with joyous expectation. E. M. Bounds says, "Trust [faith] always operates in the present tense. Hope looks toward the future. Trust looks to the present. Hope expects. Trust possesses. Trust receives what prayer acquires. So what prayer needs, at all times, is abiding and abundant trust."[24] Faith is not manufactured by man but freely provided by God (Ephesians 2:8; Galatians 2:20).

Faith is the victory!
Faith is the victory!
Oh, glorious victory
That overcomes the world. ~ John Henry Yates (1837–1900)

In dying the saint's faith is tested to its utmost, for it is to take a step into that which is known theologically but unknown experientially. No faith will bear us up in the hour of death but that only which gives the promise of Heaven real substance in our mind and soul.[25] To know by faith that upon death man will live again, as Job did, is the game changer in confronting it (Job 14:14). Jude says that if faith is weak regarding dying (or sickness, bereavement, suffering), then we should 'build it up' (Jude 20). How is that done?

Faith is built up by exposure to the Word. It is enlarged through the intake of the Word of God. Paul says, "Consequently, faith comes from hearing the message, and the message is heard through the word about Christ" (Romans 10:17 NIV). Being a faithful student of the Scriptures is the surest means of increasing one's faith. Make your sickbed, deathbed, or furnace of affliction the Word of God.

Faith is strengthened by the example of others. The observation of the availing faith of others in trusting Christ to intervene, keep His promises, and provide relief or remedy as they encounter hardships, heartaches and even death builds up faith. A. C. Dixon shared, "When I was in Boston a young man asked me for a book that would confirm his faith. I told him to go to the men's meeting on Sunday afternoon and listen for half an hour to the testimony of those who had been drunkards and criminals and are now sober, honest, happy husbands and fathers with the joy of Heaven in their faces and the music of Heaven in their voices. One live Lazarus is worth forty sermons on the resurrection."[26] "Then believed [the Israelites] his words" (Psalm 106:12). Not until they witnessed Moses' faith in God dividing the Red Sea for their safe travel across on dry ground, and the death of the Egyptian soldiers that pursued, did they believe His promises. See John 6:2.

Faith is enlarged by personal experience. Evidence of the efficacy of a display of even tiny faith increases faith when it is needed again. Faith grows with usage. George Mueller testified, "To learn strong faith is to endure great trials. I have learned my faith by standing firm amid severe testings."[27]

Faith is increased by a display of evidence. Seeing is believing, and there is much to *see* that will bolster belief. Investigation and examination of the credibility of the Bible, the resurrection of Christ and the many prophecies that He fulfilled will authenticate and substantiate the Christian faith and its worthiness of trust. Such research led Lee Strobel and Josh McDowell to exhibit faith in Christ.

Faith grows by entreaty of God. Upon acknowledgement of weak faith (with regard to his son's healing) the father prayed, "Lord, I believe; help thou mine unbelief" (Mark 9:24).

> Don't sink in your struggles, when you could float by faith.

The blessing and benefit of weak faith is great; but with strong faith, it is enormous. May we pray with the father, "Lord, I believe; help thou mine unbelief." Billy Graham said, "There is only one way to live your everyday life, and that is with your faith and your hope *permanently* on God."[28] Another said don't sink in your struggles when you could float by faith.[29]

9

5

The Anchor of the Soul

"But the righteous hath hope in his death" (Proverbs 14:32). R. C. Sproul said, "Hope is called the anchor of the soul (Hebrews 6:19), because it gives stability to the Christian life. But hope is not simply a 'wish' ('I wish that such-and-such would take place'); rather, it is that which latches on to the certainty of the promises of the future that God has made."[30] J. I. Packer writes that "The channel through which power flows, subjectively speaking, is *hope*—faith's forward look. We are to be upheld by our hope, the sure and certain hope of glory promised. God never intended humankind to live without hope, and He has in fact, given Christians the most magnificent hope that ever was."[31]

Dr. Jerome Groopman wrote, "For all my patients, hope, true hope, has proved as important as any medication I might prescribe or any procedure I might perform."[32] He continues, "Hope, I have come to believe, is as vital to our lives as the very oxygen that we breathe."[33]

What is the Christian's ultimate Hope? Paul gives answer in Philippians 1:21: "For to me to live is Christ, and to die is gain." The Christian's hope centers upon "gain" at death, hope in gaining freedom from Satan, sin, sorrow and suffering. It is hope in *gaining* an instantaneous transfer to Heaven at life's end. It is hope in *gaining* a glorified body like unto Christ's. It is hope in *gaining* fellowship supreme with Jesus and reunion with loved ones and friends. It is to *gain* incomparable joy and peace and rest from service and spiritual warfare.

Solomon states that "the righteous hath hope in his death" (Proverbs 14:32). The hope of Christians includes the assurance that whatever evil befalls them, their family, their friends or the world, Christ is Victor. See Colossians 1:5. R. G. Lee states, "Hope sees beyond the cloud, beyond the obstacle, beyond the hardship, beyond the weakness, beyond the difficulty."[34]

David Jeremiah says, "God calls us to a life characterized by hope. It's not a feeling, and it's not wishful thinking."[35] This hope is not based upon *mere wishes* or *opinions*. Christian hope is the expectation and assurance of what God promised in the Holy Scriptures. It is "the anchor of the soul" (Hebrews 6:19) maintaining its calm amidst the raging seas that threaten and frighten. Jeremiah again stated, "Just as a ship's anchor only works if it is embedded in the rock, so the anchor of hope only works if it is embedded in God's unfailing Word."[36] Packer says, "Anchored ships stay steady. Anchored Christians do the same. And the anchor that can and does hold us steady is the hope that is ours in Christ."[37]

Comfort for Troubled Hearts

In times like these you need the Bible;

In times like these, oh, be not idle.

Be very sure, be very sure,

Your anchor holds and grips the Solid Rock! ~ Ruth Caye Jones (1943)

The saint's hope of life beyond the grave is biblically (and historically) founded upon Jesus' atoning death at Calvary and resurrection, making man's access to God and Heaven possible. The Bible says, "that through death he [Jesus] might destroy him that had the power of death, that is, the devil" (Hebrews 2:14). His payment for man's sin at so great a cost and subsequent resurrection assures the believer that death will execute no power whatsoever upon him.

The Christian may say loudly and with all certainty to the face of death, "O death, where is thy sting? O grave, where is thy victory?" (1 Corinthians 15:55). Why? "The sting of death is sin; and the strength of sin is the law. But thanks be to God, which giveth us the victory through our Lord Jesus Christ" (verses 56–57). Paul explains, "If our hope in Christ is for this life only, we should be pitied more than anyone else in the world. But Christ has truly been raised from the dead—the first one and proof that those who sleep in death will also be raised. Death has come because of what one man did, but the rising from death also comes because of one man. In Adam all of us die. In the same way, in Christ all of us will be made alive again" (1 Corinthians 15:19–22 NCV). See Colossians 1:5.

There's nothing Satan or sin or death can do to extinguish the reality of the Christian's hope, for on Easter Christ proved His power over them through His resurrection. And as He lives, even so shall we! "We are conquerors of death when [by faith] we are able to look beyond it."[38]

> A HOPE of future happiness affords strong consolation under present trials.
> Charles Simeon

The saint that possesses firm hope in Heaven beyond the grave based upon the death and resurrection of Jesus Christ "can take death by its cold hand and bid him welcome."[39] "I can smile on death," said a dying saint, "because my Savior smiles on me."[40] Christian hope triumphs over fear and doubt. William Gurnall says, "Let your hope of Heaven master your fear of death."[41]

The famous preacher George Whitfield, in dying, exemplified the believer's hope: "My breath is short, and I have little hopes, since my late relapse, of much further usefulness. A few exertions, like the last struggles of a dying man, or glimmering flashes of a taper [a slender candle] just burning out, is all that can be expected from me. But, blessed be God! the taper will be lighted up again in

Heaven."[42] Charles Simeon said, "A HOPE of future happiness affords strong consolation under present trials."[43]

Spurgeon writes, "Our hope in Christ for the future is the mainspring and the mainstay of our joy here. It will animate our hearts to think often of Heaven, for all that we can desire is promised there. Here we are weary and toilworn, but yonder is the land of rest where the sweat of labor shall no more bedew the worker's brow and fatigue shall be forever banished....Through the Spirit of God the hope of Heaven is the most potent force for the product of virtue; it is a fountain of joyous effort; it is the cornerstone of cheerful holiness."[44]

Richard Baxter comments, "Oh! if we did but truly believe that the promise of this glory *is* the Word of God and that God does truly mean as He speaks and is fully resolved to make it good. If we did truly believe that there is, indeed, such blessedness prepared for believers as the Scripture mentions, surely we should be as impatient of living as we are now fearful of dying and should think every day a year till our last day should come....If a man that is desperately sick today did believe he should arise sound the next morning, or a man today in despicable poverty had assurance that he should tomorrow arise a prince, would he be afraid to go to bed, or rather think it the longest day of his life till that desired night and morning came?"[45]

I know that my Redeemer lives;
What comfort this sweet sentence gives!
He lives, He lives, who once was dead;
He lives, my ever living Head.

He lives triumphant from the grave;
He lives eternally to save.
He lives all-glorious in the sky;
He lives exalted there on high.

He lives to grant me rich supply;
He lives to guide me with His eye.
He lives to comfort me when faint;
He lives to hear my soul's complaint.

He lives to silence all my fears;
He lives to wipe away my tears.
He lives to calm my troubled heart;
He lives all blessings to impart.

He lives, my kind, wise, heav'nly Friend;
He lives and loves me to the end.
He lives, and while He lives, I'll sing;
He lives, my Prophet, Priest, and King.

He lives and grants me daily breath;
He lives and I shall conquer death.
He lives my mansion to prepare;
He lives to bring me safely there.

He lives, all glory to His name!
He lives, my Jesus, still the same.
Oh, the sweet joy this sentence gives:
"I know that my Redeemer lives!" ~ Samuel Medley (1775)

Hope's reality is not one iota diminished by weakness in the believer to express it or by the seeming abandonment by God of His promises. It always remains firm, its eternal verities unchanged. "The righteous then," states Matthew Henry, "have *the grace of hope in them*; though they have pain, and some dread of death, yet they have hope. They have before them the good hoped for, even the blessed hope which God, who cannot lie, has promised."[46] George Lawson says, "His hopes may be weak and languishing, but still he has so much hope in Christ as to venture his soul in His hands; and if his faith is mingled with fears, these fears shall vanish as a thin cloud; and these anxieties, when he is leaving his body, will add to the triumphant joy which he will feel when angels appear to convey his soul to the regions from whence fear and sorrow are forever banished."[47]

This hope is available freely by the mercy of God to all that believe in and receive Jesus Christ as Lord and Savior. The unbeliever lives and dies in utter hopelessness. "Hopelessness constricts and withers the heart, rendering it unable to sense God's blessings and grace."[48]

6

Coping with Pain

Pascal (the great mathematician) said, "From the day that I was eighteen, I do not know that I have ever passed a single day without pain."[49] F. W. Robertson (English minister) experienced sleepless nights and torture-filled days with pain in the back of the head and neck that made life dreadful to him. Often he would clench his teeth to prevent cries of pain.[50] Robert Hall (English Baptist minister) lived in such pain that often he would roll on the carpet in agony over the pain in his back.

13

When the Rain Comes

Fittingly, the inscription on his tomb reads, "Neither shall there be any more pain."[51] With these men, and myriads of others like them, you may well identify; torturing, unrelenting agonizing pain is your lot in life. Chuck Swindoll said of pain, "It communicates its own message, whether to statesman or servant, preacher or prodigal, mother or child."[52] And no one can understand it save the one who bears it.

In Revelation 21:4, John distinguishes "pain" from sorrow, death and tears. "Neither shall there be any more pain." "Pain" refers to bodily suffering that racks man with agonizing and debilitating discomfort and torture. Negatively, torturing pain may mar the enjoyment of life and impede work, since one cannot perform his best while under pain's control. It can lessen interaction with family and friends, injure dreams, cause fretting and impatience, and generate a disposition of irritability. It has led some to become addicted to pain-relieving drugs and even embittered toward God. Oswald Chambers stated, "We all know people who have been made much meaner and more irritable and more intolerable to live with by suffering. It is not right to say that all suffering perfects. It only perfects one type of person—the one who accepts the call of God in Christ Jesus."[53]

On its positive side, pain works for good in the sufferer.

(1. Pain teaches us our frailty and utter dependence upon God. Tim Keller writes, "You don't really know Jesus is all you need until Jesus is all you have."[54] Elizabeth Elliot said, "I am not a theologian or a scholar, but I am very aware of the fact that pain is necessary to all of us. In my own life, I think I can honestly say that out of the deepest pain has come the strongest conviction of the presence of God and the love of God."[55]

(2. "Pain is something to remind us of the evil of sin. You never would have had a headache if it had not been for sin. You never would have known a sleepless night, a shooting pain through the nerves, or a dull weight at the heart if it had not been for sin."[56]

(3. It helps us in some minute measure identify with the horrendous pain Christ experienced at Calvary to make possible our redemption from sin. Isaiah says, "He was beaten, he was tortured, but he didn't say a word. Like a lamb taken to be slaughtered and like a sheep being sheared, he took it all in silence. Justice miscarried, and he was led off—and did anyone really know what was happening? He died without a thought for his own welfare, beaten bloody for the sins of my people. They buried him with the wicked, threw him in a grave with a rich man, Even though he'd never hurt a soul or said one word that wasn't true. Still, it's what God had in mind all along, to crush him with pain. The plan was that he give himself as an offering for sin so that he'd see life come from it—life, life, and more life. And God's plan will deeply prosper through him" (Isaiah 53:7–10 MSG). Jesus, having been inflicted with torturing pain, relates to us in our pain; for 'He is acquainted

with our grief.' He knows our pain-filled sleepless nights, our bouts with indescribable torturing pain, and is committed to grant grace to bear it. His promise, "My grace is sufficient for you," takes the teeth out of suffering and pain.

(4. Pain humbles the proud, softens the hard and rebellious.[57] Certainly not all, but many over the years have testified of its work in their soul to bring about conversion or restoration.

(5. Pain has a designed purpose. Tim Keller states, "There is a purpose to it, and if faced rightly, it can drive us like a nail deep into the love of God and into more stability and spiritual power than you can imagine."[58]

(6. Pain builds endurance to face perhaps a greater episode of its affliction down the road.

(7. Pain might be a disciplinary infliction for sinful conduct (Hebrews 12:5–6). George Morrison states, "But never forget, pain when it is willingly accepted is one of the choicest instruments of purifying that is wielded by the love of Heaven."[59] Tim Keller says, "Some suffering is given in order to chastise and correct a person for wrongful patterns of life (as in the case of Jonah imperiled by the storm), some suffering is given not to correct past wrongs but to prevent future ones (as in the case of Joseph sold into slavery), and some suffering has no purpose other than to lead a person to love God more ardently for Himself alone and so discover the ultimate peace and freedom."[60]

(8. Pain develops great saints and leaders. Chuck Swindoll said, "I can't find in history a person whom God used greatly until He let him be hurt deeply."[61]

(9. Ultimately, pain is enveloped in the love of God for the sufferer (Romans 8:28). And He that allows it will accompany it with coping grace. John Wesley says, "Even in the greatest afflictions, we ought to testify to God, that, in receiving them from His hand, we feel pleasure in the midst of the pain, from being afflicted by Him who loves us and whom we love."[62] "Lo, I see four men loose, walking in the midst of the fire, and they have no hurt; and the form of the fourth is like the Son of God" (Daniel 3:25). "There is no fire so fierce that He will not bear the heat and be by my side. Very thankful I should be that I have a Savior touched with the feeling of my infirmities."[63] The furnace may be one of sickness, bereavement or adversity, yet Christ abides faithfully in its midst with us.

> Pain knocked upon my door and said
> That she had come to stay;
> And though I would not welcome her
> But bade her go away,

When the Rain Comes

She entered in. Like my own shade
    She followed after me,
And from her stabbing, stinging sword
    No moment was I free.

And then one day another knocked
    Most gently at my door.
I cried, "No. Pain is living here;
    There is no room for more."

And then I heard His tender voice,
    "'Tis I; be not afraid."
And from the day He entered in,
    The difference it made!

For though He did not bid her leave
    (My strange, unwelcome guest),
He taught me how to live with her.
    Oh, I had never guessed

That we could dwell so sweetly here,
    My Lord and Pain and I,
Within this fragile house of clay
    While years slip slowly by! ~ Martha Snell Nicholson

A place where pain is not. Find solace and hope in knowing that in Heaven, 'there will be no more pain.' There you will shout,

Free at last!
Free at last!
Praise God Almighty, I'm free at last.

"The parting pain which the believer feels in leaving this world is the very last that he shall ever feel at all."[64]

No more night,
No more pain,
No more tears,
Never crying again,
And praises to the great I Am—
We will live in the light of the risen Lamb. ~ Walt Harrah (1983)

7

Understanding Romans 8:28

"And we know that all things work together [conspire together] for good to them that love God, to them who are the called according to his purpose" (Romans 8:28). Jon Courson remarked, "We usually rewrite Romans 8:28 to read: 'Most things' or 'some things work together for good.' Paul says even though there's groaning and suffering as we're being adapted for Heaven, know this: It's all working for good."[65] See Romans 8:22.

The source of the promise that God works good out of *everything*. The context in which the promise is cited indicates that it flows directly from Heaven's throne room. It's not merely the word of a great saint like Paul or a potentate, but of Almighty God.

The surety of the promise that God works good out of everything. Paul doesn't say, "We hope" but, "We know." It's not a conjecture, opinion or wishful thinking; it's a firm declaration of absolute certainty.[66] Every saint that wants to "know" may know ("We know") that God works good out of everything that happens to him. The credibility and reliability of that are underwritten by God Himself that "cannot lie" (Titus 1:2). Its truthfulness is attested and substantiated by the experiences of saints over the ages. Paul includes himself among its verifiers ("*We* know").

The scope of the promise that God works good out of everything. What are the confines and perimeter of the promise, its inclusions and its exclusions? Paul said "All things" work together for good to him that loves the Lord—it's all-encompassing and non-exempting. J. A. Fitzmyer states that "all things" in all likelihood include everything listed in Romans 8:18–27.[67] "No matter what our situation," comments John MacArthur, "our suffering, our persecution, our sinful failure, our pain, our lack of faith—in those things, as well as in all other things, our heavenly Father will work to produce our ultimate victory and blessing."[68] MacArthur continues, "*All things* includes circumstances and events that are good and beneficial in themselves as well as those that are in themselves evil and harmful."[69] W. A. Criswell states, "Mystery may engulf us, enemies may assail us, friends may desert us, Satan may buffet us, sorrows may overwhelm us, poverty may threaten us, sickness may weaken us, despair may overtake us, dark clouds may swallow us up, but Paul says in this text that all things—those things and a thousand other unnamable things—they all work together for good to them that love God."[70]

The specificity of the promise that God works good out of everything. The sum and substance of the promise is that God orchestrates everything that happens in life for man's good and His glory. Matthew Henry says, "That is good for them which does their souls good. Either directly or indirectly, every providence has a tendency to the spiritual good of those that love God, breaking them off from sin, bringing them nearer to God, weaning them from the world, fitting them for Heaven."[71] God uses the good and bad in the events of life "to accomplish both our temporal and eternal benefit."[72] It is God's wisdom (thankfully, not man's) that discerns the form of "good" that flows out of even the worst of troubles and trials. Albert Barnes says, "'For good' means 'for our real welfare; for the promotion of true piety (holiness, devotion), peace, and happiness in our hearts.'"[73] All of life's blissful and blastful happenings will mutually cooperate and contribute to our good.[74] Adrian Rogers says, "In the chemistry of the cross, God takes things that in and of themselves are bad, and He puts them together, much as a chemist might take chemicals that in and of themselves may be deleterious [harmful], and mixes them to make a medicine that brings healing."[75]

The strength of the promise that God works good out of everything. The promise instills peace of mind and strength in soul in facing the giants of adversity, despair, death and bereavement. God hath all things at His disposal in Heaven and on earth to fulfill the promise proffering "a peace or serenity that passes all understanding."

The sphere of the promise that God works good out of everything. "According to His purpose." Adrian Rogers states, "That's the key. What is the good that all things are working together for? To make us like Jesus. To be conformed to the image of His Son. There is no higher good than to be like the Lord Jesus Christ. Many times this promise has been trivialized. For example, someone may be driving down the road and a tire will blow out. The person may say, 'Oh, well. The Bible says that "all things work together for good." Maybe there's a sale on tires.' That isn't what this verse means. The good is not to make us necessarily healthy or happy but to make us holy, to make us like Jesus."[76]

The subjects of the promise that God works good out of everything. It's not assigned to all, but only to them that "love God" or "the called of God," as believers (true Christians) are often referred to as being. Criswell says, "The man who is in the will and in the purpose of God, the man who is on God's side, the man whose heart is with Christ—to that man in God's plan and in God's purpose and in God's infinite love, whatever comes, whatever happens, works together, conspires together, and reaches out toward the thing that is finally, blessedly, marvelously good."[77] The eye may be blind to the "good" promised that will be the outcome of present suffering, sickness and sorrow. Exhibit patience and trust in the Lord until all shall be known (see John 13:7). Then, you will join with other saints that have walked the same path, testifying, "We went through fire and water, but you brought us to a place of abundance" (Psalm 66:12 NIV).

Comfort for Troubled Hearts

Praise to the Lord, the Almighty, the King of creation!
O my soul, praise Him, for He is your health and salvation!
Come, all who hear; now to His temple draw near.
Join me in glad adoration.

Praise to the Lord, above all things so wondrously reigning,
Shelt'ring you under His wings and so gently sustaining!
Have you not seen all that is needful has been
Sent by his gracious ordaining?

Praise to the Lord, who will prosper your work and defend you;
Surely his goodness and mercy shall daily attend you.
Ponder anew what the Almighty can do,
If with His love He befriends you.

Praise to the Lord! Oh, let all that is in me adore Him!
All that has life and breath, come now with praises before Him.
Let the amen sound from His people again,
Gladly forever adore him. ~ Joachim Neander (1680)

8

Stagger Not at the Promises of God

"He staggered not at the promise of God through unbelief; but was strong in faith, giving glory to God; And being fully persuaded that, what he had promised, he was able also to perform" (Romans 4:20–21). Abraham is the believer's example for unfailing and unwavering trust in the promises of God even when they seem to be unreasonable and irrational. Paul cites two promises that substantiate Abraham's unhesitating faith in God. First was the promise that his posterity would multiply as the stars in Heaven, becoming numerous like the sand of the sea; he would be the father of many nations (verse 18). The second promise was that Sarah, Abraham's wife, at age 90 (Abraham was 100) would conceive a son (verse 19). The promise defied the biological nature of the body; people their age just don't have babies. What appeared to be ludicrous and absurd, Abraham believed even when Sarah "laughed" at the notion (How many of us would have laughed with Sarah?). The gift of the Savior of the world through whom all that believed would be blessed would descend from Abraham's seed—something that wouldn't happen for 2,000 years, yet Abraham did not stumble at the promise. Jesus commended his faith, saying, "Your father Abraham rejoiced to see my day: and he saw it, and was glad" (John 8:56).

When the Rain Comes

What are the causes of stumbling at the promises of God (hesitation to believe what God said)?

(1. *Unbelief causes man to stagger at the promises of God.* The foundational reason for distrust in the promises of God is mere unbelief (skepticism, doubt). But honest research of the veracity of Holy Scriptures and credibility for God's existence led agnostics Josh McDowell and Lee Strobel and others like them to become strong believers in the Christian faith. Light dispels the dark; it opens blinded eyes to the truth. God said, "And you will seek Me and find Me, when you search for Me with all your heart. I will be found by you, says the LORD" (Jeremiah 29:13–14 NKJV).

(2. *Unreasonableness causes man to stagger at the promises of God.* Even among the saints, there is hesitation to believe a promise that defies medical science, natural law and human rationalism. The real question here is not whether the promise is irrational; the real question concerns God's power. Is God able to really do this thing? And to that question the Bible, history and human experience testify, 'Nothing is impossible with Him' (Luke 1:37). With God in the equation, all is possible. Matthew Henry says, "We can depend on God to fulfill His promise, even when all roads leading to it are closed. For no matter how many promises God has made, they are 'yes' in Christ."

> With God in the equation, all is possible.

(3. *Untruth causes man to stagger at the promises of God.* To discount the Bible as truth makes its promises *seem* dubious at best. The Bible has internal and external support for its veracity. John MacArthur states, "Fulfilled prophecy is perhaps the greatest proof that the Word of God is true. It carries the weight of proof for the Word of God further than any other single element of Scripture."[78] For example, there are at least thirty prophecies about the birth, the death, and the resurrection of the Messiah that were fulfilled in Jesus Christ. Josh McDowell says, "Compared with other ancient writings, the Bible has more manuscript evidence to support it than any ten pieces of classical literature combined."[79] C. H. Spurgeon wrote, "Since God wrote it [Bible], mark its truthfulness. Come, search, ye critics, and find a flaw; examine it from its Genesis to its Revelation and find an error. This is a vein of pure gold unalloyed by quartz or any earthly substance. O Bible! It cannot be said of any other book that it is perfect and pure, but of thee we can declare all wisdom is gathered up in thee without a particle of folly. This is the judge that ends the strife where wit and reason fail. This is the Book untainted by any error but is pure, unalloyed, perfect truth. Why? Because God wrote it."[80]

Comfort for Troubled Hearts

WORTHY of homage and of praise;
Worthy by all to be adored:
Exhaustless theme of heavenly lays!
Thou, Thou art worthy, Jesus, Lord. ~ Miss F. T. Wigram (1831–1871)

(4. *Unreliability causes man to stagger at the promises of God.* A promise is only as good as its promiser. Doubt in God's ability to perform all that is promised infuses distrust. But there is indisputable substantiation for God's omnipotence.

(a. In creation God made the world out of nothing. See Psalm 90:2.

(b. In the administration of the cosmos, God's power holds the oceans in bound, the stars in orbit, the sun at the exact right distance from earth, and the earth's rotation exactly right.

(c. In the intrinsic design of the human body His power is displayed. For example, the circulatory system of arteries, veins, and capillaries stretch about 60,000 miles, and the heart beats in excess of 2.5 billion times in an average lifetime (about 93,000 times per day, 655,000 times per week, 34 million times per year). Such precision operation of the heart didn't happen just by chance, nor does it continue by chance. God controls it.

(d. Throughout the history of the world men have documented again and again by their personal experience how God has been proven to be trustworthy to all He said. C. H. Spurgeon argues, "On the bed of death the truth generally comes out, yet who ever heard a solitary believer declare that it is a mistake to confide in the blood of Jesus or to rest in the faithfulness of God? Somewhere or other this thing would have come out if it had been so."[81] But it hasn't. At times in revival meetings I have asked the oldest of saints to bear testimony of two things: the time frame of their Christian walk and the faithfulness of God to keep His Word to them over that period of time. The testimony has been the same from saint to saint and church to church: God has been faithful and true to His promises.

In light of these truths (there are numerous more), God asks, "Behold, I am the LORD, the God of all flesh: is there anything too hard for me?" (Jeremiah 32:27). And *honesty* answers, "'Ah Lord God! Behold, You have made the Heavens and the earth by Your great power and by Your outstretched arm! There is nothing too difficult or too wonderful for You'" (Jeremiah 32:17 AMP). "We ought to give God strong faith, because there is no evidence which could justify mistrust."[82] There is no justified cause to stumble at the promises of God.

We may not touch His hands and side	Help then, O Lord, our unbelief,
Nor follow where He trod,	And may our faith abound
Yet in His promise we rejoice	To call on You when You are near
And cry, "My Lord and God!"	And seek where You are found.
	~ Henry Alford (1844)

9
Ministry of Sacred Songs

Former Secretary of State and senator, John Foster Dulles, found comfort in his painful illness through such hymns as "The Spacious Firmament on High," "When Morning Gilds the Skies," and "Through the Night of Doubt and Sorrow." His waning spirit was rekindled daily by listening to the great hymns of Christian faith.[83] Songs and hymns about eternal bliss assist the soul in sickness, frailty, and in its transfer to Heaven, through instilling comfort and peace. Paul exhorts, "Speaking to one another with psalms, hymns, and songs from the Spirit" (Ephesians 5:19 NIV).

Multitudes of saints' sickbeds (and deathbeds) have been and are being made *softer* through the singing or hearing of inspirational songs such as: "My Latest Sun Is Sinking Fast"; "When We All Get to Heaven"; "Beulah Land"; "The Sweet By and By"; "The Unclouded Day"; "That Shall Be Glory for Me"; "Shall We Gather at the River?"; "My Savior First of All"; "Face to Face with Christ My Savior"; "This World Is Not My Home"; "The New Jerusalem" and "I Can Only Imagine." Whether such songs are personally sung by or to you or heard by radio or CD, their melodious tune and inspiring message will soothe your troubled heart, uplift your soul, *fix* your mind on "things above" (Colossians 3:1–2) and instill hope for what lies ahead. John Henry Jowett said, "Let us sing even when we do not feel like it, for in this way we give wings to heavy feet and turn weariness into strength."[84]

Oh, sing to me of Heaven
      When I am called to die!
Sing songs, sing songs of holy ecstasy
      To waft my soul on high. ~ Mary Dana Shindler (1840)

10
The Vale of Deep Darkness

All saints (the "born-again" ones) eventually "walk in darkness" (vale of sickness, suffering, sorrow). See Isaiah 50:10a. And how dark that darkness is at times, none but he who walks in it understands. Its misery, gloom and discomfort defy tongue or pen to accurately tell. Its despair and distress are horrendous and bewildering. Its "blinding" darkness is like seeking passage through a deep fog, not knowing where to place the next foot. To walk in the vale of darkness and tears "sets all his songs to a minor key. It gives to all his prayers a wailing pathos. It takes away much of his buoyancy and elasticity for work."[85]

Comfort for Troubled Hearts

In such times what ought the believer to do? Isaiah says, "Let him trust in the name of the LORD, and stay upon his God" (Isaiah 50:10b). This is the anchor that will secure footing when our world tumbles into pieces. To "trust in the name" of the Lord is to confidently place the cause and condition of the exceedingly *dark darkness* in the hands of the God revealed in Holy Scripture.

God's trustworthiness is directly linked to and based upon His "name"; the divine nature is love, mercy, holiness, righteousness, and justice. The Bible says, "The name of the LORD is a strong tower: the righteous runneth into it, and is safe" (Proverbs 18:10). God's name is like "a strong tower" that keeps us safe and secure from the enemy. A tower in biblical days provided protection for the people from the enemy. God's name is like that strong tower to which we may flee for "help in the hour of need." In that tower is refuge for the soul, light to illuminate the night, and the balm of Gilead to heal the troubled soul.

> There is power
> In the name of Jesus;
> There is power,
> Power in His name. ~ Lincoln Brewster

"And stay upon his God" (Isaiah 50:10c). Isaiah is saying, "You trust in the name of the Lord; now rely upon it." Don't waver in dependence upon God or His promises to make a way when there is no way medically, financially or otherwise. "We are not fitfully to trust, and then to fear; but to come to a stay in God, even as ships enter a haven, cast their anchors, and then stay there till the tempest is overpast."[86] Don't allow the darkness to dictate your peace, joy, hope or future. Let that be determined by reliance upon the Lord and His promises. "The security of the saint is rooted in the fact that God has hold of him, and not at all in his consciousness that he has hold of God. His comfort may be affected by the latter, but his safety is due entirely to the former."[87] Looking to self, others, money or schemes to deliver from the darkness will be utterly futile. The Bible says if you "walk in the light of your fire, and in the sparks that ye have kindled" then you will "lie down in sorrow" (Isaiah 50:11).

> When nothing whereon to lean remains,
> When strongholds crumble to dust,
> When nothing is sure but that God still reigns,
> That is just the time to trust.

23

When the Rain Comes

'Tis better to walk by faith than sight
   In this path of yours and mine;
And the pitch-black night, when there's no outer light,
   Is the time for faith to shine.[88]

Why are we to trust and rely upon the Lord in the dark and dismal days?[89] *Because our faith displayed will glorify Christ.* It will show His power and faithfulness in both preserving us in the darkness and lifting us out of it. C. H. Spurgeon says, "It does not glorify God to trust Him when you have a thousand other props and assistances."[90]

Why trust in the Lord in dark days? *Because God's grace and promises are designed for such days.* "What God brings you to, He will bring you through" is not just a catchy cliché but a truth rooted in God's Word. Samuel Rutherford states, "No created powers in Hell or out of Hell can mar the music of our Lord Jesus nor spoil our song of joy. Let us then be glad and rejoice in the salvation of our Lord, for faith had never yet cause to have wet cheeks and hanging down brows or to droop or die."[91]

Why trust in the Lord in times of deep darkness? *Because the darkness will pass.* It is but momentary. "Weeping may endure for a night, but joy cometh in the morning" (Psalm 30:5). Soon heavenly "rays" will burst through the dark clouds, granting illumination. Confidently you may say, "Do not gloat over me, my enemies! For though I fall, I will rise again. Though I sit in darkness, the LORD will be my light" (Micah 7:8 NLT).

Why trust in the Lord in dark days? *Because it is but trivial in contrast with the eternal glory we will receive in Heaven.* "For our light affliction, which is but for a moment, worketh for us a far more exceeding and eternal weight of glory" (2 Corinthians 4:17).

Why trust in Christ in the dark days? *Because it strengthens faith* (assurance of God's control), *increases patience, enhances prayer and purifies, refines, and sharpens us spiritually* (Acts 14:22). Oswald Chambers wrote, "Sorrow burns up a great amount of shallowness."[92]

Charles Simeon says, "Take this for your pattern, brethren. You may be brought into trials which may seem to menace your very existence, but however the storm may rage, your Savior is embarked in the vessel with you—yea, and is also sitting at the helm. Only reflect on His conflicts, victories, and triumphs, and you will see the way that is marked out for you; and as He fought and overcame and is set down upon his Father's throne, so shall you also overcome and enjoy the full recompence of your trials upon your Father's throne for ever and ever."[93] John of the Cross said, "In the dark night of the soul, bright flows the river of

God."[94] C. S. Lewis says, "God whispers to us in our pleasures, speaks to us in our conscience, but SHOUTS in our pain. It is His megaphone to rouse a deaf world."[95]

Light after darkness, gain after loss,
Strength after weakness, crown after cross,
Sweet after bitter, hope after fears,
Home after wandering, praise after tears,

Sheaves after sowing, sun after rain,
Sight after mystery, peace after pain,
Joy after sorrow, calm after blast,
Rest after weariness, sweet rest at last,

Near after distant, gleam after gloom,
Love after loneliness, life after tomb—
After long agony, rapture of bliss,
Right was the pathway leading to this. ~ Frances R. Havergal

11

The Shepherd's Care

Perhaps the best-known biblical text, outside John 3:16, is Psalm 23. Millions have been comforted and strengthened from reading and studying it. Its theme is the Great Shepherd's care for His sheep (the redeemed).

David first states *the Good Shepherd justifies the sheep* (verse 1a). Spurgeon says, "No man has a right to consider himself the Lord's sheep unless his nature has been renewed, for the scriptural description of unconverted men does not picture them as sheep but as wolves or goats."[96] Jesus warns of "wolves" in "sheep's" clothing (Matthew 7:15).

The Good Shepherd supplies the sheep (verses 1b–2). Sheep, though animals that flock together, receive individualized care from the Shepherd. He makes sure no sheep in the fold lacks any needful thing ("shall not want").

The Good Shepherd quiets the sheep (verse 2). "He maketh me to lie down in green pastures: he leadeth me beside the still waters." Green pastures and still waters picture tranquility and peace. Allow Him to grant peace to your soul when the rain comes.

When the Rain Comes

Beside the still waters how calmly we rest,
When in the rough journey of life sorely pressed.
The din of the world comes but faint to our ears,
Like faraway music each murmur appears.

Beside the still waters, we rest and grow strong,
Then pass on our way with a smile and a song.
Up to the green hills of that Paradise bright,
Where faith shall be lost in a glorious sight!

Beside the still waters no storm cloud can rise
To hide from our vision the blue of the skies.
A touch of God's Heaven we find here below,
Alone with the Master whose goodness we know.

Beside the still waters to linger a while,
Then taking our burdens, pass on with a smile,
For soon by the river of peace we shall stand
And praise our Redeemer in Eden's fair land. ~ Lizzie DeArmond

The Good Shepherd revives the sheep (verse 3). "He restoreth my soul." He grants the sheep refreshing reinvigoration spiritually and mentally.

The Good Shepherd guides the sheep (verse 3). He orchestrates the entirety of their life to their delight and His glory. *Yea, though I walk through the valley of the shadow of death*. Death is pictured as a mere *shadow*. And shadows cannot bring harm. *I shall not fear*. "Why? Because I will meet my loved ones by and by? Because the separation is very brief? Yes, but the principal reason is because "THOU ART WITH ME; thy rod and Thy staff they comfort me." The SHEPHERD is with us, and joy comes through His presence."[97] To know that when facing death "thou art with me" is the soul's strong refuge and comfort. He will walk the road with us all the way.

The Good Shepherd abides with the sheep (verse 4b). Joseph Parker says, "Thou art with me"—my hand is locked in Thine, my life is drawn from Thine, my future is involved in Thine. God and the saint are one."[98] Even in the midst of the storm or the shadow of approaching death, He promises to be with us providing protection, comfort, strength and help. The God of the mountain is also the God of the valley.

I will dwell in the house of the Lord forever. At the last Christ's sheep will be satisfied with their new home in Heaven (John 14:1–3). Paul said, "Eye hath not seen, nor ear heard, neither have entered into the heart of man, the things which God hath prepared for them that love him" (1 Corinthians 2:9).[99] "We will not step

26

out into the dark when we leave this world," states John R. Rice, "but as the lost sheep feels so secure on the shepherd's shoulders, so all God's children are clasped safely in the hand of Christ and no one can take us away from Him. He wants us to be with Him."[100]

F. B. Meyer stated, "The Oriental shepherd was always ahead of his sheep. He was in front. Any attempt upon them had to take him into account. Now God is down in front. He is in the tomorrows. It is tomorrow that fills men with dread. But God is there already, and all tomorrows of our life have to pass before Him before they can get to us."[101] What a joy, comfort and peace to say, "The Lord is *my* shepherd." "Now the God of peace, that brought again from the dead our Lord Jesus, *that great shepherd of the sheep,* through the blood of the everlasting covenant, make you perfect in every good work to do his will, working in you that which is wellpleasing in his sight, through Jesus Christ; to whom be glory for ever and ever. Amen." (Hebrews 13:20–21).

My Savior the good Shepherd is;
    He'll never leave the flock.
The One Who truly loves the sheep
    Became the Lamb of God.

Despised, afflicted in my stead,
    He spent His soul for me.
And to the slaughter He was led,
    That I not thirsty be.

My Shepherd is the Lamb of God;
    He calls to me each day
To drink the waters flowing free
    From His pierced side of grace.

Yet when I stray or choose my way,
    He still would search for me
And bring me home on shoulders strong.
    Do I not His love see?

My Shepherd's face is how I live;
    I love to look at Him.
Though He might lead through shearing trial,
    But still I follow Him.

27

When the Rain Comes

Just as the Father's presence cheered
    Him through each suffering day,
'Tis once I saw His tender care
    That here I want to stay.

O Father, thank You for Your Son;
    He shares Your heart for us,
That gladly He would bear us to
    The bosom of Your love.

No greater Shepherd could there be,
    That He would not lose one
And lead us all to dwell with You,
    Sweet Pasture, Living Stream! ~ Author Unknown

12

Weep with Those That Weep

Christians ought to exhibit sympathy for the grief others experience. Paul admonishes, "Weep with them that weep" (Romans 12:15). Matthew Henry states, "It is our duty, and well becomes us, to lay to heart the sickness, and sorrow, and death of our near relations."[102] David did, for he says, "But as for me, when they were sick, my clothing was sackcloth: I humbled my soul with fasting; and my prayer returned into mine own bosom" (Psalm 35:13). The depth of David's grief and sympathy is pictured by the change of dress ("sackcloth"), denial of food ("fasting") and fervency in prayer. Albert Barnes says, "He subjected himself to the pains of hunger, that he might be better prepared to offer fervent and acceptable prayer."[103] When tears of compassion flow from our cheeks for a friend, their tears are diminished or dried up. J. J. Perowne paraphrases the last part of the text: "The prayer I offered for them is a prayer I might have offered for myself. So true a prayer was it, so full of love, that I could wish nothing more than that the blessings I asked for them should be vouchsafed to me."[104]

> When tears of compassion flow from our cheeks for a friend, their tears are diminished or dried up.

That's how we ought to pray for the sick, sorrowing and suffering—with the same intensity, fervency and passion as if praying for our own recovery. "True love will interest us in the sorrows and joys of one another and teach us to make them our own."[105] See Isaiah 63:9. If a mighty man of war like David could manifest affection, love, tenderness and pity for the sick and distressed, certainly its possible for every saint. D. L. Moody said, "My friends, if you want to get in sympathy with people, consider how you would feel in their place."[106] Spurgeon said, "I would go to the deeps a hundred times to cheer a downcast spirit. It is good for me to have been afflicted, that I might know how to speak a word in season to one that is weary."

Rejoice with those who rejoice and weep with those who weep. "What a beautiful spirit of sympathy with the joys and sorrows of others is here inculcated! But it is only one charming phase of the unselfish character which belongs to all living Christianity. What a world will ours be when this shall become its reigning spirit! Of the two, however, it is far easier to sympathize with another's sorrows than his joys, because in the one case he needs us; in the other, not. But just for this reason the latter is the more disinterested, and so the nobler."[107]

Father of mercies! send Thy grace
    All-powerful from above,
To form, in our obedient souls,
    The image of Thy love.

Oh, may our sympathizing breasts
    The generous pleasure know,
Kindly to share in others' joy
    And weep for others' woe!

When the most helpless sons of grief
    In low distress are laid,
Soft be our hearts their pains to feel
    And swift our hands to aid. ~ Philip Doddridge (1702–1751)

13

Lean upon Your Staff

Scripture states that when Jacob was dying, he did three things. He bestowed a blessing upon his two grandsons, worshipped God, and 'leaned on the top of his staff' (Hebrews 11:21). The first two are noble, worthy of our imitation and self-explanatory. But why does the writer of Hebrews find it necessary to say Jacob 'leaned on the top of his staff'?

Obviously, the staff supported Jacob's weak and feeble body, preventing a fall. After all, he was dying. But perhaps the staff provided not only physical but also spiritual bracing through the memories with which it was associated. Perhaps the old staff was the one with which he tended Laban's flock for twenty years; with him

29

when his name was changed by the Lord to Israel; with him when he was reconciled with Esau, his brother; with him when he made the long journey to Egypt to be reunited with Joseph, his son; by his bedside at Bethel when he beheld the wondrous vision of the angels ascending and descending upon a ladder stretched from Heaven and with him at Bethel when he was spiritually restored. *Leaning on the top of his staff* evoked memories that comforted, consoled and calmed as the end of life drew nigh.

Every saint's *staff,* when he leans upon it, will do the same—an old picture; correspondence stored from cherished friends; mementos received; awards and honors; a ragged, tattered and worn-out chair; diary or journal; Sunday school lectern or old country church pulpit; rock pile (prayer spot); place of an unusual encounter with the Lord; last words of a loved one. What might be the *staff* upon which you may lean for uplift, comfort and hope?

For me it's the parcel of ground located at the backside of the cemetery beneath an old oak tree at Calvary Baptist Church, Pregnall, South Carolina. That spot is holy ground to me, for when I was the church's teenage pastor, it was there where God met me in the solitude with anointing, affirmation, authorization and "Holy Ghost" power for preaching and ministry. It was there on my knees and often prostrated before the Lord that my entire life and ministry were shaped.

Don't lay your staff aside just yet. Lean on it for the precious remembrances of the mercies, kindness, faithfulness of God, and the loyalty, love and support of family and friends. And thereby be richly encouraged and deeply consoled.

> Precious memories, unseen angels
>> Sent from somewhere to my soul.
> How they linger ever near me,
>> And the sacred past unfolds. ~ J. B. F. Wright (1877)

14

Hezekiah's Miracle

Hezekiah, being informed by Isaiah that death was imminent, immediately pleaded with tears for an extension of time (2 Kings 20:2–3). God graciously added fifteen years to his life (verse 6). The willingness of God to answer the prayer reveals it was honorable and right. The motive behind the request determined its appropriateness: not for selfish benefit or pleasure but the glory of God (verses 3–4).

We can glean some lessons from Hezekiah's deathbed experience.

(1. It is always timely to "set thine house in order" (2 Kings 20:1). A successor (Hezekiah's preference) to the throne needed to be named. Greater still, the

spiritual affairs of his heart required preparation. Both, regardless of Hezekiah's immediate death or prolonged life, were expedient. An old song provides great advice: "Live as if you were dying."

(2. Embrace the dreaded news. The king's terminal condition was confirmed by Isaiah, God's prophet. Though bitter news, it was accepted. Man is most reticence to talk about death or accept its approach, but ignorance or rejection of it changes it not.

(3. Setting one's house in order for death is not synonymous with giving up on life. Hezekiah didn't; you mustn't.

(4. Look to God for help (2 Kings 20:2). In wake of the solemn news, Hezekiah turns "his face to the wall, and prayed unto the LORD." He realized the illness could possibly be reversed and life extended; what physicians were incapable of doing, the Great Physician could and might do. Matthew Henry remarks, "We have not if we ask not, or ask amiss. If the sentence was irreversible, yet prayer is one of the best preparations for death, because by it we fetch in strength and grace from God to enable us to finish well."[108] Therefore, nothing is loss in such entreaty.

(5. God has authority and power over sickness (2 Kings 20:5). Obviously, it's not His will or plan to heal all who are stricken with illness. The why of God's favor in answering Hezekiah's prayer with healing (temporarily) is an unknown. Hezekiah presumed such a decision might be made based upon his spiritual walk: "Remember now how I have walked before thee in truth and with a perfect heart, and have done that which is good in thy sight" (2 Kings 20:3). And what he said was truthful, for history states, "After him was none like him among all the kings of Judah, nor any that were before him" (2 Kings 18:5). However, it is more likely the healing was due to the need of the world more than his good deeds of life (2 Kings 20:6). The apostle Paul testified that though he possessed a strong desire to depart this world to be with Christ (which was far, far better than remaining), "yet to remain in my body is more necessary and essential for your sake" (Philippians 1:24 AMP). Bernard says, "For Christ to be with Paul was the greatest security—but for Paul to be with Christ was the chief happiness!"

(6. Fight for life until the end is known (2 Kings 20:5–6). Until the Lord manifests clearly that healing will not come, battle for it passionately in prayer (in praying, "he wept sore") and medical treatment, as did Hezekiah (2 Kings 20:1b). Such a spirit was manifested by David on behalf of his dying child; he refused to give up on the possibility of the critical sickness being reversed. He said, "Who can tell whether GOD will be gracious to me, that the child may live?" (2 Samuel 12:22). He was relentless in prayer and fasting until the word arrived the child had died.

(7. God often uses medical means to heal (2 Kings 20:7). The miracle of Hezekiah's healing was facilitated by God's use of "a lump of figs" applied to the

infection. Therefore, it is no sign of weak faith that in praying for healing, medical remedies are sought and utilized.

(8. God is able to do immeasurably more than all we ask or imagine (Ephesians 3:20). Hezekiah simply asked for healing (without a specified time frame either as to when it was to happen or its duration after it happened). But God promptly granted the request and added fifteen years to the king's life (2 Kings 20:4–6).

(9. Stay in the "saddle" (sickbed or well bed) accomplishing *what is possible* for the Lord. King Hezekiah did—certainly not in all respects but with regard to Jerusalem. "Unless the work is done here, it will not be done yonder."[109] Resolve to leave life as a "flaming fire."

(10. If life's clock is extended, make full and valuable use of the additional time allotted. That which was begun well (upon healing Hezekiah went up to the house of the Lord on the third day—2 Kings 20:8) didn't continue well. Sadly, Hezekiah was led astray by the pride of his own heart (2 Kings 20:12–18). It is said in 2 Chronicles 32:25, "Hezekiah rendered not again according to the benefit done unto him; for his heart was lifted up." A life of humility prior to "healing" evolved afterward into one of haughtiness. Bear in mind that Manasseh (the son of Hezekiah) was born during the fifteen-year extension. He became the king at age 12 and perpetrated widespread evil. The Bible tells us, "He did what was evil in the Lord's sight, following the detestable practices of the pagan nations that the Lord had driven from the land ahead of the Israelites. He rebuilt the pagan shrines his father, Hezekiah, had destroyed. He constructed altars for Baal and set up an Asherah pole, just as King Ahab of Israel had done" (2 Kings 21:2–3 NLT). Manasseh was one of the wickedest kings that ever lived. In retrospect it would have been better had Hezekiah been content to die on the sickbed. "There is often a great mystery to us when good men seem prematurely taken away. But God knows the reason why, and He doeth all things well. Let us leave the time of our own departure and the departure of our friends contentedly in God's hands."[110] It's always best to couch prayers for healing "in accordance with thy holy will, my best end and that of others."

(11. Restoration to health, if granted, is temporary (2 Kings 20:6). "And Hezekiah slept with his fathers" (2 Kings 20:21). Hezekiah died fifteen years later as foretold by the Lord. Delay in death doesn't mean ultimate escape from it.

15

The Medicine of Laughter

The mental state impacts the physical. Dark, despairing thoughts often promote worsening of the physical. "A broken spirit drieth the bones, destroys all life and vigor."[111] But the opposite also is true. Solomon says, "A cheerful heart is good medicine, but a broken spirit saps a person's strength" (Proverbs 17:22 NLT). Laughter and gaiety of heart are medicine prescribed by the *Great Physician* for a broken, crushed spirit to aid its healing. Granted, laughing is not something we want to do in times of devastating grief. In fact, it's seen as inappropriate. Nonetheless, though undesired and viewed unnecessary (as are some medical prescriptions), it speeds up the healing.

The Mayo Clinic states, "Whether you're guffawing at a sitcom on TV or quietly giggling at a newspaper cartoon, laughing does you good."[112] Research indicates that laughter produces endorphins in the body that produce the sense of well-being. Other physical benefits of laughing noted by health care professionals include decrease in stress hormone levels, strengthening of the immune system, muscle relaxation, pain reduction, lowering of blood pressure, and cardiovascular conditioning. It is also a natural antidepressant.[113] Dr. Marvin E. Herring, New Jersey's School of Osteopathic Medicine, said, "The diaphragm, thorax, abdomen, heart, lungs and even the liver are given a massage during a hearty laugh."[114] Neuroscientist Jodi Deluca, Ph.D., of Embry-Riddle Aeronautical University said, "It doesn't matter why you laugh. Even in small doses, it improves our overall quality of life."[115] The Mayo Clinic says, "When you start to laugh, it doesn't just lighten your load mentally; it actually induces physical changes in your body."[116]

So find ways to incite laughter and cheerfulness of disposition. The psalmist said, *"Then was our mouth filled with laughter, and our tongue with singing"* (Psalm 126:2). Discover what spurs the "then" moments that incite laughter and joy and visit them regularly. Follow the "DOCTOR'S" advice and daily take your laughter medication for the benefit of the mind and body.

Laughter Medicine

In a job interview, a young college graduate in the field of engineering was asked, "And what starting salary are you looking for?"

The engineer replied, "In the area of $150,000 a year, depending on the benefits package."

The interviewer inquired, "Well, what would you say to a package of five weeks' vacation, fifteen paid holidays, full medical and dental coverage, company matching retirement fund to fifty percent of salary, and a new company car leased every two years—say, a red Jaguar?"

The engineer sat up straight and said, "Wow! Are you kidding?"

The interviewer replied, "Yeah, but you started it."[117]

When the Rain Comes

A guy spots a sign outside a house that reads "Talking Dog for Sale." Intrigued, he walks in. "So what have you done with your life?" he asks the dog.

"I've led a very full life," says the dog. "I lived in the Alps rescuing avalanche victims. Then I served my country in Iraq. And now I spend my days reading to the residents of a retirement home."

The guy is flabbergasted. He asks the dog's owner, "Why on earth would you want to get rid of an incredible dog like that?"

The owner says, "Because he's a liar! He never did any of that!"[118]

A grandson asked his grandfather how old he was. He teasingly replied, "I'm not sure."

"Look in your underwear, Grandpa," he advised. "Mine says I'm 4 to 6."

A cement mixer and a prison bus crashed on the highway. Police advised citizens to look out for a group of hardened criminals.[119]

Why does Humpty Dumpty love autumn? Because he always has a great fall.[120]

A man asks a lawyer, "What is your fee?"

The lawyer says: "One thousand dollars for three questions."

The man replied, "Wow—so much! Isn't it a bit expensive?"

The lawyer answered, "Yes. What is your third question?"

A poodle and a collie were out for a walk when the poodle suddenly unloads on his friend. "My life is a mess," he says. "My owner is mean, my girlfriend ran away with a schnauzer, and I'm as jittery as a cat."

"Why don't you go see a psychiatrist?" suggests the collie.

"I can't," says the poodle. "I'm not allowed on the couch."[121]

16

The Bondage of Fear Thwarted

"My heart is sore pained within me: and the terrors of death are fallen upon me" (Psalm 55:4). "Are you afraid?" asked a minister to one of his seriously ill church members. The man was at the point of death and beyond any further medical help. "I've never been afraid of anything in my life," he replied. He then looked at the minister with tears flowing from his eyes and said, "For the first time in my life, I'm terrified—I'm afraid to die." Most identify with the man upon their dying bed. Most live in slavish bondage to the fear of death (Hebrews 2:15). Death is often a terrifying experience for any of five reasons.

(1. Death is feared because of the uncertainty of what's beyond the grave, the unknown.

(2. It is feared because it means separation from spouse, children and friends.

(3. It is feared because of the future judgment that awaits.

(4. It is feared because of the dying process.

(5. It is feared, because ultimately it is something man faces alone. The famous evangelist Dwight L. Moody said, "When it comes to death, some men say, 'I do not fear it.' I feared it and felt terribly afraid when I thought of being launched into eternity, to go to an unknown world. I used to have dreadful thoughts of God, but they are all gone now. Death has lost its sting. And as I go on through the world and the bell is tolling, I can shout now, 'O death, where is thy sting?' And I hear a voice come rolling down from Calvary: 'Buried in the bosom of the Son of God.' He robbed death of its sting; He took away the sting of death when He gave His own bosom to the stroke."[122]

Christ by His death at Calvary nullified the true reason to fear death, which is the curse and condemnation of the law of God (1 Corinthians 15:56).[123] Richard Sibbes states, "Why should we then fear death, which is but a passage to Christ? It is but a grim sergeant that lets us into a glorious palace, that strikes off our bolts, that takes off our rags that we may be clothed with better robes, that ends all our misery and is the beginning of all our happiness. Why should we therefore be afraid of death? It is but a departure to a better condition. It is but as Jordan to the children of Israel, by which they passed to Canaan. It is but as the Red Sea by which they were going that way. Therefore, we have no reason to fear death."[124]

"To overcome the fear of death," states C. H. Spurgeon, "we must look to Jesus Christ on the cross atoning for us, in the resurrection rising for us, in the Glory taking possession of our home for us, and at the right hand of God preparing our place for us, possessing all power and using it so that He may bring us unto His eternal Kingdom—and soon to come again, in all the glory of the latter days, to raise the bodies of His people from the dead unless they are still alive at His coming. This is He who conquers for us the fear of death! It is to Him we are to look—'looking unto Jesus.' Let your eyes be always looking to Him—then the fear of death will not make you subject to bondage."[125]

The disciples were at sea when a terrifying storm developed. Fearful of drowning, they shouted to Jesus who was asleep, "Lord, save us!" Jesus "got up and rebuked the wind and waves, and suddenly there was a great calm" (Matthew 8:26 NLT).

When the Rain Comes

He that quenched the disciples' fear is more than capable and willing to extinguish yours upon request.

> When I tread the verge of Jordan,
>> Bid my anxious fears subside;
> Death of deaths and hell's destruction,
>> Land me safe on Canaan's side.
>
> ~ William Williams (Guide Me, O Thou Great Jehovah)

Relating the safe passage of the priests bearing the ark of the covenant across the Jordan River (Joshua 3:17) to the Christian at death, T. DeWitt Talmage remarks, "Obstacles that may appear tremendous in the distance depart when we advance upon and touch them with courage. Many now are afraid of the *Jordan of death*. But when you come up to it, when your time has come to cross it, it will disappear. Christ your Priest, with bruised feet will go ahead of you. His feet touching the waters will cause them to roll away (as did the touch of the priests' feet with the ark), and you will go through on dry ground."[126]

A father's business required him to take a long walk through the Alps early in the morning and back home after dark. As his son grew up, he begged to be taken on these trips, but the father thought his little legs too weak to make the journey. Finally, after years of refusal, the father gave in and agreed to take him on the next trip. In the early morning walk they crossed a high rope bridge, with a few missing slats, suspended over the valley. With daylight and dad leading the way it posed no problem for the young boy to cross. Once completing their business in the city, they set out for home. The boy began to worry about crossing the rope bridge at dark and shared that fear with his father. The missing slats, the deep gorge, the thick darkness all were of grave concern. Unable to cross the bridge until they came to it, the father was unable to give the boy assurance that everything would be just fine. With strong arms and a loving heart, he placed his son on his back, seeking to assure him. The next thing the boy remembered was awaking to early rays of sunlight and seeing a silhouette of his father standing in the doorway. "Dad, what happened?" the boy inquired. "What about the bridge?" he worried out loud.

"Well, Son, you fell asleep with your arms around my neck. I carried you across the bridge and laid you safely in your own bed. You've just awakened on the other side."[127] What a beautiful picture of the death of a child of God!

The following poem, entitled "Afraid?" was written by Presbyterian missionary E. H. Hamilton after learning of the martyrdom of J. W. Vinson, a fellow missionary, at the hands of rebel soldiers in northern China in 1931. A young Chinese girl that escaped the same attack related how the incident unfolded and in doing so inspired Hamilton's poem.

"Are you afraid?" the bandits asked Vinson as they menacingly waved a gun in front of him.

"No," he replied with complete assurance. "If you shoot, I go straight to Heaven." His decapitated body was found later.[128]

Afraid? Of what?
To feel the spirit's glad release,
To pass from pain to perfect peace,
The strife and strain of life to cease?
Afraid—of that?

Afraid? Of what?
Afraid to see the Savior's face,
To hear His welcome, and to trace
The glory gleam from wounds of grace?
Afraid—of that?

Afraid? Of what?
A flash—a crash—a pierced heart;
Darkness—Light—oh, Heaven's art;
A wound of His a counterpart?
Afraid?—of that?

Afraid? Of what?
To do by death what life could not—
Baptize with blood a stony plot
Till souls shall blossom from the spot?
Afraid? —of that? ~ E. H. Hamilton (1931)

17

The Faith Will Not Fail Us

"What is your only comfort in life and in death? So states the first article in the Heidelberg Catechism of 1563. Christians answer, "It is the hope of eternal life made possible through the resurrection of Jesus Christ (1 Corinthians 15:20)." Without that expectation all is bleak and dismal both in living and in dying. Saints that embrace this "hope" (confident certainty of afterlife in Heaven with Christ) testify that it not only sustains in life but in the throes of death. The courageous, bold and patient deaths of Ignatius, Polycarp, Latimer and Ridley, Baxter and the hosts of martyrs successfully argue for the truthfulness and validity of the Christian faith.[129]

Such deathbed witnesses give more direct proof of the reality of the Christian faith than any abstract argument,[130] for what they endured, heard and saw testify of the constantly abiding and sustaining hand of God to His children as life ebbs away. Far from abandoning them, He tabernacles with them, supplying sufficient grace in the hour of need.

Under the shadow of Your throne
    Your saints have dwelt secure;
Sufficient is your arm alone,
    And our defense is sure. ~ Isaac Watts (1719)

"What an argument for the truth of religion," states Albert Barnes, "what an illustration of its sustaining power, what a source of comfort to those who are about to die, to reflect that religion does not leave the believer when he most needs its support and consolation, that it can sustain us in the severest trial of our condition here, that it can illuminate what seems to us of all places most dark, cheerless, dismal, repulsive—'the valley of the shadow of death.'"[131]

His love in time past forbids us to think
He'll leave us at last in trouble to sink;
Each sweet Ebenezer we have in review
Confirms His good pleasure to help us quite through.
                    ~ John Newton (1725–1807)

Lee Roberson said, "Nothing but encouragement can come to us as we dwell upon the faithful dealing of our Heavenly Father in centuries gone by. Faith in God has not saved people from hardships and trials, but it has enabled them to bear tribulations courageously and to emerge victoriously."[132]

The dawn is not distant,
Nor is the night starless;
    Love is eternal!
God is still God, and
His faith shall not fail us;
    Christ is eternal. ~ Henry Wadsworth Longfellow

18

The Anchor Holds in Spite of the Storm

"Remember the word unto thy servant, upon which thou hast caused me to hope" (Psalm 119:49). Hengstenberg says, "'Remember the word' to thy servant is exactly the same as our phrase *to keep one's word*."[133] David's experiences with trial and trouble revealed over and over again that God was true to His promises, that God could be trusted regardless of the furious and frightening storm encountered. Spurgeon remarked, "The Psalmist does not fear a failure in the Lord's memory, but he makes use of the promise as a plea, and this is the form in which he speaks after the manner of men when they plead with one another."[134]

Matthew Henry said, "That God, who had given him the promise in the Word, had by His grace wrought in him a hope in that promise and enabled him to depend upon it and had raised his expectations of great things from it."[135] Put God in *remembrance of His Word* in times of distress, difficulty, death, defeat, discouragement and danger, for in doing this faith is exhibited and God is pleased. W. S. Plumer says, "God will never disappoint expectations authorized and encouraged by His own promises."[136] See 2 Peter 1:4 and Titus 1:2.

> God will never disappoint expectations authorized
> and encouraged by His own promises.
> W. S. Plumer

In the Catacombs of Rome where Christians hid in times of persecution, one symbol is found written upon the walls more than any other—that of an anchor.[137] Believers have always found strength and comfort in life's storms knowing that they have an Anchor that holds them safe and secure. The Anchor is the sure promises of God recorded in the Holy Scripture. "So God has given both his promise and his oath. These two things are unchangeable because it is impossible for God to lie. Therefore, we who have fled to him for refuge can have great confidence as we hold to the hope that lies before us. This hope is a strong and trustworthy anchor for our souls" (Hebrews 6:18–19 NLT). The text is an analogy of olden days when most ships had sails. When such a ship approached a harbor difficult to navigate, the captain would send a seaman ahead in a small boat with the anchor attached to a rope that extended back to the ship. Once in the bay, the seaman would drop the anchor. The captain then would give orders to the crew to pull the rope little by little, drawing the ship safely into the harbor. In the Christian life, Christ has gone before us to drop the anchor within the harbor of Heaven.[138] The anchor (God's promises) ensures security, strength and stability amidst life's storms until life's journey ends in the harbor of the Celestial City.

When the Rain Comes

Christ Jesus is my anch'rage ground;
No firmer ever can be found.
And anchored here, I cannot fail
To ride in triumph ev'ry gale. ~ Mary D. James (1884)

Hold fast to the Anchor's rope, for it is the believers' indispensable source of strength and comfort. The promises of God (the anchor's *rope*) are drawing you heavenward and prevents drifting off course. Regarding His promises, the famous evangelist D. L. Moody stated, "When a man says, 'I will,' it may not mean much. We very often say 'I will' when we don't mean to fulfill what we say. But when we come to the 'I will' of Christ, He means to fulfill it. Everything He promised to do, He is able and willing to accomplish. I cannot find any Scripture where He says 'I will' do this or 'I will' do that but that it will be done."[139] Therefore Spurgeon says, "Banquet your faith upon God's own Word, and whatever your fears or wants, repair to the Bank of Faith with your Father's note in hand, saying, 'Remember the word unto Thy servant, upon which Thou hast caused me to hope.'"[140]

Standing on the promises that cannot fail,
When the howling storms of doubt and fear assail,
By the living Word of God I shall prevail,
Standing on the promises of God.

Standing on the promises of Christ the Lord,
Bound to him eternally by love's strong cord,
Overcoming daily with the Spirit's sword,
Standing on the promises of God. ~ Russell Kelso Carter (1886)

W. A. Criswell said, "When our trials come, when we feel pain and suffering, when our tears flow again, it is our joy and comfort to lift our faces heavenward and to go on, standing on the promises of God."[141] Corrie ten Boom gives the troubled soul great counsel: "Let God's promises shine on your problems."[142] God's promises are like unseen pillars of rocks in deep, troublesome waters that support the believer who exhibits faith in them.

19

The Physician's Sickbed Care

Merciful saints are assured of the Great Physician's special loving care and support when languishing upon the "sickbed." David says, "The LORD will strengthen him upon the bed of languishing: thou wilt make all his bed in his sickness" (Psalm 41:3). The promise is for one who had been compassionate to the needy, hurting and sick when he was healthy. Adam Clarke says, "Good, benevolent, and merciful as he is, he must also die. But he shall not die as other men; he shall have peculiar consolations, refreshment, and support while passing through the valley of the shadow of death."[143] The Lord will "strengthen him upon the bed of languishing" (the NEB says, "He nurses him"). Albert Barnes says "means to support; to uphold; to sustain. The idea here is that God would enable him to bear his sickness or would impart strength—inward strength—when his body failed or when but for this aid he must sink under his disease and die."[144]

"Thou wilt make all his bed in his sickness" (not necessarily recovery to health, though that happens). John Gill says "making him easy and comfortable on a bed of sickness, which, in a literal sense, is done when a sick person's bed is turned or made or he is turned upon it from side to side; so the Lord, by the comforts of His Spirit, makes a sickbed or a deathbed easy to them that believe in Christ and often puts that triumphant song into their mouths in their dying moments: 'O death, where is thy sting?' and this is the peaceful end and blissful state of such who wisely consider Christ and believe in him.'[145]

Barnes says, "He will relieve his suffering and make him comfortable on his bed. It does not mean that He will turn his sickness to health, but that he will relieve and comfort him, as one is relieved and soothed on a sickbed by having his bed made up."[146] W. S. Plumer says, "It represents God as exercising the office of a nurse, smoothing the pillow and making the bed of His sick and distressed servants."[147] What a wondrous picture of Christ's care for the sickly of His fold. "How tender and sympathizing is this image; how near it brings our God to our infirmities and sicknesses!"[148]

Hopefully in life you have been merciful toward others with your goods, gifts and time, for such strikes at the heart of the Christian faith. See Matthew 25:31–40. But even if not, Christ yet will "make your sickbed"—similarly, not equally, and just as assuredly. To have the greatest physician in the world at the bedside watching over and caring for you constantly instills comfort, peace and hope like nothing else. "Sometime when you are sick," says H. A. Ironside, "and nervous and tired and people do not understand you and everything is going wrong, sit down and take this forty-first Psalm and see if it does not make a wonderful prayer for you."[149]

20

Death: Friend or Foe

To the believer death is a friend in that it ushers him into the presence of Christ in Heaven. However, it remains a foe in that its process is interwoven with suffering and pain.[150] "Death, like an unfinished symphony, leaves fragments of many promising careers and lives."[151] It is the Christian's final enemy (1 Corinthians 15:26), but one that has already been conquered through Jesus' death at Calvary and subsequent resurrection.

James Gwither, a preacher of the nineteenth century, makes a wondrous contrast between the tomb of nature and that of Christ Jesus. "Now a vista is opened (by Christ's resurrection) through the dark valley of death, and the eye of faith may descry (glimpse) the glory which waits to be revealed. The gloom of death is illuminated, its solitude cheered, its bitterness destroyed by the light, comforts, promises, hopes of the Gospel. In the tomb of Jesus Christ are dissipated all the terror which the tomb of nature presents. In the tomb of nature, thou beholdest thy frailty, thy subjection to the curse and bondage of corruption; in the tomb of Jesus Christ, thy strength and deliverance. In the tomb of nature, the punishment for sin stares thee in the face; in the tomb of Jesus, thou findest the expiation of it. From the tomb of nature thou hearest the dreadful sentence pronounced against every child of Adam: 'Dust thou art, and unto dust thou shalt return'; but from the tomb of Jesus Christ issue those assents of consolation: 'I am the resurrection, and the life: he that believeth in me, though he were dead, yet shall he live' (John 11:25). In the tomb of nature, thou hearest this universal, this irrevocable doom written: 'It is appointed unto man once to die'; but in the tomb of Jesus Christ, thy tongue is loosed into this triumphant song of praise: 'O death, where is thy sting? O grave, where is thy victory?...But thanks be to God, which giveth us the victory through our Lord Jesus Christ.'"[152]

> Shrinking from the cold hand of death,
>   I too shall gather up my feet,
> Shall soon resign this fleeting breath
>   And die, my fathers' God to meet.
>
> Numbered among thy people, I
>   Expect with joy thy face to see;
> Because Thou didst for sinners die,
>   Jesus, in death remember me!
>
> Oh, that without a lingering groan
>   I may the welcome word receive,
> My body with my charge lay down
>   And cease at once to work and live!
>
> Walk with me through the dreadful shade,
>   And, certified that Thou art mine,
> My spirit, calm and undismayed,
>   I shall into thy hands resign.

No anxious thoughts, no guilty gloom,
    Shall damp whom Jesus' presence cheers.
My light, my life, my God is come,
    And glory in his face appears! ~ Charles Wesley (1762)

Paul knew the joy of living and the glory of death.[153] He contrasts the two in Philippians 1:21–24: "To me the only important thing about living is Christ, and dying would be profit for me. If I continue living in my body, I will be able to work for the Lord. I do not know what to choose—living or dying. It is hard to choose between the two. I want to leave this life and be with Christ, which is much better, but you need me here in my body" (NCV).

R. C. Sproul says the contrast is not that one is good and the other bad but that one is good and the other "far better."[154] Paul certainly therefore did not count death as a foe but a friend that would take him to a far, far better place, a place where he would be forever with Christ. So emphatically certain that death is a friend, not a foe, Paul included it in the long list of things that cannot separate a saint from God (Romans 8:38). After all, how can that which ushers us into the presence of Christ and loved ones to live eternally without sickness, suffering, pain and sorrow be not a friend!

Thomas Brooks, in agreement, says, "A man that sees his propriety (condition of being right) in God knows that death shall be the funeral of all his sins, sorrows, afflictions, temptations, desertions, oppositions, vexations, oppressions, and persecutions. And he knows that death shall be the resurrection of his hopes, joys, delights, comforts, and contentments, and that it shall bring him to a more clear, full, perfect, and constant enjoyment of God."[155]

Death is my friend,
For after it is no end.
It but opens the door
To Heaven's beautiful shore.

The Devil and sin there do not exist,
Nor else of earth that brought pain in its midst.
To be with Christ and saints about the throne
Is to experience joy that hasn't been known.

How can that which brings this to be
Be anything but a friend to me? ~ Frank Shivers (2020)

When the Rain Comes

Billy Graham summarizes, "Though the Christian has no immunity from death and no claim to perpetual life on this planet, death is to him a friend rather than a foe, the beginning rather than the end, another step on the pathway to Heaven rather than a leap into a dark unknown."[156]

Joseph Parker wrote, "The graciousness of death! What pain he has relieved; what injuries he has thrust into the silent tomb; what tumult and controversy he has ended! Men have found an altar at the tomb, a house of reconciliation in the graveyard, music for the heart in the toll and throb of the last knell. Even death must have his tribute."[157]

21
The Benefits of Trouble

"We are troubled on every side, yet not distressed; we are perplexed, but not in despair; Persecuted, but not forsaken; cast down, but not destroyed; Always bearing about in the body the dying of the Lord Jesus, that the life also of Jesus might be made manifest in our body" (2 Corinthians 4:8–10). Paul states that trouble is a blessing to the saint in disguise. In what ways is trouble a benefit to those that love the Lord?

Trouble identifies the saint. Trouble brings out the real man. In how a person responds to the pressure, pain and punch of infirmity, calamity and sorrow, others are brought to see the reality of or depth to his faith. The Bible says, "These trials will show that your faith is genuine (1 Peter 1:7a NLT). It is the ship at sea in the midst of a storm, not the one in the harbor, that tests it true mettle. Some saints thought strong are proven not to be when under fire.

Trouble purifies the saint. Adversity purges the impurities (chaff) from the saint's life (wheat), refining him into "pure gold." See Lamentations 4:1. Birch said, "Afflictions are to us like sandpaper, to make us smooth and polished to take our place in the society of Heaven."[158] The psalmist testified, "Before I was afflicted I went astray: but now have I kept thy word" (Psalm 119:67). With regard to the adversity, he said, "It is good for me that I have been afflicted" (Psalm 119:71). The spiritual restoration, renewal and revival that results from the saints' deep trouble and hardship makes it a friend, not a foe. Lying down, we are forced to look up. Elizabeth Elliot writes, "Our vision is so limited we can hardly imagine a love that does not show itself in protection from suffering....The love of God did not protect His own Son....He will not necessarily protect us—not from anything it takes to make us like His Son. A lot of hammering and chiseling and purifying by fire will have to go into the process."[159]

Comfort for Troubled Hearts

Trouble solidifies the saint. It is in the furnace of affliction that *faith* is strengthened and crystalized. Paul explains, "This doesn't mean, of course, that we have only a hope of future joys—we can be full of joy here and now even in our trials and troubles. Taken in the right spirit these very things will give us patient endurance; this in turn will develop a mature character, and a character of this sort produces a steady hope, a hope that will never disappoint us" (Romans 5:3–4 PHILLIPS). The strength of a sapling increases by the force of the storm, driving its roots deeper into the sod for support. The storms of life do that for the saints' faith and spiritual walk.

Trouble unifies the saint. Adversity is a magnet the Lord uses to bring saints together to render support to its victim. Often it is in times of grave trouble that divided saints become united saints and that "broken" relationships with family and friends are reconciled.

Trouble prospers the saint. Paul testified about his troubles, "Now I want you to know, brothers and sisters, that what has happened to me has actually served to advance the gospel" (Philippians 1:12 NIV). Christ's power is at work in adversities to further the good work which He began in us at conversion (Philippians 1:6). But its how (God's plan for our good and His glory) may be hidden. Henry Ward Beecher said, "We are always in the forge or on the anvil; by trials God is shaping us for higher things."[160]

Trouble cheers the saint. Paul said, "We also have joy with our troubles" (Romans 5:3 NCV). The good that proceeds from trouble (not necessarily at its time) prompts joy and song (Acts 16:25–34). Fanny Crosby (blinded for life by a medical mistake at six weeks of age) possessed such joy and song. As a teenager she wrote in her first poem:

> Oh, what a happy soul I am!
>   Although I cannot see,
> I am resolved that in this world
>   Contented I will be.
>
> How many blessings I enjoy
>   That other people don't!
> To weep and sigh because I'm blind,
>   I cannot, and I won't!

With David the saint says, "I will praise the Lord no matter what happens. I will constantly speak of his glories and grace" (Psalm 34:1 TLB).

When the Rain Comes

Trouble utilizes its affliction of the saint to the comfort of others. The saint's forbearance in trial engenders courage, comfort and hope to others. It enables the saint to console others in their sorrow with genuine sympathy and empathy, having experienced what the others now are encountering. W. E. Sangster states, "Sympathy is a shallow stream in the souls of those who have not suffered. There is something unheeding and harsh in the man who has known nothing of pain. And sympathy is far too precious in this needy world to begrudge the price at which it must be purchased."[161]

Trouble amplifies the bliss of Heaven to the saint. Spurgeon says, "Severe trouble in a true believer has the effect of loosening the roots of his soul earthward and tightening the anchor hold of his heart heavenward."[162]

Trouble clarifies truth to the saint. "Affliction frequently opens truths to us and opens us to truths. Many a text is written in secret ink which must be held to the fire of adversity to make it visible."[163]

Trouble magnifies the Savior to the world through the saint. The ultimate goal in the time of trouble is the magnification and glorification of Christ unto an unregenerate world. W. A. Criswell states, "The glory of God is found in the fire and the flame and the trial of His people, singing songs in the night, praising God in the midst of indescribable sorrow and heartache."[164]

William Gurnall said, "Let this encourage those of you who belong to Christ: the storm may be tempestuous, but it is only temporary. The clouds that are temporarily rolling over your head will pass, and then you will have fair weather, an eternal sunshine of glory."[165]

Sorrows multiplying,
Prospects overcast,
Weeping, groaning, sighing,
Still I'm anchored fast.~ William P. Breed (1869)

22

Light at Eventide

That which makes evening is the gradual lessening of the light of day. Evening eventually gives way to night. Life for you may presently be "evening time"; night is closing in. Common thought is that "night" is to be equated with gloom, sorrow and adversity, therefore looked upon with fear, dread and horror. But for the Christian the Bible "studs the night with stars of hope and suns of promise."[166] "At evening time it shall be light" (Zechariah 14:7). As the terrible night of death approached Job, he testified, "My days have passed, my plans are shattered. Yet the desires of my heart

46

turn night into day; *in the face of the darkness light is near*" (Job 17:11–12 NIV). Job's experience is that of all the redeemed. Death which is thought to be horrifying and gloomy is lit up by the brilliant light of Christ's holy and majestic presence, promises, peace and provision. Unlike the way it is in nature, God's *light,* instead of growing dimmer and dimmer, shines brighter and brighter as the night unfolds.

"At evening time it shall be light." T. DeWitt Talmage wrote, "Life is a short winter's day. Baptism and burial are near together. But thanks be to God, who giveth us the victory. 'At evening time it shall be light.'"[167] G. Victor Macdona said, "When the darkness grows deepest, the light begins to glow."[168] *Lux E Tenebris,* "At evening time it shall be light."

Multiplied millions of deathbeds bear witness to this promise. "Instead of a great darkness, celestial radiance! Instead of dismay, a peace unspeakable!"[169] Claim the promise. Cling to the promise. Confide in the promise. Capitulate to the promise. And find calm and comfort in the promise.

In 1915 Fanny Crosby wrote her final hymn, *At Evening Time It Shall Be Light.* With her being in her ninety-fifth year at the time of its writing, the hymn doubtlessly is based upon her experience.

At evening time it shall be light, when fades the day of toil away,
No shadows deep, no weary night; at evening time it shall be light.
At evening time it shall be light; immortal love from realms above
Is breathing now the promise bright: At evening time it shall be light.

At evening time it shall be light; we'll gather flowers from rural bowers.
Oh, sacred hope of glory bright, at evening time it shall be light!
At evening time it shall be light—sweet evening time of joy divine
That makes the Christian's life so bright; at evening time it shall be light.

At evening time it shall be light. No cares shall harm; no fears alarm.
If one in Christ, our souls unite; at evening time it shall be light.
At evening time it shall be light. The heart will glow; no tears will flow.
It cannot lose its promise bright; at evening time it shall be light.

At the evening time there shall be light at last. "When the Christian's little day has drawn to its close, when the Christian's earthly sun has set, then there should be to him the beginning of a day whose sun shall never go down and whose brightness shall be lessened by no intrusion of the dark."[170] "It is a dark passage through which you are passing now," said a young man as he sat beside his dying mother. Her whole countenance lighted up as she said, "Oh, no, my son; there is too bright a light at the other end to have it dark," and she departed to Heaven.[171] 'At the evening time it was light.' "Unto the upright there ariseth light in the darkness: he is gracious, and full of compassion, and righteous" (Psalm 112:4).

> Abide with me; fast falls the eventide.
> The darkness deepens; Lord, with me abide.
> When other helpers fail and comforts flee,
> Help of the helpless, oh, abide with me.
>
> Swift to its close ebbs out life's little day.
> Earth's joys grow dim; its glories pass away.
> Change and decay in all around I see.
> O Thou who changest not, abide with me.
>
> I fear no foe with Thee at hand to bless;
> Ills have no weight, and tears no bitterness.
> Where is death's sting? Where, grave, thy victory?
> I triumph still, if Thou abide with me.
>
> Hold Thou Thy cross before my closing eyes;
> Shine through the gloom and point me to the skies.
> Heav'n's morning breaks, and earth's vain shadows flee.
> In life, in death, O Lord, abide with me. ~ Henry Francis Lyte (1793–1847)

23

Under the Shadow of His Wings

"How excellent is thy lovingkindness, O God! therefore the children of men put their trust under the shadow of thy wings" (Psalm 36:7). "The figure is very beautiful. The Lord overshadows his people as a hen protects her brood or as an eagle covers its young, and we as the little ones run under the blessed shelter and feel at rest."[172] The word for "shadow" means protection and defense; underneath God's shadow is safety from danger. In the covert of His wings saints find a strong and loving refuge as the body grows frail, feeble and fatigued. See Deuteronomy 32:11; Ruth 2:12; Psalm 17:8; Psalm 57:1 and Matthew 23:37. *Find refuge* ("to put their trust") means to flee for refuge "like a man guilty of manslaughter fleeing from the avenger of blood. They mean to flee with haste and intensity, stopping for nothing, until by the full thrust of their entire natures they find safety and deliverance beneath the wings and in the unfailing mercy of Almighty God."[173] In times of trouble saints quickly flee to their safety zone, under the shadow of His wings. Charles Simeon said, "The more we know of man, the more shall we see the folly of trusting in an arm of flesh; but, the more we are acquainted with God, the more enlarged will be our expectations from Him, and the more unreserved our confidence in His power and grace."[174]

John Ortberg says, "There is something you can't fix, can't heal or can't escape; and all you can do is trust God. Finding *ultimate refuge* in God means you become so immersed in His presence, so convinced of His goodness, so devoted to His lordship that you find even the cave is a perfectly safe place to be because He is there with you."[175] Knowing He is there with us, wherever the "there" is, gives peace and lionlike courage to face the trial or trouble triumphantly. "Thus far the LORD has helped us" (1 Samuel 7:12 NIV). Knowing that God helped us in our yesterdays gives assurance of His help in our todays and tomorrows.

> Other refuge have I none;
>> Hangs my helpless soul on thee.
> Leave, ah! leave me not alone;
>> Still support and comfort me.

> All my trust on thee is stayed;
>> All my help from thee I bring.
> Cover my defenseless head
>> With the shadow of thy wing. ~ Charles Wesley (1740)

C. H. Spurgeon wrote, "Those who commune with God are safe with Him. No evil can reach them, for the outstretched wings of His power and love cover them from all harm. *The Almighty Himself is where His shadow is,* and hence those who dwell in His secret place are shielded by Himself. What a shade in the day of noxious heat! What a refuge in the hour of deadly storm! The more closely we cling to our Almighty Father, the more confident may we be."[176] See Psalm 91:1. The psalmist said, "God is our refuge and strength, a very present help in trouble. Therefore will not we fear, though the earth be removed, and though the mountains be carried into the midst of the sea; Though the waters thereof roar and be troubled, though the mountains shake with the swelling thereof. Selah" (Psalm 46:1–3). As chicks cuddle with their mother in danger, never hesitate to flee to the safety of God's outstretched wings in the time of trouble for sufficient refuge.

> Under His wings I am safely abiding.
>> Though the night deepens and tempests are wild,
> Still I can trust Him; I know He will keep me.
>> He has redeemed me, and I am His child. ~ William O. Cushing (1823–1902)

24

The Old Ship of Zion

In fifty-five years of ministry and biblical study, my eyes failed to see the beautiful truth of 2 Peter 1:11. That is, until now. "For so an entrance shall be ministered unto you abundantly into the everlasting kingdom of our Lord and Savior Jesus Christ" (2 Peter 1:11). View it through nautical lenses, as saints in voyage. The ship's Captain is Christ; its Navigator, the Holy Spirit; and the redeemed of the Lord, its passengers. All aboard are happy and hopeful. Its destination is "the everlasting kingdom." The kingdom is opposite from the kingdoms of the world that flourish and perish. It is marked with permanence and perfection. Its government and administration are monarchal, for King Jesus rules from the throne without dissent. It is a kingdom in which there are no Democrats, Republicans or Independents or revolutions or riots. Unallowable in the kingdom is that which defiles the soul (sin), inflicts sorrow and suffering, and brings disease, decay and death. Happiness, joy and peace reign throughout its domain.

Though the ship passes through storms, some unexpected and violent, the passengers remain calm, knowing the *Captain* is at the helm. Excitement is inflamed at first sight of the heavenly shore. Faint sounds are heard of the people and angels gathered there to give welcome upon arrival at port. In moments the Old Ship of Zion ports. How is it that saints get from the ship to the shore? No worry, 'for an entrance shall be ministered unto you abundantly into the everlasting kingdom.' The plank from ship to shore is death. But not to fear—it is extremely short and brief to travel. It is carpeted with the riches of Christ's mercy and grace and enveloped in His love, care and comfort.

Not all disembark simultaneously. It is divinely orchestrated and administered for each believer by Christ Jesus. Job said that the number of months we live is already decided by God (Job 14:5). The place, time and means of death are designed by His purpose. What consolation, assurance and joy it is to know that my Savior administers each facet of my 'entrance into the everlasting kingdom'—and does so "abundantly."

I was standing by the banks of a river
Looking out over life's troubled sea,
When I saw an old ship that was sailing.
Is that the old ship of Zion I see?

Its hull was bent and battered
From the storms of life, I could see.
Waves were rough, but that old ship kept sailing.
Is that the old ship of Zion I see?

At the stern of the ship was the Captain;
I could hear as he called out my name.
Get on board; it's the old ship of Zion.
It will never pass this way again.

As I step on board I'll be leaving
All my troubles and trials behind.
I'll be safe with Jesus the Captain,
Sailing out on the old ship of Zion. ~ Thomas A. Dorsey (1899–1993)

25

Death Is Precious to Him

A. W. Pink wrote, "If the Lord's people would more frequently make a prayerful and believing study of what the Word says upon their departure out of this world, death would lose much, if not all, of its terrors for them. But, alas, instead of doing so, they let their imagination run riot; they give way to carnal fears; they walk by sight instead of by faith."[177]

The Bible states that the death of the saint is *precious* in the sight of God (Psalm 116:15). The word "precious" used in other texts means "honorable" (Isaiah 43:4); "dear" (Jeremiah 31:20); "splendid and glorious" (Job 31:26).[178] Combined, these definitions teach that the death of a saint is precious, honorable, dear, splendid and glorious to God.

C. H. Spurgeon states, "The Lord watches over their dying beds, smooths their pillows, sustains their hearts, and receives their souls. Those who are redeemed with precious blood are so dear to God that even their deaths are precious to him."[179] Death is not a matter of unconcern to God for either the saint who dies or their loved ones who remain. A. C. Dixon wrote, "As we see death, it means decay, removal, absence—things which we do not prize. But as God sees death, He beholds something really precious to Him and, we may justly infer, precious to us, for whatever is against us cannot be precious to our Father. We are looking at the wrong side of the tapestry, where all is tangle and confusion. God sees the right side, where the design is intelligent and the colors harmonious. We are without the veil and see but the dim light through the curtain; within is the Shekinah glory. We stand in the dark, believing and hoping; God is in the light, seeing and knowing."[180]

But why does God count our deaths precious?

(1. The death of saints is precious in His sight because they are His dearly beloved. A. W. Pink wrote, "They ever were and always will be dear to Him. His saints! They were the ones on whom His love was set before the earth was formed or the Heavens made. These are they for whose sakes He left His Home on high and

51

whom He bought with His precious blood, cheerfully laying down His life for them. These are they whose names are borne on our great High Priest's bosom and engraved on the palms of His hands. They are His Father's love-gift to Him, His children, members of His body; therefore, everything that concerns them is precious in His sight"[181]—even their death. Phillips Brooks, commenting on Psalm 23:3 ("For His name's sake") states, "The poor soul loves to think that God is taking care of him for his own sake, because it is precious to himself. Many a time the soul has to flee from the sense of its own little value to the thought that God values it because it is dear and precious to Him."[182]

(2. It is precious due to its freeing (terminating) power from suffering, sorrow, and sickness. It provides the vehicle away from the curse of sin and its ravaging power to inflict pain and sorrow, into His holy, loving presence of peace and joy in Heaven safely.

> No tongue can describe, no language can paint
> How dear to the Lord is the death of the saint;
> Till journey be ended and valley be past
> And sinner meets Savior in glory at last!
>
> Precious is the death of the saint!
>   Sinner by redemption restored!
> Precious are his footsteps, passing thro' the vale,
>   Precious in the sight of the Lord. ~ James M. Gray (1901)

(3. It is precious in that it removes the saint from the present evil on earth and that which is yet to come (Isaiah 57:1).

(4. It is precious in that it puts on display the comforting grace of God as a witness to the world of how God sustains His children in the severest trial of sorrow, granting peace and solace.

(5. The death of a saint is precious in the sight of the Lord in that it means he/she is now with Him in Heaven. The saints' death is the answer to Christ's high priestly prayer offered on earth: "Father, I will that they also, whom thou hast given me, be with me where I am; that they may behold my glory" (John 17:24). "Love seeks the companionship of the loved."[183]

(6. It is precious in the fact that it may be the means of the conversion of family and friends.

(7. It is precious to the Lord in that He made possible their redemption. Francis Dixon comments, "The time is coming when our Savior 'shall see of the travail of his

soul, and shall be satisfied' (Isaiah 53:11); in other words, when He shall see some of the fruits of His death and resurrection. What is it that brings satisfaction to His heart? Is it the wonderful thousand years of millennial reign which we are anticipating (Revelation 20: 1–7)? Is it the final banishment of Satan and of all evil (Revelation 20:10)? Is it the new Heaven and the new earth that are going to be brought into being (Revelation 21:1)? No, not these, primarily—but it is the gathering into His presence of all whom He has redeemed (Revelation 7:9–17)."[184] Warren Wiersbe states, "The death of God's children is so precious to Him that it will not be an accident. It is an appointment. We are immortal until our work is done."[185]

> The death of God's children is so precious to Him that it will not be an accident. It is an appointment. We are immortal until our work is done.
> ~ Warren Wiersbe

26
But Three Little Words

The three most powerful words of tongue or pen, *I love you*, are too seldom spoken. See I Corinthians 13:13.

I love you. But three little words; when said they bridge hurt and misunderstanding; affirm value and worth; communicate care, concern and affection; manifest soul oneness and unconditional trust and support.

I love you. But three little words; they are so full of nectar and honey that repetition in use never depletes them of their fragrance and sweetness.

I love you. But three little words; simple, yet difficult to utter for some. Max Lucado states, "There is a time for risky love. There is a time for extravagant gestures. There is a time to pour out your affections on one [ones] you love. And when the time comes—seize it; don't miss it."[186] And that time, as never before, is when approaching death. Choke down the reluctance or fear in expressing love verbally and/or in writing.

I love you. But three little words; they are enormous in depth, profound in substance, simple in understanding and eternal in impact.

I love you. But three little words; they are always welcome, never "overplayed" when spoken in sincerity, and self-explanatory in nature.

President George H. W. Bush's last words to his son were: "I love you, too." Those last words captured the headlines in newspapers across the nation, highlighting their significance to his son. Obviously, much was shared between the two presidents (father and son) in those final hours. But that which bore the greatest impact were three little words.

27

The Indissoluble Bond

"Who shall separate us from the love of Christ?" (Romans 8:35). That is, is there anything at all that can dissolve the saint's union with Christ? Paul answers the question in Romans 8:37—39, stating that absolutely nothing can divorce Christ from the saint.

The argument for the guarantee of an indissoluble bond with Christ.

(1. There is nothing which can sever Christ's love from the saints, because His love was not their doing. Christ initiates it, bestows it and sustains it.

(2. There is nothing which can sever Christ's love from the saints, because it is promised that it will be everlasting. The Bible says, "'But with *everlasting love* I will have compassion on you,' says the Lord, your Redeemer" (Isaiah 54:8 NLT). And Christ keeps His word (Titus 1:2). John Piper comments, "The reason Paul can say that nothing will separate us from the love of Christ is because Christ is alive and is still loving us now. He is at the right hand of God and is therefore ruling for us. And He is interceding for us, which means He is seeing to it that His finished work of redemption does in fact save us hour by hour and bring us safe to eternal joy. His love is not a memory. It is a moment-by-moment action of the omnipotent, living Son of God, to bring us to everlasting joy."[187]

(3. There is nothing which can sever Christ's love from the saints, because of the immutability of Christ (Hebrews 13:8). The unchangeable character of Christ prevents the dissolution of His love for the saints. Jeremiah said, "The LORD hath appeared of old unto me, saying, Yea, I have loved thee with an everlasting love" (Jeremiah 31:3). Paul wrote, "If we are faithless, He remains faithful [true to His word and His righteous character], for He cannot deny Himself" (2 Timothy 2:13 AMP). J. C. Ryle said, "There is no fickleness about Jesus; those whom He loves, He loves to the end."

> O God, the Rock of Ages, who evermore hast been;
> What time the tempest rages, our dwelling place serene;
> Before Thy first creations, O Lord, the same as now;
> To endless generations, the Everlasting Thou!
>
> ~ Edward H. Bickersteth (1860)

(4. There is nothing which can sever Christ's love from the saints, because it is safekept by His omnipotent power and abiding presence. Satan, man or affliction are powerless to remove His love. Peter said, "Who are kept by the power of God through faith unto salvation ready to be revealed in the last time" (1 Peter 1:5).

(5. There is nothing which can sever Christ's love from the saints, because of the reasoning of Romans 8:32. Matthew Henry comments, "God having manifested his love in giving his own Son for us, and not hesitating at that, can we imagine that anything else should divert or dissolve that love?"[188]

The enumeration of things that cannot sever Christ's love from the believer grants assurance.

The first "cluster" of things Paul states that cannot separate the saint from Christ are the troubles of life (tribulation, distress, hunger, and being destitute—lack of sufficient clothing). Calamities do not remove but rather serve to prove the steadfast love of Christ to His children. He never abandons "ship" despite the fierceness of the storm or the impoverishment of life.

The second cluster of things that cannot divorce the saint from Christ is the hostility of man (persecution, danger, and the sword). The saint may be deprived of food and water, stripped of earthly possessions, cast into a rat-infested prison, tormented heinously and thrust through with a sword for the cause of the Gospel, but Christ's companionship and compassion never can be killed or taken away.

The third cluster of things that cannot remove the love of Christ from the saint are the unseen powers of Heaven and Hell (angels, God's Heavenly army; and principalities, Satan and the demons). Warren Wiersbe rightly says, "Angels would not and demons could not undo God's relationship with His redeemed ones."[189] All the battalions of Hell combined are unable to divorce Christ and His love from the redeemed.

The fourth cluster of things that cannot sever the love of Christ from the saint are the two sides of existence (life and death). The love of Christ is not bound to life but extends into death. Paul said, "For whether we live, we live unto the Lord; and whether we die, we die unto the Lord: whether we live therefore, or die, we are the Lord's" (Romans 14:8).

The fifth cluster of things that cannot shake the love of Christ from the saint are the extremes of time (things present and things to come).[190] The hardships, infirmity, sorrow or suffering being experienced now and whatever may be experienced tomorrow cannot thwart the love of Christ one iota.

The sixth cluster of things that cannot deprive the saint of the love of Christ are the powers in space (height and depth). There is no possibility of anything suddenly appearing from overhead or underneath the believer to sever the love of Christ.[191]

The seventh and final cluster of things that cannot injure the love of Christ for the saint are the forces in the created world (powers and "any other created thing"). Paul underscores a second time the impotency of the host of Hell to sever the love of Christ from the saint. Just as incompetent for that task is any government antagonistic to the Christian. "Any other created thing" comprehensively includes anything that Paul may have omitted among the things that cannot defeat the love of Christ in the saint ("personal or impersonal, animate or inanimate, known or unknown"[192]). "Many waters cannot drown His love, nor the floods quench it."[193]

With Paul, every believer may attest, "I stand convinced that nothing can sever a saint from the love of Christ" (Romans 8:38). What awesome assurance the saint possesses with regard to the certainty of Christ's ever-present love, guardianship and help. There is nothing any more sure and secure than personal salvation wrought and preserved by Christ. Come what may, the love of Christ for you is unshakable, immoveable and changeless.

> Oh, love of God, how rich and pure!
>   How measureless and strong!
> It shall forevermore endure,
>   The saints' and angels' song. ~ Frederick M. Lehman (1917)

28
The Defeat of Death

G. Campbell Morgan states, "Death is not robed in beauty. It is named an enemy. Its long persistent power is realized....Death to humanity is always hostile and hateful. Death continues, age after age, century after century, defying every attempt that man has made to discover its secret and abolish it....Death is the wounder of hearts. It is the assailant of faith. It is the challenger of hope. Deny the *resurrection of Christ* and you have no comfort—the thud of the clod on the coffin, and that is all. Blessed be God, for He is risen."[194] "Death to the saints," says C. H. Spurgeon, "is not a penalty; it is not destruction; it is not even a loss. It is a privilege."[195] Further he stated, "It is the very joy of this earthly life to think that it will come to an end."[196]

In 1 Corinthians 15 Paul uses the doctrine of "the two Adams" to instruct about the origin and defeat of death. Through the first Adam's sin, death entered the world (Genesis 3:1–7). But through the "Last Adam" (Jesus Christ), death was conquered at Calvary (1 Corinthians 15:21–22). Jesus, in rising from the dead on Easter, became the "firstfruits of the resurrection"; the first in the line of many that will be raised at death to be with Him in Heaven (1 Corinthians 15:23). "Christ is God's 'Last Adam,' and He will reverse the wrong that the first Adam brought into this world."[197]

The battle of Waterloo (June 18, 1815) pivoted on the seizure of a stone house, according to Napoleon Bonaparte.[198] Effort upon effort was attempted to capture it, but without success, which ultimately meant defeat for the French. Satan and the demonic host's strategy for victory over Christ and the forces of righteousness pivoted on the "empty tomb." The prevention of the resurrection of Christ would make him and the powers of darkness the victors. But that effort was utterly thwarted on Easter morning when Jesus broke the chains of death and arose.

> Death cannot keep his prey.
> Jesus, my Savior!
> He tore the bars away.
> Jesus, my Lord!

> Up from the grave He arose
> With a mighty triumph o'er His foes.
> He arose a Victor from the dark domain,
> And He lives forever with His saints to reign.
> He arose! (He arose)
> He arose! (He arose)
> Hallelujah! Christ arose! ~ Robert Lowry (1826–1899)

Death, though delivered a decisive and destructive blow by Christ at the cross and empty tomb, remains the saint's final enemy. For Christians, "death's stinger" has been removed (its fear, terror, fright) because of Christ's triumphant resurrection. However, its lingering and languishing last *kick,* all experience in the dying process. Jesus will ultimately put death under His feet (Romans 16:20 and Ephesians 1:22). All other foes will be utterly defeated "before" the final resurrection. The enmity (hostility against God) of the human heart, the false religion systems of the world, and the reign of Satan as the "prince of this world" all will be thwarted victoriously by Christ.[199] Death, the final foe, will then be subdued at the final resurrection, with the power of death wrested from Satan's hands (no more will die).[200] The effects of the curse upon sin will cease. The redeemed will live forever without the dread or fear of death in Heaven's new kingdom. Jon Courson comments, "When at last the kingdom of death is cast into outer darkness, Christ will rule and reign unchallenged. What a day that will be! The last enemy to be destroyed, nevermore to haunt or burden anyone, will not only be physical death, but the death of marriage, the death of joy, the death of peace, the death of everything that brings about hopelessness, heaviness, and sorrow."[201] Hallelujah for the funeral of death!

> Come, ye saints, with one accord;
> Join the triumph of the Lord.
> Bruised is the serpent's head;
> Jesus lives, and Death is dead.

When the Rain Comes

Death is dead, for Jesus lives;
Gift of life to all He gives.
Jesus died that death might die;
Jesus wins the victory.[202]

John Stott said, "Of course dying can be very unpleasant, and bereavement can bring bitter sorrow. But death itself has been overthrown, and 'blessed are the dead which die in the Lord' (Rev. 14:13). The proper epitaph to write for a Christian believer is not a dismal and uncertain petition, 'R.I.P.' (*requiescat in pace*, 'may he rest in peace'), but a joyful and certain affirmation 'C.A.D.' ('Christ abolished death')."[203]

29

Ultimate Healing

Paul's prayers for healing were denied. He writes, "Three times I begged the Lord for it to leave me, but his reply has been, "My grace is enough for you: for where there is weakness, my power is shown the more completely." Therefore, I have cheerfully made up my mind to be proud of my weaknesses, because they mean a deeper experience of the power of Christ. I can even enjoy weaknesses, suffering, privations, persecutions and difficulties for Christ's sake. For my very weakness makes me strong in him" (2 Corinthians 12:8–10 PHILLIPS). Trophimus likewise had to endure sickness (2 Timothy 4:20).

> Yes, ask it for ourselves, if we need healing,
>   Pleading those instances of olden cure;
> But if He then refuse, we still will trust Him,
>   And He will make it happier to endure.
>
> Aye, happier to bear with Him the suffering,
>   Or even death itself, with Him close by,
> For in His presence there is joy forever,
>   And with Him near, it is not death to die.[204]

Paul said that it's not loss to die; it is a gain (Philippians 1:21). Included in the "gain" is complete healing from our bodily parts' dysfunction wrought by disease, sickness, injury and age.

Look with me into Heaven through the lens of Holy Scripture. There yonder standing fully erect at the Throne is Joni who was a quadriplegic down here. Is that not gain? See Fanny that was blind in life adoring Jesus and admiring Heaven's streets of gold, pearly gates and the foundation of its walls made of jasper, sapphire, emerald and other precious jewels. Is that not gain? See David whose body was plagued with cancerous pain here fully clothed in newness of health. Again, I ask, is that not gain? These and the myriads of others in Heaven unitedly shout to us on our sickbeds here, "Death is not by any means a loss; it's a huge gain." What is not in the physician's power to do for us here, the Great Physician does in Heaven. Is that a loss? No, Paul answers, for it is *great gain*.[205]

Ultimately sick saints will experience complete healing.

During Baxter's dying moments, friends visited. Almost the final word spoken by him were in answer to the question, "Dear Mr. Baxter, how are you?"

"Almost well," he said.[206]

C. H. Spurgeon says, "Death cures; it is the best medicine, for those who die are not only almost well, but healed forever."[207] Ultimately sick saints will experience complete healing. Fanny Crosby puts it beautifully: "Chords that were broken will vibrate once more."

Sown in weakness, raised in power, ready to live in Paradise,
I'll have a new body, praise the Lord; I'll have a new life.
~ Luther G. Presley (1887—1974)

Not being healed also has present gain. Outside personal growth in the Lord, ponder the numerous books, hymns, sermons, blogs, movies and testimonies spurred in times of relentless suffering and pain that have greatly benefited the saints and enlarged the kingdom of God.

30

For the Christian, Death Is Merely Sleep

What the many call death, the early saints called sleep. In fact, *sleep* is the most frequently used term to describe the Christian's death in the New Testament. In hearing news of the death of Mary and Martha's brother, Jesus told the disciples, "Our friend Lazarus sleepeth; but I go, that I may awake him out of sleep" (John 11:11). Stephen, in dying from the stones of his persecutors, "kneeled down, and cried with a loud voice, Lord, lay not this sin to their charge. And when he had said this, he fell asleep" (Acts 7:60). Paul said of David, "After he had served his own generation by the will of God, [he] fell on sleep" (Acts 13:36), and of the more than five hundred brethren that saw the resurrected Christ, "of whom the greater part remain unto this present, but some are fallen asleep" (1 Corinthians 15:6). Peter, referencing the rise of scoffers of the faith in the last days, said they would say, "Where is the promise of his coming? for since the fathers fell asleep, all things continue as they were from the beginning of the creation" (2 Peter 3:4).

The term *sleep,* therefore, was a common one to describe the death of a saint by the early church. And yet the name remains with us in strong force in every "cemetery" of the world. The word *cemetery* is derived from the Greek word *koimētērion*, which literally means "sleeping place."

John Howe wrote, "How apt and obvious is the analogy between our awakening out of natural sleep and the holy soul's rising up out of the darkness and torpor ["a state of mental and motor inactivity with partial or total insensibility," *Merriam-Webster*] of its present state into the enlivening light of God's presence."[208] See Psalm 17:15.

We dread or fear death no more than sleep.[209] We have toiled long and hard through life's short day; exhausted we lay down to sleep only to awake to dawn's new day in Heaven fully refreshed and fully alive in the presence of Christ. The "sleep" is momentary. It lasts less than the twinkling of an eye, and we awake in His presence. "To die is to go at once to be with Him—no chasm, no interval, no weary delay in purgatory."[210] To be absent from the body is to instantly be present with the Lord (2 Corinthians 5:8). The soul ascends to Heaven; the body goes to the grave to await the *great resurrection* when Christ returns (1 Thessalonians 4:16–17).

Charles Simeon summarizes, "The separation that will take place between their souls and bodies will only introduce them to a higher state of existence, which they shall enjoy until the day that their bodies shall be awakened from their slumbers to participate and enhance their bliss."[211] Of death says another, "It is but the envelope torn open; the letter is elsewhere. The body did not constitute the person."[212]

> Asleep in Jesus—blessed sleep
> From which none ever wakes to weep,
> A calm and undisturbed repose
> Unbroken by the last of foes!
>
> Asleep in Jesus—oh, how sweet
> To be for such a slumber meet,
> With holy confidence to sing
> That death has lost his venomed sting!
>
> Asleep in Jesus—peaceful rest
> Whose waking is supremely blessed;
> No fear, no woe shall dim that hour
> That manifests the Savior's power.

60

Asleep in Jesus—far from thee
Thy kindred and their graves may be,
But there is still a blessed sleep
From which none ever wakes to weep. ~ Margaret Mackay (1832)

31

Why the Christian's Death Is Called Sleep

The Christian's death resembles sleep in the "unclothing" that transpires. In dress for sleep, the work clothes are discarded. In the saint's sleep of death, he is "unclothed." Job said, "Naked came I out of my mother's womb, and naked shall I return thither: the LORD gave, and the LORD hath taken away; blessed be the name of the LORD" (Job 1:21). Paul writes, "We know that when these bodies of ours are taken down like tents and folded away, they will be replaced by resurrection bodies in Heaven—God-made, not handmade—and we'll never have to relocate our 'tents' again. Sometimes we can hardly wait to move" (2 Corinthians 5:1–2 MSG).

The Christian's death resembles sleep because of its felt need. Man feels the need of the pillow and bed; that is what drives him toward it. Without pushing the metaphor too far, let me say that the Christian often *feels* the need of eternal rest. His body ravaged with incurable sickness, racked with horrendous pain, fatigued with battling illness—he gets "sleepy" (longs to go Home).

The Bible clearly states that believers should take comfort in knowing that death is mere sleep—"So David slept with his fathers, and was buried in the city of David" (1 Kings 2:10). "But we do not want you to be uninformed, brothers, about *those who are asleep,* that you may not grieve as others do who have no hope" (1 Thessalonians 4:13 ESV).

The Christian's death resembles sleep because of its commonality to all men. Sleep is normal to all men regardless of status, race or creed; no man can live long without it. Just so is death common to all. "It is appointed unto men once to die" (Hebrews 9:27). All men must "sleep the sleep of death."

The Christian's death resembles sleep because of its tranquility. To behold a child tired from play or a worker exhausted at the end of a long day sleeping pictures peacefulness and calm like that of a beautiful sunset viewed from a majestic mountain peak. What a comforting picture of death!

The Christian's death resembles sleep because of its short span or brevity. How often we go to sleep only to awake saying, "I can't believe it's already morning." It passes so quickly. The sleep of death is but an 'instant.'

The Christian's death is like sleep in that it happens rapidly. In the twinkling (blink) of an eye upon death we are in the presence of Christ in Heaven. And then it will be exclaimed, "I can't believe I'm already here." As Paul says, "To be absent from the body, and to be present with the Lord" (2 Corinthians 5:8).

The Christian's death resembles sleep because of the change it brings. We go to bed tired and weary only to awake refreshed and cheerful. The Christian in death experiences a great change. Paul says, "For this corruptible must put on incorrupt-tion, and this mortal must put on immortality. So when this corruptible shall have put on incorruption, and this mortal shall have put on immortality, then shall be brought to pass the saying that is written, Death is swallowed up in victory. O death, where is thy sting? O grave, where is thy victory?" (1 Corinthians 15:53–55). Upon awaking from "sleep," the believer will be clothed with a glorified body free from the frailties and sicknesses and sorrows of this life. It will be a body that cannot decay or die, yet fully recognizable by family and friends. It will be a body resembling that of Christ's upon His resurrection.

The Christian's death resembles sleep because of its aftermath. Just as sleep does, death awakens the saint to a bright, sunny new day—but not here, in Heaven. Sleep ushers in the morning of "everlasting day" made possible through the resurrection of Christ. His resurrection is the believer's pledge that all like Him will awake in Glory.

The Christian's death resembles sleep because of the benefits it renders. Sleep experts say that sleep provides fuel for the brain cells, rejuvenation to body muscles and organs. The sleep of death for the child of God benefits him with a new body, new Home, new labor, new peace and joy, new worship and reunion with the saints, and a Homeland free from all that brings tears to the eyes.

The Christian's death resembles sleep because of the relief it gives. The man at sleep is "unconscious" of the pressing cares and griefs of life. It is his only *oasis* of escape. However, it lasts but a short time. The believer's sleep of death removes the grief, sorrow, hardship, trouble and pain permanently. He is finally "at rest." Through the sleep of death, he enters 'the rest which remains for the people of God' (Hebrews 4:9).

The Christian's death resembles sleep because of its calmness in coming. As the exhausted man leisurely, calmly, without fear or dread lays his head upon the soft pillow to sleep, the Christian in the sleep of death, often without struggle, gradually shuts his eyes to this world only to open them in the "New World."

The Christian's death resembles sleep because of God's sovereign control in both. Spurgeon said, "Sleep is the gift of God." Were it not for God shutting the eyelids there would be no sleep. Likewise, the sleep of death for the believer is controlled by God. He orders our steps, even that of death.

Spurgeon says, "Well, if we know Christ, it shall be ours by-and-by to sleep in Him. You who believe in Christ ought no more to dread death than you dread going to sleep at night. You will, ere you sleep, commit yourself to God, and as you put your head on the pillow, the similitude of death will be upon you, even sleep, which one has called "death's cousin." You will not be afraid of that. Why then should any dismay seize you in prospect of that which is but another sleep?"[213]

32
Flawed Reasoning for the Rain

In seeking an answer regarding our infirmity, our adversity-flawed reasoning often overrules reliable faith, intensifying the discomfort and strain. Faith always trumps the best of spurious reasoning, and it comforts far better.

For example, in serious sickness, flawed reasoning says, "If God really loved me, He would not have allowed my illness and suffering." But reliable faith says, "The fabric of my sickness is sewn in God's love and stitched with nothing but His best for me and is for His glory; in and through it He is giving the world a window to see how He compassionately cares for His child."

In bitterest bereavement, flawed reasoning says, "God failed me by taking my loved one or friend; if He truly loved me, He would not have done so. He was wrong. He made a mistake." But reliable faith says, "God never makes a mistake; what He does always is purposed for man's best and for His honor. Though bringing misery to me, death was merciful to my loved one, for it spared him from the evil to come in this life; it ushered him into the presence of Christ in Heaven. Out of his death much good will come for the cause of Christ. I will see him again soon."[214]

In severest suffering, flawed reasoning says, "God has abandoned me." Reliable faith says, "In the furnace of affliction there is always a 'fourth man in the fire' with me, the Lord Jesus Christ (Daniel 3:25). It's not important that I have an explanation from God for the 'furnace'; it is sufficient to know that He is with me in it and will see me through it. He [God] may intend me to suffer in something for His will to be done....Don't constantly be looking for a way to escape what God is doing in your life."[215] Billy Graham said, "The book of Job does not set out to answer the problem of suffering, but to proclaim a God so great that no answer is needed."[216]

In the calamities and tribulations of life, flawed reasoning says, "Curse God, and die" (Job 2:9). Reliable faith says, "Most gladly therefore will I rather glory in my infirmities, that the power of Christ may rest upon me" (2 Corinthians 12:9). "The compound verb ['may rest upon'] means 'to fix a tent or a habitation upon'; and the figure is that of Christ abiding upon him as a tent spread over him during his temporary stay on earth."[217] Faith says in loss or suffering that Christ spreads a tent over me in protection, peace and comfort while accomplishing His plan.

I heard the voice of Jesus say,
  "Come unto me and rest;
Lay down, thou weary one, lay down
  Thy head upon My breast."

When the Rain Comes

I came to Jesus as I was,
Weary and worn and sad;
I found in Him a resting place,
And He has made me glad. ~ Horatius Bonar (1808–1889)

C. H. Spurgeon strikingly says, "It is a poor faith which can trust God only when friends are true, the body full of health, and the business profitable; but that is true faith which holds by the Lord's faithfulness when friends are gone, when the body is sick, when spirits are depressed, and the light of our Father's countenance is hidden. A faith which can say in the direst trouble, 'Though he slay me, yet will I trust in him,' is Heaven-born faith."[218] Don't cater to the "knee-jerk" reaction to infirmity, bereavement and adversity with flawed reasoning. Instead, steadfastly trust God with what is happening, though the stars fall from the sky. "For we walk by faith, not by sight" (2 Corinthians 5:7).

33

Consolation in Bereavement

Commenting on Job 5:26, "Thou shalt come to thy grave in a full age," C. H. Spurgeon said, "'Ah!' says one, 'that is not true. Good people do not live longer than others. The most pious man may die in the prime of his youth.' But look at my text [Job 5:26]. It does not say thou shalt come to thy grave in old age—but in a 'full age.' Well, who knows what a 'full age' is? A 'full age' is whenever God likes to take His children home....There are two mercies to a Christian. *The first is that he will never die too soon; and the second, that he will never die too late.*"[219]

Jamieson, Faussett and Brown agree with Spurgeon's interpretation: "'full of days' is not mere length of years, but ripeness for death, one's inward and outward full development not being prematurely cut short."[220] Adam Clark adapts the text to say, "Thou shalt not die before thy time; thou shalt depart from life like a full-fed guest, happy in what thou hast known and in what thou hast enjoyed."[221] Matthew Henry says, "If the providence of God do not give us long life, yet if the grace of God give us to be satisfied with the time allotted us, we may be said to come to a full age. That man lives long enough that has done his work and is fit for another world."[222]

Dietrich Bonhoeffer states, "Who can comprehend how those whom God takes so early are chosen? Does not the early death of young Christians always appear to us as if God were plundering His own best instruments in a time in which they are most needed? Yet the Lord makes no mistakes. Might God need our brothers for some hidden service on our behalf in the heavenly world? We should put an end to our human thoughts, which always wish to know more than they can, and cling to that which is certain. Whomever God calls home is someone God has loved. For their souls were pleasing to the Lord, therefore he took them quickly from the midst of wickedness."[223]

> Death is God's grace at work protecting saints who die from future heartache of immeasurable proportion.

Isaiah states saints die (at the time they do) to spare them from the evil days ahead (Isaiah 57:1–2). What a thought! Death is God's grace at work protecting saints who die from future heartache of immeasurable proportion. Thus, death is a merciful friend! The bottom line: we die when God deems it best for us, perhaps for our family or others, and His glory. Earth's perspective fails to see Heaven's perspective (Isaiah 55:8–9) when death occurs. Our shortsightedness conceals what awaits down the road. In and by faith we now say with the psalmist what later will be substantiated a million times over: "Everything God does is right—the trademark on all his works is love. God's there, listening for all who pray, for all who pray and mean it. *He does what's best* for those who fear him—hears them call out, and saves them. God sticks by all who love him, but it's all over for those who don't" (Psalm 145:17–20 MSG). Missionary Henry Martyn (1781–1812) said, "I am immortal until God's work for me to do is done." Whatever age that arrives at shall be "my full age." (For Martyn that "full age" was age 31 when he died near the shores of the Black Sea in missionary service.)

Life on earth is a transient affair,
Just a few brief years in which to prepare
For a life that is free from pain and tears
Where time is not counted by hours or years.

So death is not sad...it's a time for elation,
A joyous transition—the soul's emigration
Into a place where the soul's safe and free
To live with God through eternity. ~ Helen Steiner Rice

34

Ministering Saints

Paul, in 2 Corinthians, presents the case for saints comforting saints that are walking through the valley of sickness, sorrow, trials and tears. He writes, "Thank God, the Father of our Lord Jesus Christ, that he is our Father and the source of all mercy and comfort. For he gives us comfort in our trials so that we in turn may be able to give the same sort of strong sympathy to others in theirs. Indeed, experience shows that the more we share Christ's suffering the more we are able to give of his encouragement. This means that if we experience trouble we can pass on to you comfort and spiritual help; for if we ourselves have been comforted we know how to encourage you to endure patiently the same sort of troubles that we have ourselves endured. We are quite confident that if you have to suffer troubles as we have done, then, like us, you will find the comfort and encouragement of God" (2 Corinthians 1:3–7 PHILLIPS).

Adrian Rogers said regarding the text, "To some people, tribulation is a prison. For others, tribulation is a hospital from which they get well. But, friend, tribulation is to be a seminary where we learn to become stewards of the comfort we receive so that we can pass on our encouragement to others."[224]

An old song ("Reverend Mr. Black") says,

> You gotta walk that lonesome valley;
>   You gotta walk it by yourself.
> Oh, nobody else can walk it for you.
>   You gotta walk it by yourself. ~ The Kingston Trio

The song is untruthful, thankfully so! Christians nearing Heaven are surrounded by fellow believers, making the deathbed more serene and bearable. The uplifting medicine they provide is that prescribed by Paul in 1 Thessalonians 4:13–18: comfort and hope based upon the resurrection of Christ and His promise of eternal life to all that trust in Him. The "medicine" is delivered through prayer, music, song, testimony, reminiscing and Scripture in person or by mail or phone. Sometimes it is ministered simply by presence without words or through stories that invoke laughter. Ultimately, the soothing medicine is gladly heard and received just by "being there." Literally 1 Samuel 23:16 reads, "Jonathan helped David strengthen his grip on God." The act of instilling in the life of another the words of God that will encourage him in times of grave difficulty; enlighten him in times of spiritual darkness; enhance his joy, peace and hope, strengthening his grip on God, is the invaluable ministry afforded by the saints to each other.

William Barclay wrote, "One of the highest of human duties is that of encouragement. It is easy to laugh at men's ideals, to pour cold water on their enthusiasm, to discourage them. The world is full of discouragers; we have a Christian duty to encourage one another. Many a time a word of praise or thanks or appreciation or cheer has kept a man on his feet. Blessed is the man who speaks such a word."[225] See Hebrews 10:24. Splash out sunshine into someone else's dark cloud.

Many have burdens too heavy to bear;
Help somebody today!
Grief is the portion of some everywhere;
Help somebody today! ~ Mrs. Frank A. Breck (1904)

The saints long to share the *medicine* with you. Don't shut them out. Don't forfeit the rich comfort, peace, hope and joy they provide. Little is the danger of an "overdose." Welcome the hugs, embraces, gentle touches, the clasp of hands, smiles, cheers, companionship and encouragement. And in doing so, gain increased comfort. It's just what the DOCTOR ordered. See Romans 12:15; Philippians 2:26–28 and Job 30:25.

35

A Glimpse Beyond the Grave

The Bible gives at best a glimpse into that which awaits the saint beyond death. But it is sufficient. The rest remains a mystery and surprise until it is experienced (Deuteronomy 29:29). Scripture reveals that immediately at death the soul is ushered into the presence of Christ in Heaven to share in His glory forever (2 Corinthians 5:8). C. H. Spurgeon remarks, "He will take me out of the tomb, up to Heaven. My spirit God will receive, and my body will sleep in Jesus till, being raised in His image, it will also be received into glory."[226]

Here are some further things that Scripture reveals about Heaven.

Heaven is a *Place of Reception* by Jesus. Jesus, not an angel, will meet and greet the believer at Heaven's door (John 14:3).

Heaven is a *Place of Reunion* with saints. The saint will fellowship with not only those who were known on earth like redeemed parents, children, grandparents, and friends, but also with the host of the redeemed that we did not know, like the prophets, disciples, patriarchs, missionaries and evangelists. Those we knew on earth will be recognized in Heaven (1 Corinthians 13:12). Spurgeon says, "The distance between glorified spirits in Heaven and militant saints on earth seems great, but it is not so."[227]

When I have heard the Heavenly choir
    And left this temporal shore,
I'll thrill with rapture here unknown
    As Jesus I adore.

When the Rain Comes

Old friends I've known long years ago
    Will bid me welcome Home;
Delighted in that bliss I'll rest,
    This earth no more to roam.

What joy will be my portion then,
    All free from sin and pain!
With death forever past for me,
    Don't wish me back again.

When you see this old shell of mine,
    Don't think that I am there.
I've traveled on to live with God;
    I've climbed the golden stair! ~ Unknown

Heaven is a *Place of Release*. Everyone is healthy and happy, having been freed from the grip of pain, sickness, crippling illness or accident, suffering, and the constant pull of Satan toward sin (Revelation 21:4).

Heaven is a *Place of Rest*. The saint gets tired and worn with the demands of making a living and battling the foes of darkness, but "a day of rest" (Hebrews 4:9) is coming for the redeemed when he "will lay down his sword down by the riverside and study war no more."

Heaven is a *Place of Rejoicing* (Revelation 5:11–12). In Heaven, the saints' joy will overflow into a song of praise and adoration to the King for making salvation possible. On earth, mankind is plagued with troubles and disappointments that rob us of joy and peace, but this is not so in Heaven.

Heaven is a *Place of Reward* (Revelation 22:12). The race will soon be finished. Then, following the rapture, provided you have faithfully endured to the end in your service, the King of Glory will place upon your head the earned victor's crown(s) you have won.

Heaven is a *Place of Responsibility.* Heaven is a place not only of worship but also of work. Christians will serve God in various capacities for all eternity (Revelation 22:3).

Heaven is a *Place of Refuge*. Considering the things that are absent from Heaven is almost as wonderful as thinking about what is present—all the things that brought trouble, trial, sorrow, suffering, sickness and weeping are not permitted within its heavenly gates (Revelation 21:4).

Comfort for Troubled Hearts

> Man's grandest imagination and proclamation of Heaven
> fails to touch the hem of its glorious garment.

Paul states in 1 Corinthians 2:9, "But as it is written, Eye hath not seen, nor ear heard, neither have entered into the heart of man, the things which God hath prepared for them that love him." Granted, these words are not in reference to Heaven, but heavenly wisdom. Nonetheless, no harm or biblical injustice is done in applying them to Heaven, for that which it states is expressly true of that glorious city. Man's grandest imagination and proclamation of Heaven fails to touch the hem of its glorious garment.

They tell me of a land so fair,
    Unseen by mortal eyes,
Where spring in fadeless beauty blooms
    Beneath unclouded skies.

Eye hath not seen, ear hath not heard,
    Neither hath it entered into the heart of man,
The things which God hath prepared for them,
    Prepared for them that love Him.

They tell me of a land so fair,
    Where all is light and song,
Where angel choirs their anthems join
    With yonder blood-washed throng.

O land of light and love and joy,
    Where comes no night of care,
What will our song of triumph be
    When we shall enter there! ~ Fanny Crosby (1890)

36

Finishing Strong

You have run a good race and fought a good fight; don't let up in the final lap. Finish strong.

Even if you have not run as strongly as you should for the entire race, the last "leg" provides an opportunity to finish strong. The apostle Paul finished strong. As he sat in a Roman prison, anticipating an imminent death, he wrote to Timothy: "For I am already being poured out as a drink offering, and the time of my departure has come. I have fought the good fight, I have finished the race, I have kept the faith." (2 Timothy 4:6–7 ESV). Paul tells young Timothy with calm repose that he was "dying." The words "poured out as a drink offering" refer to a pagan custom of the day in which *wine and oil were poured* upon the head of a victim about to be offered as a sacrifice.[228] Paul was in the same state of the victim on whose head the wine and oil already was poured "and which was just about to be put to death; that is, he was about to die."[229] He was prepared for it, thus ready for it when death's toll sounded.

My departure is at hand. The word "departure" is a nautical term used to describe the casting off of the ropes or chains that bound a ship to the dock in preparation to sail. Here Paul pictures death as the loosening of the "ropes" that bind us to the world, releasing and freeing us to sail Home.[230] Albert Barnes well says, "With such a view of death, why should a Christian fear to die?"[231] During the war, when the Royal Air Force was Britain's main stay for victory, some of its pilots were killed. However, they were never referred to as being killed but always as having been "posted to another station."[232] The Christian in dying is simply "posted to another station."

I have finished the course. Paul looked backward to the good fight he had fought for Christ, downward to the grave where nothing but victory and glory awaited, upward to Heaven where His Savior and friends awaited, and inward to his preparation and readiness to die. He said, "I have fought a good fight, I have finished my course, I have kept the faith." It is one thing to start a race; it is another to finish it strong. J. I. Packer, as one nearing the finish line, wrote: "Runners in a distance race, like jockeys in a horse race, always try to keep something in reserve for a final sprint. And my contention is that, so far as our bodily health allows, we should aim to be found running the last lap of the race of our Christian life, as we would say, flat out. The final sprint, so I urge, should be a sprint indeed."[233]

> In your manner of life, look like the country to which you are going.
> Thomas Boston

With Paul and Packer, resolve to finish strong. *When Heaven draws near,* sprint wide-open to the *finish line* in holy demeanor, loyal devotion, rapturous delight and disciplined duty. Richard Baxter concisely says to help finish strong, "spend your time in nothing which you know must be repented of, in nothing on which you might not pray for the blessing of God, in nothing which you could not review with a quiet conscience on your dying bed, in nothing which you might not safely and properly be found doing if death should surprise you in the act."[234] Thomas Boston also advises, "Let the heirs of the kingdom behave themselves suitably to their character and dignity. Live as having the faith and hope of this glorious kingdom: Let your conversation be in Heaven. Let your souls delight in communion with God while you are on earth, since you look for your happiness in communion with Him in Heaven. Let your speech and actions savor of Heaven; and in your manner of life, look like the country to which you are going."[235]

John Newton told friends in his latter days, "I am like a parcel packed up and directed, only waiting for the carrier to take me to my destination."[236] May all meet death with that same "readiness."

In Heavenly love abiding,
    No change my heart shall fear;
And safe is such confiding,
    For nothing changes here.

His wisdom ever waketh;
    His sight is never dim.
He knows the way He taketh,
    And I will walk with Him.

The storm may roar without me,
    My heart may low be laid,
But God is round about me,
    And can I be dismayed?

Green pastures are before me,
    Which yet I have not seen;
Bright skies will soon be o'er me,
    Where darkest clouds have been;

Wherever he may guide me,
    No want shall turn me back;
My Shepherd is beside me,
    And nothing can I lack:

My hope I cannot measure;
    My path to life is free.
My Savior has my treasure,
    And he will walk with me.

~ Anna Letitia Waring (1850)

37
The Future Life of the Believer

David in one sentence encapsulates the future life of the believer. He says, "As for me, I will behold thy face in righteousness: I shall be satisfied, when I awake, with thy likeness" (Psalm 17:15).

(1. David says we are going to "awake" from the sleep of death. John Howe wrote, "How apt and obvious is the analogy between our awakening out of natural sleep and the holy soul's rising up out of the darkness and torpor ["a state of mental and motor inactivity with partial or total insensibility"[237]] of its present state into the enlivening light of God's presence."[238] Tholuck remarked, "Wondrously enlightened by the Holy Ghost, David speaks with a clearness, which seems possible to Christian minds only, of the glories of Heaven, where the struggle with sin shall be changed into perfect righteousness, faith into face-to-face vision, satiation [to be completely satisfied] with the divided goods of this life into satiation with the one perfect good, which renders everything besides unnecessary."[239]

When the Rain Comes

(2. David attests that man's escape from Hell and entrance into Heaven is determined by "righteousness." Not his own goodness, for it is as "filthy rags" full of corruption and impurity, but the imputed righteousness of Jesus Christ. "And therefore it was imputed to him for righteousness. Now it was not written for his sake alone, that it was imputed to him; But for us also, to whom it shall be imputed, if we believe on him that raised up Jesus our Lord from the dead" (Romans 4:22–24).

(3. David states the believer will be satisfied with his glorified body and heavenly home. The Christian is out of place in this world, a sojourner whose citizenship is in another land. He cannot be satisfied with the pervasiveness of abortion, murder, suicide, immorality, political corruption or the blatant disdain for God that many exhibit. But he is soon to go home to a place where he shall be fully satisfied in the likeness and presence of the Lord. W. S. Plumer says, "I shall be delivered from these impending evils and shall thus be assured of thy love; or above all, when I awake from my last sleep of death and in the glories of a resurrection state, I shall see God face to face. Then my discoveries of him shall bring everlasting satisfaction to my soul."[240]

C. H. Spurgeon remarked, "And there will be satisfaction. "I shall be satisfied." Imagination, intellect, memory, hope—all will be satisfied. But when shall this satisfaction be? 'When I awake in Thy likeness'—not till then. On the resurrection morn, when complete in soul and body, they will awake. Their bodies till then are in their graves. But then they shall be restored. When a Roman conqueror had been at war and won great victories, he would very likely come back with his soldiers, enter into his house and enjoy himself till the next day, when he would go out of the city and then come in again in triumph. Now the saints, as it were, steal into Heaven without their bodies; but on the last day, when their bodies wake up, they will enter in their triumphal chariots, and the body is to be in the likeness of Christ. The spirit already is."[241]

(4. David reveals the believer will see Jesus ("behold thy face") instantly upon death. He will see Jesus as He is in all His glory, holiness, and majesty. William Jay said, "The beholding of God's face meant the enjoyment of His favor. This is its constant meaning. And in Heaven 'they shall see His face.'"[242] Owen declared, "It is Christ alone who is the likeness and image. When we awake in the other world with our minds purified and rectified, the beholding of him shall be always satisfying to us. There will be then no satiety, no weariness, no indispositions; but the mind being made perfect in all its faculties, powers and operations, with respect unto its utmost end, which is the enjoyment of God, is satisfied in the beholding of him forever."[243]

Leonardo da Vinci requested a friend's opinion on his masterpiece of the "Last Supper." Upon examining it, the friend remarked: "The most striking thing in the picture is the cup." The artist with brush in hand erased the cup, saying, "Nothing in my painting shall attract more attention than the face of my Master." In Heaven, nothing shall attract more focus to the saint then the face of His Lord and Savior. Jonathan Edwards said, "To go to Heaven fully to enjoy God is infinitely better than the most pleasant accommodations here. Fathers and mothers, husbands, wives, or children, or the company of earthly friends are but shadows; but the enjoyment of God is the substance. These are but scattered beams, but God is the sun. These are but streams, but God is the fountain. These are but drops, but God is the ocean."[244] That's why Heaven is Heaven—Christ's majestic presence among His people. All else, though wondrously glorious and eternally enjoyable, are, as the saying goes, "second fiddle."

Face to face I shall behold Him
    Far beyond the starry sky;
Face to face in all His glory,
    I shall see Him by and by!

What rejoicing in His presence,
    When are banished grief and pain,
When the crooked ways are straightened
    And the dark things shall be plain.

Face to face! Oh, blissful moment!
    Face to face—to see and know!
Face to face with my Redeemer,
    Jesus Christ who loves me so! ~ Mrs. Frank A. Breck (1855–1934)

38
A Happy Farewell

Just before his death, Tennyson said, "Death, be not proud! A short sleep and I will wake again eternally! A short voyage and I will meet my Maker face to face!" At age 81 he wrote the poem *Crossing the Bar,* which is counted his farewell to life.[245]

Sunset and evening star
    And one clear call for me!
And may there be no moaning of the bar
    When I put out to sea,

But such a tide as moving seems asleep,
    Too full for sound and foam,
When that which drew from out the boundless deep
    Turns again home.

When the Rain Comes

Twilight and evening bell
    And after that the dark!
And may there be no sadness of farewell
    When I embark;

For tho' from out our bourne of Time and Place
    The flood may bear me far,
I hope to see my Pilot face to face
    When I have crossed the bar. ~ Alfred Lord Tennyson (1809–1892)

When the moment arrives to loosen the rope from the dock to sail Home, let it be done with joy in what is gained, not sorrow in what is lost. C. H. Spurgeon remarks that when that time arrives and we bid farewell to earth, "it shall not be with bitterness in the retrospect. There is sin in it, and we are called to leave it; there has been trial in it, and we are called to be delivered from it; there has been sorrow in it, and we are glad that we shall go where we shall sorrow no more. There have been weakness and pain and suffering in it, and we are glad that we shall be raised in power; there has been death in it, and we are glad to bid farewell to shrouds and to knells ["a stroke or sound of a bell especially when rung slowly"[246]]. But for all that there has been such mercy in it, such lovingkindness of God in it, that the wilderness and the solitary place have been made glad and the desert has rejoiced and blossomed as a rose. We will not bid farewell to the world, execrating it [a great loathing], or leaving behind us a cold shudder and a sad remembrance, but we will depart, bidding adieu to the scenes that remain and to the people of God that tarry therein yet a little longer, blessing Him whose goodness and mercy have followed us all the days of our life and who is now bringing us to dwell in the house of the Lord forever."[247]

Farewell vain world; I must be gone.
    I have no Home or Stay in Thee.
I take my staff and travel on
    Till I a better world can see.

Why art thou loth, my heart; oh, why,
    Dost thou recoil within my breast?
Grieve not, but say farewell and fly
    Unto the Ark, my Dove; there's rest.

I came, my Lord, a pilgrim's pace;
    Weary and weak, I slowly move.
Longing, but yet can't reach the place,
    The gladsome place of rest above.

I come, my Lord; the floods here rise.
>   These troubled seas foam naught but mire.
My dove back to my bosom flies;
>   Farewell, poor world, Heav'n's my desire.

Stay, stay, said earth; whither fond one?
>   Here's a fair world; what would'st thou have?
Fair world, oh, no! thy beauty's gone;
>   A heav'nly Canaan, Lord, I crave.

Thus th' ancient travellers, thus they,
>   Weary of earth, groan'd after Thee.
They are before; I must not stay
>   Till I both Thee and them may see.

Put on, my soul, put on with speed;
>   Though th' way be long, the End is sweet.
Once more, poor world, farewell, indeed!
>   In leaving thee, my Lord I meet. ~ Samuel Crossman (1774)

Dietrich Bonhoeffer said, "Death is grace, the greatest gift of grace that God gives to people who believe in him. Death is mild; death is sweet and gentle. It beckons to us with heavenly power, if only we realize that it is the gateway to our homeland, the tabernacle of joy, the everlasting kingdom of peace."[248]

39
The Saint's Resurrection Body

Paul states the believer at death undergoes a great change. He writes, "For the perishable must clothe itself with the imperishable, and the mortal with immortality" (1 Corinthians 15:53 NIV). The physical body is subject to decay, so at the *great resurrection* it will be replaced with one that is incapable of deterioration. Four times over the word "put on" is used (1 Corinthians 15:53–54) which means to "go into," as into a place of covering or shelter.[249] Therefore, it means to "go into one's clothes, to attire, to array oneself" (2 Corinthians 5:2).[250] Death is the unclothing of the bodily house (perishable, mortal) to be clothed with immortal garments (imperishable, eternal) at the great resurrection. It is the same identity, yet with a changed composition (glorified body). The fourfold use of the word "this" (twice in 1 Corinthians 15:53 and twice in 1 Corinthians 15:54) indicates "clear continuity of identity (*this body*) even in the midst of radical transformation."[251]

When the Rain Comes

Sweet to rejoice in lively hope,
    That when my change shall come,
Angels will hover round my bed
    And take my spirit home.

There shall my disembodied soul
    Behold Him and adore,
Be with his likeness clothed upon
    And grieve and sin no more;

Shall see him wear that very flesh
    On which my guilt was laid.
His love intense, His merit fresh,
    My sin debt He has paid.

Soon, too, my slumbering dust shall hear
    The trumpet's quickening sound,
And, by my Savior's power rebuilt,
    At His right hand be found.

These eyes shall see Him in that day,
    The God that died for me;
And all my rising bones shall say,
    Lord, who is like to thee?

If such the views which grace unfolds
    Weak as it is below,
What raptures must the church above
    In Jesus' presence know!

Oh, may the unction of these truths
    Forever with me stay,
Till from her sinful cage dismissed
    My spirit flies away. ~ Augustus Toplady (1740–1778)

The *glorified bodies* of the saints will be free from the illnesses and injuries and frailties of life. "There will be no Paul there troubled with a thorn in the flesh, no Moses slow of speech, no Jacob with a thigh out of joint, no Lazarus afflicted with sores, no Job covered with boils, and no Methuselah bowed down with age and infirmities."[252] Why are new bodies necessary? Jon Courson says, "Our present bodies of flesh and blood cannot move into the kingdom because they're not designed for Heaven. That is what death is all about. For the believer, death is simply a way of leaving our earthly tabernacles and moving into our new bodies, exchanging our crusty brown bulbs for creations of beauty."[253] The "Great Change" will take place in "a moment, in the twinkling of an eye" at the great resurrection (1 Corinthians 15:52; 1 Thessalonians 4:13–17). That is, it will happen more quickly than the "blink" of an eye.

When the Son of Man shall come in His glory
    To take the saints on high,
What a shouting in the skies
From the multitudes that rise,
    Changed in the twinkling of an eye.

Changed in the twinkling of an eye,
Changed in the twinkling of an eye,
The trumpet shall sound, the dead shall be raised,
Changed in the twinkling of an eye.

When He comes in the clouds descending
    And they who loved Him here
From their graves shall awake and praise Him
    With joy and not with fear;
When the body and the soul are united
    And clothed no more to die,
What a shouting there will be
When each other's face we see,
    Changed in the twinkling of an eye. ~ Fanny Crosby (1898)

Augustine comments, "People are amazed that God, who made all things from nothing, makes a heavenly body from human flesh....Is He who was able to make you when you did not exist not able to make over what you once were?"[254]

40

Heaven's Ferryboat

T. DeWitt Talmage, in the sermon "The Ferryboat of the Jordan" (2 Samuel 19:18), likens the believer's departure from earth to Heaven to that of the transportation of David and his family from one side of the river Jordan to the other. Aptly he states that the ferryboat had to be sent from the other side by the tribe of

When the Rain Comes

Judah. And there is a ferryboat being sent from the other side (Heaven) named mercy, grace, and salvation for the Christian. Heavenbound ferries built by man on this side will shipwreck (the ferry of morality, religion, good works) and at once must be deboarded. See Ephesians 2:8–9 and Matthew 7:21–23.

Second, note that the king with his family was aboard the ferry. This assured the passengers that the best of precautions had been undertaken to ensure safe travel. Talmage says, "When a soul goes to Heaven, it does not go alone. The King is on board the boat. Was Paul alone in the last exigency [the finale of life]? Hear the shout of the scarred missionary as he cries out, 'I am now ready to be offered up, and the time of my departure is at hand.' Was John Wesley alone in the last exigency? No. Hear him say, 'Best of all, God is with us.' Here is the promise: 'When thou passeth through the waters, I will be with thee, and through the rivers, they shall not overflow thee.' Christ at the sick pillow to take the soul out of the body; Christ to help the soul down the bank into the boat; Christ midstream; Christ on the other side to help the soul up the beach! Be comforted about your departed friends. Be comforted about your own demise when the time shall come. Tell it to all the people under the sun that no Christian ever dies alone. The King is in the boat."[255]

Knowing not only that the King has sent a ferry for our exodus into the next world but that He is aboard should calm our fears, stop our trembling and marshal confident assurance that the trip will be successful. The saint with this knowledge can shout to death, "O death, where is your victory? O death, where is your sting? For sin is the sting that results in death, and the law gives sin its power. But thank God! He gives us victory over sin and death through our Lord Jesus Christ." (1 Corinthians 15:55–57 NLT). Spurgeon states that when the saint is "dying, and the cold chilly waters of Jordan are gathering about him up to the neck, Jesus puts His arms around him, and cries, 'Fear not, beloved; to die is to be blessed. The waters of death have their fountainhead in Heaven. They are not bitter; they are sweet as nectar, for they flow from the throne of God.' As the departing saint wades through the stream and the billows gather around him and heart and flesh fail him, the same voice sounds in his ears, 'Fear not; I am with thee; be not dismayed; I am thy God.' As he nears the borders of the infinite unknown and is almost affrighted to enter the realm of shades, Jesus says, 'Fear not; it is your Father's good pleasure to give you the kingdom.' Thus strengthened and consoled, the believer is not afraid to die; nay, he is even willing to depart, for since he has seen Jesus as the morning star, he longs to gaze upon Him as the sun in his strength."[256]

My latest sun is sinking fast;
    My race is nearly run;
My strongest trials now are past;
    My triumph is begun!

Oh, come, angel band, come and around me stand.
Oh, bear me away on your snowy wings
    To my immortal home.
Oh, bear me away on your snowy wings
    To my immortal home.

I know I'm nearing holy ranks
    Of friends and kindred dear.
I brush the dew of Jordan's banks;
    The crossing must be near.

I've almost gained my heav'nly home;
    My spirit loudly sings.
The holy ones, behold, they come!
    I hear the noise of wings,

Oh, bear my longing heart to Him
    Who bled and died for me,
Whose blood now cleanses from all sin
    And gives me victory. ~ Jefferson Hascall (1860)

41

Christians Don't Die Alone

The Christian never dies alone, even if family and friends are absent during the process, "for thou art with me." F. B. Meyer says, "The soul in the dark valley becomes aware of another at its side."[257] "In that silent chamber of yours," says C. H. Spurgeon, "there sitteth by your side One whom thou hast not seen, but whom thou lovest. Thy friend sticks closely to thee. Thou canst not see Him, but thou mayest feel the pressure of His hands. Dost thou not hear His voice?"[258] Listen, for He gently is saying "Fear thou not; for I am with thee: be not dismayed; for I am thy God: I will strengthen thee; yea, I will help thee; yea, I will uphold thee with the right hand of my righteousness" (Isaiah 41:10). Hear David saying, "Though I walk through the valley of the shadow of death, I will fear no evil: for thou art with me" (Psalm 23:4). G. Campbell Morgan reminds us, "He [God] is nigh when He seems absent. He is watching when He seems blind. He is active when He seems idle."[259]

When I come to the river at the ending of day,
    When the last winds of sorrow have blown,
There'll be somebody waiting to show me the way.
    I won't have to cross Jordan alone.

When the Rain Comes

I won't have to cross Jordan alone;
Jesus died all my sins to atone.
In the darkness I see,
He'll be waiting for me;
I won't have to cross Jordan alone.

Often times I'm weary and troubled and sad,
　　When it seems that my friends have all flown.
There is one thought that cheers me and makes my heart glad:
　　I won't have to cross Jordan alone.

Though the billows of trouble and sorrow may sweep,
　　Christ the Savior will care for his own.
Till the end of my journey my soul he will keep,
　　And I won't have to cross Jordan alone. ~ Thomas Ramsey (1934)

The Bible says, "For he hath said, I will never leave thee, nor forsake thee" (Hebrews 13:5). Based upon Kenneth Wuest's Greek interpretation, *The Amplified Bible* translates the verse: "Himself has said, I will not in any way fail you nor give you up nor leave you without support. *I will not, I will not, I will not* in any degree leave you helpless nor forsake nor let you down (relax My hold on you)! Assuredly not!" Four times in this one verse God promises never to leave you alone! Not even *when Heaven draws near.* Jesus knows what it is to die utterly alone, for at Calvary He cried, "My God, my God, why hast thou forsaken me?" He promised that no child of His would ever have to experience such abandonment in dying. Claim and embrace personally His promise "I will never leave thee, nor forsake thee" to gain peace and comfort in sorrow, sickness or dying.

Though all around me is darkness,
　　Earthly joys all flown,
My Savior whispers His promise:
　　"I never will leave thee alone." ~ Unknown

42

The Death That Glorifies God

"This spake he, signifying by what death he should glorify God" (John 21:19). Peter was told by Jesus that the *death he would die* would glorify God—death by crucifixion (John 21:18). Known unto God are man's birthday, death day and "by what death we should glorify God." After all, God is omniscient, knowing "the end from the beginning" (Isaiah 46:10). Until the proper time, the manner of the "death" is concealed from us. Upon its disclosure and our submission to it, God is glorified. With David, the saint attests, "My times are in thy hand" (Psalm 31:15).

My times are in Thy gracious hand;
    I'm glad my times are there.
There's much I do not understand—
    Enough that Thou dost care.

My times are in Thy guiding hand,
    And this my peace would be;
For Thou wilt guide as Thine hast planned,
    And that will prosper me.

My times are in Thy giving hand;
    Thus till my race is run,
Till I reach the heavenly land
    Of cares I need have none. ~ J. Danson Smith

Regardless of the type of death experienced, saints glorify God in and through it in several ways.

(1. By resignation of self to accept it; whatever my beloved Savior thinks best, to that I submit.

(2. By demonstration of unflinching trust in, dependence upon and unflagging devotion to Christ.

(3. By manifestation of joyous expectation and anticipation of eternal life.

(4. By appropriation of Christ's promises, proving them to be trustworthy.

(5. By declaration and affirmation of Christ's faithfulness throughout its concourse.

(6. By exemplification of holy demeanor and patience.

When dying, a saint remarked to his friends, "It was never till today that I got any personal instruction from our Lord's telling Peter by what death he should glorify God. Oh! what a satisfying thought it is that God appoints those means of dissolution (death) by which He gets most glory to Himself. It was the very thing I needed; for of all the ways of dying, that which I most dreaded is that which I'm experiencing. But, O my dear Lord, if by this death I can most glorify Thee, I prefer it to all others and thank Thee that by this means Thou art hastening my fuller enjoyment of Thee in a purer world."

When the Rain Comes

When I walk through the shades of death,
Thy presence is my stay;
One word of Thy supporting breath
Drives all my fears away.

Thy hand, in sight of all my foes,
Doth still my table spread.
My cup with blessings overflows;
Thine oil anoints my head. ~ Isaac Watts (1719)

43

Readiness for Departure

In Simeon's *Nunc Dimittis*, adoration and praise upon seeing Christ in the Temple, he begs for dismissal from this world that he might gain the next in Heaven. He prayed, "Lord, now lettest thou thy servant *depart* (die) in peace, according to thy word: For mine eyes have seen thy salvation" (Luke 2:29–30). Warren Wiersbe remarks, "The word *depart* tells us something about the death of a Christian. It means 'to release a prisoner, to untie a ship and set sail, to take down a tent (2 Corinthians 5:1–8), and to unyoke a beast of burden (Matthew 11:28–30).'"[260] Simeon was *ready* to be set free as a prisoner from the world, set sail as a ship from the harbor, be packed up as tent to move to "Home" and unburdened from the cares of this life like a donkey that is unyoked. Matthew Henry says Simeon's words "bespeak a believing expectation of a happy state on the other side death through this salvation he now had a sight of, which not only takes off the terror of death but makes it gain (Philippians 1:21). Note, those that have welcomed Christ may welcome death."[261]

Every Christian should likewise be ready to thrust off the old garment of this life to put on the Heavenly attire of the next, to exchange burdens for blessings. Such readiness for death is only realized by sweet assurance of salvation, abiding communion and fellowship with Christ and completion of Heaven's assigned task. Since it is God that dictates the day of death ("lettest thou servant die") we must ever live prepared for it so that the day of its arrival will be no surprise. It is most fitting therefore to hoist up anchor, unloose the rope, set the sails and steadily await at the dock both eager and ready for departure. Jeremy Taylor said, "He that would die well must always look for death, every day knocking at the gates of the grave; and then the gates of the grave shall never prevail upon him to do him mischief."[262] Adoniram Judson said, "I am not tired of my work; neither am I tired of the world. Yet when Christ calls me home, I shall go with gladness."[263]

Comfort for Troubled Hearts

Ready in life, ready in death,
Ready for His return. ~ S. E. L. and A. C. Palmer (1845–1882)

Willing, desirous and ready for death, Simeon prays that he might "die in peace." And all that live devoted to Christ may die in peace—peace with Him, the conscience, death, future judgment and in the unseen afterlife that awaits in Heaven. To know peace in life is to possess it in death. Joseph Addison, the renowned author and linguist, following great physical suffering, sent for Lord Warwick. He came and said, "Dear sir, you sent for me. I believe and hope you have some commands. I shall hold them most dear."

"See," said the dying saint, "in what peace a Christian can die!" and breathed his life out like a sleeping infant."[264]

Ridley, the night prior to his execution (burned alive at the stake) had a friend offer to sit up with him in the prison. "Oh, no!" said the good man, "what would you do with yourself? I mean to go to bed and sleep as quietly as ever I did in my life. My breakfast tomorrow will be sharp and painful, but I am sure my supper will be right pleasant and sweet!" Christ grants His children (servants) sweet peace in the valley of the shadow of death. This Isaiah affirms (Isaiah 57:2), "For those who follow godly paths will rest in peace when they die" (NLT). Charles Simeon states, "It is the knowledge of Christ only that affords a scriptural hope of acceptance with God; therefore, it is that alone which will enable us to view with comfort the approach of death."[265] But such is not so with the ungodly for about their deathbed hopelessness thickens and terror monopolizes.

Forever with the Lord!
    Amen! So let it be.
Life from the dead is in that word;
    'Tis immortality.

Here in the body pent
    Absent from Him I roam,
Yet nightly pitch my moving tent
    A day's march nearer home.

My Father's house on high,
    Home of my soul, how near
At times to faith's foreseeing eye
    Thy golden gates appear!

Ah, then my spirit faints
    To reach the land I love,
The bright inheritance of saints,
    Jerusalem above!

Forever with the Lord!
    O Father, 'tis Thy will.
The promise of that faithful word
    E'en here to me fulfil.

So when my dying breath
    Shall set my spirit free,
By death I shall escape from death
    To endless life with Thee. ~ James Montgomery (1835)

44

Battling Adversity Victoriously

George Müller was en route to Quebec aboard ship for a speaking engagement when a dense fog threatened a late arrival and cancellation of the service. When the ship's Captain was invited to pray with him in the chartroom about the matter, he said to Müller, "Do you realize how dense the fog is?"

"No," he replied, "my eye is not on the dense fog but on the living God who controls every circumstance of my life." No sooner had Müller prayed than the dense fog lifted and his engagement was made possible.[266] In battling adversity of any kind, do as Müller did: glance at the "dense fog" but gaze upon the living God who *controls* every circumstance of your life. Whether He chooses to lift the fog or guide you through it matters not as long as He is in control. The Bible says, "The steps of a good man are ordered [controlled] by the LORD" (Psalm 37:23).

A. W. Tozer wrote, "To the child of God, there is no such thing as an accident. He travels an appointed way. Accidents may indeed appear to befall him and misfortune stalk his way, but these evils will be so in appearance only and will seem evils only because we cannot read the secret script of God's hidden providence and so cannot discover the ends at which He aims. The man of true faith may live in the absolute assurance that his steps are ordered by the Lord. For him, misfortune is outside the bounds of possibility. He cannot be torn from this earth one hour ahead of the time which God has appointed, and he cannot be detained on earth one moment after God is done with him here."[267] As the Bible says, 'Our times are in His hands' (Psalm 31:15). In the extremities of life, "when you can't trace His hand, trust His heart."

Spurgeon comments, "Look back, believer; think of your doubting God when He has been so faithful to you. Think of your foolish outcry of 'Not so, my Father,' when He crossed His hands in affliction to give you the larger blessing; think of the many times when you have read His providences in the dark, misinterpreted His dispensations, and groaned out, 'All these things are against me,' when they are all working together for your good!"[268]

He leadeth me; oh, blessed thought!
Oh, words with Heavenly comfort fraught!
Whate'er I do, where'er I be,
Still 'tis God's hand that leadeth me.

Sometimes mid scenes of deepest gloom,
Sometimes where Eden's flowers bloom,
By waters calm, o'er troubled sea,
Still 'tis God's hand that leadeth me.

Lord, I would clasp Thy hand in mine,
Nor ever murmur nor repine,
Content, whatever lot I see,
Since 'tis my God that leadeth me.

And when my task on earth is done,
When, by thy grace, the victory's won,
E'en death's cold wave I will not flee,
Since God through Jordan leadeth me. ~ Joseph H. Gilmore (1862)

45

Discard the Tear Bottle

The Psalmist states that God treasures up our tears induced by trials, trouble, and sorrow *in His* "bottle" (Psalm 56:8). Matthew Henry comments, "David comforts himself in his distress and fear that God noticed all his grievances and all his griefs. He observes them with tender concern."[269] See Psalm 56:11–13. Alexander Maclaren writes, "What does He keep them [tears] for? To show how precious they are in His sight and perhaps to suggest that they are preserved for a future use. The tears that His children shed and give to Him to keep…will be given back one day to those who shed them, converted into refreshment, by the same Power which of old turned water into wine."[270]

When the Rain Comes

Sufficient it is to allow God to count and store the tears. Some suffering and sickly saints keep their own "tear bottle" by their bedside to store their many tears (great and small) of woe and sorrow to share repeatedly with family and friends. And seemingly they add to it daily! The practice is not only unwarranted, since God already is doing it, but potentially unhealthy mentally; it may contribute to a gloomy outlook. By the grace of God, maintain positivity amidst negativity. With Christ in the equation, regardless of affliction, we have every right to be optimistic instead of pessimistic. After all, "the Lord is good, a stronghold in the day of trouble; he knows those who take refuge in him" (Nahum 1:7 ESV) and "a joyful heart is good medicine, but a crushed spirit dries up the bones" (Proverbs 17:22 ESV).

This is not to say that we should never share burdens and woes or pretend they don't exist. In fact, that should be done to allow Christian brothers and sisters to assist in bearing the heavy load in prayer and giving any other help they can (Galatians 6:2). Just keep the motivation right behind the sharing; exhibit care not to play on another's emotion for selfish gain, sympathy or attention. Even in our serious sickness or injury, attention ought to be placed on Jesus Christ that He may receive glory in and through it. "Not unto us, O LORD, not unto us, but unto thy name give glory, for thy mercy, and for thy truth's sake" (Psalm 115:1).

46
Stay Near the Cross

Calvary robbed death of its power and destroyed its sting (1 Corinthians 15:55–57). The consolation of the cross is the dying saint's mainstay, for through Jesus' death and resurrection, eternal life in Heaven was made available. Acquaint thyself with what transpired upon Calvary's cross. Reflect upon it. Seek deeper implications of its meaning in Holy Scripture and illumination from the Holy Spirit. Greater knowledge of the *cross* gives deeper understanding which provides its soul-enriching approbation. Open up your heart to its inflow of comfort and strength and courage. Abiding near the cross impacts the anticipation and encountering of death; no longer is it viewed with dread but with delight, not with defeat but with victory, not with doubt but with certainty. Forever rest beneath its shade.

W. S. Plumer wrote, "If men would duly meditate on death, surely they would not be so wild and extravagant as they are. But the mere contemplation of death will neither make it easy nor safe to die. The death of Christ alone rightly viewed and believed can make our death comfortable and truly blessed."[271]

Because of Christ's victory over sin and death, Paul exhorts believers to 'be steadfast, unmovable' (1 Corinthians 15:58). What happened at Calvary provides us a sure and secure anchor for hope at death; therefore, don't quake or quiver before it. "Death is swallowed up in victory" (1 Corinthians 15:54). Death is no longer a dead end; it's a thoroughfare to Heaven. Charles Simeon states, "Through His atoning blood, you may look forward to death and judgment with far other eyes than they can be viewed by the ungodly world. You may regard death as the commencement of life and the very gate of Heaven."[272] Adrian Rogers said, "While death is a decided fact, Death is also a defeated foe. We are able to laugh in the face of Death if we know the Lord Jesus Christ."[273] Stay anchored to the cross of Calvary.

> Near the cross! O Lamb of God,
>> Bring its scenes before me;
> Help me walk from day to day
>> With its shadow o'er me.

> Near the cross I'll watch and wait,
>> Hoping, trusting ever,
> Till I reach the golden strand
>> Just beyond the river. ~ Fanny Crosby (1820–1915)

47

Scriptures to Calm and Comfort

"Our hope," states Billy Graham, "must be built on Christ alone and on the promises God has given us in His Word."[274] Dr. Everek R. Storms said that there are 7,487 divine promises God has made payable to His children.[275] C. H. Spurgeon said, "There may be a promise in the Word which would exactly fit your case, but you may not know of it, and therefore you miss its comfort. You are like prisoners in a dungeon, and there may be one key in the bunch which would unlock the door, and you might be free; but if you will not look for it, you may remain a prisoner still, though liberty is so near at hand. There may be a potent medicine in the great pharmacopoeia of Scripture, and you may yet continue sick unless you will examine and search the Scriptures to discover what He hath said."[276] See John 5:39 and Acts 17:11.

> Amidst the uncertainty, doubt and pain
> That dying is said to often bring,
> Trust in His promises, upon them rely.
> In their comfort and assurance richly abide. ~ Frank Shivers (2020)

Bible promises and truths for the hurting, grieving and dying

[1] Calm and Peace

"And the peace of God, which passeth all understanding, shall keep your hearts and minds through Christ Jesus" (Philippians 4:7).

When the Rain Comes

[2] Trouble and Difficulties

"Though I walk in the midst of trouble, thou wilt revive me: thou shalt stretch forth thine hand against the wrath of mine enemies, and thy right hand shall save me" (Psalm 138:7).

[3] Healing and Recovery

"He healeth the broken in heart, and bindeth up their wounds" (Psalm 147:3).

[4] Fear and Dread

"Fear thou not; for I am with thee: be not dismayed; for I am thy God" (Isaiah 41:10a).

[5] Strength and Help

"I will strengthen thee; yea, I will help thee; yea, I will uphold thee with the right hand of my righteousness" (Isaiah 41:10b).

[6] Grief and Heartache

"The LORD is close to the brokenhearted; he rescues those whose spirits are crushed" (Psalm 34:18 NLT).

[7] Courage and Boldness

"The LORD is my light and my salvation; whom shall I fear? the LORD is the strength of my life; of whom shall I be afraid?" (Psalm 27:1).

[8] Wisdom and Guidance

"I will instruct thee and teach thee in the way which thou shalt go: I will guide thee with mine eye" (Psalm 32:8).

[9] Supply and Provision

"But my God shall supply all your need according to his riches in glory by Christ Jesus" (Philippians 4:19).

[10] Belief and Assurance

"You know and fully believe that the Lord has done great things for you. You know that he has not failed to keep any of his promises" (Joshua 23:14 NCV).

[11] Eternal Life and Freedom

"He will swallow up death in victory; and the Lord GOD will wipe away tears from off all faces; and the rebuke of his people shall he take away from off all the earth: for the LORD hath spoken it" (Isaiah 25:8).

[12] Security and Protection

"He will cover you with His feathers; you will take refuge under His wings. His faithfulness will be a protective shield" (Psalm 91:4 HCSB).

[13] Anxiety and Stress

"Come to me, all of you who are weary and over-burdened, and I will give you rest! Put on my yoke and learn from me. For I am gentle and humble in heart and you will find rest for your souls. For my yoke is easy and my burden is light" (Matthew 11: 28–30 PHILLIPS).

Comfort for Troubled Hearts

[14] Sleep and Rest

"I laid me down and slept; I awaked; for the LORD sustained me" (Psalm 3:5).

[15] Encouragement and Uplift

"I waited patiently for the LORD; he turned to me and heard my cry. He lifted me out of the slimy pit, out of the mud and mire he set my feet on a rock and gave me a firm place to stand. He put a new song in my mouth, a hymn of praise to our God. Many will see and fear the LORD and put their trust in him" (Psalm 40:1–3 NIV).

[16] Comfort and Consolation

"Praise be to the God and Father of our Lord Jesus Christ, the Father of compassion and the God of all comfort, who comforts us in all our troubles, so that we can comfort those in any trouble with the comfort we ourselves receive from God" (2 Corinthians 1:3–4 NIV).

[17] Sovereignty and Separation

"Can anything separate us from the love of Christ? Can trouble, pain or persecution? Can lack of clothes and food, danger to life and limb, the threat of force of arms?...No, in all these things we win an overwhelming victory through him who has proved his love for us. I have become absolutely convinced that neither death nor life, neither messenger of Heaven nor monarch of earth, neither what happens today nor what may happen tomorrow, neither a power from on high nor a power from below, nor anything else in God's whole world has any power to separate us from the love of God in Jesus Christ our Lord!" (Romans 8:35–39 PHILLIPS).

[18] Heaven and Homes

"Let not your heart be troubled: ye believe in God, believe also in me. In my Father's house are many mansions: if it were not so, I would have told you. I go to prepare a place for you. And if I go and prepare a place for you, I will come again, and receive you unto myself; that where I am, there ye may be also" (John 14:1–3).

[19] Return and Rapture

"For the Lord himself will descend from heaven with a cry of command, with the voice of an archangel, and with the sound of the trumpet of God. And the dead in Christ will rise first" (1 Thessalonians 4:16 ESV).

[20] Death and Fright

"Yea, though I walk through the valley of the shadow of death, I will fear no evil: for thou art with me; thy rod and thy staff they comfort me" (Psalm 23:4).

[21] Resurrection and Rejoicing

"But those who die in the LORD will live; their bodies will rise again! Those who sleep in the earth will rise up and sing for joy! For your life-giving light will fall like dew on your people in the place of the dead!" (Isaiah 26:19 NLT).

When the Rain Comes

[22] Calamity and Tribulation

"When thou passest through the waters, I will be with thee; and through the rivers, they shall not overflow thee: when thou walkest through the fire, thou shalt not be burned; neither shall the flame kindle upon thee" (Isaiah 43:2).

[23] Weary and Worn

"He gives strength to the weary and increases the power of the weak" (Isaiah 40:29 NIV).

[24] Prayer's Agreeing and Asking

"Again I say to you that if two of you agree on earth concerning anything that they ask, it will be done for them by My Father in Heaven" (Matthew 18:19 NKJV).

[25] Prayer's Rule and Certainty

"This is the confidence we have in approaching God: that if we ask anything according to His will, He hears us" (1 John 5:14 NKJV).

[26] Prayer's Persistency and Promise

"Ask and keep on asking and it will be given to you; seek and keep on seeking and you will find; knock and keep on knocking and the door will be opened to you. For everyone who keeps on asking receives, and he who keeps on seeking finds, and to him who keeps on knocking, it will be opened" (Matthew 7:7–8 AMP).

[27] Care and Compassion

"I will not leave you comfortless: I will come to you" (John 14:18).

[28] Discouragement and Despair

"The weapons of our warfare are not physical [weapons of flesh and blood]. Our weapons are divinely powerful for the destruction of fortresses. We are destroying sophisticated arguments and every exalted and proud thing that sets itself up against the [true] knowledge of God, and we are taking every thought and purpose captive to the obedience of Christ, being ready to punish every act of disobedience, when your own obedience [as a church] is complete" (2 Corinthians 10:4–6 AMP).

[29] Deliverance and Preservation

"Thou art my hiding place; thou shalt preserve me from trouble; thou shalt compass me about with songs of deliverance" (Psalm 32:7).

[30] Hope and Patience

"I wait for the LORD, my soul doth wait, and in his word do I hope" (Psalm 130:5).

[31] Trust and Confidence

"But as for me, I know that my Redeemer lives, and he will stand upon the earth at last. And after my body has decayed, yet in my body I will see God! I will see him for myself. Yes, I will see him with my own eyes. I am overwhelmed at the thought!" (Job 19:25–27 NLT).

Comfort for Troubled Hearts

[32] Loneliness and Aloneness

"Turn to me and have mercy on me, because I am lonely and hurting" (Psalm 25:16 NCV).

[33] Resistance and Victory

"Ye are of God, little children, and have overcome them: because greater is he that is in you, than he that is in the world" (1 John 4:4).

[34] Anointing and Prayer

"Is any sick among you? let him call for the elders of the church; and let them pray over him, anointing him with oil in the name of the Lord" (James 5:14).

[35] Frustration and Fretting

"Humble yourselves, therefore, under the mighty hand of God so that at the proper time he may exalt you, casting all your anxieties on him, because he cares for you" (1 Peter 5:6–7 ESV).

[36] Reunion and Recognition

"For now we see through a glass, darkly; but then face to face: now I know in part; but then shall I know even as also I am known" (1 Corinthians 13:12).

[37] Endurance and Contentment

"Be content with such things as ye have: for he hath said, I will never leave thee, nor forsake thee" (Hebrews 13:5).

[38] Despondency and Delight

"I will turn their mourning into joy; I will comfort them, and give them gladness for sorrow" (Jeremiah 31:13 ESV).

[39] Conversion and Confirmation

"And this is the record, that God hath given to us eternal life, and this life is in his Son. He that hath the Son hath life; and he that hath not the Son of God hath not life. These things have I written unto you that believe on the name of the Son of God; that ye may know that ye have eternal life, and that ye may believe on the name of the Son of God" (1 John 5:11–13).

[40] Grace and Grit

"And he said unto me, My grace is sufficient for thee: for my strength is made perfect in weakness. Most gladly therefore will I rather glory in my infirmities, that the power of Christ may rest upon me" (2 Corinthians 12:9).

Additional promises and truths may be found through use of the concordance in the back of most Bibles. It works in a way similar to a dictionary, with one exception; instead of providing definitions, it indicates passages in the Bible where a certain word occurs. Words, as in dictionaries, are listed alphabetically. Thus, in looking for passages on *peace,* the reader would look in the concordance under the word "peace" and select the appropriate texts.

48

Saying Peace, Peace When There Is No Peace

"'Peace, peace,' they say, when there is no peace" (Jeremiah 6:14 NIV). A false peace is that which is based on fraudulent reasoning and theology. Perceived as genuine, life and death are founded upon it. But, lo, in the end it avails naught and disappoints its possessor. "Peace of heart alone is not always the peace of God."[277]

There is false peace given by ministers and theologians. To inspire peace when there is no justification biblically for it is a lie that sends the dying to the grave and judgment ill-prepared. To say or infer that God will not exclude anyone from Heaven or that He is unconcerned with man's sin and faults or that the sacraments assure of salvation or that personal goodness, religious deeds and church affiliation merit eternal life is all a sham based upon liberal theology and human philosophy that are rooted in satanic deceit. It is no wonder that God will judge the false prophet (minister, priest, teacher) that proclaims such "peace" with vehemence. See 2 Peter 2:1–3.

C. H. Spurgeon cautions, "The physician who should pamper a man in his disease, who should feed his cancer or inject continual poison into the system, while at the same time he promised sound health and long life—such a physician would not be one half so hideous a monster of cruelty as the professed minister of Christ who should bid his people take comfort, when, instead thereof, he ought to be crying, 'Woe unto them that are at ease in Zion: be troubled, ye careless ones.'"[278]

Pretense of peace doth not procure it. It prevents it.

The Bible warns about false prophets that, *dressed* in sheep's clothing (Matthew 7:15), sway people by their pleasing and captivating words to buy into their "counterfeit peace" (2 Timothy 4:3). True ministers speak sound, unadulterated doctrine couched in love. See Titus 2:1 and 1 Timothy 6:3–5. Though all ministers may "sound" and "look" the same, they are not.

How shall I leave my tomb?
  In triumph or regret?
A fearful or joyful doom?
  A curse or blessing meet?

Who can resolve the doubt
  That rends my anxious breast?
Shall I with the damned be cast out
  Or numbered with the blest? ~ Charles Wesley

Comfort for Troubled Hearts

There is false peace generated by a false hope embraced by the religious. Of this Jesus warns in Matthew 7: 21–23: "Not everyone that saith unto me, Lord, Lord, shall enter into the kingdom of heaven; but he that doeth the will of my Father which is in heaven. Many will say to me in that day, Lord, Lord, have we not prophesied in thy name? and in thy name have cast out devils? and in thy name done many wonderful works? And then will I profess unto them, I never knew you: depart from me, ye that work iniquity." For example, Nicodemus was at peace with his soul's condition; yet Jesus said He needed to be born again (John 3:3).

There is a false peace manufactured in the mind of the ungodly. Through the vain imagination of their heart they claim to know peace. Rooted first in pride, this imagination is contentment, worth, and peace predicated upon comparison with people of lesser good than oneself. Second, the ungodly embrace false peace founded upon human reasoning. They deliberate with themselves only to formulate unbiblical notions about salvation and tranquility that are utterly futile to secure genuine peace. Of these Paul says they "became vain in their imaginations, and their foolish heart was darkened. Professing themselves to be wise, they became fools" (Romans 1:21–22). When man 'leans to his own understanding' (reasoning) instead of the revealed Word of God, the danger of false peace emerges (the hanging of peace on something other than God alone). See Proverbs 3:5. An example of such foolish reasoning is found in Deuteronomy 29:19 where the "renegade" say they can have peace while living in blatant sin.

How is it that man is hoodwinked into cleaving to a false peace with God, death and the hereafter?

(1. By erroneous views of Holy Scripture regarding the means of procurement of peace. He is lulled into its embrace by convincing himself that despite the enormity of sin committed, ultimately God mercifully will overlook it, granting entrance into Heaven. See Acts 17:30–31. He wrongly reasons that God loves man too much to cast him into the lake of fire.

(2. By desensitization of the conscience through continual unscrupulous and wicked conduct. The conscience seared with the red-hot iron of repetitive sin accepts as truth that which is false (1 Timothy 4:2).

(3. By the blinding deceit of Satan (2 Corinthians 4:4). Satan is the great counterfeiter of peace.

(4. By the brainwashing of the heretical. See Ezekiel 13:10 and Psalm 1:1.

(5. By religious orthodoxy (trust in beliefs; intellectual assent to biblical truth apart from faith placed in Christ).

(6. By self-righteousness. To cloak oneself with personal goodness prompts him to egoistically count himself justified to stand before the Lord. See Romans 3:10.

When the Rain Comes

False peace is dangerous both presently and in the hour of death. Pretense of peace doth not procure it. It prevents it. Therefore, to say "peace, peace" when there is no peace is meaningless and futile both presently and in the hour of death. It is totally impotent to help. As long as false peace is perceived as authentic it will soothe the conscience with its warped contentment, deadening it to the need of the true peace found in a personal relationship with Jesus Christ. See John 14:27.

> As long as false peace is perceived as authentic, it will soothe the conscience with its warped contentment, deadening it to the need of the true peace found in a personal relationship with Jesus Christ.

D. Martyn Lloyd-Jones said, "Apart from justification, apart from that which has been done for us in and through the Lord Jesus Christ, there is no peace between God and man. There is no peace either on God's side or on man's side, 'for the wrath of God is against all ungodliness and unrighteousness of men.'"[279] Here is the acid test for genuine peace. Are you in Christ Jesus? Do you possess Him as Lord and Savior? If not, then regardless of the surety of the peace you embrace, it is a false peace, for true peace flows in and through His person alone. The peace Christ affords not only sustains in life but in the throes of death. If you are not in possession of such peace then shake yourself loose from the false peace and immediately claim and cleave unto that which is true. See Philippians 4:7.

What a treasure I have in this wonderful peace
    Buried deep in the heart of my soul,
So secure that no power can mine it away
    While the years of eternity roll.

I am resting tonight in this wonderful peace,
    Resting sweetly in Jesus' control,
For I'm kept from all danger by night and by day,
    And His glory is flooding my soul.

And methinks when I rise to that city of peace
    Where the Author of peace I shall see,
That one strain of the song which the ransomed will sing
    In that Heavenly kingdom shall be:

Peace, peace! wonderful peace
    Coming down from the Father above,
Sweep over my spirit forever, I pray,
    In fathomless billows of love.

Ah! soul, are you here without comfort and rest,
　　Marching down the rough pathway of time?
Make Jesus your friend ere the shadows grow dark;
　　Oh, accept this sweet peace so sublime! ~ W. D. Cornell (1920)

49
Redeeming the Time That Remains

The biblical admonition to 'redeem the time' applies to the end of life as much as it does to its first (Ephesians 5:16). No one realizes the preciousness of time more or values it as much as the man that has so little of it left. To him moments are as particles of gold to be treasured and used wisely, not foolishly wasted. How might the dying saint make the best use of what time remains?

(1. Weave into the tapestry of every moment the thread of the spiritual.

(2. Cultivate greater intimacy with Christ through prayer and His Word.

(3. Set affairs in order with Christ and man.

(4. Love on people.

(5. Invest in people the knowledge and wisdom you have gained throughout life.

(6. Contribute generously financially to the work of Christ—set something in motion that will continue to benefit the kingdom long after your death.

(7. Make personal arrangements—minister(s) and/or others to participate in the memorial service; music/poems for the service; pallbearers; funeral home and place of interment and the obituary.

(8. Help family and friends cope with the impending departure.

(9. Bear witness to the world how a child of God copes with dying and death—fearlessly, victoriously and triumphantly.

(10. Testify of saving grace to doctors, nurses, family and friends.

Francis Schaeffer as a missionary in Switzerland reached thousands of European students for Christ who were searching for truth. In 1978 he was diagnosed with an advanced case of lymphoma and given six to eight weeks to live. God intervened, extending his life five years, during which time he manifested unusual power in ministry on both sides of the Atlantic. Nearing death, he said, "By God's grace, I have been able to do more in these last five years than in all the years before I had cancer."[280] Francis Schaeffer redeemed the extended time God granted. As in life, so in death he leaned heavily upon the Word of God, specifically Psalm 84:5–7 (NKJV): "Blessed is the man whose strength is in You, whose heart is set on pilgrimage. As they pass through the Valley of Baca [Valley of Weeping], they make it a spring; the rain also covers it with pools. They go from strength to strength; each one appears before God in Zion." Nothing can be done to retrieve squandered time of yesterday. It's irretrievable; it cannot be recalled despite bitterness of tears over its misuse. But we can resolve to use what time remains wisely unto the glory of God (1 Corinthians 10:31). And now is the moment to begin.

50
Chains and Shackles That Confine

"Remember my chains" (Colossians 4:18 NIV). Paul discovered that the loss of freedom, opportunity, and comfort caused by the prison chains that shackled him was great "gain."[281] In what ways were the "chains" a gain to Paul? His chains gave him opportunity to witness to Felix (Acts 24:22–27). His chains gave him opportunity to preach to Agrippa that almost led to his salvation (Acts 26:28–32). His chains gave him opportunity to preach on a storm-battled ship to a distraught captain and crew (Acts 27:22). His chains gave him opportunity to testify of Christ to the Roman Praetorian guard in Caesar's palace (Philippians 4:22 and Acts 28:31). His chains gave him opportunity to write the prison epistles under house arrest in Rome (Acts 28:30). His chains gave him opportunity to inspire boldness in the disciples to stand firm and brazen for Christ (Philippians 1:14). It is no wonder in light of all this that he said, "The things which happened unto me ['my bonds'] have fallen out rather unto the furtherance of the gospel" (Philippians 1:12). For the child of God, there is the possibility of gain in loss in all circumstances, as was the case with Paul, if it is only sought. "Our limitations may become our opportunities."[282]

Various "chains" like sickness, suffering, sorrow and frailty limit what the saint can do for the Lord. He longs to do more, but the infirmity, adversity or bereavement hinders and prohibits.

The final Christmas letter John R. Rice wrote (December, 1980) vividly portrays the restrictive power of the "chain" of illness. He dreamed of preaching and soul winning, but the chains of infirmity hindered.

"I still, from my armchair, preach in great revival campaigns. I still envision hundreds walking the aisles to accept Christ. I still feel hot tears for the lost. I still see God working miracles. Oh, how I long to see great revivals, to hear about revival crowds once again! I want no Christmas without a burden for lost souls, a message for sinners, a heart to bring in the lost sheep so dear to the Shepherd, the sinning souls for whom Christ died. May food be tasteless and music a discord and Christmas a farce if I forget the dying millions to whom I am debtor, if this fire in my bones does not still flame! Not till I die or not till Jesus comes will I ever be eased of this burden, these tears, this toil to save souls."[283]

Comfort for Troubled Hearts

Many saints identify with Rice in the imposed limitation to ministry by medical adversity or emotional (sorrow) chains. That is understandable, defensible and unavoidable; the failure to extend one's chains to their furthermost as Paul did, however, is not. Chains hindered Paul from doing what he *would* for Christ; not what he *could*. Do what is doable, like Paul. The river may flow through a different channel, yet it keeps flowing. Handel, with loss of health, his right side paralyzed, and creditors threatening imprisonment, almost despaired of life. By God's grace he survived the ordeal and later composed his greatest work, *Messiah*. Handel stretched his chain to its furthest extent, making maximum use of its potential. We all must. Tension will be manifest at the chain's maximum extension; at that point nothing more may be done.

> Chains bound Paul's hands, not his heart.

The secret to Paul's endurance and effectiveness while in chains was "prayer, and the supply of the Spirit of Jesus Christ" (Philippians 1:19). He was dependent upon the prayers of the saints (as well as his own) and the "supply" (the provision of all that is necessary to cope, endure and be victorious in infirmities, adversities) of the Spirit of Jesus Christ. That same "supply" is available to every Christian.

Chains bound Paul's hands, not his heart. Despite the pain, suffering, agony and hardship of our chains, he still have a "song" to sing at midnight (Philippians 4:4, 11–13). A. C. Dixon states, "There are some birds that sing beautifully in the cage, and there are other birds that just beat out their lives against the bars of the cage; they cannot understand the limitation. When GOD in His providence puts us in the cage, let us learn to sing. It is better for the birds in the cage, and better for the birds outside, and better for the people who look into the cage that we should sing rather than beat against the bars; and the singing will open the door more readily than beating the bars."[284]

It really doesn't matter if others understand our "chains" and their ministry limitations or not. Obviously, many didn't understand Paul's or else he would not have told them to "remember my bonds." To know that God understands them is all sufficient. Making the best use of our chains will enable us to say at life's end, "Lord, I didn't do all I wanted to do for you, but remember my bonds"! He then in reply will say, "Well done, thou good and faithful servant: thou hast been faithful over a few things, I will make thee ruler over many things: enter thou into the joy of thy lord" (Matthew 25:21).

The Mamertine Prison dungeon in Rome was a dark, dismal and damp place situated three stories beneath the ground. Paul was lowered through a hole in the "Carcer's floor" into the "Tullianum" (dungeon). Void of windows for light, or ventilation it was here where Paul lived. (It is noteworthy that the Mamertine Prison in the seventh century became a place of worship.) Paul accepted his "bonds" as the will of God and was determined to therefore make the best use of them. Into whatever dark and deep dungeon that you are placed by the will of God, gladly accept and bear it for His glory and your highest good. And look for opportunities it creates to further the cause of the Gospel.

51

Coping with the Storms of Life

It's been well said that "you're either heading into a storm, going through a storm or coming out of a storm." At times the voyage of life is peaceful, "the south winds blow softly." But then suddenly, "not long after that," you meet with a "tempestuous wind" that is frightening and rattles your life (Acts 27:13–14). What are we to do when such trouble rocks our boat with threats of capsizing it? The narrative of Paul's shipwreck at Malta suggests there are seven immediate things that ought to be done in confronting the storms of life successfully.

(1. *Retire to prayer*. With hope of rescue from the storm abandoned, Paul disappears from the deck of the ship for a long time (Acts 27:20). Paul's "long abstinence" obviously was time spent alone in prayer (Acts 27:21) in a quiet and private chamber.[285] The first recourse in the time of trouble is earnest prayer seeking God's perspective, protection and deliverance.

(2. *Reckon on God's presence.*[286] An angel was dispatched from Heaven to tell Paul not to be afraid and to give assurances of deliverance (Acts 27:23–24). The presence of God is always with His child in the midst of the storm, saying, "Fear not, for I am with thee." Reckon on it. Depend on it. I read of a saint whose faith was severely tried with a serious illness. The man confided in his Christian doctor, saying, "Doctor, I feel so alone. I am afraid. I fear facing the experience of death."

The doctor put a chair next to the man's bed, pointed to it and said, "I want you to remember that Jesus is here with you all the time. He will never leave you nor forsake you. Reckon upon the presence of the Lord so strongly that you can imagine Him sitting in that chair."

Over the ensuing days the dying saint constantly retained a tight grip on the arm of the chair, as if he literally was holding to the hand of Christ. The day arrived when the saint with his hand upon the arm of the chair quietly went to Heaven. When the doctor was told of this, he said, "He was holding to the nail-scarred hand of Jesus and was conscious of His presence until He died."[287] Solomon said, "When the storms of life come, the wicked are whirled away, but the godly have a lasting foundation" (Proverbs 10:25 NLT).

(3. *Rely upon God's promises.*[288] What God told Paul (no life would be lost), he believed as a certainty to happen (Acts 27:24–25). And it did (Acts 27:44). C. H. Spurgeon said, "The best praying man is the man who is most believingly familiar with the promises of God. After all, prayer is nothing but taking God's promises to Him and saying, "Do as Thou hast said." Prayer is the promise utilized. A prayer which is not based on a promise has no true foundation."[289] Claim and rely upon the "exceeding great and precious promises" of the Lord (2 Peter 1:4); they will not fail or disappoint you.

(4. *Remain calm and cheerful.* In the midst of the fright of the night, Paul said to the sailors and prisoners, "Be of good cheer"—not once, but twice (Acts 27:22, 25). And in hearing the comforting words of assured forthcoming deliverance authoritatively given by Paul, they did in fact exhibit "cheer" (Acts 27:36). The attitude and demeanor embraced by the saint in times of adversity impacts others (Acts 27:25, 27); Paul's confidence and consolation became that of those on board the ship. Knowing that God is in control of the "storm" that rocks your boat and knowing the boat's Pilot grants peace and joy in the midst of the tempest. The saint has a happy song to sing even in the "midnights" of adversity, as shown by Paul and Silas (Acts 16:25).

(5. *Resiliently stay aboard ship.* The condition for the survival of all aboard the vessel was that none bailed overboard (Acts 27:31). Don't allow panic to prompt *jumping ship*. Stay the course. James said, "Blessed is the man who remains steadfast under trial, for when he has stood the test he will receive the crown of life, which God has promised to those who love him" (James 1:12 ESV).

'Til the storm passes over,
'Til the thunder sounds no more,
   'Til the clouds roll forever from the sky,
Hold me fast; let me stand
In the hollow of Thy hand.
   Keep me safe 'til the storm passes by. ~ Mosie Lister (1958)

(6. *Render gratitude to God.* In the presence of all the crew and prisoners Paul "gave thanks to God" (Acts 27:35) for their rescue, although it had not happened. Manley Beasley well said, "Faith is acting as though a thing is so, when it is not so, in order for it to be so, because it is so." Express gratitude up front to the Lord for His divine intervention and deliverance.

(7. *Rid from the ship its unfitting cargo* (Acts 27:18). Times of trials are times of testing. Inspect the "cargo" hidden in the ship's deep hole (your heart) and toss overboard all that is unfitting to a follower of Christ. Pray with David, "Search me,

When the Rain Comes

O God,...And see if there be any wicked way in me" (Psalms 139:23–24). See Proverbs 17:3.

Oh, God will make a way
Where there seems to be no way;
He works in ways we cannot see.
He will make a way for me. ~ Don Moen (1987)

Everyone aboard the ship made it to shore safely; not one lost his life. God supernaturally orchestrated every detail of the storm's impact upon the ship so that it could withstand the intense pounding of the waves and hurricane-force winds. He still does the same for all His children experiencing "storms"; He will not put more upon them than they can possibly bear with His assistance (1 Corinthians 10:13).

Our times are in Thy hand;
    O God, we wish them there.
Our lives, our souls, our all we leave
    Entirely to Thy care.

Our times are in Thy hand,
    Whatever they may be—
Pleasing or painful, dark or bright,
    As best may seem to Thee.

Our times are in Thy hand;
    Why should we doubt or fear?
A father's hand will never cause
    His child a needless tear.

Our times are in Thy hand;
    Jesus, the Crucified,
Whose hand our many sins have pierced,
    Is now our guard and guide.

Our times are in Thy hand;
    We'll always trust to Thee,
Till we possess the promised crown
    And all Thy glory see. ~ William Freeman Lloyd (1824)

52

The Saint's Swan Song

The swan song is a metaphorical phrase for a person's final composition, gesture or performance, based on the fabled swan that never sings in its lifetime but always sings sweetly just before death. Some believers are like the *fabled* swan: they seldom or never sing (life's burdens and trials suffocate their songs), but when dying, a song is born and sung most loudly, joyfully, and melodiously as they are taken to Heaven.[290] C. H. Spurgeon says, "The best moment of a Christian's life is his last one, because it is the one that is nearest Heaven! And then it is that he begins to strike the keynote of the song which he shall sing to all eternity. Oh, what a song will that be!"[291]

While various stages of life provide the opportunity to share a *swan song* (retirement, final performance, a final farewell), the most significant is *when Heaven draws near*. To encapsulate in word or song or deed your aspirations, instructions and/or gratitude for others, Christian testimonial, story of life and charge to family members and friends to meet you in Heaven are all proper and therapeutic to others and yourself. The Holy Scriptures cite examples of powerful "swan songs" of the saints. Paul, in approaching death, said, "I have fought a good fight, I have finished my course, I have kept the faith: Henceforth there is laid up for me a crown of righteousness, which the Lord, the righteous judge, shall give me at that day: and not to me only, but unto all them also that love his appearing" (2 Timothy 4:7–8). His "swan song" was penned to young Timothy regarding holding firm to sound doctrine (2 Timothy 4:2–3). Stephen's "swan song" in death appealed to God to forgive the very people that murdered him (Acts 7:59–60). David's "swan song" was to Solomon, his son, "revealing his unfailing faith in God and his joyful confidence in his gracious covenant promises (2 Samuel 23:1–7)."[292]

But the best "swan song" of all was uttered by Jesus to the disciples in John 14:1–4: "Let not your heart be troubled: ye believe in God, believe also in me. In my Father's house are many mansions: if it were not so, I would have told you. I go to prepare a place for you. And if I go and prepare a place for you, I will come again, and receive you unto myself; that where I am, there ye may be also. And whither I go ye know, and the way ye know." Imitate the "swan songs" of the faithful, not the ungodly. Let your "swan song" be a lasting legacy, the sweetest song ever sung, as it was with the fabled swan in dying.

53

The Faithfulness of God

"When I cannot *feel* the faith of assurance," says Matthew Henry, "I live by the *fact* of God's faithfulness."[293] God keeps His promises. He is truthful; He does what

When the Rain Comes

He says. He is totally trustworthy. Isaiah declared, "O LORD, thou art my God; I will exalt thee, I will praise thy name; for thou hast done wonderful things; thy counsels of old are faithfulness and truth" (Isaiah 25:1). Moses said, "Know therefore that the LORD thy God, he is God, the faithful God, which keepeth covenant and mercy with them that love him and keep his commandments to a thousand generations" (Deuteronomy 7:9). "Not one thing hath failed or shall fail of all that the Lord hath spoken."[294]

Man may fail you, but never the Lord. Even in our unfaithfulness to Him, He remains faithful to us (2 Timothy 2:13)—what comforting news! He is faithful to believers in provision (Philippians 4:19); pardon (Isaiah 1:18); protection (Psalm 18:2); prevention (Psalm 24:1–8); promises (Deuteronomy 7:9) and preservation (John 6:39). Augustine said, "God is not a deceiver that He should offer to support us and then, when we lean upon Him, should slip away from us."[295] William Arthur Ward remarks that God's faithfulness is sufficient and secure: "God's strength behind you, His concern for you, His love within you, and His arms beneath you are more than sufficient for the job [adversity, infirmity, bereavement] ahead of you." The faithfulness of God led Jeremiah to break out in praise, exclaiming, "It is of the LORD's mercies that we are not consumed, because his compassions fail not. They are new every morning: great is thy faithfulness" (Lamentations 3:22–23).

> "Great is Thy faithfulness!" "Great is Thy faithfulness!"
>   Morning by morning new mercies I see.
> All I have needed Thy hand hath provided;
>   "Great is Thy faithfulness," Lord, unto me!
>   ~ Thomas Obadiah Chisholm (1866–1960)

Over a century ago a ship sank off the coast of England. Many lives were lost. Clinging to a rock all night, a sixteen-year-old boy was saved from the turbulent sea. Upon being rescued, he was asked, "Didn't you shake as you were clinging all night to that rock?"

The boy replied, "Yes, of course. But the rock never shook once."

Samuel Rutherford said, "Trust God's Word and His power more than you trust your own feelings and experiences. Remember, your Rock is Christ, and it's the sea that ebbs and flows with the tides, not Him."[296]

The blind Scottish preacher George Matheson, in 1882 during a time he later called "the most severe mental suffering," composed a hymn ("O Love That Will Not Let Me Go") in five minutes that has stirred the church worldwide. Make it your confession and declaration. Cloak yourself within its affirmation and experience

Christ's loving consolation. Rejoice in knowing the love of Christ for you is permanent and non-vacillating.

Alexander Smellie says, "God's care of me is particular and minute. He is my Keeper, O my heart! Mine, as though I were alone in all His universe! He knows my separate case, my necessities, my temptations, my foes. He calls me by name. He has millions upon millions for whom to provide—but He never forgets me for one moment! I live day and night in His thought and love."[297]

> O Love that will not let me go,
> I rest my weary soul in thee;
> I give thee back the life I owe,
> That in thine ocean depths its flow
> May richer, fuller be. ~ George Matheson (1882)

54
It's But a Step

David describes the distance between life and death as but a step: "There is but a step between me and death" (1 Samuel 20:3). A step, even for the tall in stature, is but a short span that may be taken in mere seconds.

The step of death is *a certain step* that all will take regardless of position, power or possessions. Yet, Young says, "All men think all men are mortal but themselves." Doth not the manner in which you live indicate the truth of the statement? An end is coming. "What will ye do in the end?" (Jeremiah 5:31). Billy Graham states, "All mankind is sitting on death row. How we die or when is not the main issue, but where we go after death."[298]

> All mankind is sitting on death row. How we die or when is not the main issue, but where we go after death.
> Billy Graham

Death is an uncertain step as to when it will be taken. Man's life is as frail as grass that "withers." The metaphor of short-lived grass is used often in Scripture to depict life's frailty. See Psalm 90:6; Isaiah 40:6–7; James 1:10 and 1 Peter 1:24. The length or duration of life is uncertain, for sickness, accident, or murder may unexpectedly and suddenly snatch it away. Every man, regardless of his age, is only one heartbeat away from death and eternity. Knowing this, man ought to pray with Moses, "So teach us to number our days, that we may apply our hearts unto wisdom" (Psalm 90:12). Of the death of friends and loved ones, Tuck says, "Nothing so effectively convinces one of the uncertainty of life. Nothing better pleads for the faithful doing of the duty of every hour. Nothing more effectively convinces one that no man is necessary to God's work in the world. It teaches us that as our lifework may be 'rounded off' at any moment, it should always be ready for 'rounding off.'"[299]

It is *a parting step* from family and friends (temporarily if you and they are believers).

It is *a final step* in that it strikes finality to the saint's earthly pilgrimage; battles with sin, sickness, suffering and sorrow are over.

It is *a solemn step* requiring the utmost seriousness in consideration; accountability to God will be rendered.

It is *a decisive" step* sealing man's eternal destiny: Heaven or hell. C. H. Spurgeon comments, "What I am when death is held before me, that I must be forever. When my spirit departs, if God finds me hymning His praise, I shall hymn it in heaven; if He finds me breathing out oaths, I shall follow up those oaths in Hell."[300]

It is *a welcoming step* by Christ and the host of Heaven for the redeemed; no more does the saint's foot strike the ground in death than it reaches the throne of God. Be cheered and comforted in knowing that the "step" may be taken in stride without fear or trembling, for He that ordains us to take it sustains us in it. Augustine said, "We want to reach the kingdom of God, but we don't want to travel by way of death. And yet there stands Necessity saying: 'This way, please.' Do not hesitate, man, to go this way, when this is the way that God came to you."[301]

If unprepared for the "step," make ready now. Spurgeon says, "If there is but a step between you and death, yet there is only a step between you and Jesus. There is only a step between you and salvation. God help you take that step."[302] Pascal said, "Between us and Hell or Heaven there is nothing but life, the most fragile thing in existence."[303] See James 4:14 and Mark 13:33.

When engulfed by the terror of the tempestuous sea,
　　Unknown waves before you roll;
At the end of doubt and peril is eternity,
　　Though fear and conflict seize your soul.

When surrounded by the blackness of the darkest night,
　　Oh, how lonely death can be;
At the end of this long tunnel is a shining light,
　　For death is swallowed up in victory!

But just think of stepping on shore—and finding it Heaven!
Of touching a hand—and finding it God's!
Of breathing new air—and finding it celestial!
Of waking up in Glory—and finding it Home! ~ Don Wyrtzen (1971)

55

Settle the Doubt of the Night

Horrendous physical or mental suffering, illness, fatigue and strong medications can play havoc with a person's long-embraced faith in Christ, the Word of God and Heaven. The safe and best course to take should such happen is not to doubt in the night (suffering, sickness, sorrow) what was trusted in the light (health, mental well-being) regarding the spiritual. God certainly understands (as should others) when *reasoning about faith* is altered through infirmity and prescription drugs.

Why shrinks my weak nature? Ah! what can it mean?
Why flutters my heart, which till now was serene?
Why ling'ring and trembling, while glory's so near?
Oh, whence the enchantment that fetters me here?
~ Hymns and Spiritual Songs for Christians (1812)

Never allow present circumstance ("night") to toy or tamper with longstanding religious beliefs. It was Peter's fear of dying that precipitated his doubt in walking on the water to Jesus (Matthew 14:31). It was John the Baptist's dire circumstance in prison awaiting probable execution that prompted doubt about Jesus' being the Messiah (Matthew 11:2–3). The same God of the mountains is God of the valleys. The promises believed in health and prosperity are still true in illness and adversity. The same God that walked life's journey with you is He that yet watches over you relentlessly in sickness, sorrow and suffering. The eternal realities of life after death, Heaven and reunion with the departed saints, remain unaltered by present circumstances. Don't frantically jump ship in the eleventh hour. Hold steadfastly to that which was believed and embraced in the *light,* despite the *night terrors and doubts* that envelope the soul. "Never question in the night what was believed in the light."

O doubting, struggling Christian,
    Why thus in anguish pray?
Oh, cease to doubt and struggle;
    There is a better way.

When the Rain Comes

Oh, settle it all with Jesus;
    Oh, settle it all today.
Oh, cease to doubt and struggle;
    Oh, cease to plead and pray.
Oh, rest in His word forever
    And settle it all today.

Give up thy will to Jesus
    And trust Him though He slay;
Hush all thy fears and questions
    And settle it today.

O soul so tossed with tempest,
    Upon His promise stay;
Cast out faith's strong sheet anchor
    And settle it today.

Lord, I give up the struggle,
    To Thee commit my way;
I trust Thy word forever
    And settle it today. ~ Albert Benjamin Simpson (1843–1919)

56

The Day of Death Is Better Than That of Birth

"A good name is better than precious ointment; and the day of death than the day of one's birth" (Ecclesiastes 7:1). The proverb is only true of him that "dies in the Lord," the redeemed of Jesus Christ by His precious blood whose good name is written in the Lamb's Book of Life. The validity of the statement is accentuated and demonstrated in Holy Scripture.

(1. The day of birth clothes man with mortality; the day of death clothes him with immortality (2 Corinthians 5:1–3).

(2. The day of birth brings imperfection due to sin and its curse; the day of death frees man from sin's curse, enabling perfection (Hebrews 12:23).

(3. The day of birth brings man into a world of sickness (some incurable), suffering, and sorrow; the day of death transports him to a city where these do not exist (Revelation 21:4).

(4. The day of birth brings man into a world of toil and labor; the day of death gives him eternal rest from life's work (Revelation 14:13).

(5. The day of birth envelops man with frail flesh that experiences grave pain and weeps bitter tears; the day of death heals the pain and wipes the tears away (Revelation 21:4).

(6. The day of birth commences man journey of life; the day of death concludes it (Ecclesiastes 7:8). C. H. Spurgeon explains: "He who is newly born and is ordained to endure through a long life is like a warrior who puts on his harness for battle; and is not he in a better case who puts it off because he has won the victory? Ask any soldier which he likes best, the first shot in the battle or the sound which means 'cease firing, for the victory is won.'"[304]

(7. The day of birth cloaks man with the propensity to sin; the day of death abolishes that natural inclination (Revelation 7:14).

(8. The day of birth brings man into a world of death; the day of death transports him into a world of life (Mark 10:30).[305] Death to the believer is not leaving the land of the living for the land of the dying, but the exact opposite.

(9. The day of birth shrouds man with imperfect knowledge; the day of death enlightens man with complete knowledge (1 Corinthians 13:12).

(10. The day of birth limits unbroken fellowship with family and friends; the day of death enables permanent, glorious reunion with loved ones in Heaven (1 Thessalonians 4:14).

(11. The day of birth welcomes man into a world that is antagonistic to God and the Christian faith; the day of death ushers him into a domain where all men bow in adoration and submission to God and His rule (Revelation 5:9–14).

(12. The day of birth thrusts man into a universe saturated with horrendous and harmful evil instigated by Satan; the day of death spares him from its influence and injury (Isaiah 57:1). Henry Ward Beecher comments, "You have come into a hard world. I know of only one easy place in it, and that is the grave."[306]

(13. The day of birth encompasses us with uncertainties as to life's duration (long or short), health and illness, godly or evil course (choices), and success or failure; the day of death is filled with absolute certainties which include life after death with God in Heaven, reunion with redeemed family and friends, cure from the diseases and heartaches and sorrows of life (2 Corinthians 5:1–8).

Therefore, the day of death ought to be celebrated and welcomed more than the day of birth. To make pungently clear, a person must be born again (saved by Christ's atoning work at Calvary), or else the proverb is invalid. For the unsaved, "though the day of your birth was a bad day; the day of your death will be a thousand times worse."[307] Driven from God's presence into Hell to experience the tormenting terrors of that abode day and night, their death will be one of eternal darkness and suffering (Revelation 20:15 and Matthew 25:41). In that awful abode men will bemoan that they ever were born.

When the Rain Comes

My latest sun is sinking fast;
    My race is nearly run.
My strongest trials now are past;
    My triumph is begun!

Oh, come, Angel Band; come and around me stand.
Oh, bear me away on your snowy wings
To my immortal home.
Oh, bear me away on your snowy wings
To my immortal home.

I know I'm nearing holy ranks
    Of friends and kindred dear.
I brush the dew of Jordan's banks;
    The crossing must be near.

I've almost gained my heav'nly home;
    My spirit loudly sings.
The holy ones, behold, they come!
    I hear the noise of wings.

Oh, bear my longing heart to Him
    Who bled and died for me,
Whose blood now cleanses from all sin
    And gives me victory. ~ Jefferson Hascall (1860)

57

The Antidote to Anxiety

"Worry is putting tomorrow's possible cloud over today's sunshine."[308] It has been said, "Worry is like a rocking chair. It will give you something to do, but it won't get you anywhere!" Arthur Somers Roche (1883–1935) remarked, "Worry is a thin stream of fear trickling through the mind. If encouraged, it cuts a channel into which all other thoughts are drained."[309]

"Why art thou cast down, O my soul? and why art thou disquieted within me? hope in God" (Psalm 43:5). The Psalmist, in a state of mental anguish and gloom, arouses himself through self-interrogation not to fret but to trust in God for relief and consolation. J. M. Boice states, "It is a case of the mind speaking to the emotions rather than the emotions dictating to the mind."[310] Then quoting D. Martyn Lloyd-Jones, he adds: "You have to take yourself in hand; you have to address yourself, preach to yourself, question yourself. You must say to your soul, 'Why art thou cast down'—what business have you to be disquieted? You must turn on yourself, upbraid yourself, condemn yourself, exhort yourself, and say to yourself, 'Hope thou in God'—instead of muttering in this depressed, unhappy way."[311] Talk to yourself like David talked to himself (Psalm 43:5a) about the anxiety in an effort to talk yourself out of it as he did (Psalm 43:5b). Discipline the mind to bring "into captivity every thought to the obedience of Christ" (2 Corinthians 10:5).

> Talk to yourself as David talked to himself about the anxiety in an effort to talk yourself out of it as he did.

Oswald Chambers said, "Fretting means getting ourselves 'out of joint' mentally or spiritually. It is one thing to say, 'Do not fret,' but something very different to have such a nature that you find yourself unable to fret. Worrying always results in sin. We tend to think that a little anxiety and worry are simply an indication of how wise we really are, yet it is actually a much better indication of just how wicked we are. Set all your opinions and speculations aside and "abide under the shadow of the Almighty" (Psalm 91:1). Deliberately tell God that you will not fret about whatever concerns you. All our fretting and worrying are caused by planning without God."[312] Give no room in the mind to that which steals peace, contentment, hope, joy and usefulness; rebuke it in Jesus' name the moment it enters (Ephesians 4:27). Hudson Taylor remarked, "It doesn't matter how great the pressure is. What really matters is where the pressure lies, whether it comes between me and God or whether it presses me nearer His heart."[313]

The worried cow
Would have lived till now,
   If she had saved her breath;
But she feared her hay
Wouldn't last all day,
   And she mooed herself to death. ~ Unknown

"In the multitude of my thoughts [anxiety] within me thy comforts delight [soothe] my soul" (Psalm 94:19). What are the "comforts" of the Lord for anxious and troublesome thoughts that weigh us down? There are many of them which flow from Heaven's throne ("thy comforts").

(1. They are the *comforting* promises in Holy Scripture. See 2 Peter 1:4. God's promises should be fastened to the mind so that in times of disturbing and burdensome thoughts they may be recalled to put the injurious thoughts to flight. Cherish the promises of God and allow them to expel the negative thoughts that

choke out joy and peace. The psalmist declared, "This is my comfort in my affliction, for Your word has given me life" (Psalm 119:50 NKJV).

(2. They are the *comforting* musing of the doctrinal themes of God's encompassing love, atonement, resurrection of Christ, the second coming and rapture, glorification of the saint, Heaven and God's sovereignty (Psalm 39:3).

(3. They are the *comforting* remembrances of His loving-kindness and manifold blessings. "Hitherto the Lord has helped me." Therefore, I am assured of His help now. See Psalm 94:22. "As a general principle, if we would exercise our memories more wisely, we might, in our very darkest distress, strike a match which would instantaneously kindle the lamp of comfort."[314]

> Ponder anew
> What the Almighty can do,
> Who with His love doth befriend thee. ~ Joachim Neander (1650–1680)

(4. They are the *comforting* musings of the majesty of nature; her calm, beauty, magnificence, and awe uplift the downhearted.

> O Lord, my God, when I in awesome wonder
>   Consider all the worlds Thy Hands have made.
> I see the stars; I hear the rolling thunder
>   Thy power throughout the universe displayed.
> Then sings my soul, my Savior God, to Thee,
> How great Thou art; how great Thou art. ~ Stuart K. Hine (1899–1989)

(5. They are the *comforting* ministries of the Holy Spirit. See John 14:26. Upon the occasion of the text, David's psychic (mental) state was changed (agitation quieted), not his circumstance. He still was in the same "place" coping with the same issues, but without the fret and worry. The Holy Spirit (when allowed and trusted) grants a peace in mind 'that surpasses all understanding' when the body is shaken with sorrow, sickness and suffering. He sustains even when the trouble is retained.

Comforting thoughts from the Lord will "delight" the soul. They will soothe and cheer the soul. They will restore the soul. They will keep the soul in "perfect peace" (Isaiah 26:3). They will encourage the soul. They will give the soul "songs in the night." See 1 Peter 5:7 and Philippians 4:6–7. "The notable efficacy of these divine comforts—they do not only pacify the mind, but they joy it; they do not only satisfy it but ravish it; they do not only quiet it but delight it."[315]

C. H. Spurgeon remarks, "By anxious thought you cannot add an inch to your stature nor turn one hair white or black; take, then, no anxious thought for the morrow, for the morrow shall take thought for the things of itself. Lean upon your

God and remember His promise that as your day is so shall your strength be. 'I would have you,' says the apostle, 'I would have you without carefulness' (Philippians 4:6). He does not mean, I would have you without economy, without prudence and without discretion, but he means he would have you without fretfulness, without distrustful care. I would have you be without care for yourself, because the Lord's eyes will be upon you."[316] William Osler said, "The load of tomorrow added to that of today makes the strongest falter. Shut off the future as tightly as the past."[317]

> The load of tomorrow added to that of today makes the strongest falter. Shut off the future as tightly as the past.
> William Osler

58
Bear a Good Witness When It Rains

The great pastor of yesteryear George W. Truett strongly exhorts, "Mind, when trouble comes, how you behave. No matter what the trouble is, mind how you behave. Many a man has dishonored God when trouble came. No matter what the trouble is, no matter what brought it, no matter who brought it, no matter how it came about, God is dishonored if a Christian does not bear his fiery trial like he ought to bear it. You will either dishonor Him egregiously, or you will honor Him gloriously, according to your behavior when trouble is on. Trouble rightly borne will surely honor God. Remember that."[318] "When you are living by faith," writes Alan Redpath, "through the darkness of circumstances, other people become aware of the radiance and sweetness of your life, and they are truly blessed."[319] The opposite is also true.

> No matter what the trouble is, no matter what brought it, no matter who brought it, no matter how it came about, God is dishonored if a Christian does not bear his fiery trial like he ought to bear it.
> George W. Truett

John Wesley, Methodist minister and theologian, was feeling miserable at breakfast. Sensing the situation, his wife momentarily left the room to redress in black, and then rejoined him.

"Who is dead?" Wesley asked.

"God," she replied.

"Oh, no!" he said.

Mrs. Wesley responded, "I thought so, from your countenance and conduct."[320]

In your present circumstance despite its deepening darkness, uncertainty, fear, and suffering, give none the faintest idea that "God is dead," but passionately seek to reflect (to doctors, nurses, friends, etc.) the faithfulness of His presence, the trustworthiness of His promises and the goodliness of His provision. Adrian Rogers stated, "A Christian with a glowing witness is worth a library full of arguments."[321]

How we react to adverse circumstances may either fuel the choice of an unbeliever to begin a quest for God or sadly, dismiss Him altogether; enlarge hope in the life of a believer or diminish it; honor or dishonor the Lord. Martyn Lloyd-Jones states, "As we face the modern world with all its trouble and turmoil and with all its difficulties and sadness, nothing is more important than that we who call ourselves Christian, and who claim the Name of Christ, should be representing our faith in such a way before others as to give them the impression that here is the solution, and here is the answer. In a world where everything has gone so sadly astray, we should be standing out as men and women apart, people characterized by a fundamental joy and certainty in spite of conditions, in spite of adversity."[322] Aristides bears witness to such observation. Around A.D. 125 he wrote to a friend about the reasons for the extraordinary success of Christianity since its inception. In part he said, "If any righteous man among the Christians passes from this world, they rejoice and offer thanks to God, and they escort his body with songs and thanksgiving as if he were setting out from one place to another nearby."[323] What a testimonial the early saints manifested in the hour of deepest sorrow!

Whether the form of the rain that comes is bereavement, adversity, or sickness, saints ought to genuinely (not fakery or self-manipulation) manifest the hope that they possess in Christ Jesus, as the early saints did. Why?

(1. Because it is a *real hope* founded in Christ's death, burial, and resurrection.

(2. Because it is a *hope that will not disappoint* (Romans 5:5 NCV) despite the difficulty confronted. Both the Bible and experience testify to this truth. The hope in Christ Jesus that sustained you in the sunshine will not disappoint you in the rain.

(3. Because it is a hope that is founded upon *the love of God* that is unfailing, always abounding, and sustaining. He hath said, "I will never leave thee, nor forsake thee." He promises, and we are certain that He will never desert or abandon us regardless of the storm that rages. William MacDonald says, "We will never be disappointed or find that we have rested on a false confidence. How can we be so sure? Because the love of God has been poured out in our hearts."[324]

(4. Because it is a hope *undergirded by God's divine promise* to work good out of our adversity (Romans 8:28). Put this hope on display (the hope that God is in control, providing care, comfort, and consolation) despite the affliction, adversity or sorrow.

When someone asks, "How did you react to adversity?" let the resounding reply be: "I reacted as one that possessed eternal hope in the Lord Jesus Christ." See 1 Thessalonians 4:13.

Comfort for Troubled Hearts

Tho' your heart may be heavy with sorrow and care,
    You may others to gladness beguile,
If a face like the light of the morning you wear
    And carry your cross with a smile!

Carry your cross with a smile;
Carry your cross with a smile.
You may others from sadness to gladness beguile,
If you carry your cross with a smile.

Let the well by the wayside that flows unto all
    Strength impart for each step of the mile;
Let your faith the great promises often recall,
    And carry your cross with a smile! ~ Ina D. Ogdon (1916)

To test the genuineness of a diamond, it may be placed in clear water, in which it will sparkle with brilliance. A fake stone on the other hand, sparkles slightly. When both stones are placed side by side in clear water the difference is obvious. It is when Christians are in the crucible of adversity, tragedy and sorrow that they are distinguished from unbelievers, carnal saints and mere professors. Their radiance (which testifies of Christ's all-sufficient grace and comfort and eternal hope), despite similar trouble and suffering, is vastly different.[325]

59

The Never-Forsaking God

"For he hath said, I will never leave thee, nor forsake thee. So that we may boldly say, The Lord is my helper" (Hebrews 13:5–6).

The perimeter of the promise. Wherever the locale—hospital, assisted living facility, land or sea, prison, home or foreign soil—the promise stands. Whatever the circumstance—sickness, suffering, loneliness, bereavement, utter hopelessness, fear, deathbed—it is included in the promise. Whenever the time—now, tomorrow, or anytime ('never will I leave thee')—the promise applies. It pertains to all times of the believer's life—good or bad, ups and downs, joys and sorrows.

The Promiser of the promise. "For he hath said." A promise is only as good as its giver. Some make promises they are unable or unwilling to keep. But it is not so with the Promiser of this promise, for He is "the faithful God, which keepeth covenant and mercy with them that love him and keep his commandments to a thousand generations" (Deuteronomy 7:9). "The inviolable faithfulness of the

113

When the Rain Comes

Promiser is good security for the accomplishment of the promise."[326] His omnipotence, omniscience, immutability and omnipresence assure us that the thing which was promised is capable of being done. C. H. Spurgeon said, "A promise is nothing unless I have good security that it shall be fulfilled. It is in vain for men to promise largely unless their fulfillment shall be as large as their promise, for the largeness of their promise is just the largeness of their deception. But here every word of God is true. God has issued no more notes for the bank of Heaven than He can cash in an hour if He wills. There is enough bullion in the vaults of Omnipotence to pay off every bill that ever shall be drawn by the faith of man on the promises of God."[327] None but God may say truthfully, "I will never leave thee, nor forsake thee." John Owen, in a letter dictated to his friend Charles Heetwood, says, "Live and pray, hope and wait patiently, and do not despond; the promise stands invincible that He will never leave nor forsake us."[328]

The pledge of the promise. Christ promises, "I will never leave thee, nor forsake thee." He pledges to personally walk with the saint (never leave *thee*), being their helper in every circumstance of life. J. B. Hutson expresses the *aloneness* of dying when family and friends are absent (in Heaven) in the poem *All Gone*. (No one understands and consoles that aloneness better than Christ!)

All gone! dear ones I loved so well,
    And I am left alone;
One house we had in which to dwell,
    One family—but they are gone.

Father and mother long since gone,
    And others as dear as life;
Brother and sister, all my own;
    And now my poor, sweet wife.

All gone but me, and yet I see
    Their forms and looks of love
And almost hear them speak to me
    From their sweet home above.

Gone! gone! I think of things they said,
    No voice like theirs so sweet;
And can it be that they are dead,
    On earth no more to meet?

Yes, they are gone, all gone! all gone!
    I might as well give up
And all alone the grief endure
    And drink the mournful cup.

All gone! and soon it will be true
    That I with all the rest
Will too be gone, all gone! all gone!
    To mansions of the blest. ~ J. B. Hutson

The profit of the promise. The assurance of Christ's unwavering constant companionship secures peace amid life's storms, averts the fear of His abandonment, assures His help in the hour of need, emboldens with strong courage and bravery to face the darkest of trials, and fills the heart with satisfying contentment, knowing the Great Physician and the Holy Comforter are always available. The promise fully embraced by faith will be confirmed in experience. To act upon it in acceptance and trust will banish despondency, dread, drudgery and despair, giving delight.

Keith poses Christ's word to the saint in poetic form:

The soul that on Jesus hath leaned for repose
I will not, I will not desert to His foes;
That soul, though all Hell should endeavor to shake,
I'll never, no, never, no, never forsake. ~ attributed to George Keith (1787)

60
"Ne Plus Ultra" or "No More Beyond"

Prominent mountains flank the entrance to the Sea of Gibraltar (separates the Atlantic Ocean from the Mediterranean Sea) from the East. These mountains from antiquity have been known as the Pillars of Hercules. Spain etched across the pillars three Latin words centuries ago: *"Ne plus ultra,"* or "No more beyond" to warn sailors not to enter the Atlantic Ocean, for it was thought there was nothing beyond them. So certain of this claim, the three Latin words were even written on the edges of their maps. The great sailor Christopher Columbus ignored the warning only to discover the New World. In Valladolid, Spain, where Christopher Columbus died in 1506, stands a monument erected to his honor. Depicted on the memorial is the statue of a Lion eating away one of the three Latin words, *Ne* (No), to make it read *Plus Ultra* which means "More Beyond."

Prior to the resurrection of Jesus, across every cemetery entrance were etched (figuratively speaking) *Ne plus ultra* (No more beyond). But in defeating and conquering death, Jesus swallowed up the *Ne* (No), leaving *plus ultra* ("more beyond"). As Randy Alcorn states, "Death is not a wall but a turnstile."[329]

61

"Oh, No, You Never Let Go of Me"

A small boy went for a swim in the old swimming hole behind his home. Unknowingly, as he swam toward the middle of the lake, an alligator was swimming toward him. The watchful eye of his father saw what was transpiring and he quickly ran to the water, shouting the danger to his son. The lad made a U-turn to swim to him. Reaching from the dock, the father grabbed his son's arms just as the alligator snatched his legs. An incredible tug-of-war raged. Battling a strength greater than his own, the father would not let go. A farmer passing by in his truck heard the screams, raced to the water and shot the alligator. Miraculously, following weeks of hospitalization, the young boy recovered. The severe scars on his legs bore witness to the traumatizing and almost fatal encounter with the alligator while the deep scratches on his arms showed the marks of his father's fingernails that dug into his flesh to hang onto him. A reporter asked to see the scars. The boy pulled up his pant legs. And then the boy said, "But look at my arms. I have great scars on my arms, too, because my dad wouldn't let go."

The application of this lesson is that regardless of the *alligators* that afflict and assail, bringing hurt and pain, the heavenly Father will not let go of you—even when you want to let go, like Elijah (1 Kings 19:4) and Jonah (Jonah 4:3) did. The scars in His hands, feet and side bear indisputable testimony to that. Matt Redman rightly sings of Christ, "Oh, no, You never let go. You never let go of me."

> Jesus will walk with me, guarding me ever,
> Giving me victory through storm and through strife;
> He is my Comforter, Counselor, Leader,
> Over the uneven journey of life. ~ Haldor Lillenas (1922)

God securely grips your hand in the storms of life, refusing to let go. He says, "That's right. Because I, your God, have a firm grip on you and I'm not letting go. I'm telling you, 'Don't panic. I'm right here to help you'" (Isaiah 41:13 MSG). Our grip on Him may waver, but not His upon us. Knowing He holds our hand tightly and firmly, what have we to dread or fear from the "alligators"?

62
Two Strings on My Bow

An infidel and simpleton argued about the truthfulness of the Christian faith. In the midst of the discussion, the infidel said to the poor countryman, "Well, Hodge, you really are so stupid that there is no use arguing with you. I cannot get you out of this absurd religion of yours."

"Ah! well," said Hodge, "I dare say I am stupid, but do you know we poor people like to have two strings to our bow?"

"Well," said the critic, "what do you mean by that?"

"I'll show you. Suppose it should all turn out as you say; suppose there is no God and there is no hereafter, don't you see I am as well off as you are? Certainly it will not be any worse for me than it will be for you if we both get annihilated. But don't you see if it should happen to be true as I believe what will become of you?"[330]

Blaise Pascal (1623–1662) put the countryman's argument similarly. He said, "Belief is a wise wager. Granted that faith cannot be proved, what harm will come to you if you gamble on its truth and it proves false? If you gain, you gain all; if you lose, you lose nothing. Wager, then, without hesitation, that He exists."[331] Christians are utterly content in the need for only one string on their bow, for they possess all assurance and certainty of eternal life in Heaven with Christ beyond the grave, founded upon biblical documentation, verification of Christ's life, death and resurrection historically as well as biblically, and the credible witness of the Holy Spirit to their soul. To them the fact of life after death is not a gamble; it's a surety. But the ungodly and spiritually immature may need two strings on their bow until they are enlightened.

63
Burdens Are Lifted at Calvary

"Cast thy burden upon the LORD, and he shall sustain thee" (Psalm 55:22). "Burdens" are the hardships of life that weigh us down with anxiety, worry, fear, despair, hurt, suffering and dread, filling our hearts with pain and our eyes with tears.

The problem with life's burdens ("thy burden"). Burdens are part and parcel of every man's life regardless of status or saintliness. The Bible says, "For every man shall bear his own burden" (Galatians 6:5). William Shakespeare says it's not hard to bear the toothache of another, but when one's own jaw is throbbing, that's a different story. Sometimes the burden is beyond our ability to bear it. So says Paul in 2 Corinthians 1:8, "For we do not want you to be unaware, brethren, of our affliction...that we were burdened excessively, beyond our strength, so that we

117

despaired even of life" (NASB). That is, Paul counted his situation virtually hopeless. Sooner or later, even God's children embrace a hopeless situation where neither they nor anyone else can grant deliverance from its clutches. In fact, you may presently be in the midst of such a season battling terminal illness, horrendous grief over the death of a family member or friend, and/or excruciating suffering mentally or physically.

The provision for life's burdens ("cast thy burden upon the Lord"). The Hebrew word for "cast" means "to throw down, to hurl away forcefully, to dispose of and to reject." Relief is possible and available for life's burdens, but it requires trusting God with them by vigorously casting them at His feet. Obviously, the more faith one exhibits in the Lord to completely manage the burden, the greater will be the relief. H. A. Ironside says, "A burdened heart is the portion of the one who tries to carry his own sorrows and daily cares and fails to turn all over to Him who so delights to bear them for us. Nothing breaks the spirit like hidden grief, but such need not be the portion of any saint who will allow the Lord Jesus to be not only his Sin-bearer but his Burden-bearer too."[332]

The promise for life's burdens ("And he shall sustain thee"). The Hebrew word for "sustain" means "support, clasp, contain and manage." It pictures a vessel that contains cargo. The Lord is man's "vessel" in which life's burdens (heavy cargo) are to be contained and managed. Note, the promise is not that God will remove the burden (though He may), but that He will grant increased strength and stamina to equal its weight. Paul's burden, "the thorn in the flesh" (unknown as to its nature), was cast upon the Lord three times. Though it was not removed, he was given sufficient grace to bear it (2 Corinthians 12:9).

The premise for the promise is revealed in 1 Peter 5:7 AMPC: "Casting the whole of your care [all your anxieties, all your worries, all your concerns, once and for all] on Him, for He cares for you affectionately and cares about you watchfully." Charles Weigle (1932) poetically illustrates the text, saying, "No one ever cared for me like Jesus; there's no other friend so kind as He." God willingly bears our burdens out of compassionate concern.

> Cast your care on Jesus today;
>   Leave your worry and fear.
> Burdens are lifted at Calvary;
>   Jesus is very near.

> Troubled soul, the Savior can feel
>   Every heartache and tear.
> Burdens are lifted at Calvary;
>   Jesus is very near.

Burdens are lifted at Calvary, Calvary, Calvary.

Burdens are lifted at Calvary; Jesus is very near. ~ John M. Moore (1952)

A minister in study asked his young son to retrieve a large book located upstairs. Soon the father heard sobbing on the staircase and went to investigate. He found his son on the top of the stairway crying bitterly with the large book he had tried to lift and carry lying at his feet. "Oh, Daddy," he cried, "I can't carry it. It's too heavy for me." In an instant, the father was upstairs. Stooping down, he picked up both the book and the child in his strong arms and carried them to the room below. *And that,* he found himself thinking later, *is how God deals with His children.*[333] He carries both our "burdens" and us.

64
The Unexplainable Why

Asking why the illness, terminal disease, crippling accident or death has come is natural. The ultimate, complete and satisfying answer to the question, however, is unknown. What is known is that its primary cause springs from the fallen world in which we live. Sickness, suffering, sorrow, and death were unknown in the Garden of Eden prior to man's fall into sin. Vance Havner said, "You need never ask why, because Calvary covers it all. When before the throne we stand in Him complete, all the riddles that puzzle us here will fall into place, and we shall know in fulfillment what we now believe in faith—that all things work together for good in His eternal purpose. No longer will we cry, "My God, why?" "Alas" will become "Alleluia," all question marks will be straightened into exclamation points, sorrow will change to singing, and pain will be lost in praise."[334]

Across some of our days, God marks, "Will explain later."[335] Until then, we trust His heart and live by His promise that "all things work together for good to them that love God, to them who are the called according to his purpose" (Romans 8:28). Presently, the "good" that will evolve from your sickness, suffering, or sorrow may not be known. But Jesus is still saying, "What I do thou knowest not now; but thou shalt know [if not now, then] hereafter" (John 13:7). Upon that you may confidently depend.

When my troubles take the blue from the sky
And all my asking is futile as to why,
In Christ will I trust to use all not understood
For His divine purposes and my best good.

119

When the Rain Comes

Through grace He will help me to bear all the pain
And then at death give me Heaven to gain.
There the why of life's trials will be clearly shown
And my best "good" from them will be completely known.

'Til then to His promise to work good I will cling,
Though not knowing exactly what that may bring.
Knowing He watches all that happens to me
Gives hope while accepting it on bended knee.

Its weight will not be beyond my strength to bear
As I lean upon Christ for enabling care.
A constant Companion and Friend will He be,
Until this difficult journey ends for me. ~ Frank Shivers (2020)

Whatever answers the doctor, friends, family, or perhaps even your minister gives for your present adversity or sorrow may simply not satisfy you or ease the hurt. They may never. In truth, no answer is sufficient. It's not explanations but a *fresh* revelation of Jesus that gives consolation. Scott Wesley Brown agrees, saying, "When answers aren't enough, there is Jesus."[336]

Dark midnight was my cry;
Dark midnight was my cry;
Dark midnight was my cry;
Give me Jesus.

Give me Jesus; give me Jesus.
You may have all this world; give me Jesus. ~ Afro-American spiritual

65

Rest from the Griefs of Life

"They may rest from their labors" (Revelation 14:13). At times it appears that no sooner do we come through one grievous experience than another arrives on its heel—pain heaped upon pain, sorrow heaped upon sorrow, and despair heaped upon despair. If not for the grace of God, the best of us would have been overcome by grief's dark, dismal, dreary, and destructive power long ago. But though the throes of grief may temporarily knock the saint down, it never will knock him out. He has incredible bounce-back capabilities supplied by Christ.

Comfort for Troubled Hearts

Author Edgar Jackson poignantly describes the grief of bereavement: "Grief is a young widow trying to rear her three children alone. Grief is the man so filled with shocked uncertainty and confusion that he strikes out at the nearest person. Grief is a mother walking daily to a nearby cemetery to stand quietly and alone a few minutes before going about the tasks of the day. She knows that part of her is in the cemetery, just as part of her is in her daily work. Grief is the silent, knifelike terror and sadness that comes a hundred times a day when you start to speak to someone who is no longer there. Grief is the emptiness that comes when you eat alone after eating with another for many years. Grief is teaching yourself to go to bed without saying good night to the one who has died. Grief is the helpless wishing that things were different when you know they are not and never will be again. Grief is a whole cluster of adjustments, apprehensions, and uncertainties that strike life in its forward progress and make it difficult to redirect the energies of life."[337]

But all griefs, though possibly not as grievous as those mentioned by Jackson in bereavement, are horrendously painful and emotionally taxing.

The Bible informs us of glorious news. At death the Christian *gains rest from the griefs* (sorrows, sufferings, heartaches, burdens) experienced on earth. In Heaven, Jacob mourns no Joseph, David and Bathsheba weep for no child, Mary and Martha bewail no Lazarus, Job does not cry for his children, Hezekiah loathes no disease, David is not bereaved of Absalom. That which produces grief beyond measure (the curse of sin) is absent and forever banned from Heaven. "He will wipe every tear from their eyes. There will be no more death or mourning or crying or pain, for the old order of things has passed away" (Revelation 21:4 NIV). Samuel Rutherford said, "One tear, one sigh, one sad heart, one fear, one loss, one thought of trouble cannot find lodging there. Sorrow and the saints are not married together; or, suppose it were so, Heaven would make a divorce."[338]

There is no grief in Heav'n,
For life is one glad day
And tears are of those former things
Which all have passed away. ~ Francis M. Knollis (1859)

The Scottish Presbyterian Covenanters (Christians that revolted against the monarch's claim of authority over the church in Scotland), in dying for their faith, would often climb the scaffold shouting, "Good-bye world! Good-bye pain! Good-bye suffering! Good-bye sorrow! Good-bye heartache! Welcome life! Welcome joy! Welcome Heaven! Welcome eternity! Welcome Jesus!"[339] All Christians can "shout" the same as they depart for Heaven. Thanks be unto God for the promise of rest from *grief* in Heaven!

66

God Is Able, More Than Able to Help

"[He] is able to do immeasurably more than all we ask or imagine, according to his power that is at work within us" (Ephesians 3:20 NIV). The divine ability of God enables Him to do infinitely more than prayer may utter or the mind conceive. He is the saints' omnipotent and almighty helper in any and all circumstances, regardless of their horrendous nature. Arthur W. Pink stated, "To the one who delights in the sovereignty of God, the clouds not only have a 'silver lining,' but they are silver all through, the darkness only serving to offset the light!"[340]

The Israelites wandering in the wilderness committed the sin of "limiting God." See Psalm 78:41. Believers are prone to do likewise with regard to little trust in His ability to provide help in the most serious crisis or calamity. James Hastings says, "What we need most is certainty of God, that we may hold fast our faith in Him."[341] The Holy Scripture provides ample reason to exhibit uninhibited trust (faith) in the Lord with every care. He is our *refuge* in the time of trouble and tribulation (Psalm 46:1–2); *strong tower* in the time of personal conflict (Psalm 61:3); *strong Rock* in times of weakness and frailty (Psalm 31:2); that *friend that sticketh closer than a brother* in times of horrendous grief, sorrow and loneliness (Proverbs 18:24); *the potter* who takes the broken pieces of one's life and molds them into something beautiful (Isaiah 64:8); *the vine* supplying nutriment to the branches (His children) that they may experience abundant life and bear much fruit for the kingdom of God (John 15:5); *the wonderful counsellor* to impart wisdom for handling life's problems and pains (Isaiah 9:6 and John 14:16); *the Good Shepherd* that lays down His life for His sheep that they might be saved and secured (John 10:11); *the light of the world* illuminating the spiritual darkness, showing man the right path to travel (John 8:12); *the great emancipator* setting the prisoner free from the strongholds of satanic bondage (John 8:36); *the bread of life* that satisfies the longing of the soul (John 6:35–51); and *the sympathizing Jesus* who "speaks the drooping heart to cheer."[342] See Matthew 9:12; Mark 1:41 and Isaiah 66:13.

But not only does the Word of God substantiate God's power to rescue or grant relief in the hour of severest trial, but so also does personal experience. Adam Clarke, commenting on Psalm 46:1 (God "is a very present help in trouble"), says that our Lord is "*a help* found to be very powerful and effectual in straits and difficulties. The words are very emphatic *in the Hebrew*. 'He is found an exceeding or superlative (magnificent, unparalleled) help in difficulties.' Such we have found Him, and therefore celebrate His praise."[343] He that trusts Him wholly finds Him wholly able to render the assistance needed. Oswald Chambers wrote, "Faith is a tremendously active principle which always puts Jesus Christ first—'Lord, Thou hast said so and so (Matthew 6:33); it looks mad, but I am going to venture on Thy word.' To turn head faith into a personal possession is a fight always, not sometimes."[344] Alexander Maclaren says, "Trust [God] as what He is, and trust Him because of what He is, and see to it that your faith lays hold on the living God Himself and on nothing besides."[345]

> He is able, more than able
> To accomplish what concerns me today.
> He is able, more than able
> To handle anything that comes my way.
>
> ~ Gregory F. Ferguson and Rory J. Nolan

67
The Beatitude of Dying

The Christian looks upon Death as a "blessing" while the ungodly view it as a "curse."[346] "The Christian who dies," writes Warren Wiersbe, "experiences rest and reward; the unbeliever, however, experiences eternal torment and loss of everything."[347] John wrote what the Holy Spirit prompted, saying, "Blessed are the dead which die in the Lord from henceforth: Yea, saith the Spirit, that they may rest from their labors; and their works do follow them" (Revelation 14:13). Happiness ("Blessed"), restfulness and reward for service are promised by the Holy Spirit to all that "die in the Lord," not just those who are martyrs. The Beatitude promise does not include all, only those who "die in the Lord."

What then does it mean to *"die in the Lord"*? It means to be identified and united with Christ through the new birth, to manifest a genuine attachment to Him. Compare John 3:3 with Matthew 7:22–23. It means "to have been faithful unto death" (hoping, depending, and trusting in Christ unto the end). See Revelation 2:10.

They may rest from their labors. Albert Barnes explains, "It is used here *(labors)* in the sense of wearisome toil in doing good, in promoting religion, in saving souls, in defending the truth. From such toils the redeemed in Heaven will be released."[348] Believers will work in Heaven, yet without fatigue or weariness.

> There is much about a man that cannot be put into a coffin. The life and character of men are impressed on society deeply, indelibly.
> W. L. Watkinson

Their works do follow them. Believers will be recompensed in Heaven for their faithfulness on earth to Christ and His cause. Barnes says, "This is all that can follow a man to eternity. He can take with him none of his gold, his lands, his raiment; none of the honors of this life; none of the means of sensual gratification. All that will go with him will be his character and the results of his conduct here, and in this respect, eternity will be but a prolongation of the present life."[349]

When the Rain Comes

The man "that dies in the Lord" will leave on earth a gigantic footprint of impression for Christ that will continue to make impact long after his exodus. Solomon says, "*The memory of the just is with praises*: and the name of the wicked shall rot" (Proverbs 10:7 Douay-Rheims Bible). W. L. Watkinson wrote, "We think that when a man dies he has done with the world and that the world has done with him. That view, however, needs revision. There is much about a man that cannot be put into a coffin. The life and character of men are impressed on society deeply, indelibly....We can speak confidently about the immortality of the influence of the good. Abel being dead yet speaketh; we are not told that Cain does. It is a reassuring thing to know that the good which men do is not buried with their bones. Not only do remarkable saints influence posterity beneficially; all saints do so, although it may be to a lesser degree."[350] What a glorious thought; the saints' present spiritual walk and work set streams in motion that will flow long after their exodus. Especially in that sense, the Christian, though "being dead yet speaketh" (Hebrews 11:4).

68

A Juniper-Tree Experience

The spiritual giant Elijah prayed that he might die, due to pressing circumstances and burdens (1 Kings 19:4). Death to him would have been an escape from it all. But God had something far better in store for Elijah—a journey to Heaven in a chariot of fire (2 Kings 2:11). Similarly, the believer's prayer to die to escape adversity, suffering and sickness is often denied or delayed by the Lord in order that something exceedingly better may be experienced. And that something better just might be departure to Heaven through the rapture, the second coming of Christ (1 Corinthians 15:51–55).

Weariness, despondency, illness, fatigue, fear and loneliness often run ahead of sound judgment. From the human perspective it's understandable why some say with Elijah, 'It is enough. Let me die.' It is the calamity that has clouded rational thinking. It's imperative in horrendous grief and pain not to allow emotions to dictate the when and how of death, but to leave that to the Lord, as Elijah did (he didn't give in to the cry of painful emotions). It is never right to usurp God's authority governing the climax of life.

In denying Elijah's request, the Lord provided provision for coping with the adversity successfully (1 Kings 19:5–7). This He does for all saints that pray similarly, through ministering angels, fellow believers, physicians, ministers, the promises of His Word, and the Holy Spirit. God changes the suffering saint's words from "it is enough; let me perish" to "God is enough; let me persevere."

Jesus Christ is made to me, all I need, all I need.
He alone is all my plea; He is all I need.
Wisdom, righteousness and power, holiness this very hour,
My redemption full and free, He is all I need. ~ Anonymous

In retrospect, Elijah, realizing that his work was not over, was elated that his prayer to die was denied. (For example, he passed the baton of authority and power of his office to Elisha. See 1 Kings 19:19–20.) The reason "juniper-tree" prayers are often denied, as they were with Elijah, is because God is not finished with the saint, regardless of what circumstances seem to say.

69
Divine Testing

"The fining pot is for silver, and the furnace for gold: but the LORD trieth the hearts" (Proverbs 17:3). "The fining pot" is a container that melts metals into liquid form under intense heat. A "furnace" would likewise be used to melt metal. Both removed the impurities from the silver and gold. Solomon states that God likewise tests, refines or judges ("trieth") man's heart. As the furnace of fire determines the purity of gold, removing any impurities if they are present, just so, through intense testing of a man, our righteous God purges out the dross of sin. Job testified, "But he knoweth the way that I take: when he hath tried me, I shall come forth as gold" (Job 23:10). Peter states, "Pure gold put in the fire comes out of it proved pure; genuine faith put through this suffering comes out proved genuine" (1 Peter 1:7 MSG).

In Jeremiah the Lord elucidates the testing, saying, "I the LORD search the heart, I try the reins, even to give every man according to his ways, and according to the fruit of his doings" (Jeremiah 17:10). The Lord examines (tests) man's heart, detecting its darkest secrets, darlingest sin, deviating defiance and devotional deficiency to reveal all such impurities, that through confession and repentance the person may be pure inside and outside (a holy, sanctified vessel). Malachi explains, "For He is like a refiner's fire and like fullers' soap. He will sit as a smelter and purifier of silver, and He will purify the sons of Levi and refine them like gold and silver, so that they may present to the LORD offerings in righteousness. Then the offering of Judah and Jerusalem will be pleasing to the LORD as in the days of old and as in former years" (Malachi 3:2–4 NASB). The testing or refining is to make the believer more like Jesus (righteousness), that he may live "pleasing to the Lord" in every dimension of life.

"We have all read how they try the great guns before they use them in the Queen's service. So God tries us to prove whether we are fit for the service of Christ's militant here on earth. As the brightest jewels have to be cut and ground, and some tried in a fierce fire, so the brightest gems, on the day when God makes up His jewels, will be those people who have suffered and passed through the fire of affliction, of whom it can be said, 'Blessed is the man that endureth temptation [testing].'"[351] (see James 1:12)

> By trials God is shaping us for higher things.
> Jeremy Taylor

W. A. Criswell further explains, "Now when Satan tries you, he tries to ruin you, to destroy you, to plow you up, to bury you deep. But when God tries you, what God is doing is like a refiner's fire to make pure gold out of you. Any trial that comes from God—if it's from Heaven, if it's providence—there's in it some great and blessed thing. It's not a vicious thing, and it's not a wicked thing, but it is a holy and heavenly thing. The providential trials of our life are to make true sons of us, to reveal the gold of God that is in us; a refiner's fire."[352]

C. H. Spurgeon, in the sermon "Whither Goest Thou?" says, "God appoints the weight and number of all our adversities—if He declares the number ten, they cannot be eleven. If He wills that we bear a certain weight, no one can add half an ounce more. Every trial comes from God. Take courage. The rod is one of the tokens of the child of God. If you were not God's child, you might be left unchastised; but inasmuch as you are dear to Him, He will whip you when you disobey. If you were only a bit of 'common clay,' God would not put you into the furnace. But as you are 'gold' and He knows it, you must be refined; and to be refined it is needful that the fire should exercise its power upon you. Because you are bound for Heaven, you will meet with storms on your voyage to Glory. I cannot tell what troubles may come nor what temptations may arise. But I know in whose hands I am, and I am persuaded that He is able to preserve me, so that when He has tried me, I shall come forth as GOLD. I go into the fire, but I shall not be burned up in it; 'I shall come forth.'"[353]

Warren Wiersbe comments, "When God puts His own people into the furnace, He keeps His eye on the clock and His hand on the thermostat. He knows how long and how much. We may question why He does it to begin with or why He doesn't turn down the heat or even turn it off, but our questions are only evidences of unbelief. Job 23:10 is the answer: "But He knows the way that I take; when He has tested me, I shall come forth as gold" (NKJV). Gold does not fear the fire. The furnace can only make the gold purer and brighter."[354]

The man that endures the testing will be rewarded ("blessed") in at least six ways. "Blessedness of thankfulness for being sustained; of holy dependence under conscious weakness; of peace and submission under God's hand; of fearlessness as to result of further trial; of familiarity with God enjoyed in the affliction; of growth in grace through the trial. He who, being tested, is supported in the ordeal and comes out of the trial approved, is the blessed man."[355] C. H. Spurgeon says, "Trials teach us what we are; they dig up the soil and let us see what we are made of."[356] Jeremy Taylor states, "By trials God is shaping us for higher things."[357] Therefore, James says, "My Christian brothers, you should be happy when you have all kinds of tests [trials, troubles]. You know these prove your faith. It helps you not to give up" (James 1:2–3 NLV).

70
Assurance of Eternal Life

Make full proof of salvation sooner rather than later. Nothing induces fright in dying more than an uncertainty of Heaven on its other side. The Scriptures instruct, "Examine yourselves to see if your faith is genuine. Test yourselves. Surely you know that Jesus Christ is among you; if not, you have failed the test of genuine faith" (2 Corinthians 13:5 NLT).

The person. All believers ought to make sure as they approach life's end that they possess genuine salvation, not a counterfeit. This is a divine command, not a suggestion. It is you, not parents, spouse, minister or friends, who must decide the question.

The purpose. Were mistaken hope of salvation not possible, the inquiry commanded would not have been issued. Its possibility is confirmed multiple times in Holy Scriptures in precept and example. Matthew 7:22–23 indicates its hazardous reality in the church. Other biblical texts clearly reveal there are tares among the wheat; professors among possessors; the reformed among the reborn; goats among the sheep; the religious among the redeemed, and the lost among the saved. One may preach like Nicodemus, be devoted to his religion like Saul of Tarsus, be baptized like Simon Magus, and be a respected and trusted officer among the saints (church) like Judas (disciple band) and still miss Heaven. Unto all who are religious but not reborn, Jesus will say at the judgment, "I never knew you." Make certain that you are not just a believer but a regenerated and converted sinner. Watchman Nee said, "There is nothing more tragic than to come to the end of life and know we have been on the wrong course."[358]

Amazing grace! how sweet the sound
   That saved a wretch like me!
I once was lost, but now am found;
   Was blind, but now I see. ~ John Newton (1725–1807)

When the Rain Comes

The procedure. To ascertain proof of salvation, Paul says to "prove yourselves." Assurance of salvation is obtainable, knowable. Question your heart inside and out to determine whether it is genuine or counterfeit based upon the Word of God. Did you repent of sin and exhibit faith in Jesus Christ as Lord and Savior (Acts 20:21)? Does a change in conduct back up that *experience* as genuine (2 Corinthians 5:17)? Implore the Holy Spirit's help and verdict (Romans 8:16). Be truthful and thorough, for mistake in examining and proving it cannot be rectified upon death.

The profit. The benefit of seriously examining one's faith is a positive all the way around. Either it confirms authenticity and genuineness of faith, enabling the believer to say earnestly, "I know whom I have believed, and am persuaded that he is able to keep that which I have committed unto him," or it reveals a false hope which enables the embracing of genuine salvation through repentance and faith.

> But it's real; it's real;
> Oh, I know it's real.
> Praise God, the doubts are settled,
> For I know, I know it's real. ~ Homer L. Cox (1907)

71

The Dark Night of the Soul

James Montgomery Boice says the dark night of the soul "is a state of intense spiritual anguish in which the struggling, despairing believer feels he is abandoned by God."[359] Adrian Rogers comments, "If you will read biographies of great Christians, almost all of them will talk about something they call the dark night of the soul. I mean, they're serving God; they're loving God; and then, things come—perplexities. They can't understand."[360] Warren Wiersbe remarks, "At times even the most dedicated Christian feels 'in the dark' and wonders why God seems so far away. During the Boxer Rebellion, the China Inland Mission suffered greatly; and its founder, J. Hudson Taylor, said to a friend, 'I cannot read, I cannot think, I cannot even pray, but I can trust.' It was a dark time, but God eventually gave light."[361] Voicing the feelings of many in the dark time of the soul, C. S. Lewis states, "We're not necessarily doubting that God will do the best for us; we are wondering how painful the best will turn out to be."[362]

What ought the saint to do in experiencing such darkness? *With the psalmist he should seek the Lord* (Psalm 77:2) as the only source or means for help and rescue. He ought to say, "I will lift up mine eyes unto the hills, from whence cometh my help. My help cometh from the LORD, which made heaven and earth" (Psalm 121:1–2). It is futile to rely upon the arm of flesh for deliverance. H. A. Ironside writes, "In the New Testament we see each Person of the blessed Trinity engaged in this ministry of comfort. GOD the Father is called 'the God of all comfort' (2 Corinthians 1:3). GOD the Holy Spirit is spoken of four times in our Lord's last discourse to His disciples as the 'Comforter' (John 14:16, 26; 15:26; 16:7). One character of our Lord's work and ministry is 'to comfort all that mourn' (Isaiah 61:2). He is also called our 'advocate with the Father' (1 John 2:1). The word for 'advocate' is exactly the same in the Greek as that for 'Comforter' in John's Gospel. How blessed to be in fellowship with the Father, the Son, and the Holy Spirit, so that one can enter into and enjoy the comfort They delight to give! What greater privilege can we have on earth than to enjoy the abiding presence of the GOD of all comfort as we face the perplexities and bitter disappointments that we are called upon to endure? If we never knew grief or pain, we would never be able to appreciate what GOD can be to His suffering people. When we cry to the Lord in hours of distress, He does not remove the cause of our trouble in every case, but always gives the needed grace to bear whatever we are called upon to endure."[363]

> Those He saves are His delight;
>> Christ will hold me fast.
> Precious in His holy sight,
>> He will hold me fast.

> He'll not let my soul be lost;
>> His promises shall last.
> Bought by Him at such a cost,
>> He will hold me fast. ~ Ada Habershon (1861–1918)

With the psalmist he should cry unto the Lord for deliverance (Psalm 77:1). The Lord hears both audible and mental prayer, but the former at times is immensely therapeutic, enabling one to vent the pent-up agony, anger and pain. Audible praying also helps one retain focus in praying.

With the psalmist he should pray with incessant importunity (Psalm 77:2). Albert Barnes says, "In his (the psalmist's) painful meditations in the night watches—in thinking on God and His ways as he lay upon his bed—he stretched out his hand in fervent prayer to God."[364] Keep knocking on Heaven's door until it opens (Luke 11:8 and Matthew 7:8). C. H. Spurgeon says, "Importunity prevailed. The gate opened to the steady knock. It will be so with us in our hour of trial; the God of grace will hear us in due season."[365] In praying, claim the promise of Psalm 50:15.

With the psalmist the saint should remember God's goodness in the past (Psalm 77:11). Remember God's former mercies unto you (Psalm 77:10–15 and 1 Samuel 7:12). Matthew Henry remarks, "The remembrance of the works of God will be a powerful remedy against distrust of His promise and goodness, for He is God and changes not."[366]

But unlike the psalmist, the distraught saint should not refuse to be comforted with the comfort provided (Psalm 77:2). C. H. Spurgeon said, "When you hear the Gospel and refuse to be comforted by it, there is a wrong done to the minister of God. He sympathizes with you, he desires to comfort you, and it troubles him when he puts before you the cup of salvation and you refuse to take it. See Psalm 116:12– 13. But worse than that, you wrong God's Gospel. You put it away as though it were a thing of naught. You wrong this precious Bible. It is full of consoling promises, and you read it, and you seem to say, 'It is all chaff.' Oh, but the Bible does not deserve to have such a slur cast upon it. You do wrong to the dear friends who try to comfort you. Above all, you do wrong to your God, to Jesus, and to His Holy Spirit."[367] Up and be done with such refusal and avail yourself at once of the consolation afforded by Christ through the Holy Spirit in sundry ways (ministers, Bible promises, hymns and songs, fellow saints, etc.). See John 14:26 and 2 Corinthians 1:3–4.

His oath, his covenant, his blood
Support me in the whelming flood.
When all around my soul gives way,
He then is all my hope and stay.

On Christ the solid rock I stand;
All other ground is sinking sand;
All other ground is sinking sand. ~ Edward Mote (1797–1874)

There ariseth light in the darkness. See Psalm 112:4. "Light is the emblem and sum of all good, as darkness is of all evil."[368] The rain falls upon the just as it does upon the unjust (raindrops of sickness, bereavement, depression, suffering and trouble). Though not immune to adversities similar to those of the unbeliever, the Christian is assured that God will be with him in the midst of the storm to comfort, encourage and deliver. Albert Barnes wrote, "The peculiarity in regard to those who fear God is that these things will not always continue, that they shall not be overwhelmed by them, that it will not be uninterrupted and unmitigated gloom, that the sky shall not be always overcast."[369]

What you trusted God for in the "light," don't doubt in the "dark." Ellicott says, "The Hebrew verb ["ariseth"] is commonly used of the sunrise. See Psalm 97:11 and Isaiah 58:8. For the good man the darkest night of trouble and sorrow will have a dawn of hope."[370] It has been said that faith is like film. It's developed in the dark. It's in the dark times of life that we learn to trust God implicitly. John Ker said, "If there are hours in our life when we know that there is a living God and an eternal world, it is in such a crisis when we are compelled to cling to Him in the dark and feel, as we cling, a strength beneath that lifts us up. This could never be, if there were not a God."[371]

72
A Mighty Friend in Jesus

"Henceforth I call you not servants; for the servant knoweth not what his lord doeth: but I have called you friends" (John 15:15). "Friend" is the Greek word *philos* which means more than mere friendship—it means "love-friends."[372] It entails "the idea of loving as well as being loved."[373] A friend is one that loves me forever; loves me for who I am, not what I possess; and loves me despite my faults! And he loves me without expectation of anything in return. A friend exhibits unflinching faithfulness to me in health and sickness, prosperity and poverty, smiles and sorrows and in the throes of death as in the bliss of life. A friend's heart throbs with my grief and thrills in my joy.[374] When necessary, a friend sacrifices for me without thought to its cost; only my personal good and well-being is that which matters. As Cicero wrote, "A friend is, as it were, a second self."[375] Such a friend is a rare treasure to possess.

The best friendship pales in contrast to that of Christ's. He is "a friend that sticketh closer than a brother" in the time of need (Proverbs 18:24).

There is no grief that He does not understand. Unlike some who condemn our grieving conduct as overboard or weird or even unchristian, Jesus understands. If our "Job type friends" only knew the reason for the "peculiar" behavior, they would be compassionate rather than condemnatory.[376] Recall that Eli called Hannah a drunkard, only to discover afterwards that she was simply praying with a broken spirit (1 Samuel 1:13).[377] Christ always is sympathetic with our case.

There is nothing that will drive Him away. "There is one Friend whom the slanderer cannot alienate. No falsehood breathed against any man ever injured him in the estimation of Jesus, but on the contrary, made him more peculiarly the object of the Savior's care."[378]

There is no grief that He cannot comfort, no adversity or trial through which He cannot sustain, no turbulent storm that will not obey His "peace, be still," and no difficulty which He cannot resolve. And, amazing as it is, He calls us "friend" (John 15:14).

> There's not a Friend like the lowly Jesus,
> > No, not one! no, not one!
> None else could heal all our souls' diseases,
> > No, not one! no, not one!

When the Rain Comes

Jesus knows all about our struggles;
    He will guide 'til the day is done.
There's not a Friend like the lowly Jesus,
    No, not one! no, not one!

There's not an hour that He is not near us,
    No, not one! no, not one!
No night so dark but His love can cheer us,
    No, not one! no, not one!

Did ever saint find this Friend forsake him?
    No, not one! no, not one!
Or sinner find that He would not take him?
    No, not one! no, not one! ~ Johnson Oatman (1895)

J. C. Ryle wrote, "Jesus is indeed the Brother born for adversity. He is the Friend that sticketh closer than a brother, and He alone can comfort His people. He can be touched with the feeling of their infirmities, for He suffered Himself (Hebrews 4:15). He knows what sorrow is, for He was a Man of sorrows. He knows what an aching body is, for His body was racked with pain. He cried, 'All my bones are out of joint' (Psalm 22:14). He knows what poverty and weariness are, for He was often wearied and had not where to lay His head. He knows what family unkindness is, for even His brethren did not believe Him. He had no honor in His own house. And Jesus knows exactly how to comfort His afflicted people. He knows how to pour in oil and wine into the wounds of the spirit, how to fill up gaps in empty hearts, how to speak a word in season to the weary, how to heal the broken heart, how to make all our bed in sickness, how to draw nigh when we are faint, and say, "Fear not: I am thy salvation" (see Lamentations 3:57). There is no sympathy like that of Christ. In all our afflictions He is afflicted. He knows our sorrows. In all our pain He is pained, and like the good Physician, He will not measure out to us one drop of sorrow too much. How a believer gets through all his troubles appears wonderful. How he is carried through the fire and water he passes through seems past comprehension. But the true account of it is just this—that Christ is not only justification and sanctification, but consolation also."[379] See Philippians 2:1.

"You should never forget," states Charles Simeon, "what an Almighty Friend you have. How many times in this Psalm [121] are you reminded, that the LORD, even the Almighty God, is your Helper and Deliverer! Were He less powerful or less vigilant or less worthy of credit, you might well fear. But what ground can he have for fear who has God Himself for his refuge? Only rely on God, and you are safe."[380] Jonathan Edwards, upon his deathbed, said, "Now where is Jesus of Nazareth, my true and never failing Friend?" and so saying he fell asleep (died)."[381] He that has Jesus as Friend can die as peacefully as Edwards did, for even in the valley of the shadow of death He will not forsake us. W. S. Plumer states, "When we find Him, we need seek no further. He is all-sufficient. The more He is tried, the more He is found to be the very Friend we need."[382]

> Can we find a friend so faithful,
>> Who will all our sorrows share?
> Jesus knows our every weakness;
>> Take it to the Lord in prayer. ~ Joseph Scriven (1752)

73

What to Do When You Don't Know What to Do

"My soul, wait thou only upon God; for my expectation is from him" (Psalm 62:5). The word David uses for "expectation" in the Hebrew language means "to rescue, save, deliver from illness, physical peril, enemies, or death—anything that threatens the well-being or life of the one who prays."[383] A good synonym for *expectation* is hope, "my hope" is from God. In times of adversity and infirmity, God alone was the foundation for David's hope and confidence, his Refuge and Strong Tower in the time of need.

What are you to do when you don't know what to do?

(1. Exhort your soul to be still ("my soul, wait thou only upon God"). Restrain impulsive reaction while waiting for divine interaction. Don't panic. Remain calm. Let God speak, instruct and console.

> Be still, my soul; your God doth undertake
>> To guide the future as He has the past.
> Your hope, your confidence let nothing shake;
>> All now mysterious shall be bright at last.
> Be still, my soul; the waves and winds still know
> His voice who ruled them while He dwelt below.
>> ~ Katharina von Schlegel (1855)

(2. Trust God explicitly ("only upon God"). To place one foot on the rock and the other in quicksand doth not avail. "Put not your trust in princes, nor in the son of man, in whom there is no help" (Psalm 146:3)." Alexander McLaren said, "If God sends us on stony paths, He will provide us with strong shoes."[384]

When the Rain Comes

James McConkey writes, "When He leads you into paths that wound your faltering feet, confronts you with a future that lowers dark and threatening, hems you in with providence that seem harsh and mysterious—in all these stand still; whisper to yourself, 'It is God that worketh'; and TRUST Him. It matters not that His dealings with you are strange, mysterious, even confusing; that this is not the way in which you would like Him to work. You may not indeed understand all this, but He does, 'for it is God which worketh in you.' But you would not dare take your case out of His hands even if you could—would you? Therefore, trust Him while He in you works."[385] See Philippians 2:13.

(3. Place hope ("thy expectation") in God. C. H. Spurgeon says, "We expect from God because we believe in him. *Expectation* is the child of prayer and faith and is owned of the Lord as an acceptable grace. We should desire nothing but what it would be right for God to give. The vain expectations of worldly people come not; our expectations are on the way and in due course will arrive to satisfy our hopes. Happy is the person who feels that all he has, all he wants, and all he expects are to be found in his God."[386] W. M. Statham says, "There is nothing that fills life with such joy and rest as expectation!"[387]

> We must trust him no less when we see no way for our deliverance than when the promised relief is visibly at hand.
> Charles Simeon

(4. Confidently anticipate God's intervention ("my expectation *is* from him"). Don't stagger at His promises, readiness and eagerness to help. Charles Simeon states, "If He sees fit to delay His answer, we must not be discouraged, but wait His time, assured that 'the vision shall not tarry' beyond the precise moment that He sees to be best for us. We must trust Him no less when we see no way for our deliverance than when the promised relief is visibly at hand."[388]

My soul with expectation depends on God indeed;
My strength and my salvation doth from Him alone proceed.
My soul, wait thou with patience upon thy God alone;
On him dependeth all my hope and expectation.

He only my salvation is, and my strong rock is He.
He only is my sure defense; I shall not moved be.
In God my glory placed is and my salvation sure;
In God the rock is of my strength, my refuge most secure.

~ Scottish Psalter and Paraphrases

74

Nevertheless, Thy Will Be Done

"O my Father, if it be possible, let this cup pass from me: nevertheless not as I will, but as thou wilt" (Matthew 26:39). What was in the bitter "cup" that Jesus prayed thrice to have taken away? In the cup we find sin's penalty and payment for its absolution and man's justification, the depravity and wickedness of man, the ingratitude and rejection of man, and the agonizing and tormenting torture of the cross. All these troubled and vexed Christ's soul grievously to the degree that as He prayed, "his sweat was as it were great drops of blood falling down to the ground" (Luke 22:44). In humility and submission to the Father, despite the bitter distaste for the "cup," Jesus says, "nevertheless not my will, but thine, be done" (Luke 22:42). Jesus drank the "cup," and man was provided the means of salvation (rightness with God and eternal life).

You may be going through a Gethsemane experience. The "cup" is that of severe illness or sorrow or suffering. It's a hard and difficult "cup" to drink. You recoil from it. You denounce it. You even try denying it. You pray fervently and persistently for its removal. But it remains. That which remains to be done, which you have struggled not to do, is submissively to say, "Father, let this cup pass from me; nevertheless, not my will, but thy will be done. Lord, I accept the cup and drink it if that is thy divine purpose and intent for my life." "The entire resignation of our wills to the disposing will of God is the indispensable duty of Christians under the sharpest afflictions."[389] If we must drink the bitter "cup" of sorrow, sickness or suffering, His gentle hands will hold it to our lips with care and compassion (and grant grace to cope with what happens).

> Whate'er my God ordains is right;
> > Though now this cup, in drinking,
> May bitter seem to my faint heart,
> > I take it, all unshrinking.
> My God is true; each morn anew
> Sweet comfort yet shall fill my heart,
> And pain and sorrow shall depart. ~ Samuel Rodigast (1675)

Jon Courson remarked, "The key to prayer is not so much 'name it and claim it.' Rather, the key to prayer is 'request and rest.' That's the way Jesus prayed: 'Father, if it be possible let this cup pass from Me. That's My request. Nevertheless, not My will, but Thy will be done. That's where I will rest.'"[390] D. L. Moody said, "Spread out your petition before God, and then say, 'Thy will, not mine, be done.' The sweetest lesson I have learned in God's school is to let the Lord choose for me."[391] Curtis Hutson said, "He [God] has purposes of love to accomplish through

When the Rain Comes

disease and pain, of which we may know nothing at present."[392] Have you discovered the secret to peace despite the storms that assail life? The famous poet Henry Van Dyke reveals the secret in the poem *Peace*.

> With eager heart and will on fire
> I sought to win my great desire.
> "Peace shall be mine," I said, but life
> Grew bitter in the endless strife.
>
> My soul was weary, and my pride
> Was wounded deep. To Heaven I cried,
> "God give me peace, or I must die."
> The dumb stars glittered no reply.
>
> Broken at last, I bowed my head,
> Forgetting all myself, and said:
> "Whatever come, His will be done."
> And in that moment peace was won.

It was in praying "not my will, but thine be done" that F. G. Browning was able to say,

> I cannot say
> Beneath the pressure of life's care today,
>   "I joy in these."
> But I can say
> That I had rather walk this rugged way,
>   If Him it please.
>
> I cannot feel
> That all is well when darkening clouds conceal
>   The shining sun.
> But this I know:
> God lives and loves; and I can say, since it is so,
>   "Thy will be done."
>
> I cannot speak
> In happy tones; the teardrops on my cheek
>   Show I am sad.
> But I can speak
> Of grace to suffer with submission meek,
>   Until made glad.

Comfort for Troubled Hearts

I do not see
Why God should e'en permit some things to be,
      When He is love.
But I can see
Though often dimly, through the mystery,
      His hand above.

I may not try
To keep the hot tears back; but hush that sigh,
      "It might have been"
And try to still
Each rising murmur and to God's sweet will
      Respond—"Amen."

Submissively and trustingly pray, "Not my will, but thine be done" (that is, I trust you Lord to do what is best for me and others), and a peace that is independent of circumstances (unaffected by adversities and infirmities) will possess your soul. See Philippians 4:7 and John 14:27. Alexander Smellie said, "Let me suffer and be still in the name of Jesus. When the dark days come, the desert place, the sickroom, the weakness and impotence, let me imitate Him who took the cup and said, "Not My will, but Yours be done." Let me walk, my hand in His, through the shadows, and over the crags and torrents. Let me enter Heaven at last in the name of Jesus."[393]

In acceptance lieth peace;
Oh, my heart be still.
Let thy restless worries cease
And accept His will.

In His plan there cannot be
Aught to make thee sad;
If this is His choice for Thee,
Take it and be glad.

Cease from sighs and murmuring;
Sing His loving grace.
This thing means thy furthering
To a wealthy place.
From thy fears He'll give release;
In acceptance lieth peace. ~ Hannah Hurnard (1905–1990)

The Tyranny of Fear

C. H. Spurgeon describes the devastating power of "fear": "O Fear, thou art the rock upon which many a ship hath been wrecked. Yea, and where fear doth not work utter destruction, it is capable of doing much damage to the spirit. Fear hath paralyzed the arm of the most gigantic Christian, stopped him in his race, and impeded him in his labors. Faith can do anything; but fear, sinful fear, can do just nothing at all, but even prevent faith from performing its labors. Fear hath made the Christian to sorrow, both by night and day. A cankering fear lest his wants should not be provided for and his necessities supplied has driven the Christian to unworthy thoughts; and distrustful, doubting fear hath made him dishonor God and prevented his sucking the honey out of the promises. Fear hath kept many a child of God from doing his duty, from making a bold profession; hath brought bondage into his spirit. Fear, thou art the Christian's greatest curse, and thou art the sinner's ruin. Nothing can be worse than this sinful fear; it hath slaughtered its myriads and sent thousands to Hell."[394] William Beveridge said that "God can secure us from fear, either by removing the thing feared or by subduing the fear of the thing."[395]

"There is no fear in love; but perfect love casteth out fear: because fear hath torment. He that feareth is not made perfect in love" (1 John 4:18). Fear arises with regard to something dreaded or beyond one's ability to control or comprehend. Fear is the coiled snake ready to strike in the heart of every man about disease, the dying process, death, judgment and the afterlife. It strikes suddenly and viciously the most ardent saint, imparting poisonous venom of terror, horror and fright all purposed to "torment" (mental pain and physical suffering, worry and stress of future woe). Unless checked, it brings bondage to the soul (slavish fear), prompting irrational thoughts, actions, decisions, restlessness and panic.

> If I understand that God really, truly loves me, I can have absolute confidence that whatever happens at any given moment is the best for me.
> Jon Courson

The antidote to fear is "perfect love." S. S. Smalley says, "Real love, he (John) claims, which results in spiritual boldness, 'flings fear out of doors.'"[396] God's abiding love for us (1 John 3:1) and ours for Him (1 John 4:19; John 15:9–10) expels the tyranny of fear. How so? Jon Courson says, "If I understand that God really, truly loves me, I can have absolute confidence that whatever happens at any given moment is the best for me. Regardless of what the doctor may say, what the IRS may declare, or who wins the election—when you are sure of God's love for you,

you don't have fear. The answer to fear is to become saturated in God's love, because His perfect love casts out fear."[397]

There is no fear in love. "Fear has no place in love. Bold confidence (1 John 4:17), based on love, cannot coexist with fear."[398]

But perfect love casteth out fear. "That is, love that is complete, or that is allowed to exert its proper influence on the soul...delivers the mind from alarms. If it should exist in any soul in an absolutely perfect state, that soul would be entirely free from all dread in regard to the future.

Because fear hath torment. It is a painful and distressing emotion. Thus, men suffer from the fear of poverty, of losses, of bereavement, of sickness, of death, and of future woe. From all these distressing apprehensions, that love of God...delivers us."[399]

To summarize, it is because of Christ's immeasurable, indescribable and unspeakable love for the redeemed that they need "not be afraid for the terror by night; nor for the arrow that flieth by day" (Psalm 91:5). W. Jones states, "Some men are dreading painful and lingering illness; others, death; others, judgment; others, God Himself. Such fears agitate and distress souls; they have torment. Perfect love will expel each and all of these tormentors. It clothes our life and its experiences in new aspects by enabling us to regard them in a different spirit. This love is of God; it proceeds from Him and returns to Him, and it cannot dread Him or His appointments in relation to us. In this way it banishes from the heart the dread of death and of the judgment."[400] See 2 Timothy 1:7.

Love of the Father, love of God the Son
From whom all came, in whom was all begun,
Who formest heavenly beauty out of strife,
Creation's whole desire and breath of life.

Thou the all holy, Thou supreme in might,
Thou dost give peace; Thy presence maketh right.
Thou with Thy favor all things dost enfold
With Thine all kindness, free from harm wilt hold.

Hope of all comfort, splendor of all aid
That dost not fail nor leave the heart afraid,
To all that cry Thou dost all help accord,
The angels' armor and the saints' reward.

When the Rain Comes

Eternal glory, all men Thee adore,
Who art and shalt be worshipped evermore;
Us whom Thou madest, comfort with Thy might
And lead us to enjoy Thy heavenly light. ~ Author Unknown

Leighton said, "When God is in the midst of a kingdom or city, *He makes it as firm as Mount Zion, that cannot be removed.* When He is in the midst of a soul, though calamities throng about it on all hands and roar like the billows of the sea, yet there is a constant calm within, such a peace as the world can neither give nor take away. What is it but want of lodging God in the soul, and that in His stead the world is in men's hearts, that makes them shake like leaves at every blast of danger?"[401] It is the perfect and enduring love of God for and embraced by the believer that enables him in times of fear to say, "Surely I know that it shall be well with them that fear [reverence, honor] God, which fear before him" (Ecclesiastes 8:12). *Perfect love casteth out all fear.*

76

The Ministry of Suffering

"Suffering may be defined," states J. I. Packer, "as getting what you do not want while wanting what you do not get. This definition covers all forms of loss, hurt, pain, grief, and weakness; all experiences of rejection, injustice, disappointment, discouragement, frustration, and being the butt of others' hatred, ridicule, cruelty, callousness, anger, and ill-treatment—plus all exposure to foul, sickening, and nightmarish things that make you want to scream, run, or even die. Suffering in some shape or form is everyone's lot, though some know far more of it than others."[402] It is to be expected and valued by each believer, for it produces character (Romans 5:3), glorifies God (2 Corinthians 12:9–10) and fulfills the law of the harvest (before the blessing, there must come suffering, John 12:24).[403]

B. R. Lakin states, "Perhaps God has allowed a crushing blow to fall upon your life. It may seem for the moment to be an appalling mistake. But it isn't. You are "in His hand," and no man can take you out. In His infinite wisdom and love He may allow you to suffer for a season, but He will bring you out as gold "tried by fire." More eloquent than the ministry of preaching, singing or teaching *is the ministry of suffering*. If you are in the "furnace of affliction," then rejoice that He considered you strong enough to endure such a difficult ministry and serve Him faithfully."[404]

Christians are prone to connect all suffering with sin, unjustifiably. Granted, it is taught in Scripture that suffering may be the result of sin, but it is egregiously wrong to equate all suffering with sin. Biblical examples are cited of people making this wrong assessment. Seeing a blind man, the disciples asked Jesus, "Master, who did sin, this man, or his parents, that he was born blind?" Jesus replied, "Neither hath this man sinned, nor his parents: but that the works of God should be made manifest in him" (John 9:2–3). When a poisonous snake fastened to Paul's hand on the island of Malta, the islanders thought it proved he was a murderer (Acts 28:3–4). "But after they had looked a great while, and saw no harm come to him, they changed their minds" (Acts 28:6).

The friends of Job suggested that the cause of his great suffering was sin. Zophar repeated what Eliphaz and Bildad told Job: "If iniquity is in your hand, put it far away, and let not injustice dwell in your tents. Surely then you will lift up your face without blemish; you will be secure and will not fear....your life will be brighter than the noonday" (Job 11:14–15, 17 ESV). But their assessment wasn't true, for God said of Job, "There is none like him in the earth, a perfect and an upright man, one that feareth God, and escheweth [turns away from] evil" (Job 1:8).

As was the case with Job, it is a devastating and injurious error to surmise that a person's calamity or trouble is the consequence of sin when it is not. A close examination of the cases we have mentioned reveals that in each a divine purpose, not sin, was the reason for the hardship or sorrow.

Let it be emphasized strongly that it is wrong to rashly say, "Had there been no sin there had been no sorrow."[405] Not all troubles or sorrows are punishments. "Don't then say in the case of a given sufferer 'Here is the wrath of God,' for the varied forms of affliction are often divine appliances for testing our principles, developing our graces and practicing our virtues."[406] And they are often just to "manifest the glory of Christ."

Matthew Henry elucidates "that they [suffering through trouble and trials] are sometimes intended purely for the glory of God and the manifesting of His works. God has a sovereignty over all His creatures and an exclusive right in them and may make them serviceable to His glory in such a way as He thinks fit, in doing or suffering; and if God be glorified, either by us or in us, we were not made in vain."[407] For example, the man in John 9 was born blind so Jesus could heal him, giving Him glory and honor and validating Him as the true Light to the world sent from God.[408]

E. Stanley Jones said, "He cleansed suffering! It was no longer a sign of our being caught in the wheel of existence, as Buddha suggests; no longer the result of our evil deeds of a previous birth, as our Hindu friends tell us; no longer the sign of the displeasure of God, as many of all ages and of all religions have suggested; no longer something to be stoically and doggedly borne. It is more than that. Suffering is the gift of God."[409] See Philippians 1:29 and 1 Peter 5:10. Chuck Swindoll says, "When you suffer and lose, that does not mean you are being disobedient to God. In fact, it might mean you're right in the center of His will. The path of obedience is often marked by times of suffering and loss."[410]

When the Rain Comes

No suffering is without divine purpose. Why does God allow suffering to happen to His endeared children?

(1. As previously stated, suffering *at times* (but not at all times) happens to purge the saint of impurities. "But he knoweth the way that I take: when he hath tried me, I shall come forth as gold" (Job 23:10). Not all suffering is the consequence of sin, however, some is, according to the Holy Scriptures (Lamentations 3:39–40; Hebrews 12:6–8 and 1 Corinthians 11:30).

> Oh, who would cast away the gold
>> We've gathered in the furnace flame?
> And who would wish again the dross
>> Here purged in our Redeemer's name? ~ Daniel S. Warner (1883)

(2. Suffering happens to manifest the faithfulness of Christ to care for His children. Thomas Brooks said, "A gracious soul may look through the darkest cloud and see God smiling on him."[411]

(3. Suffering happens to bear witness to the consolation of Christ to the saints (Philippians 2:1).

(4. Suffering happens to show the world the brilliance of the saint in the furnace. B. R. Lakin says, "To an inexperienced eye, a synthetic diamond is as brilliant as the genuine. But when these two stones are placed under water, the synthetic stone loses its brilliance while the genuine gains in luster. God sometimes leads His children through the 'waters of affliction' that the world may behold our brilliance in the hour of trouble."[412] See the Roll Call of the Faith, Hebrews 11.

(5. Suffering happens to prove the sufficiency of Christ's grace to enable the saint to endure the direst of circumstances and the severest of pains. Paul testified, "And he said unto me, My grace is sufficient for thee: for my strength is made perfect in weakness. Most gladly therefore will I rather glory in my infirmities, that the power of Christ may rest upon me" (2 Corinthians 12:9).

(6. Suffering happens to spur growth in likeness to Christ Jesus (Romans 8:28–30 and James 1:2–4). Spurgeon said, "I am certain that I never did grow in grace one-half so much anywhere as I have upon the bed of pain."[413] The psalmist said, "It is good for me that I have been afflicted; that I might learn thy statutes" (Psalm 119:71). "Like the growth of a muscle when one is lifting weights, resisting in time of trial causes the muscle of faith to grow stronger. It is in the heat of trials where these deficiencies in faith and character surface. It is only when they surface that God can begin to purify our hearts and motives and actions."[414]

(7. Suffering happens to sharpen the saint for more effective Christian service or ministry. Robert Hall preached better sermons due to his suffering; Spurgeon

accomplished the best work of his ministry while an invalid; Richard Baxter wrote better because of bodily infirmity.[415] Unknown to many, Susannah Spurgeon (Spurgeon's wife), due to a botched surgery, suffered tremendously the rest of her life. The suffering prompted her to form *The Book Fund* to raise money to freely distribute her husband's book *Lectures to My Students* to impoverished ministers. At her death in 1902 she had distributed 199,315 theological resources throughout England without cost to the recipients.[416]

(8. Suffering happens to ready the saint for Heaven (2 Corinthians 4:17).

(9. Suffering happens to humble the saint. Spurgeon said, "I would venture to say that the greatest blessing that God can give to any of us is health, *with the exception of sickness*. Sickness has frequently been of more use to the saints of God than health has. If some men that I know of could only be favored with a month of rheumatism, it would, by God's grace, mellow them marvelously."[417]

(10. Suffering happens to test the saint. Peter says, "So be truly glad. There is wonderful joy ahead, even though you must endure many trials for a little while. These trials will show that your faith is genuine. It is being tested as fire tests and purifies gold—though your faith is far more precious than mere gold. So when your faith remains strong through many trials, it will bring you much praise and glory and honor on the day when Jesus Christ is revealed to the whole world" (1 Peter 1:6–7 NLT). L. B. Cowman said, "He [Job] was tried so that his godliness might be confirmed and validated. In the same way, my troubles are intended to deepen my character and to clothe me in gifts I had little of prior to my difficulties, for my ripest fruit grows against the roughest wall. I come to a place of glory only through my own humility, tears, and death, just as Job's afflictions left him with a higher view of God and humbler thoughts of himself."[418]

(11. Suffering happens to profit the saint. The psalmist declared, "Thou in faithfulness hast afflicted me" (Psalm 119:75). Albert Barnes comments, "In faithfulness to my soul; in faithfulness to my own best interest—it was not arbitrary; it was not from malice; it was not that the affliction had come by chance; it was because God loved his soul, and sought his welfare. It was because God saw that there was some good reason why it should be done; that there was some evil to be checked, some improper conduct to be corrected, some lesson which he would be the better for learning, some happy influence on his life here and on his happiness in Heaven which would be more than a compensation for all that he would suffer."[419]

Sufferers become God's best comforters. "Men will never become great in divinity (ministry) until they become great in suffering. 'Ah!' said Luther, 'affliction is the best book in my library'; and let me add, the best leaf in the book of affliction is that blackest of all the leaves, the leaf called heaviness when the spirit sinks within us and we cannot endure as we could wish. And yet again, this heaviness is of essential use to a Christian if he would do good to others. There are none so tender as those who have been skinned themselves. Those who have been in the chamber of affliction know how to comfort those who are there. Do not believe that any man will become a physician unless he walks the hospitals, and I am sure that no one will become a comforter unless he lies in the hospital as well as walks through it and has to suffer himself."[420] J. I. Packer wrote, "God sanctifies our suffering to good ends. Our suffering produces character (Romans 5:3). Our suffering glorifies God (2 Corinthians 12:9–10). And our suffering fulfills the law of the harvest: Before there is blessing anywhere, there will be suffering somewhere (John 12:24)."[421]

In affliction, explanations from God are unnecessary. But belief that He is in control and watchful over you in it is imperative to endure and cope victoriously. Martin Luther rightly taught that "suffering is unbearable if you aren't certain that God is for you and with you."[422] Get that settled and suffering becomes bearable and beneficial.

77

Strength Promised for the Day

"As thy days, so shall thy strength be" (Deuteronomy 33:25). The promise is directly spoken to Asher, but its comfort and hope may be claimed by all God's children.

It promises sure strength for the day. Coping grace to enable endurance to face life's trials "today" is assured by God. Billy Graham said, "God will give us the strength and resources we need to live through any situation in life that He ordains."[423]

It promises specific strength for the day. Whatever form of strength is needed to bear the circumstances of "the day" (sickness, suffering, sorrow, service and death) shall be provided.

It promises sufficient strength for the day. Whatever the demand of the day, so shall that measure of strength be given to enable or endure. *Coping grace* is provided when *delivering grace* is withheld. Paul's request thrice for the removal of the thorn in his flesh was denied. But with the denial God said, "My grace is sufficient for thee" to bear it. And Paul discovered that to be true. See 2 Corinthians 12:7–9. Matthew Henry writes, "Though God accepts the prayer of faith, yet He does not always give what is asked for: as He sometimes grants in wrath, so He sometimes denies in love. When God does not take away our troubles and temptations, yet if He gives grace enough for us, we have no reason to complain. Grace signifies the goodwill of God toward us, and that is enough to enlighten and enliven us, sufficient to strengthen and comfort in all afflictions and distresses."[424]

It promises set strength for the day. Renewed strength is assured for each day as it arrives, not cumulative. Jesus taught us to pray, "Give us this day [day by day] our daily bread." He also said, "So don't be anxious about tomorrow. God will take care of your tomorrow too. Live one day at a time" (Matthew 6:34 TLB). Strength needed for tomorrow's pain and problems or service will be given at that time. As each new day unfolds, a fresh supply of strength will be given to cope. As with God's mercies, strength is given "new every morning: great is thy faithfulness" (Lamentations 3:23).

It promises secure strength for each day. As each day unfolds in our life, until its very last God will be faithful to supply strength according to that day's demand. "He is faithful [reliable, trustworthy, dependable] that promised" (Hebrews 10:23). "God is in control. He may not take away our trials or make detours for us, but He strengthens us through them."[425]

Frances Ridley Havergal said God "will never make you take even one step beyond what your feet are able to endure. Never mind if you think you are unable to take another step, for either He will strengthen you to make you able, or He will call a sudden halt, and you will not have to take it at all."[426] A promise is only as good as its giver. An exhausted and weary worker is given this quotation by another: "Come unto me, all ye that labor and are heavy laden, and I will give you rest!"

"Them's good words," is the reply, "but who says 'em?"

That promise and the promise of Deuteronomy 33:25 are signed by Him that is the Creator and Sustainer of all that exists—the sovereign God of the universe. He that affixed His signature to it is the same "that spared not his own Son, but delivered him up for us all," and because He did, "how shall he not with him also freely give us all things?" (Romans 8:32). He that issued the promise certainly has the authority and power to back it up. With this promise in hand and heart, the Christian may encounter whatever betides calmly, courageously and victoriously one day at a time.

> Afflicted saint, to Christ draw near;
> Your Savior's gracious promise hear.
> His faithful Word you can believe:
> That as your days your strength shall be. ~ John Fawcett (1740–1817)

78
Hymns and Poetry to Calm and Comfort

Our God, Our Help in Ages Past

Our God, our help in ages past,
    Our hope for years to come,
Our shelter from the stormy blast,
    And our eternal home,

When the Rain Comes

Under the shadow of Your throne
       Your saints have dwelt secure;
Sufficient is Your arm alone,
       And our defense is sure.

Before the hills in order stood
       Or earth received her frame,
From everlasting you are God,
       To endless years the same.

A thousand ages in your sight
       Are like an evening gone,
Short as the watch that ends the night
       Before the rising sun.

The busy tribes of flesh and blood,
       With all their lives and cares,
Are carried downward by your flood
       And lost in foll'wing years.

Time, like an ever rolling stream,
       Bears all its sons away;
They fly forgotten, as a dream
       Dies at the op'ning day.

Our God, our help in ages past,
       Our hope for years to come,
Oh, be our guard while troubles last
and our eternal home. ~ Isaac Watts (1719)

Day by Day, and With Each Passing Moment

Day by day and with each passing moment,
       Strength I find to meet my trials here;
Trusting in my Father's wise bestowment,
       I've no cause for worry or for fear.

He whose heart is kind beyond all measure
       Gives unto each day what he deems best,
Lovingly its part of pain and pleasure,
       Mingling toil with peace and rest.

Ev'ry day the Lord Himself is near me
      With a special mercy for each hour;
All my cares He fain would bear and cheer me,
      He whose name is Counselor and Pow'r.

The protection of His child and treasure
      Is a charge that on Himself He laid;
"As your days, your strength shall be in measure,"
      This the pledge to me He made.

Help me then in ev'ry tribulation
      So to trust Your promises, O Lord,
That I lose not faith's sweet consolation
      Offered me within Your holy Word.

Help me, Lord, when toil and trouble meeting
      E'er to take, as from a father's hand,
One by one, the days, the moments fleeting,
      'Til I reach the promised land. ~ Lina Sandell Berg (1865)

Immortal, Invisible, God Only Wise

Immortal, invisible, God only wise,
In light inaccessible hid from our eyes,
Most blessed, most glorious, the Ancient of Days,
Almighty, victorious, Thy great name we praise.

Unresting, unhasting, and silent as light,
Nor wanting, nor wasting, Thou rulest in might;
Thy justice like mountains high soaring above,
Thy clouds which are fountains of goodness and love.

Great Father of glory, pure Father of light,
Thine angels adore Thee, all veiling their sight.
All praise we would render; oh, help us to see,
'Tis only the splendor of light hideth Thee! ~ Walter C. Smith (1867)

Abide With Me

Abide with me; fast falls the eventide.
The darkness deepens; Lord, with me abide.
When other helpers fail and comforts flee,
Help of the helpless, oh, abide with me.

When the Rain Comes

Swift to its close ebbs out life's little day.
Earth's joys grow dim; its glories pass away.
Change and decay in all around I see.
O Thou who changest not, abide with me.

I need Thy presence every passing hour.
What but Thy grace can foil the tempter's power?
Who like Thyself my guide and strength can be?
Through cloud and sunshine, oh, abide with me.

I fear no foe with Thee at hand to bless;
Ills have no weight and tears no bitterness.
Where is death's sting? Where, grave, thy victory?
I triumph still, if Thou abide with me.

Hold Thou Thy cross before my closing eyes.
Shine through the gloom and point me to the skies.
Heaven's morning breaks and earth's vain shadows flee;
In life, in death, O Lord, abide with me. ~ Henry Francis Lyte (1847)

Safely Home

I am home in Heaven, dear ones;
>> All so happy, all so bright!
There perfect joy and beauty
>> In this everlasting light.

All the pain and grief are over;
>> Every restless tossing passed.
I am now at peace forever,
>> Safely home in Heaven at last.

Did you wonder I so calmly
>> Trod the Valley of the Shade?
Oh! but Jesus' love illumined
>> Every dark and fearful glade.

And He came Himself to meet me
>> On that way so hard to tread;
And with Jesus' arm to lean on,
>> Could I have one doubt or dread?

Then you must not grieve so sorely,
    For I love you dearly still.
Try to look beyond earth's shadows;
    Pray to trust our Father's will.

There is work still waiting for you,
    So you must not idle stand.
Do your work while life remaineth;
    You shall rest in Jesus' land.

When that work is all completed,
    He will gently call you home.
Oh, the rapture of the meeting!
    Oh, the joy to see you come! ~ Anonymous

He Leadeth Me

He leadeth me; oh, blessed thought!
Oh, words with heavenly comfort fraught!
Whate'er I do, where'er I be,
Still 'tis God's hand that leadeth me.

He leadeth me; He leadeth me;
By His own hand He leadeth me.
His faithful follower I would be,
For by His hand He leadeth me.

Sometimes mid scenes of deepest gloom,
Sometimes where Eden's flowers bloom,
By waters calm, o'er troubled sea,
Still 'tis God's hand that leadeth me.

Lord, I would clasp Thy hand in mine,
Nor ever murmur nor repine,
Content, whatever lot I see,
Since 'tis my God that leadeth me.

And when my task on earth is done,
When, by Thy grace, the victory's won,
E'en death's cold wave I will not flee,
Since God through Jordan leadeth me. ~ Joseph H. Gilmore (1862)

My Shepherd Will Supply My Need

My Shepherd, You supply my need;
    Most holy is Your name.
In pastures fresh You make me feed
    Beside the living stream.

You bring my wand'ring spirit back,
    When I forsake Your ways;
You lead me, for Your mercy's sake,
    In paths of truth and grace.

When through the shades of death I walk,
    Your presence is my stay;
One word of Your supporting breath
    Drives all my fears away.

Your hand in sight of all my foes
    Does still my table spread.
My cup with blessings overflows;
    Your oil anoints my head.

Your sure provisions, gracious God,
    Attend me all my days;
Oh, may Your house be my abode
    And all my work be praise.

Here would I find a settled rest,
    While others go and come;
No more a stranger, nor a guest,
    But like a child at home. ~ Isaac Watts (1719)

In the Cross of Christ I Glory, Towering o'er the Wrecks of Time

When the woes of life o'ertake me,
    Hopes deceive, and fears annoy,
Never shall the cross forsake me.
    Lo! It glows with peace and joy.

When the sun of bliss is beaming
    Light and love upon my way,
From the cross the radiance streaming
    Adds more luster to the day.

Bane and blessing, pain and pleasure
      By the cross are sanctified;
Peace is there that knows no measure,
      Joys that through all time abide. ~ John Bowring (1792–1872)

Looking for the Sunrise

I'm not looking for the sunset
      As the swift years come and go;
I am looking for the sunrise
      And the golden morning glow,

Where the light of Heaven's glory
      Will break forth upon my sight,
In the land that knows no sunset
      Nor the darkness of the night.

I'm not going down the pathway
      Toward the setting of the sun,
Where the shadows ever deepen
      When the day at last is done.

I am walking up the hillside
      Where the sunshine lights the way,
To the glory of the sunrise
      Of God's never ending day.

I'm not going down, but upward,
      And the path is never dim,
For the day grows ever brighter
      As I journey on with Him.

So my eyes are on the hilltops,
      Waiting for the sun to rise,
Waiting for His invitation
      To the home beyond the skies. ~ Albert Simpson Reitz (1953)

For Me to Live Is Christ

For me to live is Christ;
      To die is endless gain.
For Him I gladly bear the cross
      And welcome grief and pain.

When the Rain Comes

The dawn on distant hills
        Shines o'er the vales below;
The shadows of this world are lost
        In light to which I go.

My journey soon will end,
        My scrip and staff laid down;
Oh, tempt me not with earthly toys!
        I go to wear a crown.

Faithful may I endure
        And hear my Savior say,
Thrice welcome home, beloved child;
        Inherit endless day! ~ Anonymous (1864)

Prospice

Fear death?—to feel the fog in my throat,
        The mist in my face,
When the snows begin and the blasts denote
        I am nearing the place,
The power of the night, the press of the storm,
        The post of the foe;
Where he stands, the Arch Fear in a visible form,
        Yet the strong man must go:
For the journey is done and the summit attained
        And the barriers fall,
Though a battle's to fight ere the guerdon be gained,
        The reward of it all.
I was ever a fighter, so—one fight more,
        The best and the last!
I would hate that death bandaged my eyes and forbore
        And bade me creep past.
No! let me taste the whole of it, fare like my peers
        The heroes of old,
Bear the brunt, in a minute pay glad life's arrears
        Of pain, darkness and cold.
For sudden the worst turns the best to the brave,
        The black minutes at end,

And the elements rage; the fiend-voices that rave
Shall dwindle, shall blend,
Shall change, shall become first a peace out of pain,
Then a light, then thy breast,
O thou soul of my soul! I shall clasp thee again,
And with God be the rest! ~ Robert Browning

God Leads Us Along

In shady, green pastures, so rich and so sweet,
God leads His dear children along;
Where the water's cool flow bathes the weary one's feet,
God leads His dear children along.

Some through the waters, some through the flood,
Some through the fire, but all through the blood;
Some through great sorrow, but God gives a song
In the night season and all the day long.

Sometimes on the mount where the sun shines so bright,
God leads His dear children along;
Sometimes in the valley, in darkest of night,
God leads His dear children along.

Though sorrows befall us and evils oppose,
God leads His dear children along.
Through grace we can conquer, defeat all our foes;
God leads His dear children along.

Away from the mire and away from the clay,
God leads His dear children along;
Away up in glory, eternity's day,
God leads His dear children along. ~ G. A. Young (1903)

Guide Me, O Thou Great Jehovah

Guide me, O my great Redeemer,
Pilgrim through this barren land.
I am weak, but You are mighty;
Hold me with Your powerful hand.
Bread of Heaven, Bread of Heaven,
Feed me till I want no more;
Feed me till I want no more.

When the Rain Comes

Open now the crystal fountain,
    Where the healing waters flow.
Let the fire and cloudy pillar
    Lead me all my journey through.
Strong Deliverer, strong Deliverer,
Ever be my strength and shield,
Ever be my strength and shield.

When I tread the verge of Jordan,
    Bid my anxious fears subside;
Death of death and hell's destruction,
    Land me safe on Canaan's side.
Songs of praises, songs of praises
I will ever give to Thee;
I will ever give to Thee. ~ William Williams (1745)

Vital Spark of Heavenly Flame

Vital spark of heavenly flame,
Quit, oh, quit this mortal frame!
Trembling, hoping, lingering flying,
Oh, the pain, the bliss of dying!
Cease, fond nature, cease thy strife,
And let me languish into life.

Hark! they whisper; angels say,
Sister spirit, come away!
What is this absorbs me quite—
Steals my senses, shuts my sight,
Drowns my spirit, draws my breath?
Tell me, my soul, can this be death?

The world recedes—it disappears.
Heav'n opens on my eyes; my ears
    With sounds seraphic ring!
Lend, lend your wings! I mount! I fly!
O grave! where is thy victory!
    O death! where is thy sting? ~ Alexander Pope (1712)

The Sands of Time Are Sinking

The sands of time are sinking;
    The dawn of Heaven breaks.
The summer morn I've sighed for,
    The fair sweet morn awakes.
Dark, dark hath been the midnight,
    But dayspring is at hand,
And glory, glory dwelleth
    In Emmanuel's land.

The King there in His beauty
    Without a veil is seen;
It were a well-spent journey,
    Though sev'n deaths lay between.
The Lamb with His fair army
    Doth on Mount Zion stand,
And glory, glory dwelleth
    In Emmanuel's land.

Oh, Christ, He is the fountain,
    The deep sweet well of love!
The streams on earth I've tasted;
    More deep I'll drink above.
There to an ocean fullness
    His mercy doth expand,
And glory, glory dwelleth
    In Emmanuel's land.

The bride eyes not her garment,
    But her dear bridegroom's face.
I will not gaze at glory
    But on my King of grace,
Not at the crown He gifteth,
    But on his pierced hand;
The Lamb is all the glory
    Of Emmanuel's land. ~ A. R. Cousin (1857)

Calm Me, My God, and Keep Me Calm

Calm me, my God, and keep me calm,
    While these hot breezes blow;
Be like the night-dew's cooling balm
    Upon earth's fevered brow.

Calm me, my God, and keep me calm,
    Soft resting on Thy breast;
Soothe me with holy hymn and psalm
    And bid my spirit rest.

Calm me, my God, and keep me calm;
    Let Thine outstretched wing
Be like the shade of Elim's palm
    Beside her desert-spring.

Yes, keep me calm, though loud and rude
    The sounds my ear that greet,
Calm in the closet's solitude,
    Calm in the bustling street,

Calm in the hour of buoyant health,
    Calm in the hour of pain,
Calm in my poverty or wealth,
    Calm in my loss or gain,

Calm in the sufferance of wrong
    Like Him who bore my shame,
Calm 'mid the threatening, taunting throng
    Who hate Thy holy Name

Calm as the ray of sun or star
    Which storms assail in vain
Moving unruffled through earth's war,
    The eternal calm to gain. ~ Horatius Bonar (1857)

79

The Legend of Death's Door

"Death's Door" is the main navigational passage between the Bay of Green Bay and Lake Michigan.[427] The legends of Death's Door portray horrific winds and deadly storms that pushed ships and their crews crashing into the rocks on the shore. The legend is said to have originated around 1700. One author contends it's but a "frightful legend" devised by the French to discourage English exploration.[428]

Whether or not the legend is true, *Death's Door* exists for every man, not in Michigan, but in the straits of "the valley of the shadow of death." See Psalm 23:4 and Hebrews 9:27. Concerning this "Death's Door," Satan has concocted frightful and horrifying untruths purposed to induce fear in the believer. But that's all it is, a hoax fabricated with lies, for Jesus in His triumphant resurrection disempowered death of its curse and horror (1 Corinthians 15:20–21). The Christian at Death's Door with calm, confidence and courage can shout, "O death, where is thy sting? O grave, where is thy victory?...Thanks be to God, which giveth us the victory through our Lord Jesus Christ" (1 Corinthians 15:55, 57).

Spurgeon counsels, "O child of God, death hath lost its sting, because the Devil's power over it is destroyed. Then cease to fear dying. Ask grace from God the Holy Ghost that by an intimate knowledge of and a firm belief in thy Redeemer's death thou mayest be strengthened for that dread hour. Living near the cross of Calvary, thou mayest think of death with pleasure and welcome it when it comes with intense delight. It is sweet to die in the Lord; it is a covenant-blessing to sleep in Jesus. Death is no longer banishment; it is a return from exile, a going home to the many mansions where the loved ones already dwell."[429]

However, Death's Door ought to be fearsome to the unbeliever, for upon entering it, judgment and eternal damnation in Hell await (Revelation 20:12; 21:8).

80

Last Words of Saints

F. B. Myers stated, "The dying ones are conscious of sights and sounds for which we strain eye and ear in vain."[430] Scripture records the account of Stephen, the first Christian martyr, who testified while dying, "Look, I see the heavens opened and Jesus the Messiah standing beside God, at his right hand!" (Acts 7:56 TLB). No mortal man has returned from the other side of the grave to testify of Heaven's reality and bliss. But we do have eyewitness testimonies to both from saints upon their deathbeds. Are such things possible and trustworthy? Yes, if one exercises caution based upon the scriptural consistency of what was shared and the credibility of those by whom it was shared. God's only revelation about Heaven and its beauty is in the Holy Bible, not in personal, out-of-body experiences. Therefore, dying visions about Heaven and angels that fail to agree with the Holy Scriptures are spurious and must be discounted. But don't allow the *counterfeit* to rob you of the comfort of the *authentic*.

C. H. Spurgeon, one of history's greatest ministers, stated, "Beloved, it is very probable that we shall have such a sight of our glorious King as we never had before when *we come to die*. Many saints in dying have looked up from amidst the stormy waters and have seen Jesus walking on the waves of the sea and heard Him say, "It is I, be not afraid." Ah, yes! when the tenement begins to shake and the clay falls away, we see Christ through the rifts, and between the rafters, the sunlight of Heaven comes streaming in. But if we want to see face to face the 'King in his beauty,' we must go to Heaven for the sight!"[431] And what consolation that glimpse of the King brings to the dying saint!

May the last words and/or glimpses of Heaven or angels that great saints witnessed in life's final moments comfort, cheer, encourage and assist in removing death's fear while inflaming the heart with joyous anticipation and expectation.[432] "Departing saints have uttered brave things and rare things which have made us wish that we had been going away with them, so they have made us long to see what they have seen and to sit down and feast at their banquet."[433]

C. H. Spurgeon. "Can this be death? Why, it is better than living!"

William Wilberforce. "My affections are so much in Heaven that I can leave you all without regret; yet I do not love you less, but God more."

Brownlow North. "The blood of Jesus Christ his Son cleanseth us from all sin" — that is the verse on which I am now dying. One wants no more."

Isaac Watts. "It is a great mercy that I have no manner of fear or dread of death. I could, if God please, lay my head back and die without terror this afternoon."

George Whitfield. "Lord Jesus, I am weary in Thy work, but not of Thy work. If I have not yet finished my course, let me go and speak for Thee once more in the fields, seal the truth, and come home to die."

Comfort for Troubled Hearts

Dietrich Bonhoeffer. A prisoner wrote: "Sunday, April 8, 1945, Pastor Bonhoeffer held a little service which reached the hearts of all. He had hardly finished his prayer when the door opened. Two evil-looking soldiers came in and barked, 'Prisoner Bonhoeffer, come with us!' The words meant only one thing: the scaffold. As he bid his fellow prisoners good-bye, he said, "For me this is the beginning of a new life, eternal life."[434]

George Washington. "Doctor, I am dying...but I am not afraid to die."

Norman Macleod. On the day of his death he said, "I have had constant joy, and the happy thought continually whispered, 'Thou art with me!' Not many would understand me. They would put down much I have felt to the delirium of weakness, but I have had deep spiritual insight." Shortly before his death he said, "Now all is perfect peace and perfect calm. I have glimpses of Heaven that no tongue or pen or words can describe."[435]

Lady Powerscourt. "One needs a great many Scriptures to live by, but the only Scripture that a person needs to die by is 1 John 1:7; and that verse never was sweeter to me than at this moment."

John Pawson. "I know I am dying, but my deathbed is a bed of roses. I have no thorns planted upon my dying pillow. Heaven is already begun!"[436]

Benjamin Abbot. "Glory to God! I see Heaven sweetly opened before me!"

Martha McCrackin. "How bright the room! How full of angels!"

Phillip Heck. "How beautiful! The opening Heavens around me shine!"

John Owen. When John Owen, the great Puritan, lay on his deathbed, his secretary wrote (in his name) to a friend, "I am still in the land of the living." "Stop," said Owen. "Change that and say, I am yet in the land of the dying, but I hope soon to be in the land of the living." When dying, Owens said, "I am going to Him whom my soul loveth, or rather, who has loved me with an everlasting love."

John A. Lyth. "Can this be death? Why, it is better than living! Tell them I die happy in Jesus!"

When the Rain Comes

Augustine. "Your will be done. Come, Lord Jesus!"

Stonewall Jackson. "Let us cross the river and rest in the shade."

R. G. Lee. "I see Heaven! It's beautiful. I never did it justice." Then he said to his adopted daughter, "I see my mother, and she's beautiful; she's beautiful."[437]

Billy Graham. In his final column he wrote: "By the time you read this, I will be in Heaven, and as I write this I'm looking forward with great anticipation to the day when I will be in God's presence forever. I'm convinced that Heaven is far more glorious than anything we can possibly imagine right now, and I look forward not only to its wonder and peace, but also to the joy of being reunited with those who have gone there before me, especially my dear wife, Ruth. The Bible says, 'Now we see but a poor reflection as in a mirror; then we shall see face to face' (1 Corinthians 13:12)."[438]

Richard Baxter. "I have pain—but I have peace; I have peace."[439]

John Knox. "Live in Christ, die in Christ, and the flesh need not fear death."[440]

Joseph Everett. He said, "GLORY! GLORY! GLORY!" and continued exclaiming "GLORY!" said Billy Graham, for over twenty-five minutes until he entered Heaven.[441]

Augustus Toplady. "Oh! What delight! Who can fathom the joys of Heaven! I know it cannot be long now until my Savior will come for me." And then bursting into a flood of tears, he said, "All is light, light, light, light, the brightness of His own glory. Oh, come, Lord Jesus, come. Come quickly!"[442]

Blumbardt. Moments before death he exclaimed, "Light breaks in! Hallelujah!"

Olympia Morata. Dying, he said, "I distinctly behold a place filled with ineffable (inexpressible) light."

Lambert (a martyr under Henry VIII). While being consumed by a slow fire he exclaimed, "None but Christ; none but Christ!"[443]

Comfort for Troubled Hearts

Lawrence Saunders (martyred by the "bloody Queen Mary"). "Welcome the cross of Christ! Welcome the cross of Christ! Welcome life everlasting!"[444]

James Durham. He said to a friend, "For all that I have preached and written, there is but one Scripture that I can think of or dare to lay hold of. Tell me, brother, if I may dare lay the weight of my salvation on it: 'Whoever comes unto me, I will in no wise cast out!'"[445]

Doddridge. "I am full of confidence. There is a hope set before me; I have fled; I still fly for refuge to that hope. In Him I trust. In Him I have strong consolation and shall assuredly be accepted in the beloved of my soul."[446]

Thomas Scott (the commentator). "Lord, support me! Lord Jesus, receive my spirit! Christ is my all! He is my only hope! Oh, to realize the fullness of joy! Oh, to be done with temptation! This is Heaven begun! I am done with darkness forever! Satan is vanquished! Nothing remains but salvation with eternal glory, eternal glory!"[447]

David Brainerd. "Oh! why is the chariot so long in coming? Why tarry the wheels of His chariot? Come, Lord Jesus; come quickly!"[448]

Susannah Wesley. "Children, when I am gone, sing a song of praise to God."

Charles Wesley. "I shall be satisfied with thy likeness—satisfied, satisfied!"

Melanchthon. When Melanchthon was asked if there was anything he desired, he said, "No, Luther, nothing but Heaven."

John Brown. "I am weak, but it is delightful to feel oneself in the everlasting arms."

Locke. "Oh, the depth of the riches of the goodness and knowledge of God!"

Adrian Rogers: "I am at perfect peace."[449]

81

Look Beyond the Empty Chair

There is no greater sorrow then to be crushed in the winepress of bereavement. To say good-bye to those we love is the most difficult and painful task of life. The separation is thought unbearable, our broken heart thought incurable, the continuation of life thought impossible, a life without them thought unimaginable. And all this would be true were it not for the grace of God to bestow needed solace, serenity and strength. There is no hell on earth or sorrow of heart so deep that God's grace cannot go deeper still. Where heartache and despair abound, God's grace abounds more. Out of the fullness of Christ Jesus we have and continue to have 'grace upon grace' (John 1:16). No matter how awesome, grand, or superlative you think God's grace to be, it is yet that much greater. James underscores my point in saying, "He gives a greater grace" (James 4:6 NASB). Grace is greater than our sin but equally greater than our grief. Richard Sibbs said, "The depths of our misery can never fall below the depths of mercy."[450]

> Look beyond the empty chair
> To know a life well spent;
> Look beyond the solitude
> To days of true content.
>
> Cherish in your broken heart
> Each moment gladly shared
> And feel the touch of memory
> Beyond the empty chair. ~ Unknown

Billy Graham stated, "When we grieve over someone who has died in Christ, we are not sorrowing for them but for ourselves. Our grief isn't a sign of weak faith but of great love."[451] Crying is a healthy way to articulate grief and "great love." It's okay to cry. Jesus wept. David wept. Jeremiah wept. The only biblical restraint on crying is that we sorrow not, weep not 'as those that are without hope' (1 Thessalonians 4:13).

The Lord values and treasures the tears of His children and *keeps track of every single one* that flows down their cheek. The psalmist says, "You [God] keep track of all my sorrows. You have collected all my tears in your bottle. You have recorded each one in your book" (Psalm 56:8 NLT). Washington Irving said, "There is a sacredness in tears. They are not the mark of weakness, but of power. They speak more eloquently than ten thousand tongues. They are the messengers of overwhelming grief, a deep contrition, and of unspeakable love." And God understands and caringly sympathizes. The same tears that are bitterly wept by us will presently or in time be converted into tears of joy, peace, and comfort by the same power which turned water into wine.[452]

Weary heart, He calls you, "Come to Me and rest."
Does the path grow rugged? Yet His way is best.
Leave the unknown future in the Master's hands.
Whether sad or joyful, Jesus understands. ~ Birdie Bell (1903)

Grief is a long, twisting, painful, difficult and seemingly unending journey accompanied by a cycle of varied emotions. But it is doable through God's strength (Philippians 1:6) and comfort (Matthew 5:4) one day at a time. C. S. Lewis said in regard to sorrow, "Relying on God has to begin all over again every day, as if nothing had yet been done."[453]

C. H. Spurgeon provides counsel in handling grief: "The good news is that by God's grace, in time the sorrowing sadness will lessen more and more, giving way to sweet sadness. Though sorrow will never be completely erased, by God's promises and the testimonies of others who have walked the same path, it will evolve into a life of heightened peace, hope and joy. Sorrow is not a stage you get through, but rather a process you live with. To say, 'God, my Father,' to put myself right into His hand and feel that I am safe there, to look up to Him though it is with tears in my eyes and feel that He loves me and then to put my head right on His chest as the prodigal son did and sob my griefs out there into my Father's heart—oh, this is the death of grief and the life of all comfort. Isn't Jehovah called the God of all comfort? You will find Him so, beloved. He has been our help in ages past; He is our hope for years to come. If He had not been my help, then my soul would have utterly perished in the day of its suffering and its heartache. Oh, I bear testimony for Him this day that you cannot go to God and pour out your heart before Him without finding a wonderful comfort. When your friend cannot wipe away your tears, when you yourself with your best reasoning powers and your most courageous efforts cannot overcome your grief, when your heart beats fast and seems as if it would burst with grief, then as God's child, you will pour out your heart before Him. God is a refuge for us. He is our fortress, our refuge and defense. We only have to go to Him, and we will find that even here on earth God will wipe away every tear from our eyes."[454] The psalmist says, "The LORD hears his people when they call to him for help. He rescues them from all their troubles. The LORD is close to the brokenhearted; he rescues those whose spirits are crushed" (Psalm 34:17–18 NLT).

Although visibly absent, the person loved is with you constantly through the love and precious memories they left. Retreat to this treasure often and gain strength and repose.

When the Rain Comes

Although it's difficult today to see beyond the sorrow,
May looking back in memory help comfort you tomorrow.

~ Author Unknown

Amos J. Traver said, "Death is not a period but a comma in the story of life." In English grammar, a period at the conclusion of a sentence means "the end; nothing more is coming; the thought has been completed." In contrast, a comma loudly states, "Take a breath; relax a moment. Get prepared, for there is more to come." What a wonderful description of death! Death is not a period to one's life, only a comma indicating "the best is yet to be." When everything seems to cry out that death is the end to your loved one, remember that when Jesus rose from the dead, He forever made it a "comma." Jesus said, "I am the resurrection, and the life: he that believeth in me, though he were dead, yet shall he live" (John 11:25). In parting from another, it's common among the young to say "Later" instead of "Good-bye." That's exactly what the saint says in death to family and friends. Christians never see each other for the final time; it's not good-bye but see you "later."

Why do we mourn departing friends
    Or shake at death's alarms?
'Tis but the voice that Jesus sends
    To call them to His arms.

Are we not tending upward too
    As fast as time can move?
Nor would we wish the hours more slow
    To keep us from our Love.

Why should we tremble to convey
    Their bodies to the tomb?
There the dear flesh of Jesus lay
    And scattered all the gloom.

The graves of all His saints He blest
    And softened ev'ry bed.
Where should the dying members rest
    But with the dying Head?

Thence He arose, ascending high,
    And showed our feet the way.
Up to the Lord we too shall fly
    At the great rising day.

Comfort for Troubled Hearts

Then let the last loud trumpet sound
   And bid our kindred rise;
Awake, ye nations under ground!
   Ye saints, ascend the skies! ~ Isaac Watts

Upon the death of the only son of Sir Harry Lauder (world-famed Scottish singer and comedian), he remarked, "I had three choices. One, I could drown my sorrow in drink. Two, I could drown my sorrow in the grave; I could take my own life. Or three, I could find hope and comfort in God." And he said, "I turned to God."[455] Wise and wonderful choice that he made! W. A. Criswell states, "Sorrow will always do one of two things. It will warp your mind, embitter your soul, destroy your life; or else it will bring you closer to God."[456] By God's enabling hand, determine that sorrow will do the latter for you when you are within its grip.

No, not cold beneath the grasses,
   Not close-walled within the tomb,
Rather, in our Father's mansion,
   Living in another room;

Living, like the man who loves me,
   Like my child with cheeks abloom,
Out of sight, at desk or schoolbook,
   Busy, in another room;

Nearer than my son whom fortune
   Beckons where the strange lands loom;
Just behind the hanging curtain,
   Serving, in another room.

Shall I doubt my Father's mercy;
   Shall I think of death as doom
Or the stepping o'er the threshold
   To a bigger, brighter room?

Shall I blame my Father's wisdom;
   Shall I sit enswathed in gloom,
When I know my loves are happy,
   Waiting in another room? ~ Robert Freeman

82

My Father's House

Jesus describes Heaven as "My Father's house" (John 14:2). Death often terrorizes and horrifies. The "unknown" of what lies beyond the grave incites fear, causing dread and despair. After all, nobody comes back. Even great saints that have assurance of salvation often draw back at death. Most exhibit the knee-jerk reaction of trepidation (fear and apprehension) when the subject of death is raised. "BUT the words, 'my Father's house' gives us a gleam in the gloom."[457] It gives a vivid picture of what Heaven is like, the earthly happy home, but far happier, more expansive and perfect. Sadly, not every earthly house is a home nor every home happy. But "My Father's house" is the loving and caring Home of God. It is lit brightly with His radiant smile and immaculate holy presence. Joy and laugher flood its many rooms. All of the "family" reside together and those that have been separated through death are reunited. Its streets of pure gold, walls of jasper, foundations of twelve precious stones, and gates of pearl (Revelation 21:19–21) are breathtaking and glorious. All the Father's children in His house have new glorified but recognizable bodies which will not become sick or injured or decay or die. "My Father's house" is the sanctuary from that which hounded believers with trouble, sorrow and distress on earth. God does not permit anything into His "house" that would in any wise cause pain and weeping.

My Father's house is every believer's Home, and the "Father" personally awaits each at its heavenly gate to bid a welcome. Knowing death is the mere conveyance of transport to get us to the Father's house relieves fear and calms anxiety. The walk home from work at night was a terror to a boy. That which prompted the fear was the cemetery through which he had to pass to reach home on its other side. In fact, the light of home was visible. Suddenly the boy thought, *Why should I be afraid of walking through the cemetery when the light of home is viewable and I know my Father is watching for me to arrive safely?* Death and the cemetery hold no fear to the saint that sees the Light shining brightly from the *Father's house* on the other side and knows the Father awaits to receive him *home* safely. Matthew Henry is right in stating, "He whose head is in Heaven need not fear to put his feet into the grave."[458]

We read of a place that's called Heaven;
It's made for the pure and the free.
These truths in God's Word He hath given;
How beautiful Heaven must be!

In Heaven no drooping nor pining,
No wishing for elsewhere to be;
God's light is forever there shining.
How beautiful Heaven must be!

Pure waters of life there are flowing,
And all who will drink may be free;
Rare jewels of splendor are glowing.
How beautiful Heaven must be!

How beautiful Heaven must be,
Sweet home of the happy and free,
Fair haven of rest for the weary,
How beautiful Heaven must be!

~ Cordelia J. Whiteside Bridgewater (1920)

"Too little do we, in the rivalries and anxieties of our human life, permit the blessed influences of that holy world to allure and to occupy us."[459]

83

As a Mother Comforteth, So Doth God

"As one whom his mother comforteth, so will I comfort you; and ye shall be comforted in Jerusalem" (Isaiah 66:13). "A stranger may administer comfort, but it is in a distant way; a friend may console us, and this with kindness; a father also, with tenderness still more impressive; but none comforts like a mother."[460] How fitting it is that Isaiah says that God will comfort His children in the same manner as a mother doth console her afflicted child. It's an analogy (a striking and beautiful contrast, comparison) that all can understand, explain and apply. As a mother comforts her child sympathetically, assiduously, affectionately, strenuously, tirelessly, and tenderly, so doth also Almighty God comfort His child when he or she is brokenhearted and crushed.

Memories of my mother's comforting voice and touch now are aroused. She had a special way to "kiss" the hurt away and make everything better. Cuddled in her arms and under her caring watchfulness, I found rest without alarm, regardless of the sickness, failure, disappointment, or trouble. And that comforting did not end when I left home but continued until her death. How I sometimes yet miss my mother's comfort to minister to my hurts and pains! But thankfully I do have someone who can comfort me "as one whom his mother comforteth." The Holy Spirit has come to do this "motherly" comforting in me, and for all believers.

167

When the Rain Comes

C. H. Spurgeon remarked, "A mother's comfort! Ah, this is tenderness itself. How she enters into her child's grief! How she presses him to her bosom and tries to take all his sorrow into her own heart! He can tell her all, and she will sympathize as nobody else can. Of all comforters the child loves best his mother, and even full-grown men have found it so. Does Jehovah condescend to act the mother's part? This is goodness indeed. We readily perceive how He is a father, but will He be as a mother also? Does not this invite us to holy familiarity, to unreserved confidence, to sacred rest? When God Himself becomes "the Comforter," no anguish can long abide. Let us tell out our trouble, even though sobs and sighs should become our readiest utterance. He will not despise us for our tears; our mother did not. He will consider our weakness as she did, and He will put away our faults, only in a surer, safer way than our mother could do. We will not try to bear our grief alone; that would be unkind to one so gentle and so kind. Let us begin the day with our loving God, and wherefore should we not finish it in the same company, since mothers weary not of their children?"[461]

> Like as a mother comforteth,
>   Oh, words of gentle worth!
> So will I comfort you, declares
>   The Lord of all the earth.
>
> He bends in faithful watchfulness;
>   He slumbers not nor sleeps.
> Above His trusting child the Lord
>   A constant vigil keeps.
>
> He patient is, as mothers are
>   Who love their children well.
> Our faults and failings He forgives;
>   His mercies—who can tell!
>
> Like as a mother, grant, O God,
>   This likeness e'er may be
> A holy symbol to declare
>   The love that dwells in Thee. ~ William M. Runyan (1870–1957)

Be comforted in knowing that in times when your heart is crushed by adversity, bereavement and infirmity, the Holy Spirit stands ready to comfort you with a mother's comfort (except perfectly).

84

A Sheltering Tree in the Storm

Shortly before his death, Samuel Taylor Coleridge wrote the poem "Youth and Age" in which are compared his old age and his youth. In part, he writes,

Flowers are lovely; love is flower-like;
Friendship is a sheltering tree.

Friendship is a sheltering tree. What descriptive language to describe true friends! What an image to describe intimate friendship! The words suggest taking shelter from the raging heat of a July day in an extremely hot place under a gigantic tree whose branches and foliage block the sun, providing a cool shade. Coleridge is right. Friends provide a refuge from the trials, tribulations and troubles of life by allowing us to sit under their massive sheltering shade to be refreshed in their encouragement, strengthened by their companionship and helped by their counsel.

Chuck Swindoll writes, "When everything else fails and everybody else has turned away, there are precious few who will give you a call and say, 'I'm with you. I'm there. Count on me. Call on me any time, day or night. I'll come. I won't kick you when you're down. I'm by your side. I understand.'"[462] Fortunately, though David had his backstabbing and deserting friends, he also had groves of friends that were as sheltering trees. All David's *real* friends came through for him in a big way when he needed them the most, but for one exception (Psalm 142:3). "They had no agenda, like gaining political clout. They were there to help with his physical and emotional needs."[463] It was these friends who enabled David to make it through the toughest of days and darkest of nights. Every person needs a sheltering tree or trees.

Someone has said, *"A friend lives to make life less difficult for another."* Couple those words with Coleridge's, and you have a beautiful definition and description of a real friend. In the sicknesses and sorrows of life, friends are sheltering trees doing what is within their ability to make what we are experiencing less difficult and more bearable. They lighten the burden, relieve the heaviness of heart, strengthen our grip on God (1 Samuel 23:16) and "rejoice the heart" (Proverbs 27:9). Sheltering trees are God's gracious gift to each of us to be His ministers of comfort, peace and hope. Express gratitude for your "sheltering trees" (don't take them for granted), and inasmuch as possible be a "sheltering tree" unto others in their time of adversity or infirmity.

We all need a friend when life lays us low,
One that walks with us when other friendships go,
A friend that gives hope and peace to the heart
'Til the storm passes over and the darkness departs. ~ Frank Shivers (2021)

85

Why Did God Allow This to Happen—to Me?

"The LORD blessed the latter part of Job's life more than the former part" (Job 42:12 NIV). "Job found his legacy through the grief he experienced....At last he cried, 'Now my eyes have seen you' (Job 42:5 NIV). If I experience the presence of God in His majesty through my pain and loss so that I bow before Him and pray, 'Your will be done' (Matthew 6:10 NIV), then I have gained much indeed."[464]

The tale is told of a small and stunted plant growing beneath the shade of a tall oak. It valued the shade very much and enjoyed the quiet rest its kind friend afforded. Then the day came when a woodman with axe in hand felled the oak. The plant wept and cried, "My shelter is departed; every rough wind will blow upon me, and every storm will seek to uproot me!"

"No, no," saith the angel of that flower; "now will the sun get at thee; now will the shower fall on thee in more copious abundance than before; now thy stunted form shall spring up into loveliness, and thy flower, which could never have expanded itself to perfection shall now laugh in the sunshine, and men shall say, 'How greatly hath that plant increased! How glorious hath become its beauty, through the removal of that which was its shade and its delight!'"[465]

> Trouble never comes to someone unless it brings a nugget of gold in its hand.
> Alexander Smellie

Like the little plant, people are prone to take for granted the shade of the oak, relying upon it for what is needed to sustain them in the calm or crisis of life. However, when the oak is suddenly removed (job, money, car, house, or health), they are tossed into an emotional tailspin, crying, "Why did God allow this to happen to ME?" Perhaps that answer is revealed in part by the little plant following the felling of its oak. With no hovering limbs and leaves to block the sunshine from reaching it, the little plant was only then able to reach its fullest potential and purpose as a beautiful flower. It is in the removal of the shady oaks (comforts and benefits of life we have relied upon) that we learn that God alone is our towering "Oak" of refuge, strength and help in whom we are to trust and depend in all seasons of life. This acknowledgment enables uninhibited spiritual growth and development and fulfillment of God's best intentions for our life.

"Pain and suffering and sorrow," states W. A. Criswell, "have a purpose in our lives. They are the means and instruments and ways of God to teach us to be humble and to be compassionate and to love the Lord and lean upon His kind heart—the end of sorrow, the beginning and the end, the end of sorrow."[466] Therefore, our grievous loss translates into bountiful gain (Romans 8:28). "Trouble never comes to someone unless it brings a nugget of gold in its hand."[467]

> The doctrine of providence teaches Christians that they are never in the grip of blind forces (fortune, chance, luck, fate); all that happens to them is divinely planned.
> J. I. Packer

J. I. Packer writes, "The doctrine of providence teaches Christians that they are never in the grip of blind forces (fortune, chance, luck, fate); all that happens to them is divinely planned, and each event comes as a new summons to trust, obey, and rejoice, knowing that all is for one's spiritual and eternal good (Romans 8:28)."[468]

Spurgeon states, "The God of providence has limited the time, manner, intensity, repetition, and effects of all our sicknesses; each throb is decreed, each sleepless hour predestinated, each relapse ordained, each depression of spirit foreknown, and each sanctifying result eternally purposed. Nothing great or small escapes the ordaining hand of Him who numbers the hairs of our head."[469]

God moves in a mysterious way
    His wonders to perform;
He plants His footsteps in the sea
    And rides upon the storm.

Deep in unfathomable mines
    Of never failing skill,
He treasures up His bright designs
    And works His sov'reign will.

Ye fearful saints, fresh courage take;
    The clouds ye so much dread
Are big with mercy and shall break
    In blessings on your head.

Judge not the Lord by feeble sense,
    But trust Him for his grace;
Behind a frowning providence
    He hides a smiling face.

His purposes will ripen fast,
    Unfolding ev'ry hour;
The bud may have a bitter taste,
    But sweet will be the flow'r.

When the Rain Comes

Blind unbelief is sure to err
 And scan His work in vain;
God is His own interpreter,
 And He will make it plain. ~ William Cowper (1774)

86

Power in Prayer

James says, "The effectual fervent prayer of a righteous man availeth much" (James 5:16). What is prayer? The prolific writer upon the subject of prayer, E. M. Bounds, said, "Prayer is the helpless and needy child crying to the compassion of the Father's heart and the bounty and power of a Father's hand."[470] With regard to effective praying, James reveals four conditions and its promise. The word "effectual" is better understood as *energetic and powerful*.[471]

(1. *Prayer's power is found in its Provider and Promiser*. That is, it must be addressed to the One that authorized it and has the power to answer it. J. C. Ryle states, "The bank note without a signature at the bottom is nothing but a worthless piece of paper. The stroke of a pen confers on it all its value. The prayer of a poor child of Adam is a feeble thing in itself—but once endorsed by the hand of the Lord Jesus, it avails much."[472] Ryle continues, "The name of Jesus is a never failing passport for our prayers. In that name, a person may draw near to God with boldness and ask with confidence. God has engaged to hear him."[473]

(2. *Prayer that is power filled is not listless or cold, but passionate*. It is earnest, hearty, sincere praying.[474] Prayer ought to be addressed to Christ with divine unction. "It is not enough to say a prayer," wrote Matthew Henry, "but we must *pray* in prayer. Our thoughts must be fixed, our desires firm and ardent, and our graces in exercise; and, when we thus pray in prayer, we shall speed in prayer."[475] J. C. Ryle said, "Words said without heart are as utterly useless to our souls as the drum beating of savages before their idols. Where there is no heart, there may be lip work and tongue work, but there is no prayer."[476] The Puritan Thomas Brooks said, "As a painted fire is no fire, a dead man no man, so a cold prayer is no prayer....Cold prayers are as arrows without heads, as swords without edges, as birds without wings: they pierce not, they cut not, they fly not up to Heaven. Cold prayers do always freeze before they reach to Heaven."[477] Bill Gothard, in *The Power of Crying Out*, states that the most significant difference between the prayers of the saints in Scripture (powerfully effective) and that of believers today (highly ineffective) is this: "There was a fervency in the prayers of biblical saints—a fervency that is inherent in crying out."[478] The Bible emphasizes repetitively the specific purposes and potential of crying out or praying aloud.[479]

(3. *The propulsion of prayer is unflinching trust.* "And the prayer of faith..." (James 5:15). L. B. Cowman wrote, "Genuine faith puts its letter in the mailbox and lets go. Distrust, however, holds on to a corner of the envelope and then wonders why the answer never arrives."[480] See Matthew 21:22.

(4. *Effectual prayer is uttered by a righteous man.* A "righteous man" indicates the requirement or condition on which effective prayer hinges: not religious position or status in the church but personal *rightness* with Christ. The righteous are the ones devoted to Christ who live for His delight and glory in holiness and obedience. See Philippians 2:15 and Psalm 66:18. Note, the Christian in the pew may possess as much or more power in prayer than he that is in the pulpit, for it is not determined by religious position or status, but godliness.

> The Christian in the pew may possess as much or more power in prayer than he that is in the pulpit, for it is not determined by religious position or status, but godliness.

The promise cited about effectual prayer. James says that the fervent prayer of a godly person "availeth much." That is, it prevails with God; it is successful praying. It accomplishes very, very much. It's not a waste of time. It moves the hand of God on earth. Alfred Tennyson was right when he said that more things are wrought by prayer than this world ever dreams.[481] The *power that is in prayer* summons laborers to the harvest field; it secures power in service; it supplies need; it sustains in the hour of sorrow and suffering; it heals and restores to health (if in accordance to God's will); it squashes difficulties; it defeats temptation; it speeds the Gospel around the world; it stifles the work of Satan; and it sanctifies the soul beyond our greatest imagination. Albert Barnes states, "We have no power to control Him; we cannot dictate or prescribe to Him; we cannot resist Him in the execution of His purposes; but we may ask Him for what we desire, and He has graciously said that such asking may effect much for our own good and the good of our fellowmen."[482]

The Bible abounds with promises connected to prayer for the claiming (Matthew 21:22; John 14:13–14; John 15:7; John 16:23–24; Psalm 10:17; 1 John 5:14; Matthew 18:19; Matthew 7:7). Christ bends His ear to the bended knee of purified pleading saints (Jeremiah 29:12 and Psalm 66:18). E. M. Bounds says, "Four things let us ever keep in mind. God hears prayer, God heeds prayer, God answers prayer, and God delivers by prayer."[483] Prayers based upon the promises of God's Word in conjunction with His holy will from a clean and holy heart are effectual. Requests or supplications made inconsistent with God's will (for He knows what's always best for man) are declined or delayed in granting. "And this is the confidence that we have in him, that, if we ask any thing according to his will, he heareth us [grants it]" (1 John 5:14). Therefore, the believer must couch all that is requested by saying, "Nevertheless not my will, but thine, be done" (Luke 22:42). James H.

When the Rain Comes

Brooks cautions, "Without submission to the will of God as infinitely right and infinitely wise, prayer is not prayer."[484] David Jeremiah says, "Prayer is not to get God to change His will. If we really believe that the will of God is perfect, then why would we want to change it? Our prayers ought to be prompted out of our deep understanding of what the will of God is."[485]

At times it is unknown whether or not our request is in agreement with His will. In such times pray as if it is God's will, provided it is not in contradiction to Holy Scripture. For example, don't allow not knowing His will about healing for yourself or that of another to cripple your praying for it. Keep knocking in bold faith and confidence at Heaven's door in prayer until the request is granted or it is spiritually discerned that in this particular case healing is not in God's plan. Whatever the answer to prayer is, it's a win-win. "If the Lord does not pay in silver, He will in gold; and if He does not pay in gold, He will in diamonds."[486] Jon Courson remarks, "Brothers and sisters, pray three times, thirty times, three hundred times until you either get the answer you're asking for or you hear the Father say, 'No, and here's why not.' Don't settle for anything less. If you pray this way, I believe you'll experience successful prayer one hundred percent of the time. Talk to the Father about your thorns, your difficulties, and keep praying until the answer comes your way or until, like Paul, you have understanding and revelation and can say, 'That's a closed issue. I don't need to talk about that anymore. I get it, Father. Your grace is sufficient for me.'"[487] See Matthew 7:7–8.

The faith-based prayer of the saints uttered in purity of heart for the glory of God, though delayed or modified, will be answered. And the answer, J. I. Packer says, will be a huge "positive, though it may be 'I am adjusting the terms of your prayer to give you something better than you asked for.' Or it may be, 'I know that this isn't the moment in which answering your prayer would bring you and others most blessing, so I'm asking you to wait.' Or it may be, 'I am answering your prayer, but you don't know the strategy I'm working on, and it doesn't at the moment feel or look like an answer at all. Nonetheless, it is. Keep praying, keep trusting, and keep looking for what, down the road, I may be able in wisdom to let you see.'"[488]

No matter how hard goes the battle of life,
    God's children need never despair;
His conquering grace giveth peace 'mid the strife.
    There is wonderful pow'r in prayer.

Wonderful pow'r,
    A wonderful pow'r in prayer
For it moveth the Arm that moveth the world.
    There's a wonderful pow'r in prayer.

We know that roses not always will bloom.
    The skies will not always be fair,
But go to the Father to brighten the gloom.
    There is wonderful pow'r in prayer.

Perhaps you are seeking a soul far astray—
    That name to the mercy-seat bear;
The Shepherd himself will go with you today.
    There is wonderful pow'r in prayer.

Thro' all the swift changes that come to us here,
    Till white robes of glory we wear,
We'll look up to Jesus for comfort and cheer.
    There is wonderful pow'r in prayer. ~ Eliza E. Hewit (1909)

John Henry Jowett remarked, "God's ability to perform is far beyond our prayers—even our greatest prayers! I have recently been thinking of some of the requests I have made of Him innumerable times in my prayers. And what have I requested? I have asked for a cupful, while He owns the entire oceans! I have asked for one simple ray of light, while He holds the sun! My best asking falls immeasurably short of my Father's ability to give, which is far beyond what we could ever ask."[489]

87
Suggested Prayers for Difficult Times

In times of illness, fatigue or emotional trauma it may difficult to know how to pray or generate words to pray. That's understandable and acceptable to God. But the Holy Scripture says that in such times "the Spirit helps us in our weakness. We do not know what we ought to pray for, but the Spirit himself intercedes for us through wordless groans" (Romans 8:26 NIV). Therefore, if all you can do is *groan* or speak garbled words or sentences in prayer, pray on, for it is being translated by the Holy Spirit into the ears of Almighty God. "Groans that words cannot express," states Spurgeon, "are often prayers that God cannot refuse."[490]

Further assistance in praying is provided by the constant intercession of Christ. A. C. Dixon writes, "Our prayers ever need His intercession. He is our Daysman. He takes our prayers and makes them presentable to the Father. A little child went into the garden to gather a bouquet of flowers for mother. When mother received them, the flowers were mixed with weeds and some trash. But mother's skillful fingers soon removed the unsightly things and made the bouquet fit for a place on the table in the parlor. Our holiest acts of devotion need the touch of CHRIST to remove the selfishness, insincerity and coldness which are apt to be there. But He knows how to take our prayers and make them what they ought to be."[491] Hallelujah! Therefore, pray confidently and boldly, knowing that Christ and the Holy Spirit ever assist in getting your petitions in acceptable fashion before the throne of Almighty God.

Pray perseveringly. J. I. Packer states, "The Father's larger plans for blessing us and others may require Him to delay giving us what we ask for until the best time and circumstances for its bestowal are reached. To keep asking with patient persistence and waiting with expectation for the answer is thus sometimes necessary and is always the reverent way to go. This strengthens the muscles of our faith, as constant walking strengthens the muscles of heart and legs."[492]

> Sweet hour of prayer! sweet hour of prayer!
> That calls me from a world of care
> And bids me at my Father's throne
> Make all my wants and wishes known.
>
> In seasons of distress and grief,
> My soul has often found relief
> And oft escaped the tempter's snare
> By thy return, sweet hour of prayer!
>
> With such I hasten to the place
> Where God my Savior shows His face
> And gladly take my station there
> And wait for thee, sweet hour of prayer!
>
> Sweet hour of prayer! sweet hour of prayer!
> Thy wings shall my petition bear
> To Him whose truth and faithfulness
> Engage the waiting soul to bless.
>
> And since He bids me seek His face,
> Believe His Word and trust his grace,
> I'll cast on Him my every care
> And wait for thee, sweet hour of prayer!
>
> Sweet hour of prayer! sweet hour of prayer!
> May I thy consolation share,
> Till from Mount Pisgah's lofty height,
> I view my home and take my flight.

Comfort for Troubled Hearts

This robe of flesh I'll drop and rise
To seize the everlasting prize
And shout, while passing through the air,
"Farewell, farewell, sweet hour of prayer!" ~ W. W. Walford (1845)

Prayers cited below may assist in echoing your heart to God. Additionally, numerous prayers of Old and New Testament writers may be personalized (especially that of David in the Psalms).

A prayer for Heaven

O my Lord, may I arrive where means of grace cease and I need no more to fast, pray, weep, watch, be tempted, attend preaching and sacrament; where nothing defiles; where is no grief, sorrow, sin, death, separation, tears, pale face, languid body, aching joints, feeble infancy, decrepit age, peccant [sinful] humors, pining sickness, griping fears, consuming cares; where is personal completeness; where the more perfect the sight the more beautiful the object, the more perfect the appetite the sweeter the food, the more musical the ear the more pleasant the melody, the more complete the soul the more happy its joys; where is full knowledge of Thee.

Here I am an ant, and as I view a nest of ants, so do You view me and my fellow-creatures; but as an ant knows not me, my nature, my thoughts, so here I cannot know You clearly. But there I shall be near You, dwell with my family, stand in Your presence chamber, be an heir of Your kingdom, as the spouse of Christ, as a member of His body, one with Him who is with Thee, and exercise all my powers of body and soul in the enjoyment of You.

As praise in the mouth of Your saints is comely, so teach me to exercise this divine gift, when I pray, read, hear, see, do, in the presence of people and of my enemies, as I hope to praise You eternally hereafter. Amen.[493]

A prayer for safe travel HOME

Holy Father, all about us are weighty questions. It is not easy to live, and the journey of the earthly life is soon ended, and then we pass into a land that shall never end. O Jesus, we would follow Thee faithfully all the days, and then, when we come to the valley of the shadow, we would have Thee with us, and Thy rod and Thy staff to comfort us, and when the mists from off the sea of death come into our faces and we hear the echo of the breakers of that sea, O Thou loving Savior, be Thou the Pilot for us all, and bring us safely to the Father's house above, to the home of many mansions, where we shall be with Jesus, and be like Him forever. How we bless Thee for answering prayer, and for saving souls, and for keeping us in the love of God! Amen.[494]

When the Rain Comes

A prayer for God's intervention in despair, distress and disease

We can truly say that we delight in God....The sickbed is soft when Thou art there. The furnace of affliction grows cool when Thou art there, and the house of prayer, when Thou art present, is none other than the house of God and it is the very gate of Heaven. Come near, our Father; come very near to Thy children. Some of us are very weak in body and faint in heart. Soon, O God, lay Thy right hand upon us and say unto us, "Fear not." Peradventure, some of us are alike and the world is attracting us. Come near to kill the influence of the world with Thy superior power.

Even to worship may not seem easy to some. The dragon seems to pursue them and floods out of his mouth wash away their devotion. Give to them great wings as of an eagle, that each one may fly away into the place prepared for him, and rest in the presence of God today. Our Father, come and rest Thy children now. Take the helmet from our brow, remove from us the weight of our heavy armor for a while, and may we just have peace, perfect peace, and be at rest. Oh! help us, we pray Thee, now.

Lord Jesus, take from us now everything that would hinder the closest communion with God. Any wish or desire that might hamper us in prayer remove, we pray Thee. Any memory of either sorrow or care that might hinder the fixing of our affection wholly on our God, take it away now. Now, we have come close up to Thyself, to the light that shineth between the wings of the cherubim, and we speak with Thee now as a man speaketh with his friends. Our God, we are Thine. Thou art ours.

Our Father, we are very weak. We feel as if we would now come closer to Thee still and hide under the shadow of Thy wings. We wish to be lost in God. We pray that Thou mayest live in us, and not we live, but Christ live in us and show Himself in us and through us. Lord, sanctify us. Oh! that Thy spirit might come and saturate every faculty, subdue every passion, and use every power of our nature for obedience to God.

May every breath be for Thee, may every minute be spent for Thee. Help us to live while we live, and while we are busy in the world as we must be, for we are called to it, may we sanctify the world for Thy service. May we be lumps of salt in the midst of society. May our spirit and temper as well as our conversation be Heavenly. May there be an influence about us that shall make the world the better before we leave it. Lord, hear us in this thing.

We lift our voice to Thee in prayer, also, for all our dear ones. Lord, bless the sick and make them well as soon as it is right they should be. Sanctify to them all they have to bear. There are also dear friends who are very weak, some that are very trembling. God, bless them. While the tent is being taken down, may the inhabitant within look on with calm joy, for we shall by-and-by 'be clothed upon with our house that is from Heaven.' Lord, help us to sit very loose by all these things here below. May we live here like strangers and make the world not a house but an inn, in which we sup and lodge, expecting to be on our journey tomorrow. Lord, save the unconverted. We ask in the name of Jesus Christ Thy Son. Amen.[495]

A prayer for peace in the midst of woeful trouble

Listen to my prayer, O God. Do not ignore my cry for help! Please listen and answer me, for I am overwhelmed by my troubles. My heart pounds in my chest. The terror of death assaults me. Fear and trembling overwhelm me, and I can't stop shaking. Oh, that I had wings like a dove; then I would fly away and rest! Morning, noon, and night I cry out in my distress, and you hear my voice. I'm trusting you to help me. Amen.[496]

A prayer for absolute trust in and dependence upon God

Sovereign Commander of the Universe, I'm sadly harassed by doubts, fears, unbelief, in a felt spiritual darkness. My Heavenly Pilot has disappeared, and I have lost my hold on the Rock of Ages; I sink in deep mire beneath storms and waves, in horror and distress unutterable. Help me, O Lord, to throw myself absolutely and wholly on Thee. Give me peace of soul, confidence and enlargement of mind, morning joy that comes after night heaviness.

In my distress let me not forget this. All-wise God, thy never failing providence orders every event, sweetens every fear, reveals evil's presence lurking in seeming good, brings real good out of seeming evil. Out of my sorrow and night, give me the name Naphtali—"satisfied with favor"—help me to love Thee as Thy child and to walk worthy of my Heavenly pedigree. Amen.[497]

A prayer for comfort when smitten with grief

Dear Lord, hasten to my rescue. Consuming anguish is ravaging my life. I can't eat, sleep or have a moment's peace. My life is in constant turmoil and restlessness. I feel all alone and am frightened at the unknown of tomorrow. I feel as if there is nothing but the darkness of dread and despair ahead. My hope is in You alone for help! Please heal my broken heart and bind up my hurting wounds (Psalm 147:3). Amen.[498]

A prayer for healing and health

Almighty God, You are the only source of health and healing. In You there is calm and the only true peace in the universe. Grant to each one of us Your children an awareness of Your presence, and give us perfect confidence in You. In all pain and weariness and anxiety teach us to yield ourselves to Your never failing care, knowing that Your love and power surround us, trusting in Your wisdom and providence to give us health and strength and peace when Your time is best; through Jesus Christ our Lord. Amen.[499]

A Prayer for relief and rescue

Lord, *help* me. Amen.[500]

A Prayer for calm in the face of death

Lord Jesus, as I near the shores of Home, grant me new grace for the transition through death. I'm somewhat afraid—no, I'm terrified. Calm my anxieties, hush my worries, banish my doubts, and extinguish my fears. It's Your assurances of life after death in Heaven and Your presence with me in the crossing that I plead. Instill in my soul strong faith and firm hope about my future with You and loved ones in the city that knows no sickness, sorrow or death. Turn my mourning into singing, pouting into shouting, pessimism into optimism, doubting into confidence, and fearfulness into peacefulness. Make my pillow soft on the sickbed and my departure gentle and calm. Amen.[501]

A prayer for restoration

O Good Shepherd, seek me out and bring me home to Thy fold again. Deal favorably with me according to Thy good pleasure till I may dwell in Thy house all the days of my life and praise Thee for ever and ever with them that are there. Amen.[502]

A prayer for times of aloneness

Alone with none but Thee, my God,
    I journey on my way.
What need I fear when Thou art near,
    O King of night and day?
More safe am I within Thy hand
Than if a host did round me stand. Amen.[503]

A prayer for divine enablement

We ask you, Master, be our helper and defender. Rescue those of our number in distress; raise up the fallen; assist the needy; heal the sick; turn back those of Your people who stray; feed the hungry; release our captives; revive the weak; encourage those who lose heart. Let all the nations realize that You are the only God, that Jesus Christ is Your Child, and that we are Your people and the sheep of Your pasture. Amen.[504]

Comfort for Troubled Hearts

A prayer for deliverance from sickness, suffering and death

Father, if You are willing, take this cup away from me. Nevertheless, let Your will be done, not mine. Amen.[505]

A prayer for courage and cheer for all that suffer loneliness

God of our life, there are days when the burdens we carry chafe our shoulders and weigh us down; when the road seems dreary and endless, the skies gray and threatening; when our lives have no music in them and our hearts are lonely and our souls have lost their courage. Flood the path with light, run our eyes to where the skies are full of promise, tune our hearts to brave music, give us the sense of comradeship with heroes and saints of every age, and so quicken our spirits that we may be able to encourage the souls of all who journey with us on the road of life, to Your honor and glory.[506]

A prayer for renewed strength and peace

O God, who is the unsearchable abyss of peace, the ineffable sea of love, the fountain of blessings, and the bestower of affection; who sends peace to those that receive it, open to us this day the sea of Your love, and water us with the plenteous streams from the riches of Your grace. Make us children of quietness and heirs of peace. Kindle in us the fire of Your love; sow in us Your fear; strengthen our weakness by Your power; bind us closely to You and to each other in one firm bond of unity, for the sake of Jesus Christ. AMEN.[507]

A prayer for guidance in the time of storm

Steer the ship of my life, good Lord, to Your quiet harbor, where I can be safe from the storms of sin and conflict. Show me the course I should take. Renew in me the gift of discernment, so that I can always see the right direction in which I should go. And give me the strength and the courage to choose the right course, even when the sea is rough and the waves are high, knowing that through enduring hardship and danger, in Your name we shall find comfort and peace. Amen.[508]

A prayer for forgiveness of sin

O Lord, who hast mercy upon all, take away from me my sins, and mercifully kindle in me the fire of thy Holy Spirit. Take away from me the heart of stone and give me a heart of flesh; a heart to love and adore Thee; a heart to delight in Thee, to follow and to enjoy Thee, for Christ's sake. Amen.[509]

<u>When the Rain Comes</u>

A prayer for salvation

Lord Jesus, I acknowledge that You died upon the cross and were raised from the dead to make possible man's forgiveness and rightness with God. Underserving of such rich mercy, I cry out for it in regard to my hideous sin that I might be cleansed thoroughly and have a personal relationship with you as Lord and Savior. I do willingly and eagerly turn from my sin to live unto Your purpose and delight. In Jesus name, *amen.*[510]

A prayer for strengthening of faith

Behold, Lord, an empty vessel that needs to be filled. My Lord, fill it. I am weak in faith; strengthen Thou me. I am cold in love; warm me and make me fervent that my love may go out to my neighbor. I do not have a strong and firm faith; at times I doubt and am unable to trust Thee altogether. O Lord, help me. Strengthen my faith and trust in Thee. In Thee I have sealed the treasures of all I have. I am poor; Thou art rich and didst come to be merciful to the poor. I am a sinner; Thou art upright. With me there is an abundance of sin; in Thee is the fullness of righteousness. Therefore, I will remain with Thee of whom I can receive but to whom I may not give. Amen.[511]

A prayer for healing of sickness

Dear Lord, you are my great Physician, Him to whom I look and whom I trust for healing of my sickness. Thou art able to that which is beyond the ability of man and medicine to do. Apart from any merit of my own, based wholly upon Thy mercy and favor, grant wholeness and health to my body. But if that be not for my best and Thy glory, grant new grace, a grace never known before, to enable me to endure to the end as a good soldier of Jesus Christ. Ultimately, I will be healed—if not here and now, then there and later with You. Either way You will grant the healing for which I pray, for which I give thanks and praise. Amen.[512]

A prayer for finishing strong

Lord, take me Home before dark, lest in my languishing mental and physical state I say or do something contrary to my deeply imbedded core religious beliefs, bringing harm to my reputation as a godly person and to Your holy name. Help me finish my course with Thy stamp of divine approval, leaving a legacy that exalts and glorifies You, as Paul did. Grant a new measure of strength not to stumble in the final part of the course of life, one that I'm finding difficult, painful, distressing and fearful. It's so hard that at moments I don't think I can endure to the end. But I keep looking to You for that added help not to quit or falter. And it always comes just when it's needed most. Give me grace for each new day to face the challenges of my bodily weakness, suffering and disorientation. Keep me from falling on the last leg of the race. Help me finish strong. Amen.[513]

A prayer in facing the storms of life
When the storms of life are raging,
    Stand by me (stand by me);
When the storms of life are raging,
    Stand by me (stand by me);
When the world is tossing me
Like a ship upon the sea,
Thou Who rulest wind and water,
Stand by me (stand by me).

In the midst of tribulation,
    Stand by me (stand by me);
In the midst of tribulation,
    Stand by me (stand by me);
When the hosts of Hell assail
And my strength begins to fail,
Thou Who never lost a battle,
Stand by me (stand by me).

In the midst of faults and failures,
    Stand by me (stand by me);
In the midst of faults and failures,
    Stand by me (stand by me);
When I do the best I can
And my friends misunderstand,
Thou Who knowest all about me,
Stand by me (stand by me).

In the midst of persecution,
    Stand by me (stand by me);
In the midst of persecution,
    Stand by me (stand by me);
When my foes in battle array
Undertake to stop my way,
Thou Who saved Paul and Silas,
Stand by me (stand by me).

When the Rain Comes

When I'm growing old and feeble,
    Stand by me (stand by me);
When I'm growing old and feeble,
    Stand by me (stand by me);
When my life becomes a burden
And I'm nearing chilly Jordan,
O Thou "Lily of the Valley,"
Stand by me (stand by me).[514]

88

A Daring Confidence

"For the LORD shall be thy confidence, and shall keep thy foot from being taken" (Proverbs 3:26). In times of trouble God will be your "confidence" (trust, reliability, refuge). Matthew Henry says, "The Lord shall be not only thy *protector* to keep thee safe, but thy *confidence* to keep thee secure."[515] Martin Luther said, "Faith is a living, daring confidence in God's grace, so sure and certain that a man could stake his life on it a thousand times."[516] *A daring confidence* in the Lord that casts out all terror contained in bad news and adversity, and comforts and sustains us in the difficulties of life, instilling courage, hope, surefootedness and peace, comes from reverence and respect for the Lord and ingestion of His Word (Romans 10:17 and Ephesians 3:11–12). It provides the saint a safe hiding place, a place of refuge when the rains come (Proverbs 14:26). As noted above (No. 66), Alexander Maclaren says, "Trust [God] as what He is, and trust Him because of what He is, and see to it that your faith lays hold on the living God Himself and on nothing besides."[517]

> Faith is a living, daring confidence in God's grace, so sure and certain that a man could stake his life on it a thousand times.
> Martin Luther

To know Jesus theologically (head) and experientially (heart) is to trust Him unwaveringly and unreservedly, for both prove Him trustworthy, dependable, compassionate and faithful to those that love Him.

"Great is Thy faithfulness!" "Great is Thy faithfulness!"
    Morning by morning new mercies I see.
All I have needed Thy hand hath provided.
    "Great is Thy faithfulness," Lord, unto me!
        ~ Thomas Obadiah Chisholm (1866–1960)

89
When the Rain Comes

"In the day of my trouble [when the rain falls] I will call upon thee: for thou wilt answer me....Because thou, LORD, hast holpen me, and comforted me" (Psalm 86:7, 17).

The reality of the "day of trouble." The specific "trouble" to which David refers is unknown; multiplied troubles seemed to be his lot both before and after becoming King of Israel. Trouble (difficulty, affliction, bereavement, ill-health) is part and parcel of life that all will experience sooner or later; its measure to some will be severe, heart-wrenching and grave. R. G. Lee said, "There is no back but has its burden, no soul but has its sorrow, no heart but has its ache, and no life but has its troubles. Trouble is one word in every man's dictionary. No bars or bolts or doors can keep trouble out or away. But let us thank God for the balm He gives to troubled hearts, for the comfort and gladness He brings to those who are in grief."[518]

The resolution for the "day of trouble." In times of trouble, David resolved to call upon the Lord ("I will call upon thee"). Prayer ought to be the believer's first recourse in the hour of crisis and calamity, as it was with David. When two mountain climbers set out for a great climb in Norway, people tried to dissuade them. In response the men shouted, "There is no precipice too steep for two." Provided that God is the other, there is no precipice, storm, trouble, trial, calamity "too steep for two."[519]

The readiness in the "day of trouble." The Hebrew text implies that David habitually made God his refuge in times of trouble;[520] it was as natural to him as breathing. That habit made him always ready for trouble when it surfaced unexpectedly and/or suddenly. We all are only one phone call, knock on the door or doctor visit away from bad news. It behooves us to be prepared for it by adapting David's resolution.

The relief from the "day of trouble." "For thou wilt answer me." "This implies a fixed and steady assurance of mind, applicable not only to this case, but to all similar cases."[521] It never was a surprise to David when God answered his prayer, granting help and comfort. In spreading troubles before the Lord, in confident trust and reliance, expect Him to answer, just as David did. "The Psalmist can ask great things when he is well assured that He who has given much grace can give more grace."[522] R. G. Lee says, "Paul speaks of God as the God of hope (Romans 15:13 and 1 Thessalonians 4:13). Back of all our troubles is God; back of all our sorrows, all our sins, is God—God wanting to bring comfort in sorrow, God anxious to forgive and deliver us out of all our troubles and distresses. God is not feeding His children on false hopes."[523]

When the Rain Comes

We are out upon an ocean;
    We are far, far out from land,
And the billows' angry motion
    Beat and drive us from the strand;

But our hope is in our Captain.
    He the bark will steer aright,
So we'll journey on and trust Him
    Till we reach the "beacon light."

Oh, we'll trust Him, trust Him ever,
    And we'll toil without a frown,
For His love will fail us never.
    He'll reward us with a crown.

Fierce and wild the waves are dashing
    As the storm-king passes by
And the lurid lightning's flashing
    Brightly lumes the western sky;

But our hearts are calm and peaceful,
    Tho' our eyes are dimmed with tears,
Since in ev'ry time of trouble
    Jesus doth dispel our fears.

So by faith we'll travel ever,
    Battling with the tempest wild,
Heed His Word and falter never,
    For He'll guide and guard his child.

Oh, how sweet the music falling
    From our Father's glory throne
As we hear Him gently calling,
    "Weary one, come home; come home." ~ D. B. Towner (1883)

The revelation to the ungodly in the "day of trouble." David prays, "Show me evidence of your favor. Then those who hate me will see it and be ashamed" (Psalm 86:17 NET). "More than renewed help and protection were asked. The Psalmist entreated God to answer his prayer in such a conspicuous way as to impress the godless."[524] Pray that in our deliverance from or endurance in trouble the ungodly will see the hand of God at work and be converted.

Comfort for Troubled Hearts

The reasoning David used in prayer in "the day of trouble." David reasoned with God in prayer for help, saying, "For You, O LORD, have helped me and comforted me" (BSB). Charles Spurgeon taught believers ought to pray with *argument* or reasoning based upon the Word of God to make their case authoritatively. The inability to cite clear reasons as to why God should answer prayer may indicate their need of revising.[525] J. M. Boice says, "David buttresses his prayers with sound arguments."[526] His plea (argument) for help and comfort is based upon God's response in the past. In prayer, argue the intervention of God based upon His promises, loving-kindness and mercy, help provided in former days of trouble, and the glory it will bring to His name (Psalm 115:1).

When our way is hedged about us
    And our cross too great to bear,
How the soul to God is lifted
    Thro' the wondrous power of prayer.

Only trust the Savior's promise.
    Do His will, whate'er it be;
Then our faith will hear Him saying,
    "Come and find a rest in Me."

Oh, 'tis prayer that brings a blessing
    When our hope on Him is stayed,
Prayer that gives us joy and comfort,
    Tho' the answer be delayed.

Oh, the joy of sweet communion,
    When we know that He is near,
When we feel His love within us,
    Casting out our every fear.

Why, oh, why should we be troubled,
    When the Lord Himself declares,
If we call on Him believing,
    He will grant our fervent prayers. ~ Fanny Crosby (1903)

90
The Brevity of Life

"LORD, make me to know mine end, and the measure of my days, what it is; that I may know how frail I am" (Psalm 39:4). David's prayer is for understanding of his mortality. Being mindful of and influenced by the brevity of life prompts man to redeem the time that remains wisely and profitably. Man is prone to skirt the subject of death; it's the last thing desired to be discussed or considered. It was Caesar's Praetorian Guard that whispered as the parade roared down the avenue, "Remember, Caesar, thou art mortal."[527] Every man needs to hear those words personalized: Remember thou art mortal. You are not indestructible. You will die. Your rendezvous with death may be sudden and unexpected. Today thy soul may be required of thee.

Life, the Bible states, is like a mere "handbreadth" in duration (Psalm 39:5), the measurement of four fingers, "one of the smallest measures in the Hebrew system of measuring,"[528] and it passes as quickly "as a tale that is told" (Psalm 90:9). The hands on the wall clock or the watch, the display on the cell phone, the passing of one day to the next, the throb of the heart, the sudden death of others, and the growing decay of the body all are testament to life's frailty and brevity. The life of the strongest and healthiest may snap at any moment, just like that of the weakest and sickest. Every man, regardless of status or wealth, has a birthday and a death day.

> Knowing the frailty of life is important in order to prioritize life's affairs, prune away life's possessions, plan for life's closure, and prepare for life's departure.

David's prayer is for himself: 'Teach *me* to know my end, and the measure of *my* days.' All would do well to make that prayer for themself. But, alas, often we urge the prayer upon others while neglecting it for ourselves. Edward Young said, "All men think all men are mortal, but themselves." Charles Dickens pictures an attorney who was always harping on the need for people to make a will while healthy, only to die intestate (without a will).[529] Get the point?

David's prayer encompasses his personal cry for divine help to assist in knowing his end and the measure of his days. Of this need, Charles Simeon remarks, "Speculatively indeed he [David] knew well enough that man's days are but few at all events and quite uncertain as to their continuance, but the deep and practical and influential sense of it he had not in any degree equal to its importance; nor could he impress it on his own soul without the powerful assistance of God's Holy Spirit. Hence he poured forth this earnest petition to his God: 'Lord, make me to know my end! make me to know how frail I am!'"[530] Divine illumination is needed likewise by all to understand how little time remains. Knowing the frailty of life is important in order to prioritize life's affairs, prune away life's possessions, plan for life's closure, and prepare for life's departure.

Someday I'll embark on my final trip
    On an unknown, uncharted sea;
And now is the time to start building my ship,
    For to build it there's no one but me.

My ship must be seaworthy, sturdy and staunch,
    Lest the way be stormy and cold;
I must have a pilot and crew ere I launch,
    For that ship is to carry my soul.

The Carpenter of Nazareth furnished the plans
    For building the ship of my life;
If I can but imitate His skillful hands,
    I'll weather the worst storms and strife.

The material used must be truth, which prevails
    Against all the tempest of sin;
I must cut out the badness of hate from sails
    And use only good will toward men.

And then ere I go I must have faith in God,
    For He is the Way and the Light;
I call my ship Hope, and tho' the way be hard
    A compass of Love guides me right. ~ Edwin Youmans

91

When Friends Abandon and Forsake

"I look for someone to come and help me, but no one gives me a passing thought! No one will help me; no one cares a bit what happens to me" (Psalm 142:4 NLT). David was in sore distress ("my spirit was overwhelmed within me," Psalm 142:3) and "looked" for someone to *care for his soul* in vain. He had known many, but none *at this time* 'knew him.' It appears that even Jonathan on this occasion was not to be found or at least didn't come forward for fear of reprisal by David's enemies. C. H. Spurgeon paraphrases David: "'Whether I lived or died was no concern of anybody's. I was cast out as an outcast. No soul cared for my soul. I dwelt in no-man's-land, where none cared to have me, and none cared about me.' This is an ill plight—no place to lay our head and no head willing to find us a place."[531]

You may identify with David's aloneness upon the sickbed of affliction—no phone calls, cards, emails or visits; no cheering or comforting voices about the bed;

no friend in which to confide; none to depend upon for what you need. To be deserted by all and left alone to face perhaps life's greatest battle brings indescribable despair and horror. Spurgeon remarks, "The fact is that in times of desertion it is not true that no man did know us, *but no man would know us*. Their ignorance is willful."[532] And that's the *piercing dagger* to the heart. The willful neglect of able "friends" in the time of adversity is inexcusable by them and unalterable by us.

What, then, is the believers' only recourse for help in such an hour? It is that of David in a similar circumstance. "'But,' said he, 'I cried unto Thee, O Lord! who knowest me and carest for me when none else will, and wilt not fail me nor forsake me when men do'; for God is constant in His love."[533] With David, pray, "Be not far from me; for trouble is near; for there is none to help" (Psalm 22:11). Make thy God an all-sufficient refuge; in the 'shadow of His wings' are safety and peace. When family and friends abandon us, He takes us up (Psalm 27:10). He promises, "When thou passest through the waters, I will be with thee; and through the rivers, they shall not overflow thee" (Isaiah 43:2). He says, "Fear thou not; for I am with thee: be not dismayed; for I am thy God: I will strengthen thee; yea, I will help thee; yea, I will uphold thee with the right hand of my righteousness" (Isaiah 41:10), and "I will never leave thee, nor forsake thee" (Hebrews 13:5). With God in the equation, even in our aloneness we are not ever "alone."

No, never alone,
   No, never alone—
He promised never to leave me,
   Never to leave me alone.

No, never alone,
   No, never alone—
He promised never to leave me,
   Never to leave me alone. ~ Ludie Day Pickett (1897)

92

How to Get a Good Night's Sleep

"I laid me down and slept; I awaked; for the LORD sustained me" (Psalm 3:5). Sleep deprivation caused by anxiety (worry), fear, guilt or shame has a remedy. It is not to be found in the medicine cabinet but in the Lord. In sleep He will 'sustain me'; the Hebrew word for *sustain* means "to place an open hand under an object to give it support." When the saint sleeps, God holds him up in the 'palms of His hands' (as He does when the saint is awake) to assure his safety and rest.

Comfort for Troubled Hearts

I laid me down and slept. This testimonial of a peaceful sleep is most remarkable considering that while David slept Absalom was hard on his trail seeking to slay him. In his shoes, might you have done that?[534] Upon awaking the next morning, he said, "I awaked; for the Lord sustained me." In other words, 'I just had a real good sleep with all the foes seeking my destruction.'[535] H. A. Ironside says, "It is only when you hand everything over to God that such a thing can be possible."[536]

> And while I rest my weary head,
>   From cares and business free,
> 'Tis sweet conversing on my bed
>   With my own heart and Thee.
>
> Thus with my thoughts composed to peace,
>   I'll give mine eyes to sleep;
> Thy hand in safety keeps my days
>   And will my slumbers keep. ~ Isaac Watts (1719)

C. H. Spurgeon remarks, "The sleep of the body is the gift of God. He rocks the cradle for us every night, He draws the curtain of darkness, He bids the sun shut up his burning eyes, and then He comes and says, 'Sleep, sleep, my child; I give thee sleep.'"[537] He continues, "Not a man would close his eyes, did not God put His fingers on his eyelids; did not the Almighty send a soft and balmy influence over his frame which lulled his thoughts into quiescence, making him enter into that blissful state of rest which we call sleep."[538] The Lord is the believer's hiding place in the night as in the light. David declared, "Thou art my hiding place; thou shalt preserve me from trouble; thou shalt compass me about with songs of deliverance" (Psalm 32:7). Hide thyself confidently in the pavilion of God's embrace, closing out the world and its concerns, trusting Him to keep you secure and safe in sleep. Solomon states, "When thou liest down, thou shalt not be afraid: yea, thou shalt lie down, and thy sleep shall be sweet [peaceful, restful]" (Proverbs 3:24). David says, "I will both lay me down in peace, and sleep: for thou, LORD, only makest me dwell in safety" (Psalm 4:8).

> The sleep of the body is the gift of God. He rocks the cradle for us every night, he draws the curtain of darkness, he bids the sun shut up his burning eyes, and then he comes and says, "Sleep, sleep, my child; I give thee sleep."
> C.H. Spurgeon

Billy Graham defines peace as "the ability to sleep in the storm."[539] To sleep in peace requires peace with the peace-giver. Make sure 'it is well with thy soul.' Rid the mind of that which disturbs sleep (worry, fear, cares, etc.) through prayer.

When the Rain Comes

"Prayer is a good preparation for sleep."[540] Guard the mind from that which may disturb sleep (consciously and subconsciously). Solomon advises, "Keep thy heart with all diligence; for out of it are the issues of life" (Proverbs 4:23). Focus on "whatsoever things are true, whatsoever things are honest, whatsoever things are just, whatsoever things are pure, whatsoever things are lovely, whatsoever things are of good report; if there be any virtue, and if there be any praise, think on these things" (Philippians 4:8). Be mindful of that which is viewed or read and said at bedtime, for it has potential to affect the quality and quantity of sleep. Read and mediate upon the Scriptures in the "night watches" in preparation for sleep. Calm the soul in claiming the multitudinous promises of God (Proverbs 3:24; Psalm 3:3–6; Psalm 27; Psalm 32:7; Psalm 91:5; Philippians 4:7; John 14:27; Romans 8:32–39). Clay Smith, in the sermon *Hope: Hope 101,* well stated that we are to read the Bible to change the way we think, not just for knowledge.[541] Let what is read impact belief.

Wakeful nights become sleepful nights when the soul takes refuge in the arms of God. Fear, trouble, sorrow, worry (anxiety) spur insomnia, but the Lord is the antidote. He "makes sleep possible in an impossible situation."[542] W. S. Plumer writes, "The great fountain of peace, tranquility and *security is confidence in God.* He will sustain His servants at all times. The preserving care of God over us when we are asleep is truly wonderful."[543] And it is that which enables the believer, even in great trial and tribulation, to lie down and sleep like a "baby." Martin Luther one evening noted a bird quietly settling down for the night, and he exclaimed, "That little fellow preaches faith to us all! He takes hold of his twig, tucks his head under his wing, and goes to sleep, leaving God to think for him."[544]

Now the day is over;
> Night is drawing nigh.
Shadows of the evening
> Steal across the sky.

Jesus, give the weary
> Calm and sweet repose;
With Thy tend'rest blessing
> May my eyelids close.

Through the long night watches
> May Thine angels spread
Their white wings above me,
> Watching round my bed.

Comfort ev'ry suff'rer
  Watching late in pain;
Those who plan some evil
  From their sin restrain.

When the morning wakens,
  Then may I arise
Pure and fresh and sinless
  In Thy holy eyes.

Glory to the Father,
  Glory to the Father,
And to Thee, blest Spirit,
  While all ages run. ~ S. Baring-Gould (1865)

93
When God Is Silent

A New Testament story of God's silence is John 11:1–6. Mary and Martha, the sisters of Lazarus, notified Jesus that Lazarus was deathly ill. That's all. No request was made for Him to do anything, for such is unnecessary when making such news known to a true friend. (It's always expedient to "notify" the Great Physician when sick; He alone can comfort, heal, and cheer.) Unlike the two sisters, aren't we prone to "tell" Jesus what to do instead of trusting Him to do what He deems best for our good and His glory? Jesus' affection ("loveth" refers to a friend's love for a friend) for Lazarus prompted the two sisters to fully expect His arrival in Bethany immediately. (Note, not even those whom Christ loves are exempt from adversity, calamity and infirmity.) But that didn't happen. In fact, not a word was heard from Jesus about the news of Lazarus (John 11:6). And that silence in Mary's and Martha's home in Bethany certainly was perplexing and disturbingly painful—especially when Lazarus died (John 11:14).

In the silences of Christ there are unknown divine intentions and designs at play (as was the case with Mary and Martha). Benson says, "His lingering so long after their message came did not proceed from want of concern for His friends, but happened according to the counsels of His own wisdom, for the length of time that Lazarus lay in the grave put his death beyond all possibility of doubt and removed every suspicion of a fraud, and so afforded Jesus a fit opportunity of displaying the love He bore to Lazarus, as well as His own almighty power, in his unquestionable resurrection from the dead."[545]

When the Rain Comes

The silences of Christ don't mean that He is unconcerned or is failing to answer your cry for help. Even in His physical absence from Bethany, He was yet there orchestrating all that happened for His greater glory and their best good. The unseen hand of Christ starts to work at the first cry of desperation, only later to be evidenced visibly. G. Campbell Morgan said, "He is nigh when He seems absent. He is watching when He seems blind. He is active when He seems idle."[546]

The silences of Christ cause others to second-guess what's really happening in our life. See John 11:37. Job's friends were full of reasons for his great adversity and sorrow. But they were all wrong. Well-meaning friends may misinterpret the silences of Christ, as did the companions of Job.

The reason for the silences of Christ always will be manifest, so patiently wait. See John 11:45. Good always comes when Christ delays to intervene. It was when Jesus called Lazarus to "come forth" out of the tomb that the reason for His silences became manifest. Benson says, "Indeed, so incontestable a proof of His power and authority left them no room to doubt of His character. They knew that no impostor could perform any miracle, and so great a one as the resurrection of a person who had been in the grave four days was a miracle worthy of the Messiah himself."[547] The miracle convinced the doubters that Jesus was the Christ (substantiated His Messiahship), brought "many" souls to salvation (Jews), escalated Jesus' notoriety and mission (the Pharisees and chief priests were informed of the miracle by eyewitnesses), comforted the mourners, and instilled stronger faith in the saints. And now over 2,000 years later the church is still reaping the benefits of Lazarus' resurrection that were revealed by the silences of Christ. The silences of Christ likewise will yield bountiful benefits to you. Faint not at His delay. Trustingly and patiently await His arrival.

The silences of Christ seem to last longer than they actually do, based upon Heaven's timetable. Heaven's clock differs from ours. A thousand years with Christ are as a day, and a day as a thousand years. "The longest protraction of the fulfilment of a desire will seem but as a winking of an eye when we estimate duration as He estimates it."[548] Matthew Henry states, "Cast not away your confidence because God defers His performances. That which does not come in your time will be hastened in His time, which is always the more convenient season. God will work when He pleases, how He pleases, and by what means He pleases. He is not bound to keep our time, but He will perform His word, honor our faith, and reward them that diligently seek Him."[549] Though He may delay His response, it is always on time.

The silences of Christ often are painful and disturbing, as they were for Mary and Martha. The unknown purpose for the Christ's delay in responding is wearisome and grievous if strong faith (confident trust) in His best good for us is

194

absent. See Isaiah 54:10. Spurgeon memorably says that the Christian "believes Him to be too wise to err and too good to be unkind; he trusts Him where he cannot trace Him, looks up to Him in the darkest hour, and believes that all is well."[550] Interpret the silences of Christ with the backdrop of Calvary, and the heart will remain calm. Oswald Chambers states, "When you cannot hear God, you will find that He has trusted you in the most intimate way possible, with absolute silence— not a silence of despair, but one of pleasure, because He saw that you could withstand an even bigger revelation. If God has given you a silence, then praise Him—He is bringing you into the mainstream of His purposes. The actual evidence of the answer in time is simply a matter of God's sovereignty. Time is nothing to God."[551]

94

A Father's Bereavement

David's manner of coping with the death of his young son provides helpful guidance to every parent that experiences that horrendous grief of bereavement (2 Samuel 12:18–24).

David accepted the news of the child's death (2 Samuel 12:18–20). He returned to the responsibilities and requirements of life. "Accepting" your child's death is not forgetting him or her. You will never do that. Pressing forward in responsibilities and "life" is not saying you are over the death. That will never happen.

David understood that the child's departure to Heaven was at the Father's bidding (2 Samuel 12:14). Nathan informed David of God's will with regard to the child. The time of birth and the time of death are in God's hands. The former is understood while the latter often remains a mystery as to its why and when. It may be that your child was taken to Heaven to spare him/her from the "evil days" ahead. Isaiah stated, 'The good man perishes, the godly die before their time and no one seems to care or wonder why. No one seems to realize that God is taking them away from the evil days ahead. For the godly who die shall rest in peace' (Isaiah 57:1–2). What a thought! Death is God's grace at work protecting children who die from future heartache and hardship. J. R. Macduff said, "In this life we have an incomplete view of God's dealings, seeing His plan only half finished and underdeveloped. Yet once we stand in the magnificent temple of eternity, we will have the proper perspective and will see everything fitting gracefully together!"[552] See John 13:7.

Death may be viewed as a tapestry. Looking at its backside, only threads of various colors in a maze of confusion are seen. It's only when it's flipped over that its colors are seen blended together, forming a beautiful picture. In the death of a child, a parent only sees the backside of the weaving that consists of some black

When the Rain Comes

threads mixed with others in which there is no beauty, only dark sorrow mingled with confusion. But in Heaven, the full magnificent, beautiful tapestry will be seen, making clear the "why" of its particular weaving to the understanding and satisfaction of every grief-stricken parent.[553]

Not now, but in the coming years,
　　It may be in the better land,
We'll read the meaning of our tears,
　　And there, sometime, we'll understand.

Then trust in God thro' all the days;
　　Fear not, for He doth hold thy hand.
Though dark thy way, still sing and praise;
　　Sometime, sometime, we'll understand.

We'll catch the broken thread again
　　And finish what we here began;
Heav'n will the mysteries explain,
　　And then, ah, then, we'll understand.

We'll know why clouds instead of sun
　　Were over many a cherished plan,
Why song has ceased when scarce begun;
　　'Tis there, sometime, we'll understand.

God knows the way; He holds the key;
　　He guides us with unerring hand.
Sometime with tearless eyes we'll see;
　　Yes, there, up there, we'll understand.

~ Maxwell N. Cornelius (1891)

David (in essence) didn't ask "why" but "what now?" "When parents experience the death of a child [like David did]," remarks John MacArthur "one of the first questions they are likely to ask is, 'Why did my child have to die?' Generally, the emphasis in asking the question is, 'Why did *my* child have to die?' There is no easy answer to that question. The answer begins with the fact that life is marked by difficulty and sorrow. We live in a fallen world. We live in a world flawed by disease and sin. Trouble comes to us as part of our human condition....God is omnipotent. He is also omniscient. As a result, some of His purposes and plans we cannot know this side of eternity. God may have allowed a child to die for reasons that will never be understood—reasons that may involve the lives of the parents, the lives of siblings, the life of the child himself, the lives of others unknown by the parents or child.

"There is a question even more potent than the question 'Why did my child have to die?' That question is 'What does God desire for me to do in the midst of this tragedy?' The question of 'Why?' has no satisfactory answer. The question of 'What now?' can turn a person from grief to action, from loss to healing, from sorrow to joy, and from feelings of utter devastation to feelings of purpose."[554]

Comfort in a child's death may be gained from four considerations. "Let us consider *to whom* they have gone, *from what* they have been taken, *for what* they have been taken, and *how this bereavement* will appear to us when we come to die ourselves."[555]

David embraced religious hope (2 Samuel 12:23b). He anticipated reunion with his son in Heaven. "Let the hope 'full of immortality' be our stay in our dark hour. No 'counterfeit immortality,' but the continuance, in a higher sphere of being, of the conscious, complete, personal existence, now certified by Christ's resurrection. This can give patience in suffering and solace in death."[556] It's okay for the Christian parent to cry bitterly at the death of a child as long as "ye sorrow not, even as others which have no hope" (1 Thessalonians 4:13). Grieving parents finds solace in precious memories, but utmost comfort is to be found upon the promise of life after death with Jesus and their child. Live in expectation and anticipation of that glorious day.

David believed he would recognize his child in Heaven (2 Samuel 12:23). Your child in Heaven retains his personal identity. Take comfort in knowing that in Heaven your child will know you as being his parent as you will know him being your child. W. A. Criswell, in *Heaven,* states that one's personality survives in Heaven, that we each will be who we are now but without the baggage of sin and imperfection.[557] Further, Criswell states, "We shall not know less of each other in Heaven; we shall know more. We shall possess our individual names in Heaven. We shall be known as individuals. You will be you; I shall be I; we shall be we. Personality and individuality exist beyond the grave."[558]

David leaned heavily upon his own future immortality (2 Samuel 12:23). "I can't bring him back to me, but I can go to him." See Psalm 17:15 and Psalm 16:9–11. Every parent ought to say the same with all certainty. Apart from Christ there will be no reunion with our child. The chiefest comfort in the death of a child hinges upon your soul's estate.

David understood that continual incessant grieving could not bring the child back (2 Samuel 12:22–23). As long as the child was alive, he prayed and fasted in hope of the child's survival. Upon the child's death, that stopped. "But now he is dead, wherefore should I fast? can I bring him back again?" Nothing can be done to recapture the life of your beloved child—no amount of fasting, praying, anguish,

When the Rain Comes

anger, deprivation, or weeping. David had to reconcile himself to the fact the child was dead and "move on" with life, as difficult as that was. You must do the same. With God's enablement, hope, Christian friends, the church, and your child's memories etched in your heart, the journey in grief progressively gets easier and more bearable. But it never is completely healed until you get to Heaven. Grief that is currently visible will in time be borne "invisibly."

David was misunderstood in his recovery from grief (2 Samuel 12:21). David's response to his son's death was questioned by others (and some will still do this). In the face of such inquisitiveness be dauntless. All grieve differently, even the parents of a deceased child, so don't expect your spouse to grieve like you do, and don't think you must grieve like others who have experienced the death of a child.

David's grief was enveloped in peace (2 Samuel 12:20). He went into the house of the Lord and worshiped. Peace flows from worship, communion and praise (Isaiah 26:3). Horatio Spafford and his family decided to join the D. L. Moody team on an evangelistic crusade in Europe. Spafford's wife and four daughters departed without him; he was to join them in a later. Tragically, the ship on which they were aboard collided with another vessel and sank within twenty minutes. Spafford's wife, Anna, was the family's only survivor. Ten days later, from the hospital, Anna sent her husband a message that consisted of two words: "Saved alone." He was devastated and shook uncontrollably. Major Whittle, Spafford's friend, consoled him and traveled with him to France to see his wife. En route, the captain awoke him *at the spot where his children drowned*, as he had requested. Upon looking into the dark, cold water that now was their grave, he wept. He then sat down and penned the words of a hymn that has brought comfort and hope to many in their hour of grief.

When peace like a river attendeth my way,
    When sorrows like sea billows roll,
Whatever my lot, Thou hast taught me to say,
    "It is well, it is well with my soul."

Though Satan should buffet, though trials should come,
    Let this blest assurance control,
That Christ has regarded my helpless estate
    And hath shed His own blood for my soul.

And, Lord, haste the day when my faith shall be sight,
    The clouds be rolled back as a scroll.
The trump shall resound, and the Lord shall descend—
    Even so, it is well with my soul.

Horatio Spafford, in his devastation, trusted God with his loss and grief. Every brokenhearted parent that leans on Jesus for repose will discover a peace in the midst of great grief that passeth all understanding.

David comforted Bathsheba (2 Samuel 12:24). Gender impacts the grieving process. Spouses must seek to understand each other's needs and lovingly meet them. "Parts of the death necessities can devastate you or your partner," Elizabeth Brown warns in her book *Surviving the Loss of a Child*. "Each should shoulder the responsibility for needs he or she can handle emotionally."[559] Lighten the load on your spouse, even if it seems minute. Focus on each other, making the relationship a priority—guard against injury to the marriage. Healing also is aided by looking outward to the hurts of others. Use your pain as gain to console parents that experience the death of a child.

> E'en for the dead I will not bind my soul to grief;
> Death cannot long divide.
> For is it not as though the rose that climbed my garden wall
> Has blossomed on the other side?
>
> Death doth hide
> But not divide;
> Thou art but on Christ's other side!
> Thou art with Christ, and Christ with me;
> In Christ united still are we.[560] ~ Unknown

George Müller said, "When sometimes all has been dark, exceedingly dark, with reference to my service among the saints, judging from natural appearances; yea, when I should have been overwhelmed indeed in grief and despair (had I looked at things after the outward appearance); at such times I have sought to encourage myself in God by laying hold in faith on His mighty power, His unchangeable love, and His infinite wisdom, and I have said to myself, *God is able and willing to deliver me, if it be good for me; for it is written: 'He that spared not his own Son, but delivered him up for us all, how shall he not with him also freely give us all things?'* (Romans 8:32)."

95

A Mother's Bereavement

"Run now, I pray thee, to meet her, and say unto her, Is it well with thee? is it well with thy husband? is it well with the child? And she answered, It is well" (2 Kings 4:26). The story of the Shunammite mother provides comfort and solace for every grieving mother (and father) in the death of a child. They find this comfort in identifying with her faith, empathizing with her loss and resolving their grief.

She was not exempt from bereavement in her home. The only child (a son, maybe three or four years old) of a Shunammite mother (though she was a "Christian") suddenly fell ill in the morning (while with his father playing in the field among the reapers) and was dead at noon. The child around whom her life centered, who was her heartthrob, and whom her affections engulfed was dead, according to the divine purpose of God which was then unknown. (The father, like the mother, "idolized" and treasured him.) The boy was the sunshine and happiness of the Shunem home, but now it was filled with darkness and gloom. Like the Shunammite mother, even the saintliest of mothers is not exempt from bereavement in the home.

She was not removed from grievous sorrow. "And the man of God said, Let her alone; for her soul is vexed within her" (2 Kings 4:27). The grief that she bore was so heavy that it was displayed (countenance) before Elisha. There is no grief like a mother's grief over the death of her child, especially if it is the only child as in this case. It's okay, even important, for Christian mothers to grieve the loss of a child. "There may be sorrow, there must be sorrow, under the afflictions and bereavements of life; only it should not be despondent sorrow, nor rebellious sorrow, nor murmuring sorrow, but sorrow submissive and sanctifying, like that of this woman."[561] It's okay for Christian mothers to cry. Jesus wept (John 11:35). Mary wept (John 20:15). David wept (Psalm 6:6). Ruth wept (Ruth 1:14). Jeremiah wept (Jeremiah 13:17). Paul sanctioned grief over death, provided we "sorrow not, even as others which have no hope" (1 Thessalonians 4:13).

> The heart may be heavy yet happy if it is known that God's sovereign hand purposed the death of our child.

She was not embittered toward God in her sorrow. The Shunammite mother acquiesces to the will of God.[562] While suffering horrendous grief, she tells the man of God, 'It is well with my soul.' The heart may be heavy yet happy if it is known that God's sovereign hand purposed the death. J. R. Miller, in the sermon "Afterward You Will Understand," states: "But all the mysteries in our lives will someday be revealed. They will not always, be inexplicable to us. 'What I am doing—you do not understand now; but afterward you will understand' (John 13:7). We do not see now how this or that experience can be well and can do good—but after a time, the mystery is explained.

"The plow cuts mercilessly through the field. It seems only destructive. But afterward a harvest of golden grain waves—where all seemed ruin at first. It is only afterward that many of God's providences can be clearly understood. It takes time for the full meaning to be wrought out. We do not know in the days of sorrow what 'shining blessing' will be revealed as the final outcome. We do not see in midwinter the roses that are hidden under the snow which after a while will unfold their beauty. God has given a distinct promise that the mysteries of life will be made clear. Sometimes they are clarified soon, while at other times they are left unknown. The fact is that death sometimes occurs without explanation here and now. But another life awaits the believer in Heaven where there is enough time for the deepest mysteries to be made plain."[563]

She was not controlled by her grief. Instead of allowing grief to control her, she sought to control the grief by consulting the man of God immediately for comfort and strength. Elisha was the "mouth of God" to this mother, and therefore, she sought him out for consolation and guidance (2 Kings 4:24–25). Every grieving mother ought to avail herself of the counsel and comfort afforded from the minister of God. As God's "mouthpiece," he provides the healing balm of Gilead that will soothe the heartache and pain, granting assurance of a reunion in Heaven. Grieving mothers today, unlike the Shunammite mother, also have the Holy Spirit residing in them upon which to lean for comfort and consolation (John 14:26).

She was not hopeless about the future. She told Elisha, 'It is well with the child.' She did not know all that we know about the resurrection of the dead and the splendor and majesty of Heaven.[564] But she was confident of one thing; she would see her child again in the hereafter. Therefore, she could say, 'It is well with the child.' Wow! What faith displayed by a grieving mother! Every grieving Christian mother finds consolation and peace in that same hope (certainty). "All dead children will be brought back to life. Only the body dies; the soul lives forever."[565] Jesus said, "I am the resurrection, and the life: he that believeth in me, though he were dead, yet shall he live" (John 11:25).

> The little hands are folded like white lilies on his breast;
> The busy feet, so noisy once, are evermore at rest.
> The snowdrift of his little bed is stainless, smooth, and still,
> As if waiting for the laddie back, his cozy place to fill.
>
> The hobbyhorse is saddled and gives forth a hearty neigh,
> But the rider does not heed it, for he is far away.
> He is dwelling with the angels, and though I may be late,
> I know he'll not forget me but be watching at the gate.
>
> His toys are laid upon the shelf; his clothes are put away;
> The little rug is folded up on which he knelt to pray.
> His empty chair is by the hearth, as if expecting him,
> And when I see the vacant chair, my eyes with tears are dim.

When the Rain Comes

I listen, wait and listen, for a voice that never calls,
For a step along the hallway, but the footstep never falls.
But this comfort I have always, that though I may be late,
I know he'll not forget me but be watching at the gate.[566] ~ Unknown

96

A Refuge for Every Trial

"The name of the LORD is a strong tower: the righteous runneth into it, and is safe" (Proverbs 18:10). The "name of the Lord" (reveals His character, nature, attributes) is a "strong tower" (a high wall; place of safety in the storms of life): the "righteous" (upright; Christian) "runneth" (flees into it; escapes from the pursuit of the storm or trouble) "into it, and is safe" (guarded, protected from harm). A tower in biblical days provided protection for people in times of different types of emergencies. For example, when an enemy was about to attack, the inhabitants would run into this strong tower and be kept safe. God's name is like that strong tower for the believer, providing a hiding, helping and healing place in emergencies (adversity, infirmity, bereavement). It is so deep that no bomb can undermine it, so thick that no missile can penetrate it, so high that no ladder can scale it or arrow of Hell reach it. The psalmist says, "For in the time of trouble he shall hide me in his pavilion: in the secret of his tabernacle shall he hide me; he shall set me up upon a rock" (Psalm 27:5).

His very *names*, Alexander Smellie states, are the saint's promises.[567]

In times of need run into the Strong Tower of *Jehovah-Jireh,* our provider and supplier.

In times of hurt or sickness run into the Strong Tower of *Jehovah-Rapha*, our healer and helper.

In times of temptation or attack by Satan run into the Strong Tower of *Jehovah-Nissi,* our deliverer and protector.

In times of trouble, grief or fear run into the Strong Tower of *Jehovah-Shalom,* our peace and hope giver.

In times of needed comfort run into the Strong Tower of *Jehovah-Raah,* our caring and sustaining Shepherd.

In times of sin run into the Strong Tower of *Jehovah-Maccad-Deshem,* our sanctifier and restorer.

In times of despair and bewilderment run into the Strong Tower of *EL-EL-YON,* the Sovereign ruler of the universe who controls all that touches our lives (nothing ever catches Him by surprise).

"The rich man's wealth is his strong city, and as an high wall in his own conceit" (Proverbs 18:11).

Foolishly the rich (ungodly rich) believe that which is possessed is a sure defense against life's storms and God's judgments. The mere possession of wealth and its "commodities" make it hard for them not to trust in them.[568] But the notion that the 'abundance of things possessed' is the shield and protector of a man is delusional and disastrous.[569] See Psalm 20:7. All attempts to erect castles of refuge are futile, regardless of the material used in their construction, and great will be their collapse when the rain comes (Matthew 7:26–27). His Name (trust and reliance upon Jesus) is man's only impenetrable fortress and strong tower (protection, peace, strength, and hope) that can endure *when the rain comes down*. "The Lord is like a strong tower, where the righteous can go and be safe" (Proverbs 18:10 GNT).

97
Let Me Die the Death of the Righteous

Balaam knew that death was inevitable. He saw how both the ungodly and the righteous (Christian) die and exclaimed, "Let me die the death of the righteous, and let my last end be like his!" (Numbers 23:10). Shortly after making the declaration, Balaam died in battle fighting the very "righteous" men that he wanted to imitate in death. See Joshua 13:22.

Observations:

(1. "By the *righteous man*," states C. H. Spurgeon, "we mean the man who has believed in Jesus and so has been covered with Christ's righteousness, and moreover has by the power of the Holy Spirit received a new heart, so that his actions are righteous both towards God and man."[570]

(2. Both the righteous and wicked die "outwardly" similarly. It is that which happens upon death and afterward that is different. The ungodly will be eternally separated in Hell from God and loved saved ones; the believer will reside in Heaven with Christ and the family of God forever. "My last end be like his" refers to the Christian's resurrection to newness of life in Heaven. Balaam didn't want to experience eternal damnation in separation from God.

(3. Resolve or serious desire to die the death of the righteous is commendable but not effectual. There is an old proverb which says, "Wishers and woulders make bad housekeepers." Mere hoping and wanting to die the death of the believer won't make it happen. It's the height of foolishness to think that a person who lives a bad life can die a good death by making a resolve that it be so, as Balaam did. It would be far more possible for a thorn bush to resolve to bear luscious grapes.

(4. Conviction apart from application is utterly futile. Balaam believed mentally in the honorable and peaceful death of the righteous and their afterlife but failed to embrace it spiritually in the heart. To possess knowledge of what is true and right without properly utilizing it is useless. See Revelation 2:14.

(5. Most worldly men want to die with the peace, joy, comfort, honor, hope and anticipation of the redeemed. They want to face death courageously and calmly in the arms of Christ, as the saints do, but without any change in conduct or commitment to Christ. "Charles, our people die well," said John Wesley to his brother. And it is that which the ungodly envy in the righteous. Billy Graham said, "I have talked to doctors and nurses who have held the hands of dying people, and they say there is often as much difference between the death of a Christian and a non-Christian as there is between Heaven and Hell."[571]

(6. Through the lips of the ungodly, spiritual truth may flow. Balaam, though wicked, uttered sound biblical theology about death and the future life. Therefore, refuse not all that the unsaved say, whether or not they understand all that it means.

(7. The ungodly may die the death of the godly provided he expresses repentance for sin and exhibits faith in Jesus Christ (Acts 20:21). Such was the case with the penitent thief on the Cross (Luke 23:42–43). A far better and wiser prayer for Balaam and others like him to utter is this: "Help me be prepared to die the death of the righteous through trust in you, Christ Jesus, and by leading a devoted life of holiness as they do."

(8. Balaam's desire (induced by the Holy Spirit) was intended to prompt him to prepare for death. Man must not dismiss the "flashes" of appetite for the spiritual that seemingly arise from out of nowhere, prompted by nothing. Such moments of enlightenment or illumination must be viewed as generated by the Holy Spirit to stimulate immediate action with regard to salvation, service or surrender. Heedlessness suffocates them and harms the soul. "Impressions not followed blow away like the blossoms are blown from the trees in the orchards in the springtime. Convictions not followed get fainter and die."[572]

You, like Balaam, desire to die the death of the righteous, but are you making preparation for such a death by placing your soul confidently in Christ's charge as Lord and Savior? There is a world of difference between "desire" and "decision."

98

Take the Harp off the Willow Tree

"By the rivers of Babylon, there we sat down, yea, we wept, when we remembered Zion. We hanged our harps upon the willows in the midst thereof. For there they that carried us away captive required of us a song; and they that wasted us required of us mirth, saying, Sing us one of the songs of Zion. How shall we sing the LORD'S song in a strange land?" (Psalm 137:1–4). The "LORD'S song" includes the Psalms, hymns and spiritual songs, all of which are the making of melody in the heart to the Lord (Ephesians 5:19). The "LORD'S song" may be "sung" verbally or mentally. It was this song that was silenced among the saints in Babylonian captivity due to heaviness of heart (grief and sorrow over their estate and that of Jerusalem).

Without a "song" to sing (in a "strange land", a solemn place where the believer's song is silenced by tribulation and trials), he hangs his "harp" upon the willows at the river's bank (for he has no heart to use it) and tearfully inquires "How shall we sing the LORD'S song in a strange land?" What a good question! While languishing upon a sickbed ("a strange land"), approaching death or gripped with great sorrow over the death of a loved one, how is the saint to "sing" the song of Zion? How is it that martyrs of old while dying for the faith still had a "song" as they were nailed to a cross, thrust into a den of lions, beheaded by the guillotine, or burned at the stake? How is it that saints like Fanny Crosby, blinded in infancy by a medical mistake; Joni Eareckson Tada, who through a swimming accident became a paraplegic; Horatio Spafford, whose children were drowned at sea when crossing the Atlantic; Carman Licciardello, in battling myeloma cancer; and Dave Walton, afflicted with cirrhosis of the liver, all maintained (maintain) their "song" despite the pain, suffering, sickness and sorrow? Along with multitudes of others, in their *strange land,* these testify with Job, "Though he slay me, yet will I trust in him" (Job 13:15). Sword, guillotine, lion, disease, sorrow and even death was (is) unable to silence their song.

Suffering saints like these answer the question, "How shall we sing the LORD'S song in a strange land?" with the question, "Why shouldn't we sing the Lord's song in a strange land?" They continue, "In this land God is the same God as He is outside it; not one iota has changed with regard to His loving guardianship and tender compassionate care. Every promise of the Bible remains true—possession of forgiveness of sin and eternal life through the Savior's redeeming blood has not been altered; the defiled garments of sin are still washed clean; the saints' citizenship in Heaven is unchanged; God yet remains in sovereign control of all that happens to the saint; the Holy Spirit's ministry of comfort and help to the believer is unabated; and God's mercies are still new every morning." These stupendous facts ought to cause the heart to erupt in praise songs to the King, even in sojourning in a "strange land," and to say with David, "I will bless the LORD at all times: his praise shall continually be in my mouth" (Psalm 34:1).

Matthew Henry says that the Israelites were probably at fault in hanging their harps on the trees, "for praising God is never out of season; it is His will that we should in everything give thanks."[573] See 1 Thessalonians 5:18. Keep your harp ready and tuned. Don't allow that which crushes the heart to silence the song.

When the Rain Comes

My heart can sing when I pause to remember
    A heartache here is but a steppingstone
Along a trail that's winding always upward.
    This troubled world is not my final home.

The things of earth will dim and lose their value,
    If we recall they're borrowed for a while,
And things of earth that cause the heart to tremble,
    Remembered there will only bring a smile.

This weary world with all its toil and struggle
    May take its toll of misery and strife.
The soul of man is like a waiting falcon;
    When it's released, it's destined for the skies.

But until then my heart will go on singing,
    Until then with joy I'll carry on,
Until the day my eyes behold the city,
    Until the day God calls me home. ~ Stuart Hamblen (1908–1989)

99

Don't Be Afraid of Bad News

Saint and sinner alike are only a phone call, knock on the door, doctor visit, or letter away from hearing bad news. Though both receive bad news, the Christian's reaction should be different than that of the unbeliever. The psalmist says the believer, "does not fear bad news. He is confident; he trusts in the Lord" (Psalm 112:7 NET). The man that exhibits a "fixed" trust in the Lord is not frightened when bad news is received.[574] Why?

(1. Whatever *rain* comes is permitted by God. Nothing can touch him without God's knowledge. There are no accidents or mistakes with regard to what happens to a Christian.

(2. With the rain God always provides an umbrella of His unfailing love, care, and comfort to enable us to endure it victoriously.

(3. He trusts the love of God for him, which banishes fear. John says, "There is no fear in love; but perfect love casteth out fear: because fear hath torment. He that feareth is not made perfect in love" (1 John 4:18).

(4. If God allows it, then there is an unseen purpose in it that will glorify God and edify the believer (and perhaps others).

(5. Whatever "evil" befalls, he knows that God will work good out of it (Romans 8:28).

(6. It is impossible for the "evil" that comes to take away the soul's greatest treasures: salvation; the presence, protection and promises of God; and a Home in Heaven (Philippians 1:6).

(7. God has our "back" in whatever happens. Isaiah says, "For the Lord will go ahead of you; yes, the God of Israel will protect you from behind" (Isaiah 52:12b NLT). Moses said, "And the Lord, he it is that doth go before thee; he will be with thee, he will not fail thee, neither forsake thee: fear not, neither be dismayed" (Deuteronomy 31:8).

The bottom line? Not to be afraid at the arrival of bad news is *contingent upon confident, trustfulness in the Lord*. Spurgeon states, "Those who have laid hold on Christ Jesus and are resting in the Father's love and power have no reason to be disquieted. Should all Hell be unmuzzled and all earth be unhinged, they may rejoice with a joy undamped by carnal fear or earthly sorrow."[575] A. E. Hooper remarks, "No doubt the Messenger of Sorrow will knock at all our doors, for it is not his custom to pass any by; but while we listen to his message, we can lift our glance over his shoulder; and seeing Jesus, who has overcome the world, we call, 'Be of good cheer' and say, 'Whatever thy news may be,...our heart standeth fast and trusteth in the Lord.'"[576]

100
The Right Look When All Looks Bad

"I will lift up mine eyes unto the hills, from whence cometh my help. My help cometh from the Lord, which made heaven and earth" (Psalm 121:1–2). *What is the right look when all looks bad?* In times of trouble or crisis, look up to Heaven with solicitation, meditation and expectation. Look up beyond the dark and gloomy clouds of life's vale of tears to the bright and vibrant sunshine of God's bountiful peace, comfort and help, and be lifted by that look of faith. David, in the mud and mire of the deep pit of hopeless difficulty, looked up, and that is what brought him out (Psalm 40:1–2). Instantly his song of gloom and despair was changed to a new song of praise and jubilation (Psalm 40:3). *Look up,* and despondency will change to blissfulness, the storm to calm, the panic to peace, the fear to trust, the sorrow to serenity, and the despair to hope. Looking up brings relief to life's pressures, rescue from life's burdens, release from life's sorrows and remedy to life's problems. "Looking unto Jesus" (Hebrews 12:2) is man's supreme and sure help in the hour of need and secret of contentment in times of turmoil inwardly and outwardly.

"There can come no difficulty, no entanglement, from which He cannot deliver us; there can come no sorrow in which He will not be able to support us."[577]

When the Rain Comes

Saints that have proven this to be true testify with David, saying, "My help cometh from the LORD." They declare with Matthew Henry, "Shall I depend upon the strength of the hills? upon princes and great men? No; my confidence is in God only. We must lift up our eyes above the hills. We must see all our help in God; from Him we must expect it, in His own way and time. It is almighty wisdom that contrives and almighty power that works the safety of those that put themselves under God's protection."[578]

The promise linked to the looking up is that of *divine keeping*. He "shall preserve [keep] thy going out and thy coming in" (Psalm 121:8). So much emphasis does the psalmist place upon the safekeeping of the saint that no fewer than six times in the psalm's last five verses is it reiterated. "Going out" is a synonym for sorrow; "coming in," for gladness and joy.[579] In life's ups and downs, ins and outs, calm and calamity, and gladness and grief, God will be faithful to constantly watch over and protect His own. C. H. Spurgeon says, "As a king keeps his jewels, God hides His people in the casket of His power and protects them with all His wisdom and strength."[580]

My wife often reminds me to "look up" (physically, for posture). Looking down is a habit I formed in my running over the years (lest I stumble or step on a snake) that has subconsciously carried over to the rest of life. As concerns in running have prompted my downward looking, so often the cares and troubles of life do the same spiritually to believers. Mentally and spiritually they therefore need to be reminded to look up beyond the hills whence cometh their help.

Saints, additionally, are instructed in the Holy Scriptures to look up for Christ's return: "Lift up your heads; for your redemption draweth nigh" (Luke 21:28)! Look up to Christ in prayer: "My voice shalt thou hear in the morning, O LORD; in the morning will I direct my prayer unto thee, and will look up" (Psalm 5:3). Look up to see the fields white unto harvest: "Say not ye, There are yet four months, and then cometh harvest? behold, I say unto you, Lift up your eyes, and look on the fields; for they are white already to harvest" (John 4:35). Look up to behold the majesty of God: "In the year that king Uzziah died I saw also the Lord sitting upon a throne, high and lifted up, and his train filled the temple" (Isaiah 6:1). And look up to Christ for salvation: "Look unto me, and be ye saved, all the ends of the earth: for I am God, and there is none else" (Isaiah 45:22). There is much to see, learn, adore and receive by looking up—and so much to miss by looking down. Thus, keep looking up, my brothers and sisters!

> Keep looking up; keep looking up.
> The mists will clear away.
> In God's own time His loving hand
> Will brighten up the day.

Keep looking up; keep looking up.
The eternal hills are there.
Far, far beyond these gloomy clouds
Are treasures rich and rare.

Keep looking up; keep looking up,
With Faith's aspiring eye.
The promise is that help will come
From Him who dwells on high.

Lift up thine eyes, lift up thine eyes,
And take the outstretched hand.
'Tis Jesus bids thee struggle on,
And victor thou shalt stand. ~ G. Tabor Thompson (1886)

"When something bad happens, you have three choices. You can let it define you, you can let it destroy you, or you can let it strengthen you."[581]

101
The Strength in Waiting on God

"Wait on the LORD: be of good courage, and he shall strengthen thine heart: wait, I say, on the LORD" (Psalm 27: 14). No one is more qualified to give counsel on the practice of waiting on the Lord than David was.[582] He gives keen insights into its five aspects in the text cited.

The what of waiting. "To wait" (based on the Hebrew language) means an expecting, eager, hopeful and robust waiting upon the Lord. Swanson says it involves looking "forward with confidence to that which is good and beneficial, often with a focus of anticipation in a future event."[583] Thus, to wait upon the Lord is to await His response to life's pressing circumstances and hardships with confident expectation of His divine intervention for the best good.

The who of waiting. Wait upon the Lord, for it is He alone that foresees that which is best for us and is able to bring it to pass. The psalmist says that our "expectation is from him" (Psalm 62:5). Albert Barnes remarks, "Often we are in such circumstances that we feel our only 'expectation'—our *only hope*—is in God. All our strength fails, all our resources are exhausted, our fellowmen cannot or will not aid us, our own efforts seem to be vain, our plans are frustrated, and we are shut up to the conclusion that God alone can help us."[584]

The when of waiting. In times of trial, adversity, disheartenment, sorrow and lack of wisdom as to what to do, wait (rely) upon the Lord for help.

209

When the Rain Comes

The how of waiting. Charles Spurgeon wrote, "It may seem an easy thing to wait, but it is one of the postures which a Christian soldier learns not without years of teaching."[585]

(1. Wait courageously. That is, "be stout, strong, bold, alert."[586] Don't act cowardly in the wake of hardship, sorrow and sickness. In waiting, don't let the difficulty that afflicts you deflate your trust in God. Keep facing it bravely. Confidence in eternal verities gives us courage to face the difficulties and trials of life and to manifest the fruits of the Spirit (Galatians 5:22–23).

(2. Wait prayerfully. Present the need and plead the promises.

(3. Wait patiently. "Believe that if He keeps you tarrying even till midnight, yet He will come at the right time."[587]

(4. Wait confidently. Doubt neither His willingness nor ability to come to your assistance, though His help seems tardy. Spurgeon says, "He hangeth the world upon nothing; shall He who doth this be unable to support His children? Shall He be unfaithful to His word for want of power? Who is it that restrains the tempest? Doth not He ride upon the wings of the wind and make the clouds His chariots and hold the ocean in the hollow of His hand? How can He fail thee?"[588]

(5. Wait persistently. See Luke 11:8. Don't waver in the waiting; wait until the Lord answers.

The why (benefit) of waiting. Wait on the Lord that He may "strengthen" thy heart to grow firm and strong, to be fortified against that which oppresses, opposes, obstructs, or overwhelms. Paul was granted strength (supernatural enabling) with regard to the thorn in his flesh that afflicted him sorely (2 Corinthians 12:9), and its pain (and that of other afflictions) turned into pleasure (2 Corinthians 12:10). Now that's worth waiting upon the Lord to attain!

Waiting dispels despondency, dread, despair and defeat. Waiting comforts (instills peace), enables (empowers), clarifies (illuminates the mind about the will of God), emboldens (infuses bravery sufficient for the challenge) and awakens the soul to God's perspective and purpose. Henry Blackaby and Claude King offer great advice on what to do while you wait: "Let God use times of waiting to mold and shape your character. Let God use those times to purify your life and make you into a clean vessel for His service."[589] Chuck Swindoll states, "We don't like waiting, but that's when God does some of His best work on our souls."[590]

A minister, often interrupted by annoying knocks on his door by fleeing children, hung under the knocker the polite request, "Please don't knock unless you wait for an answer." Let's not "trouble" God with our requests (knocks at His door) unless we are willing to wait for Him to answer.[591] Bring your troubles to the Lord, and then wait upon Him to grant rescue, relief or remedy. Rest assured He will answer the knock.

March on, my soul, with strength;
    March forward, void of fear.
He who has led will lead
    Through each succeeding year;
And as you journey on your way,
His hand shall hold you day by day. ~ William Wright (1859–1920)

102
Don't Look for the Undertaker; Look for the Uppertaker

I have great and glorious news! Some who are now alive may never die. The Bible says, "For this we say unto you by the word of the Lord, that we which are alive and remain unto the coming of the Lord shall not prevent them which are asleep. For the Lord himself shall descend from heaven with a shout, with the voice of the archangel, and with the trump of God: and the dead in Christ shall rise first: Then we which are alive and remain shall be caught up together with them in the clouds, to meet the Lord in the air: and so shall we ever be with the Lord" (1 Thessalonians 4:15–17). Stop looking for the signs; start listening for the shout of Christ's return. Stop looking for the undertaker; start looking for the Uppertaker!

Jesus promised to return for His bride, the church of the redeemed (John 14:1–6).

The time of His return is only known to God. Jesus said, "But of that day and hour knoweth no man, no, not the angels of heaven, but my Father only" (Matthew 24:36).

There are in excess of 320 references to the Second Coming in the Bible; one of every twenty-five verses in the New Testament refers this event. See Matthew 24:30; 24:42–51; 25:31; 2 Thessalonians 1:7–8; 1 Thessalonians 4:13–18; 5:2–3 and Titus 2:13.

At the coming of Christ Jesus to earth, all of nature will burst into resounding joy in welcome (Psalm 96:11–12). Nature supplies the "music"; the saints provide the "song." What a glorious day that will be when King Jesus returns!

Forest and flower exclaim;
    Mountain and meadow the same;
All earth and Heaven proclaim,
    Jesus is coming again. ~ John W. Peterson (1972)

There are two phases of the coming of Christ. The first is the "Rapture" in which Jesus comes *for* the saints and meets them in the *air*. It is at this time that the saint will be changed in a twinkling of an eye to be like Jesus (1 Corinthians 15:51–52), receive rewards at the Judgment Seat (1 Corinthians 4:5), and *partake* of the Marriage Supper of the Lamb. See Revelation 19:7–10). The second phase is when He comes *with* His saints to *earth* to set up His Kingdom of 1,000 years, known as the Millennial reign. See Revelation 19:11–15.

At Christ's coming man will be judged. See Hebrews 9:27. The judgment will be just and fair based upon His truth. See Psalm 96:13. The Bible does not speak of a general judgment for all mankind. There will be two judgments: one for the believer (Judgment Seat of Christ, 2 Corinthians 5:9–10) and one for the unbeliever (Great White Throne, Revelation 20:11–15). The Christian is not judged with regard to his salvation, but his conduct and service. See 1 Corinthians 3:11–15. Results of this judgment determine the Christian's reward. See Revelation 22:12 and Revelation 4:10. The unbeliever at the Great White Throne will be judged according to his sin and rejection of Christ as Lord and Savior, receiving the condemnation of eternal torment in Hell. See Revelation 21:8.

Man's eternal destiny is forever sealed or settled at Christ's appearing.

Lift up the trumpet, and loud let it ring:
    Jesus is coming again!
Cheer up, ye pilgrims; be joyful and sing,
    "Jesus is coming again!"

Echo it, hilltops; proclaim it, ye plains:
    Jesus is coming again!
Coming in glory, the Lamb that was slain—
    Jesus is coming again!

Heavings of earth, tell the vast, wondering throng,
    Jesus is coming again!
Tempests and whirlwinds, the anthem prolong:
    Jesus is coming again! ~ Jesse E. Strout (1872)

Early in World War II, General MacArthur was forced to leave the Philippines due to the invasion of the Japanese. Upon departure, he delivered the famous promise, "I shall return." In landing at Leyte Island in the Philippines, October 20, 1944, MacArthur kept that promise. Prior to departing for Heaven, Jesus promised, "I will come again." And He will keep that promise! The saint is to look forward to it eagerly (2 Timothy 4:8). All that do so will receive the Crown of Righteousness at His appearing. As He set things in motion, He will wind them down. Look up! Our "redemption draweth nigh" (Luke 21:28). Soon Jesus will come with His ring of keys and say, "It's closing time," and the saints will be raptured Home where they belong.

This which He has promised will be our reality when He comes! How stupendous is that news! Concentrate on it. Digest it. Consume it. Talk about it. Walk in it. Be encouraged in it. Joy in it—and expect it!

103
Wonderful Peace

"Thou wilt keep him in perfect peace, whose mind is stayed on thee: because he trusteth in thee" (Isaiah 26:3). It may be said that true peace is the prize which all men seek, yet seldom find. Why? They are looking for it in all the wrong places (religion, the church, possessions, pleasures, success, academic accolades, wealth, popularity). "Perfect peace" (unlike the fleeting and insufficient "peace" of the world) is obtainable only from God by His children through a fixed and steadfast trust in Him according to the verse given above. The greater the trust, the deeper the peace. He that confidently relies upon God is tranquil amid trouble. C. S. Lewis writes, "God cannot give us a happiness and peace apart from Himself, because it is not there. There is no such thing."[592] Another said, "When we put our problems in God's hands, He puts peace in our hearts."

> When we put our problems in God's hands, He puts peace in our hearts.

James McConkey writes, "For there is a peace which 'passeth all understanding'—and, as one has well said, 'all *mis*understanding'; a peace which keeps us, not we it; a peace of which it is said 'Thou wilt keep him in perfect peace whose mind is stayed on thee'; a peace which, because born not of an outer calm, but an inner Christ, cannot be disturbed by sting or storm....How wondrous must be God's peace! With Him there is no frailty, no error, no sin. With Him there is no past to lament, no future to dread, no blunders to deplore, no mistakes to fear, no plans to be thwarted, no purposes to be unmet. No death can overcome, no suffering weaken, no ideal be unfulfilled, no perfection unattained. Past, present or future; vanishing time or endless eternity; life or death; hope or fear; storm or calm—naught of these, and naught else within the bounds of the universe, can disturb the peace of Him who calls Himself the God of Peace. And it is this peace that is ours to possess."[593]

What a treasure I have in this wonderful peace
    Buried deep in the heart of my soul,
So secure that no power can mine it away
    While the years of eternity roll. ~ W. D. Cornell (1920)

The renowned evangelist D. L. Moody connected Isaiah 26:3 with verse 4 in the following words: "The tree of peace strikes its roots into the crevices of the Rock of Ages."[594] What a beautiful word picture to embrace. See Psalm 18:2 and Isaiah 44:8.

When the Rain Comes

Like a river glorious is God's perfect peace,
Over all victorious in its bright increase,
Perfect, yet it floweth fuller every day,
Perfect, yet it groweth deeper all the way.

Hidden in the hollow of His blessed hand,
Never foe can follow, never traitor stand.
Not a surge of worry, not a shade of care,
Not a blast of hurry touch the spirit there.

Every joy or trial falleth from above,
Traced upon our dial by the Sun of Love.
We may trust Him fully all for us to do;
They who trust Him wholly find Him wholly true.

Stayed upon Jehovah, hearts are fully blest,
Finding, as He promised, perfect peace and rest. ~ Francis Havergal (1876)

God's peace does not promise escape from sorrow, sickness or suffering, but a tranquility, calmness 'that surpasses all understanding' in the midst of trials (Philippians 4:7). Why is it said that the treasure of peace is beyond comprehension? Because, Billy Graham answers, "until you actually possess true peace with God, no one can describe its wonders to you."[595] Jonathan Edwards said, "The foundation of the Christian's peace is everlasting; it is what no time, no change can destroy. It will remain when the body dies; it will remain when the mountains depart and the hills shall be removed and when the heavens shall be rolled together as a scroll. The fountain of His comfort shall never be diminished, and the stream shall never be dried. His comfort and joy are a living spring in the soul, a well of water springing up to everlasting life."[596]

In Villa Franca, Italy, family members were frightened and showed uneasiness when the shock of an earthquake was felt—that is, all but one, who smiled throughout the ordeal. That man was a dying man (about a week later he died in the Lord), and he realized that the time of his departure for Heaven was nigh. It was of little matter to him if he was summoned by the slow process of dying or by the crushing blow of an earthquake. His mind was stayed upon Jehovah and was therefore kept in perfect peace when other family members trembled.[597] There is no peace to him in living or dying whose mind is stayed on worldly refuges (Isaiah 57:21). A bumper sticker states it well: "Know God; Know Peace. No God; No Peace."

104

When Heaven Draws Near

The wilderness wandering of the Israelites was about to end. Within "three days" they would depart for Canaan; therefore, immediate preparation had to be made (Joshua 1:11). "Victuals" had to be gathered, belongings had to be packed and planning undertaken. Though certain of the departure, they were uncertain as to when it actually would occur. The Israelites simply were told that it would happen, "*Within* three days." The trumpet might sound at any moment, signaling it was time to move out. Immediate readiness therefore was essential, lest they be ill prepared to cross the dangerous Jordan River into the promised land.

> Even in the best of health we should have death always before our eyes.
> Martin Luther

Just like the Israelites, Christians have received marching orders for the final part of the journey to *Home*. The divine "Exodus" may take place at any moment, "in the twinkling of an eye" (1 Corinthians 15:52); "therefore be ye also ready" (Matthew 24:44). Martin Luther said, "Even in the best of health we should have death always before our eyes. We will not expect to remain on this earth forever but will have one foot in the air, so to speak."[598] Thomas Adams well said, "Death is as near to the young as to the old; here is all the difference: death stands behind the young man's back, before the old man's face."[599] To cross the deep, dark and dreaded Jordan River (death) into Heaven's beautiful land confidently and fearlessly requires soul readiness: a passport issued by Jesus stamped with His atoning blood and holiness. Salvation ensures entrance into its gates (Revelation 22:14–16); holiness assures approval at its judgment (1 Corinthians 3:14). The Christian, like the Israelites, must store up "victuals" to make the final miles to Glory comfortable, calm and peaceful. The "victuals" are the promises of God recorded in the Holy Scriptures that guarantee safe passage through the turnstile of death to the promised land. And an exodus strategy must be planned: Last Will and Testament, funeral arrangement and final farewells.

The trumpet sounded, and the Israelites in faith pressed ahead to Canaan. "After three days" (Joshua 3:2) they arrived at the Jordan. But God removed terror and fear of crossing it; its waters were divided, enabling the people to cross "over on dry ground" (Joshua 3:17). In the saint's approach to the Jordan River (death), fear seeks to terrorize him. But there's no reason for concern, for God will part the waters and accompany the believer safely through it to the other side. Isn't it interesting that Scripture states the Israelites "clean passed over Jordan" (Joshua 4:1)? That means that not just some of them but all of them (not one was left behind) got across. Every one of God's children will make it "clean passed over Jordan."

When the Rain Comes

A remarkable comparison may be made with the resurrection of Christ. Jesus was buried following the crucifixion. However, "within three days" He was raised from the dead (Matthew 27:63; Matthew 28:1). The huge stone that sealed the tomb was miraculously rolled away (Matthew 28:2). In doing so, He parted the waters at the Jordan (death) for His children to walk across unscathed by its frightful noise and power. Death, the final enemy, was conquered (1 Corinthians 15:26). Hallelujah!

Louis XV, King of France, foolishly sought to avoid every suggestion of death and even ordered that death was never to be spoken of in his presence.[600] But avoiding the subject does not prevent its hastening approach. As Spurgeon says, "If I do not think of death, yet death will think of me."[601] Death's fear and terror are overcome by facing its reality in the light of Holy Scriptures and personal soul preparation (Romans 10:13).

Precious Lord, take my hand;
Lead me on; let me stand.
I am tired; I am weak; I am worn.
Through the storm, through the night,
Lead me on to the light.
Take my hand, precious Lord,
Lead me home.

When my way grows drear,
Precious Lord, linger near.
When my life is almost gone,
Hear my cry; hear my call;
Hold my hand, lest I fall.
Take my hand, precious Lord,
Lead me home.

When the darkness appears
And the night draws near
And the day is past and gone,
At the river I stand,
Guide my feet; hold my hand.
Take my hand, precious Lord,
Lead me home. ~ Thomas A. Dorsey (1932)

105

There Is a Balm in Gilead

"Is there no balm in Gilead; is there no physician there? why then is not the health of the daughter of my people recovered?" (Jeremiah 8:22). The balm of Gilead, though costly, was a highly effective medicine to treat wounds. It could be obtained in Gilead (a former region in modern-day Jordan). In a time when physicians were rarely successful (based on texts like Job 13:4 and 2 Chronicles 16:12–13), doctors in Gilead actually were effective, probably because they confined themselves to the balsam medicine.[602] Jeremiah's questions therefore were rhetorical—not seeking an answer but rather making a strong affirmation.[603] He was stating: "There is healing medicine in Gilead. There are reliable and effective doctors there. And yet my people are still hurting." It just didn't make sense to Jeremiah that when spiritual healing was available it wasn't obtained. In brokenness for the people (nation of Judah), he cries, "Oh that my head were waters, and mine eyes a fountain of tears, that I might weep day and night for the slain of the daughter of my people!" (Jeremiah 9:1). Along with Jeremiah, our hearts ought to weep for the hurting who know not of the healing balm of Gilead or how it may be obtained or who in ignorance or blatant stubbornness rely upon ineffective medicines prescribed by false physicians (human remedies).

There is balm in the blood of Christ Jesus. Although there is *no physician* here that possesses healing balm for a sin-sick soul, there is such a physician in Heaven. It is the Great Physician, Jesus. Charles Simeon states, "Has not God sent us a Physician from Heaven, even His only dear Son, who perfectly knows the extent of our disorders and is able to prescribe a remedy for them? Other physicians find their remedies in the productions of nature and of art, but this blessed Physician "heals his people with his own stripes." He shed His own precious blood for us upon the cross that it might be applied, as a sovereign balm, to our souls to restore us to perfect health."[604] The Bible says, 'The blood of His son, the Lord Jesus Christ cleanseth from all sin' (1 John 1:7).

> There is a balm in Gilead
> > To make the wounded whole;
> There is a balm in Gilead
> > To heal the sin sick soul.[605]

There is balm in the Holy Scriptures. C. H. Spurgeon wrote, "Within the Scriptures there is a balm for every wound and a salve for every sore!"[606] Whatever might be the hurt or hardship, grief or difficulty, anxiety or trauma, Christ provides and dispenses the needed assistance through Holy Scriptures to comfort, console, calm, combat, and cheer, and to help us cope victoriously.

There is balm in Christ's personal touch. "He [Christ] is the only universal doctor"; Spurgeon writes, "and the medicine He gives is the only true catholicon [a cure-all], healing in every instance. Whatever our spiritual malady may be, we should apply at once to this Divine Physician. There is no brokenness of heart which Jesus cannot bind up. We have but to think of the myriads who have been delivered from all sorts of diseases through the power and virtue of His touch, and we shall joyfully put ourselves in His hands. We trust Him, and sin dies; we love Him, and grace lives; we wait for Him, and grace is strengthened; we see Him as He is, and grace is perfected forever."[607]

> Come, ye disconsolate, where'er ye languish.
> Come to the mercy seat; fervently kneel.
> Here bring your wounded hearts; here tell your anguish.
> Earth has no sorrow that Heaven cannot heal.
>
> Joy of the comfortless, light of the straying,
> Hope of the penitent, fadeless and pure,
> Here speaks the Comforter, tenderly saying,
> "Earth has no sorrow that Heaven cannot cure."
>
> Here see the Bread of Life; see waters flowing
> Forth from the throne of God, pure from above.
> Come to the feast of love; come, ever knowing
> Earth has no sorrow but Heaven can remove.
>
> ~ Thomas Moore (1779–1852)

The balm of Gilead must be appropriated. The "healing balm" must be sought and applied in order to be beneficial. Jeremiah's complaint and grief were that the people of Judah neglected it when they sorely needed it, even though they knew where to find it. Avoid being like them. Seek it, seize it, and be sustained by it in time of deepest need. The psalmist declared, "He healeth the broken in heart, and bindeth up their wounds" (Psalm 147:3)—and "what He has done for others, He will do for you."

> What a Friend we have in Jesus, all our sins and griefs to bear!
> What a privilege to carry everything to God in prayer!
> Oh, what peace we often forfeit; oh, what needless pain we bear,
> All because we do not carry everything to God in prayer.
>
> ~ Joseph Scriven (1855)

The physician is in and awaits your request for His prescription of soothing and healing balm for whatever the ailment might be.

106
Grace Enough to Endure

Paul's "thorn in the flesh" (whatever it may have been) was incurable but manageable. How? By, in and through the new grace daily provided to him by Christ Jesus (2 Corinthians 12:9). That grace was amazingly sufficient to grant strength and stamina to endure the hardship and suffering of the grievous "thorn." The thorn that you bear may be equally incurable by the decree of the love of God for purposes presently unknown. If so, accept it as such, as Paul did, and rely upon a fresh supply of grace from Heaven to enable you to endure it "as a good soldier of Jesus Christ" (2 Timothy 2:3).

What is the coping grace afforded to man to bear infirmity, sorrow and suffering courageously and enduringly?

Grace's substance. It is the undeserved and unmerited loving favor and kindness of God manifested in strength, comfort and fortitude for the redeemed.

Grace's scope. It is grace that encompasses every form of trial, trouble and tribulation. Nothing is excluded.

Grace's sufficiency. It is grace that is capable of enabling one to endure in the direst of conditions or circumstances. Whatever comfort you require, His grace is sufficient to bestow it; whatever the difficulty is, His grace is sufficient to uphold you; whatever the sorrow you have, His grace is sufficient to sustain you; whatever the fear might be, His grace is sufficient to conquer it; whatever anxiety you feel, His grace is sufficient to thwart it; whatever the service called for, His grace is sufficient to enable its accomplishment; whatever gloom there is, His grace is sufficient to dispel it; and whatever danger you face, His grace is sufficient to shield you from it. Matthew Henry says, "Christ Jesus understands our case and knows our need and will proportion the remedy to our malady, and not only strengthen us, but glorify Himself."[608]

We don't have to ask Christ to make His grace sufficient to us; it already is ("IS sufficient for thee").[609] "This sufficiency is declared," states Spurgeon, "without any limiting words, and therefore Christ's grace is sufficient to uphold, strengthen, comfort thee; sufficient to make thy trouble useful to thee, to enable thee to triumph over it, to bring thee out of ten thousand like it, and to bring thee home to Heaven. Whatever would be good for thee, Christ's grace is sufficient to bestow; whatever would harm thee, His grace is sufficient to avert; whatever thou desirest, His grace is sufficient to give thee if it be good for thee; whatever thou wouldst avoid, His grace can shield thee from it if so His wisdom shall dictate."[610]

Grace's supply. It is a present benefit (*"is* sufficient") that is showered upon the saint moment by moment as needed upon request. See Hebrews 4:16 cited below. On the morrow should grace be needed, it shall be provided graciously. It's a vast, inexhaustible and unlimited supply with no danger of being depleted.

Grace's strength. Grace is Christ's strength released within man to tolerate every intolerable adversity patiently, hopefully and joyfully, to empower victorious warfare against Satan's attacks, and to enable effectual Christian service and ministry. It gives strength to stand, when the believer feels like giving up. "Man's extremity is God's opportunity; man's security is Satan's opportunity. God's way is not to take His children out of trial but to give them strength to bear up against it."[611] By grace, Paul's "strength [was] made perfect [achieved its purpose[612]] in weakness" in bearing (victoriously coping, enduring) the thorn (2 Corinthians 12:9b). The outward man may be taxed beyond measure with pain, illness fatigue, anxiety and despair and yet inwardly experience perfect peace, all because of the gracious gift of amazing grace. "John Bunyan said that he could pray for a darker, damper dungeon, because, as his physical discomforts increased, his spiritual comforts and joys were multiplied."[613] Rick Warren said, "What gives me the most hope every day is God's grace, knowing that His grace is going to give me the strength for whatever I face, knowing that nothing is a surprise to God."[614] Spurgeon says, "Whenever the Lord sets His servants to do extraordinary work, He always gives them extraordinary strength; or if He puts them to unusual suffering, He gives them unusual patience."[615] "The grace of Christ is sufficient to enable His servants to perform efficaciously unto His glory the undertakings with which He entrusts them."[616]

Grace's solace. "The grace of Christ is sufficient to give comfort under afflictions and to convert them into means of improvement in faith and holiness."[617]

Grace's source. Whence is such wondrous grace (love, strength, enablement of Christ) derived? The answer is discovered in the first word of the text, *"My* grace." It is given from Christ who is full of love and compassion to His children for their benefit and His glory. Therefore, "Let us...come boldly unto the throne of grace, that we may obtain mercy, and find grace to help in time of need" (Hebrews 4:16). Jon Courson writes, "The Father says, 'You want Me to take away the pain, to solve the problem, to get you out of the situation—but that's not what you need. *You need Me.* And the very problem you're seeking to get away from, the very situation you desire to get out of is the very one that is causing you to talk to Me, spend time with Me, and depend on Me. You'll be stronger when you're weak because you'll have no other choice than to draw strength from Me. You'll do better when you're weak because you'll have to rely on Me.'"[618]

He giveth more grace as our burdens grow greater;
    He sendeth more strength as our labors increase.
To added afflictions, He addeth His mercy;
    To multiplied trials, He multiplies peace.

When we have exhausted our store of endurance,
    When our strength has failed ere the day is half done,
When we reach the end of our hoarded resources,
    Our Father's full giving is only begun.

His love has no limits; His grace has no measure;
    His power, no boundary known unto men;
For out of His infinite riches in Jesus,
    He giveth, and giveth, and giveth again. ~ Annie Johnson Flint (1866–1932)

107

When Darkness Seems to Hide His Face

It is possible to mistake a season of darkness (the time when God seems distant and afar off) as the judgment of God. To the contrary, Isaiah says such seasons are common to the most faithful and devoted saint apart from judgment: "Who is among you that feareth the LORD, that obeyeth the voice of his servant, that walketh in darkness, and hath no light? let him trust in the name of the LORD, and stay upon his God" (Isaiah 50:10). It is clear that seasons of darkness may occur not as a result of sin but as the providential will of God. Matthew Henry explains, "It is no new thing for the children and heirs of light sometimes to walk in darkness and for a time not to have any glimpse or gleam of light. This is not meant so much of the comforts of this life (those that fear God, when they have ever so great an abundance of them, do not walk in them as their light) as of their spiritual comforts which relate to their souls. They walk in darkness when their evidences for Heaven are clouded, their joy in God is interrupted, the testimony of the Spirit is suspended, and the light of God's countenance is eclipsed."[619]

Why is this so? God allows the believer to experience "darkness" for manifold reasons: to strengthen and increase his faith (utter dependence upon Him); to show forth His ability to sustain when all props are taken away; "to let us see from whence spiritual comforts and refreshings come: that God alone has the keys of that cupboard";[620] to enable us to prize the "light" God gives more highly when it returns; to train the believer to trust Him in the dark as in the light; to humble; to prompt earnest and frequent praying;[621] to prepare the believer for a new assignment or adversity that will appear when the light returns; to help the believer understand that the Christian walk is one of faith, not feelings, of things unseen, not seen.

C. H. Spurgeon, in the sermon *Five Fears,* acknowledges that seasons of darkness are the lot even of the holiest of saints. "But shall I tell thee one thing? Dost thou know *the greatest* of God's people are often in the same condition as thou art now? 'No, no,' says the fearful soul, 'I do not believe that; I believe that when persons are converted they never have any fear,' and they look at the minister and say, 'Oh, but if I could be but like that minister; I know he never has doubts and fears. Oh, if I could be like old deacon So-and-so—such a holy man how he prays! Oh, if I could feel like Mr. So-and-so who calls to visit me and talks to me so sweetly. They never doubt.' Ah, that is because you do not know. Those whom you think to be the strongest, and are so in public, have their times of the greatest weakness when they can scarcely know their own names in spiritual things. If one may speak for the rest, those of us who enjoy the greatest portions of assurance have times when we would give all the world to know ourselves to be possessors of grace, when we would be ready to sacrifice our lives if we might but have the shadow of a hope that we were in the love of Jesus Christ our Lord. Now, little one, if the giants go there, what wonder if the dwarfs must? What if God's favorite and chosen ones; what if his valiant men, the bodyguard of Christ, those men whose swords are on their thighs and who stand up for the truth and are its champions—what if they sometimes are weak? What wonder if thou shouldest be weak? What if the heirs of salvation and the soldiers of the cross sometimes feel their knees feeble and their hands hang down and their hearts faint? What wonder if thou, who art less than the least of all saints shouldst sometimes be in trouble too? Oh, be of good cheer; fear will never kill anybody. 'Doubts and fears,' said an old preacher once, 'are like the toothache— nothing more painful, but never fatal.' They will often grieve us, but they will never kill us; they distress us much but they will never burn the soul."[622]

> God understands your sorrow;
> He sees the falling tear
> And whispers, "I am with thee."
> Then falter not, nor fear.
>
> God understands your heartaches;
> He knows the bitter pain.
> Oh, trust Him in the darkness;
> You cannot trust in vain. ~ Oswald Smith

Pardington says, "The first thing to do is do nothing. This is hard for poor human nature to do. In the West there is a saying that runs thus: 'When you're rattled, don't rush'; in other words, 'When you don't know what to do, don't do it.'

When you run into a spiritual fog bank, don't tear ahead; slow down the machinery of your life. If necessary, anchor your bark or let it swing at its moorings."[623] Wait until the light breaks through the overshadowing clouds, giving clarity of direction. Don't try to eliminate the darkness by building your own "fires."[624] Warren Wiersbe says, "In obedience to the Lord, you may find yourself in the darkness; but do not panic, for He will bring you the light you need just at the right time."[625] As a ship drops anchor in the harbor to stay until the storm passes by, just so the believer is to *stay in God* in times of life's storms.[626] If divine providence has placed you in the "darkness," don't fight to regain the "light." When its purpose has been accomplished, the light will spring forth unabated. S. D. Gordon states, "It's safe to trust God's methods and to go by His clock."[627] "It's incredible to realize," states Bill Hybels, "that what we do each day has meaning in the big picture of God's plan."[628] Therefore, embrace the darkness and its purpose.

> When darkness veils His lovely face,
> I rest on His unchanging grace;
> In every high and stormy gale,
> My anchor holds within the veil. ~ Edward Mote (1797–1874)

108

The Everlasting Arms That Cannot Be Broken

"The eternal God is thy refuge, and underneath are the everlasting arms" (Deuteronomy 33:27).

No clearer or more concise picture of the believer's security in God is found in all of Scripture than in this text. Moses depicts the everlasting arms of God "underneath" the believer holding him up through the trials and troubles of life. What are the everlasting arms of God?

They are the everlasting arms of God's power. Greek mythology embraces the view that Atlas was charged with the task of holding the terrestrial sphere upon his shoulders. But, alas, no man or army or religion has such strength. But the Almighty God that made the heavens and the earth and all that therein is certainly manifests that power and ability. He carries not only the weight of the world on His shoulders but that upon the shoulders of His children as well. Randy Alcorn states, "The Gospel infuses hope and joy into our current circumstances by acknowledging God's greatness over any crisis we'll face."[629]

They are the everlasting arms of God's love. It is out of great love for His children that He ministers to their hurts, pains and fears. It is a "love that wilt not let me go"; it resides beneath me, above me, around me and in me, ensuring my best good. Spurgeon says, "Let the thought of his special love to you be a spiritual pain killer, a dear quietus to your woe."[630]

> Let the thought of his special love to you be a spiritual pain killer, a dear quietus to your woe.
> C. H. Spurgeon

They are the everlasting arms of God's plan. His purpose and plan for the believer's life is divinely orchestrated and will not be thwarted by adversity or infirmity. In fact, it may be furthered by them. God promises to complete that work which He began in us at conversion (Philippians 1:6).

They are the everlasting arms of God's immutability. That is, they are eternal (never changing) in duration and strength. Never, ever, can a saint sink so far into the sea of trouble that God's arms "underneath" fail to sustain him. The saint's security and hope rests not in his feeble, frail and wavering faith but in the everlasting clasp of God's arms. The everlasting arms of God can never be broken; they will forever hold firmly the child of God. Hallelujah!

How long will the everlasting arms of God undergird the saint from "underneath?" For as long as life exists. See Isaiah 46:4. They sustain us when we are aware of them and when we are not, from the cradle to the grave. Where might we presently be had it not been for the unseen arms of God holding us up (for the most part unknown by us) through life's numerous evils and storms? How might our present circumstance, though hard, be even direr were it not for His arms "underneath" giving support? Even in the valley of the shadow of death God's strong arms will uphold us. John Bunyan, in the classic book *Pilgrim's Progress,* described the believer's confidence in death when picturing the pilgrims passing the river. Christian cried out to young Hopeful, "I sink in deep waters; the billows go over my head; all His waves go over me." Then said Hopeful, "Be of good cheer, my brother; I feel the bottom, and it is good." You and I shall feel the bottom of the river of death but will say, "It is good; for underneath me are the everlasting arms of God."[631]

What then?

(1. Live courageously and fearlessly. Keep looking "beneath" to see the everlasting arms of God upholding you in the direst of circumstances. Vance Havner said, "Our efficiency turns out to be a deficiency unless we have God's sufficiency."[632]

(2. Live hopefully. There is no sickness that God cannot cure, sorrow that He cannot relieve, or calamity from which He cannot deliver.

(3. Live joyfully. Don't let the troubles that push you down determine your joy and contentment, but the arms of God that hold you up.

(4. Live confidently. In times of weakness and weariness, sickness and sorrow, the everlasting arms of God will prevent tottering in doubt and fear, while providing strength and comfort to endure.

Adrian Rogers reminds the saint, "Nothing can touch the life of a child of God unless God ordains or allows it. Everything is Father-filtered through the loving hand and sovereign will of God. Therefore, even in trials and tribulations, we can rest in Him. Regardless of life's circumstances, we can experience outrageous hope and extraordinary joy!"[633]

What a fellowship, what a joy divine
   Leaning on the everlasting arms!
What a blessedness, what a peace is mine
   Leaning on the everlasting arms!

Leaning, leaning,
   Safe and secure from all alarms,
Leaning, leaning,
   Leaning on the everlasting arms.

What have I to dread; what have I to fear
   Leaning on the everlasting arms?
I have blessed peace with my Lord so near
   Leaning on the everlasting arms.

   ~ Elisha Albright Hoffman (1887)

109
We Will Meet in the Morning

F. B. Meyer, in a letter to a friend, wrote, "I have just heard to my great surprise that I have but a few days to live. It may be that before this reaches you, I shall have entered the palace. Don't trouble to write. We shall meet in the morning."[634] F. B. Meyer's words echo the sentiment of all who die in the Lord. A glad reunion day awaits with loved ones "in the morning."

I'll meet you in the morning with a "how do you do?"
And we'll sit down by the river and with rapture old acquaintance renew.
You'll know me in the morning by the smile that I wear,
When I meet you in the morning in the city that is built foursquare.

   ~ Albert E. Brumley (1956)

When the Rain Comes

We love with the greatest love our spouse, children, parents, siblings and friends. Death is not so much dreaded because *we* are departing as it is because we are leaving *them*. Leaving them is gravely difficult and grievous. My mother in dying shared the pain she felt for "us" in knowing that her death would leave a void that nothing could fill. She was saddened for my sister and me, not for herself. Deepest concern for those dearest to us is what makes the departure difficult, not the departure itself. If only we all could go together everything would be okay.[635]

In death there is not only grief on our part in departing from family and friends, but also on their part in our departure from them. And it's their grief for which we are the most grieved. "Jesus wept"—not for Lazarus but for the breakup of the Bethany home; it would never be the same.[636] He wept in compassion for Mary and Martha in their great sorrow. And this is the element of death that makes it sad and sorrowful. F. W. Robertson says, "Let him that calls death a trifle remember this—not just that one man is gone, but that Bethany is no longer Bethany. A blight is there. You open a book; there is a name. A day comes; it is a birthday—the chair is vacant. In reverie, you half rise up, but the name on your lips belongs to none on earth."[637] The saint's great comfort in dying is in knowing that Christ has promised to minister to and constantly care for loved ones that remain, and that a day will come when we will be reunited. (Jesus wept also over the curse of sin and the death it brought to man.)

Alexander Smellie says, "I am glad, too, for the wide range of Christ's tears. At Bethany He wept for a beloved friend's death; and on Olivet, I remember, He wept for a great city doomed to death. He bends over me, forlorn, heartbroken, stricken, in measureless grace. I praise Him that His tenderness is both individual and universal. And I think of the source and origin of His tears. Standing by the grave of Lazarus—He mourned for my sorrows, my desolating bereavements, the orphanhood of my life when my dear ones are snatched away. Sitting on the hillside near Jerusalem—He mourned for my sins. And then I rejoice in the outcome of the Savior's tears. They did not drain the force out of His soul. They roused and quickened Him. The new life of Lazarus was the result in the one case, the atoning death of the cross in the other."[638]

At the death of his close friend Arthur Henry Hallam, the poet Alfred Tennyson suffered grave emotional trauma. In "Break, Break, Break," he muses about the friend's death while sitting by the seashore. He sees the fisherman's children laughing and playing, the sailor singing in his boat, and the stately ships sailing away from the harbor. But Tennyson thinks, *Oh, for the touch of a vanished hand and the sound of a voice that is still!*[639] Every Christian certainly identifies with the poet when death removes ones whom they dearly love. But knowing there will be a meeting in Heaven with them "in the morning" lightens the load immeasurably. The Bible says, "The Master himself will give the command. Archangel thunder! God's trumpet blast! He'll come down from Heaven and the dead in Christ will rise—they'll go first. Then the rest of us who are still alive at the time will be caught up with them into the clouds to meet the Master. Oh, we'll be walking on air! And then there will be one huge family reunion with the Master. So reassure one another with these words" (1 Thessalonians 4:15–18 MSG).

Max Lucado writes, "If you'll celebrate a marriage anniversary alone this year, He [Christ] speaks to you. If your child made it to Heaven before making it to kindergarten, He speaks to you. If you lost a loved one in violence, if you learned more than you want to know about disease, if your dreams were buried as they lowered the casket, God speaks to you. He speaks to all of us who have stood or will stand in the soft dirt near an open grave. God transforms our hopeless grief into hope-filled grief. How? By telling us that we will see our loved ones again."[640]

110
The Futility of Worry

"Don't fret or worry. Instead of worrying, pray. Let petitions and praises shape your worries into prayers, letting God know your concerns. Before you know it, a sense of God's wholeness, everything coming together for good, will come and settle you down. It's wonderful what happens when Christ displaces worry at the center of your life" (Philippians 4:6–7 MSG). John MacArthur defines worry as "the sin of distrusting the promise and providence of God."[641] He continues to say, "And yet it is a sin that Christians commit perhaps more frequently than any other."[642] Thomas à Kempis said, "Oh, how great peace and quietness would he possess who should cut off all vain anxiety and place all his confidence in God."[643] Jesus says, "Don't worry, but trust." Worry slanders every promise of God to the believer. "Worry," states Adrian Rogers, "doesn't take the sorrow out of tomorrow; it takes the strength out of today. There are two days that can steal joy from today. One is yesterday, and the other is tomorrow. Both are days in which we as Christians should refuse to live."[644]

Darlow Sargeant comments, "What is the use of worrying? It never made anybody strong, never helped anybody do God's will, never made a way of escape for anyone out of perplexity. Worry spoils lives which would otherwise be useful and beautiful. Restlessness, anxiety and care are absolutely forbidden by our Lord."[645] Don't let anxiety control your life. Jesus said, "Take no thought for your life" (Matthew 6:25). Again, He says, "Take therefore no thought for the morrow: for the morrow shall take thought for the things of itself. Sufficient unto the day is the evil thereof" (Matthew 6:34). And this is possible if we "Seek...first the kingdom of God, and his righteousness" (Matthew 6:33). "Only the Holy Spirit," says Billy Graham, "can give us peace in the midst of the storms of restlessness and despair. We should not grieve our Guide by indulging in worry or paying undue attention to self."[646] In casting all your care upon the Lord in prayer, "the peace of God, which passeth all understanding, shall keep your hearts and minds through Christ Jesus" (Philippians 4:7). "Thinking God's thoughts" will take the place of worried, anxious concerns."[647]

Why is it foolish for Christians to worry? Francis Dixon states, "(1. It is foolish because we gain absolutely nothing by worrying. (2. It is foolish because whatever happens will only be with God's permission. (3. It is foolish because whatever happens will always be for our good. (4. It is foolish because even if the worst that we fear happens, God's grace will be sufficient. (5. It is foolish because the promises of God will never fail. (6. It is foolish because nothing can ever happen to separate us from the love of Christ."[648] George Mueller said, "The beginning of anxiety is the end of faith, and the beginning of true faith is the end of anxiety."[649]

Worry is the gong
That takes away the song.
It fills the heart with fear,
Making the outlook weary and drear.

Anxious thoughts control the life,
Causing nothing but pain and strife.
To change what is to what is not
Is to worry, a great cannot.

To rid oneself of this spoiler to peace,
Making its torturous pain to cease,
Cast all your care upon Christ in prayer,
And worry will be something you won't have to bear. ~ Frank Shivers (2020)

111

Death Just Makes a Lot of Noise

There's a lot of bothersome, disturbing noise about death that the Devil orchestrates toward the dying saint. But that's all it is, just noise. And noise has never hurt anyone. Despite all the Devil does to create havoc and chaos and fear and doubt about death, it will fall powerlessly upon the sanctified ears of the saint.

The devil invades the dying bed with chatter,
But all he says just doesn't matter.
The noise he makes is meant to terrify,
But harmless it is to the soul that's justified.

Comfort for Troubled Hearts

He assails with doubts never thought before
Of Heaven's reality on the other side of the door,
Of the soul's readiness the Savior to meet,
and the great reunion where loved ones we'll greet.

Drown out the noise by making the choice
To listen only to the Savior's calming, assuring voice.
What He says in His Word don't let the Devil deny;
In His promises of life eternal always abide. ~ Frank Shivers (2020)

A boy who was highly allergic to bee stings, while riding in the car with his father, became terrified when a bee flew in the window. The father stopped the car, allowing the boy to get out while he caught the bee. Back in the car, the boy, seeing the bee again and hearing it buzz, cried out with fear once again. The boy's fear was calmed when the father simply opened his hand, revealing the bee's stinger. Death makes a lot of fuss and noise but is powerless to harm us, for Jesus Christ bore its stinger upon the cross.

Don't you see my Jesus coming?
    See Him come in yonder cloud?
With ten thousand angels 'round Him,
    How they do my Jesus crowd!

I'll arise and go and meet Him;
    He'll embrace me in His arms.
In the arms of my dear Jesus,
    Oh, there are ten thousand charms.

Death shall not destroy my comfort;
    Christ will guide me through the gloom.
Down He'll send some Heavenly convoy
    To escort me to my spirit home.

Jordan's streams shall ne'er o'erflow me,
    While my Savior's by my side.
Canaan, Canaan lies before me;
    Rise and cross the swelling tide.

See the happy spirits waiting
    On the bank beyond the stream,
Sweet responses still repeating,
    Jesus, Jesus is their theme.

When the Rain Comes

See, they whisper! hark! they call me,
    Sister spirit come away!
Lo, I come! earth cannot contain me.
    Hail! Ye realms of endless day.

Worlds of light and crowns of glory,
    Far beyond the azure sky,
Though by faith I now explore ye,
    I'll enjoy you soon on high.

Soon I'll gain the full possession;
    Faith and hope shall henceforth cease,
Lost in love's exhaustless ocean,
    Love, that sweetest, brightest grace.

Swiftly roll, ye lingering hours;
    Seraphs lend your glittering wings.
Love absorbs my ransomed powers;
    Heavenly sound around me rings.

Worlds above are bright and glorious;
    All beneath are dark and void.
Conquest gain'd, I'll shout victorious
    In the praises of my God.

Smiling angels now surround me;
    Troops resplendent fill the skies,
Glory shining all around me,
    While my towering spirit flies.
Jesus clad in dazzling splendor
    Now, methinks, appears in view;
Brethren, could you see my Jesus,
    You would serve and love Him too.

    ~ A Choice Selection of Hymns and Spiritual Songs (1829)

112

The Dirge of Grief Is Brief

"Weeping may endure for a night, but joy cometh in the morning" (Psalm 30:5).
The promise is a pledge of God to every sorrowing believer. "Weeping" is pictured as

a stranger who lodges with the believer but for the night. The unwanted stranger causes us to toss and turn in unrest, wet our pillow with tears, become mentally and spiritually strained and drained, miserable and helpless. It appears the night will never end. The "night" (cause of weeping) includes bereavement which puts the heart in the winepress of perhaps life's deepest woe and sorrow, incurable illness, frailty of body and/or mind (dementia), suffering, and various trials and troubles. All *weeping* is relieved by a compassionate and consoling God to whom it is brought. "He heals the brokenhearted and bandages their wounds" (Psalm 147:3 NLT). Billy Graham said, "Tears become telescopes to Heaven, bringing eternity a little closer."[650]

Weeping may endure for a night. Grief is said to last for the night.

(1. The night is brief. It will not last for long.

(2. The night is under the control of God, as is the day. He that will not suffer thy foot to stumble in the day will not allow you to stumble in the night (Psalm 121:3).

(3. The night is compelled to end. It has not the power or authority to extend beyond its allotted time. The duration of grief will end by divine injunction.

(4. The night has glimpses of light. The stars in the heavens sprinkle light in the night. The Holy Spirit doth do the same for the saint in the dark nights of sorrow, sickness and suffering to comfort, sustain and strengthen. The Bible says, "LORD, you light my lamp; my God illuminates my darkness" (Psalm 18:28 CSB).

(5. The night is always followed by morning.

But joy cometh in the morning. The long night of distress and agony seems relentless and unbearable. And well it might be, were it not for the consolation and compassion of Christ. In the morning the dirge of grief gives way to the joy of relief. A. C. Dixon states, "The night makes the morning. The morning comes and drives away the night, it is true, but GOD knows how to make the night produce the morning. Jesus said, 'Your sorrow shall be turned into joy.' Your sorrow shall be transmuted into joy."[651] Dixon continues, "GOD knows how to make the morning out of the night. He can touch the black charcoal into diamonds. He knows how to speak and the darkness becomes light. The very affliction that would drag you down lifts you up; the things that are weights become wings. That which, if you could, you would have prevented lifts you up to Heaven."[652]

In the morning the dirge of grief gives way to the joy of relief.

Oh, where shall rest be found,
    Rest for the weary soul?
'Twere vain the ocean depths to sound
    Or pierce to either pole.

When the Rain Comes

The world can never give
    The bliss for which we sigh;
'Tis not the whole of life to live
    Nor all of death to die.

Beyond this vale of tears
    There is a life above
Unmeasured by the flight of years,
    And all that life is love.

Here would we end our quest;
    Alone are found in Thee
The life of perfect love, the rest
    Of immortality. ~ James Montgomery (1854)

The promise (Psalm 30:5) is known only in part but will be fully realized at the dawning of Heaven's eternal day when God 'shall wipe every tear from our eyes' (Revelation 21:4). "But you may say," remarks Alexander Maclaren, "'Ah! there are two kinds of sorrows. There are those that can be cured, and there are those that cannot. What have you got to say to me who has to bleed from an *immedicable* (incurable) wound till the end of my life?' Well, I have to say this—look beyond earth's dim dawns to that morning when the Sun of Righteousness shall arise. If we have to carry a load on an aching back till the end, be sure that when the night, which is far spent, is over, and the day, which is at hand, hath broken, every raindrop will be turned into a flashing rainbow when it is smitten by the level light, and every sorrow rightly borne be represented by a special and particular joy."[653] A. C. Dixon elucidates, "With some Christians it is winter—long nights with short days, much darkness and cold. With others it is summer—long days and short nights, with the bloom of flowers and the song of birds and beauty all about them. But with all Christians every night is followed by its morning, whether it be the long night of winter or the short night of summer."[654]

Whatever may be the night of your weeping, short or long in duration, remember that:

Joy cometh in the morning!
Weeping may endure,
May endure for a night,
But joy cometh in the morning.

Ye feeble saints, dismiss your fears,
For joy cometh in the morning!
And weeping mourners, dry your tears,
For joy cometh in the morning.

Our God will wipe our tears away,
For joy cometh in the morning!
Sorrow and sighing flee away,
For joy cometh in the morning! ~ Mrs. M. M. Weinland (1819-1899)

113
Things That Are Unshakable

"Those things which cannot be shaken" (Hebrews 12:27). Hannah Whitall Smith comments, "We will all acknowledge, I think, that if our souls are to rest in peace and comfort, it can only be on unshakable foundations. It is no more possible for the soul to be comfortable when it is trying to rest on 'things that can be shaken' than it is for the body. No one can rest comfortably in a shaking bed or sit in comfort on a rickety chair. Foundations, to be reliable, must always be unshakable."[655]

Shaky foundations for peace and comfort (those built upon the sand of unbiblical tenets, human wisdom and philosophy) erode quickly in the midst of storms, failing us when needed the most. See Isaiah 28:15. The book *The Seventeen False Rests of the Soul* identifies and warns of insecure foundations of hope and comfort. The sure and unshakable foundation on which to place trust and hope is the Solid Rock, the Lord Jesus Christ (Isaiah 33:6). It is time-tested and proven to be sure and secure. Though Satan and the hosts of Hell have sought to demolish it, it remains fixed. Though the Voltaires of the world have sought to undermine it, it remains strong. Though heretical teaching has sought to replace it, it remains intact. Though emperors and kings have sought to defeat it, it stands unconquerable. Though secularism has sought to trample it to death beneath its foot, it flourishes. Though liberals have sought to prove it untrue, its veracity is unparalleled with biblical, prophetic and historical documentation. Though death has sought to silence it, it is yet triumphant.

Upon this sure Foundation abide four unshakable things that supply comfort and consolation in the storms of life.

God's presence with you is unshakable. He will never abandon His children despite what assails their life. The Bible says, "For *He hath said*, I will never leave thee, nor forsake thee" (Hebrews 13:5). Even in the darkest night of life when God appears nowhere to be found, He faithfully abides with you. Isaiah said, "'Though the mountains be shaken and the hills be removed, yet *my unfailing love for you will not be shaken* nor my covenant of peace be removed,' says the LORD, who has compassion on you" (Isaiah 54:10 NIV).

God's promises to you are unshakable. Jesus said that heaven and earth may pass away but that His Word would stand sure forever (Matthew 24:35). Not one of His promises has ever failed or will ever fail. All that He promised will come to pass, including that which affirms that good will come out of bad to those that love Him (Romans 8:28). See Hebrews 4:12.

God's power in you is unshakable. Ephesians 1:19 states that the 'immeasurable greatness of his power' abides in the believer. See Acts 1:8. His power manifested in you enables you to conquer temptation, be calm in tempest, have comfort in trials and courage in terror. This power possesses keeping power. Peter says believers "are kept by the power of God through faith unto salvation ready to be revealed in the last time" (1 Peter 1:5). The text literally reads, 'Kept in the power of God.'[656] Francis Dixon comments, "It is nothing less than 'the power of God.' Think of His power in creation, in history, in providence, in redemption and in His final intention. Surely the same God of power can keep you? His power is absolutely sufficient, and He guarantees to make it available to you and operative in your life until the end of your earthly pilgrimage, when you will no longer need to be through faith 'shielded by God's power,' for then faith will be lost in sight."[657]

God's purpose for you is unshakable. Paul says, "God began doing a good work in you, and I am sure he will continue it until it is finished when Jesus Christ comes again" (Philippians 1:6 NCV). Jeremiah says, "'For I know the plans and thoughts that I have for you,' says the Lord, 'plans for peace and well-being and not for disaster, to give you a future and a hope'" (Jeremiah 29:11 AMP). Regardless of the form, severity or duration of the rain that pounds upon the saint's life, God's plan remains unshakable and unalterable for them.

> The anchor for our souls is Christ alone;
> Our refuge through the storm is Christ alone.
> If hope has been promised and faith is secure,
> Our confidence now is one that is sure.
> Our hope is unsinkable;
> Our faith is unshakable.[658] ~ Village Hymns Worship Leaders

Appearances are deceptive and damaging. A house built upon the shifting sands appears secure and stable. But when tested with the storms of life, it crumbles to the ground. "And great and complete was its fall" (Matthew 7:27 AMP). But the house built upon the foundation of faith in Christ Jesus victoriously withstands the rain, the floods and the torrents and winds that beat upon it (Matthew 7:24–25). It remains unshakable and invincible. Ving Rhames said, "Since God is the foundation of my life, anything that streams from that can only be positive."[659]

114
A Comforting Conscience

The conscience possesses great power to comfort or discomfort the dying. Paul says that 'the testimony of his conscience' reveals "that in simplicity and godly sincerity...by the grace of God" he had conducted all his activities and relationships in this world (2 Corinthians 1:12). The word "sincere" is derived from a Latin word meaning "without wax."[660] In Paul's day men would use wax to hide the cracks in defective pottery.[661] Paul is saying there's nothing insincere, dishonest or questionable in him hidden or covered up by "wax." Everything was done "absolutely above-board" (2 Corinthians 1:12 PHILLIPS). Paul based what was said, thought and done upon the Word of God and the glory of God (Colossians 3:17).

William Barclay suggests the addition of a new beatitude: "Blessed is the man who has nothing to hide."[662] That's advisable to all, especially when it comes to facing God at the judgment. Arthur Conan Doyle, author of the Sherlock Holmes mysteries, played a practical joke on twelve famous friends, all of whom were virtuous and greatly respected. He sent each the same telegram: "Fly at once; all is discovered!" Within twenty-four hours, the men were on a plane out of the country. Guilt plagues all, regardless of honorable reputation or status.

Adrian Rogers comments, "Guilt brings anxiety. It brings depression. The soul becomes a window covered with the dirt and grime of guilt. Everything we look at is colored or discolored by the guilt within. Guilt can make you sick. If you carry around a load of guilt, it can make you emotionally, spiritually and even physically ill." Guilt (unclear conscience) is an insidious robber of contentment, happiness, and peace of mind when approaching life's end. To help make the sickbed peaceful and the exit into eternity calmer, square the conscience with the Bible. Set things right with God, if necessary. The Bible says, *"By mercy and truth iniquity is purged"* (Proverbs 16:6). By "mercy and truth" (God's love and loyal faithfulness has provided a way for man's justification; His Word promises it; His mercy secures it) "iniquity" (sin and its guilt) is "purged" (banished, covered, forgiven, and atoned for through the blood of the Lord Jesus Christ [Jesus "by himself purged our sins"— Hebrews 1:3]). Set things right with God through confession for cleansing through the blood of Christ. "The blood of his son, the Lord Jesus Christ cleanseth us from all sin" (1 John 1:7). There are no exceptions to what Jesus is able and willing to forgive. Though your sins may be as "scarlet" or of a milder "hue," they are forgivable (Isaiah 1:18). God so forgives sin the moment it is confessed in godly repentance (Acts 20:21; 1 John 1:9) that it is *just as if you had never sinned* (justification). Yes, such forgiveness is undeserved and certainly unmerited. Yes, we should be required to pay more for the hideous sin committed mentally and physically. But because of God's awesome, all-enveloping love for man, and His graciousness, He overrules these and every other reason why we shouldn't be forgiven and says, "I, even I, am he that blotteth out thy transgressions for mine own sake, and will not remember thy sins" (Isaiah 43:25).

Correct things that are wrong with man inasmuch as it is within your power (Matthew 5:23–24). *Endeavor* to mend broken relationships with family members and others (it's never too late as long as life exists); make things right with those you have defrauded; set the unethical dealings of life right. The keyword in all this is *endeavor*, just do what is possible and others allow you to do (Romans 12:18); that's all that is required by God. Deal *only* with wrongs not righted, not righted wrongs long buried in the cemetery (Ephesians 4:27). In hearing that death was nigh, Hezekiah found great consolation in 'the testimony of his conscience.' He was able honestly and frankly to say, "Please, O Lord, just remember how I have walked before You in faithfulness and truth, and with a whole heart [absolutely devoted to You], and have done what is good in Your sight" (Isaiah 38:3 AMP). For his beloved country that was being threatened by the King of Assyria he "wept sore," but for himself he had no reason to mourn. The testimony of his conscience before God gave approval to his actions. Hezekiah therefore had no dread or fear of death or facing God at the judgment.[663]

The 'testimony of your conscience' will make your sick pillow either *soft or hard*. What saith it? "A condemning conscience is a dark shade thrown over the life."[664] But a clear conscience yields joy and peace (2 Corinthians 1:12). Purify it, if necessary (by the measures mentioned above), to be comforted by it rather than distressed in it (Philippians 4:7). "Under the old system, the blood of goats and bulls and the ashes of a heifer could cleanse people's bodies from ceremonial impurity. Just think how much more the blood of Christ will purify our consciences from sinful deeds so that we can worship the living God" (Hebrews 9:13–14 NLT). W. S. Plumer remarked, "One ingenuous acknowledgment goes farther to secure peace of mind than all false disguises. When we know that we deal honestly with God and with our own consciences, we may safely hope that Jehovah will deal mercifully with us through Jesus Christ."[665] C. H. Spurgeon said, "May Divine Grace cause you so to set this house in order that you may leave it without reluctance and enter into the next with joy, leaving your first house behind without shame, in sure and certain hope of a blessed resurrection! May you cheerfully leave the first house and joyfully surrender the key to the Great Landlord."[666] May you be able to say with Paul in Acts 24:16: "And herein do I exercise myself, to have always a conscience void of offence toward God, and toward men."

115

The Things Which Are Not Seen

"The things which are not seen" (2 Corinthians 4:18). Saints look forward to their future in Heaven, for it stimulates endurance in trial and trouble, infuses the heart with hope and expectation, and excites the soul with joy and gaiety unspeakable. Spurgeon comments, "Looking into the future we see sin cast out, the body of sin and death destroyed, the soul made perfect and fit to be a partaker of the inheritance of the saints in light. Looking further yet, the believer's enlightened eye can see death's river passed, the gloomy stream forded, and the hills of light attained on which standeth the celestial city; he seeth himself enter within the pearly gates, hailed as more than conqueror, crowned by the hand of Christ, embraced in the arms of Jesus, glorified with Him, and made to sit together with Him on His throne, even as He has overcome and has sat down with the Father on His throne. The thought of this future may well relieve the darkness of the past and the gloom of the present."[667]

Its perpetual practice.

Focusing on the "unseen" splendor of Heaven is to be engaged in habitually in every season of life, most especially in its final season. As a habit, it must be accomplished by mental discipline. See Colossians 3:1–4. Augustine remarked, "By desiring Heaven we exercise the powers of our soul. Now this exercise will be effective only to the extent that we free ourselves from desires leading to infatuation with this world."[668]

Its immense benefits.

(1. Gazing upon the future life in Heaven brings inspiration and encouragement (it uplifts the soul). Ignatius of Loyola said, "He who beholds Heaven with a pure eye sees better the darkness of earth; for although the latter seems to have some brilliancy, it disappears before the splendor of the heavens."[669]

(2. It brings hope. The present hour of infirmity, sorrow or suffering will not last forever; it will give way to wholeness of body, mind and spirit in the celestial city of God.

(3. It brings comfort and consolation. It robs the present of its deadening dominating influence, allowing Heaven to be its governing power.

(4. It prepares the saint for death. The grand anticipation of the change of bodily makeup at death, the corruptible putting on the incorruptible and the mortal clothing itself with immortality take the edge away from its fear.

(5. It makes possible victorious coping in life's present trials. Richard Sibbes states, "The life of a Christian is wondrously ruled in this world by the consideration and meditation of the life of another world."[670]

(6. It infills the soul with rapturous joy and song.

(7. It develops patience to endure the pain. Paul said the saints' "present suffering" (temporal) is not even worthy to be compared with the glory that awaits them in eternity (Romans 8:18). Paul further states, "For our light affliction...worketh for us a far more exceeding and eternal weight of glory" (2 Corinthians 4:17).

> I must keep alive in myself the desire for my true country, which I shall not find till after death.
> C. S. Lewis

(8. It elevates the tone of life.[671] "Everyone who has this hope in him purifies himself, even as he is pure" (1 John 3:3 FV). Despite the hardships and pains, life is lifted to a higher plain. The soul is optimistic, not despondent and gloomy.

(9. It enables perseverance until that which is not seen becomes full sight.

(10. It keeps eternity in focus. See Philippians 3:20. C. S. Lewis in *Mere Christianity* wrote, "When the real want for Heaven is present in us, we do not recognize it. Most people, if they had really learned to look into their own hearts, would know that they do want, and want acutely, something that cannot be had in this world. There are all sorts of things in this world that offer to give it to you, but they never quite keep their promise. If I find in myself a desire which no experience in this world can satisfy, the most probable explanation is that I was made for another world. I must keep alive in myself the desire for my true country, which I shall not find till after death; I must never let it get snowed under or turned aside; I must make it the main object of life to press on to that other country and to help others to do the same."[672]

The French author, Gustave Flaubert, remarked, "The principal thing in this world is to keep one's soul aloft."[673] Implement the "habit" of looking through the lenses of faith at the "things which are unseen" that await in Heaven, and you will be lifted from the pit of despair, distress and depression by that simple discipline. Ever look up to keep your soul aloft.

116

The Endurance of Hardship

"Thou therefore endure hardness" (2 Timothy 2:3). A. W. Pink said, "Faith endures as seeing Him who is invisible, endures the disappointments, the hardships, and the heartaches of life by recognizing that all comes from the hand of Him who is too wise to err and too loving to be unkind."[674] Despite multiple hardships, Paul learned that the secret of endurance with joy was to be content with whatever happened, trusting God for care and provision (Philippians 4:11–12). While waiting patiently for a hardship to improve or pass, don't complain, grumble or grow embittered; instead, be content knowing God is in control and somehow, someway it will be for *gain as promised,* even as it was for Paul (Philippians 1:21 and Romans 8:28).

"But they that wait upon the LORD shall renew their strength; they shall mount up with wings as eagles; they shall run, and not be weary; and they shall walk, and not faint" (Isaiah 40:31).

They that wait. To wait upon the Lord is to look with patient expectancy for His intervention in times of weakness, frailty, trouble and sorrow. It is to place confident trust in Him to help. See Psalm 25:3, 5; Psalm 27:14 and Psalm 69:3. However, it does not mean inactivity. In waiting upon God to help, the Christian must utilize the means He has provided.[675] Albert Barnes explains, "The farmer who should wait for God to plow and sow his fields would not only be disappointed but would be guilty of provoking Him. And so the man who waits for God to do what he ought to do to save him without using any of the means of grace will not only be disappointed but will provoke his displeasure."[676] In waiting, the saint has eyes fixed on Jesus, ears tuned to hear His gentle whispers of instruction and consolation and feet in readiness to obey.

Shall renew their strength. The Christian's strength may lessen amid life's many trials and troubles (illness fatigue, bereavement, suffering, conflict), causing the need for it to be renewed, restored and revived. "Fainting spells" cause soul doubt, despair and defeat. They cause lack of drive, purpose and fight. The great prophet Elijah had a "fainting spell" under a juniper tree (1 Kings 19:4). It is in such a time of decaying strength that the believer must cry out to God for heart and soul renewal.

They shall renew their strength. Spurgeon comments: "This means that they shall change their strength. They shall put off their own threadbare, worn-out, poverty-stricken strength, and they shall be clad with strength as with a garment, a garment that has been woven in celestial looms. It means among other things that the strength they have, God-given, shall be adapted to special circumstances and applied to peculiar conditions. I know how possible it is to have a goodly measure of strength and yet not know how to use it. Those who wait on the Lord are taught spiritual economy. They make the most of the little they have, and by using it, it is increased. They are as those who, having a long journey to undertake, have made arrangements previously that at each stage there shall be a fresh horse awaiting them."[677]

Praise to the Lord, who o'er all things so wondrously reigneth,
Who, as on wings of an eagle, uplifteth, sustaineth.
Hast thou not seen how thy desires all have been
Granted in what He ordaineth? ~ Joachim Neander (1650–1680)

When the Rain Comes

They shall mount up on wings of eagles. The velocity of the wings of an eagle enable it to soar fast and to heights of 10,000 feet. The eagle is the only bird that to avoid rain will fly above the storm.[678] The saint, upon renewal, is clothed with feathers (strength, power, ability) like that of an eagle, enabling him to soar above life's troubles, hardships and sorrows victoriously though they be baffling, exhausting and cause pain.

They shall run and not be weary. Barnes says, "It has been found in the experience of thousands and tens of thousands that by waiting on the Lord the heart has been invigorated, the faith has been confirmed, and the affections have been raised above the world. Strength has been given to bear trial without complaining, to engage in arduous duty without fainting, to pursue the perilous and toilsome journey of life without exhaustion, and to rise above the world in hope and peace on the bed of death."[679]

They shall walk and not faint. He that is touched with God's hand of renewal figuratively walks without weariness, runs without fatigue and flies without fainting.

Thy youth is renewed like the eagle's. Commenting on Psalm 103:5, J. A. Alexander states, "The only point of comparison with the eagle is its strength and vigor, as in 2 Samuel 1:23 and Isaiah 40:31, and the whole verse may be paraphrased as follows: 'So completely does His bounty feed thy strength, that even in old age thou growest young again and soarest like an eagle.'"[680] The secret to patient endurance in hardship is dependence upon divine strength coupled with an attitude of contentment like that of Paul (Philippians 4:11).

His grace is sufficient.
 Then why I need fear,
Though the testing be hard
 And the trial severe?

He tempers each wind
 That upon me doth blow
And tenderly whispers,
 "Thy Father doth know!"

His pow'r is sufficient.
 Then why should I quail,
Though the storm clouds hang low,
 And though wild is the gale?

His strength will not falter,
 Whatever betide,
And safe on His bosom
 He bids me to hide.

His love is sufficient—
 Yea boundless and free,
As high as the mountains,
 As deep as the sea.

Ah, there I will rest
 Till the darkness is o'er
And wake in His likeness
 To dwell evermore.

~ Avis Burgeson Christiansen

117

Bruised Reeds

"A bruised reed He will not break, and a smoldering wick He will not snuff out" (Isaiah 42:3 NIV). A reed is a plant (cane) with a thin delicate hollow stem that easily is bent (bruised) or broken due to its brittleness and frailty. Once bent or broken, it is valueless and useless. Man is a fragile "reed" (feeble, "shaken with the wind"—Matthew 11:7) whom though bruised or broken by sorrow, sickness, adversity or sin, Christ sympathetically and compassionately mends and restores upon request. Rather than worsening the bruised reed's estate (weak and frail), Christ tenderly heals it. "He healeth the broken in heart, and bindeth up their wounds" (Psalm 147:3). Christ has never, nor will He ever, break a bruised reed (oppress those that are beaten down and weakened[681]). He will never put upon the saint more than he can bear; never allow calamity, sin's torment, sorrow or adversity to crush him utterly ("break").

Alexander Smellie says, "Even if I am a bruised reed, He will not break my feebleness. Even if I am a dimly burning wick, He will not quench my flickering light. He remembers too well when they put a reed in His own hand, the one scepter which they allowed Him, and when, in the darkness of Gethsemane and Golgotha and the grave, His light seemed altogether extinct and gone."[682]

No, no. He uses and loves and transfigures bruised reeds. They become pens to write the marvels of His truth and the riches of His grace. They become instruments of sweet music to ring forth His praises in winning melody. They become columns which support and adorn His temple. They become swords and spears to rout His enemies, so that, as a poet sings, "the bruised reed is amply tough to pierce the shield of error through."

And He loves and employs and fans into bright and glowing flame dimly burning wicks. They are changed...

into lamps that shine for the guidance of wandering feet,

into beacon-fires that warn the voyagers from sandbank and iron coast,

into torches which hand on His message to the generation following,

into lighthouse rays and beams which conduct storm-tossed sailors to their desired haven."[683]

Christ, "acquainted with grief" (its sorrows and pain), identifies with and feels for *bruised reeds* (Isaiah 53:5, 10; Isaiah 50:4 and Isaiah 61:1). Therefore, tenderly He says, "Come unto me, all ye that labor and are heavy laden, and I will give you rest" (Matthew 11:28). He will prop and support you. He will heal you.

When the Rain Comes

I know not what the future hath
    Of marvel or surprise,
Assured alone that life and death
    His mercy underlies.

And if my heart and flesh are weak
    To bear an untried pain,
The bruised reed He will not break,
    But strengthen and sustain.

And so, beside the silent sea,
    I wait the muffled oar;
No harm from Him can come to me
    On ocean or on shore.

I know not where His islands lift
    Their fronded palms in air;
I only know I cannot drift
    Beyond His love and care.

~ John J. Whittier

It is thought by some that the bruised reed is a musical instrument that cannot play melodiously due to a crack or flaw, something that spoiled its music. Christ, in seeing "bruised reeds" (saints), says, "I must do something to repair it so it may again sound out beautiful music." He never says, "The rift in the lute is irreparable, its music impossible to restore, so throw it away."[684]

Shattered dreams, wounded hearts, broken toys,
Give them all, give them all,
Give them all to Jesus,
And he will turn your sorrow into joy.

~ Bob Benson, Sr. and Phil Johnson (1975)

118

Suicide Is Not the Answer

Every suicide (self-murder) is a mad rush to end "unbearable pain" without thought to its ultimate end of permanent separation from family and friends and obstruction to God's plan. Suicide is an act of selfishness; thinking of self above any consideration of a spouse, parent, child or friend. It violates the sixth commandment: "Thou shalt not murder" (Exodus 20:13 JPST). Augustine said, "In no passage of the holy canonical books can there be found either divine precept or permission to take away our own life, whether for the sake of entering on the enjoyment of immortality, or of shunning or ridding ourselves of anything whatever. Nay, the law, rightly interpreted, even prohibits suicide, where it says, 'Thou shalt not kill.'"[685] Ultimately suicide is wrong because life is a gift from God; therefore, He has the sole power to determine when it is to end. Chuck Swindoll agrees, stating, "When an individual makes the decision to commit suicide, that person has violated, in a criminal fashion, a right that is not his or hers. It is God's right alone to take life, just as it is His prerogative to give life."[686]

Comfort for Troubled Hearts

Life is full of hardships and troubles which are unavoidable. We all experience heartache, sorrow, disappointment, sickness and adversity. And some battle grave suffering. At times these afflictions seem unbearable and intolerable. But with Christ they are endurable. In college I heard a chapel speaker say something that impacted my life then and now: "There's a tolerable solution for every intolerable problem you face." I have proved that statement to be true time and again. The secret to bearing the intolerable is looking for its tolerable solution. And that solution isn't suicide. Let me repeat, suicide is not the solution to agonizing emotional pain. The solution is unflinching trust in Jesus Christ that He is in control and promises to work good out of the bad condition or circumstance. It's confident assurance that He walks with you in the storms of sorrow, suffering and sickness. It's knowledge that He will "never leave thee, nor forsake thee."

Days of emotional and physical upheaval will come, but they will PASS. The darkness eventually must give way to the light. God promises to still the boisterous winds and waves beating upon the vessel of your life, saying, "Peace, be still." Don't panic. Wait on Him. Trust in Him. Soon the raging sea will become as a sea of glass and tranquility will reign again. "In his favor is life: weeping may endure for a night, but joy cometh in the morning" (Psalm 30:5). D. L. Moody offers encouragement: "Take courage. We walk in the wilderness today and in the Promised Land tomorrow."[687]

"Humpty Dumpty sat on a wall; All the king's horses and all the king's men
Humpty Dumpty had a great fall. Couldn't put Humpty together again."[688]

Regardless of the "fall" experienced—a broken, crushed heart; illness; fatigue; adversity; or abandonment, King Jesus can do what "all the king's horses and all the king's men" cannot do—put you back together again! All that is needed for this to happen is for you to cry out to Him. "The righteous cry out, and the LORD hears, and delivers them out of all their troubles. The LORD is near to those who have a broken heart, and saves such as have a contrite spirit. Many are the afflictions of the righteous, but the LORD delivers him out of them all. He guards all his bones; not one of them is broken" (Psalm 34:17–20 NKJV). As Dietrich Bonhoeffer wrote: "A man who is on the brink of suicide no longer has ears for commands or prohibitions;…A man who is desperate cannot be saved by a law that appeals to his own strength;…One who despairs of life can be helped only by the saving deed of another, the offer of a new life which is to be lived not by his own strength but by the grace of God."[689]

Charles Spurgeon said, "We are to groan for glorification, but we are to wait patiently for it, knowing that what the Lord appoints is best. Waiting implies being ready. We are to stand at the door expecting the Beloved to open it and take us away to Himself."[690] It is He that must open it, not yourself. Peter Marshall prayed, "When we long for life without difficulties, remind us that oaks grow strong in contrary winds and diamonds are made under pressure."[691]

> Up, my drowsing eyes!
>   Up, my sinking heart!
> Up to Jesus Christ arise!
>   Claim your part
> In all the rapture of the skies.
>
> Yet a little while,
>   Yet a little way,
> Saints shall reap and rest and smile
>   All the day.
> Up! let's trudge another mile. ~ Christina Rossetti

119
Can't Stop the Music

Death can't stop the music of the Christian's life. It plays on even more melodiously in a different sphere—Heaven. A. W. Tozer said, "Death is not annihilation. Death is not cessation of existence. Death is a changed relationship in a different form of existence."[692] Spurgeon remarks, "Even death itself, with all its terrible influences, has no power to suspend the music of a Christian's heart, but rather makes that music become more sweet, more clear, more heavenly, till the last kind act which death can do is to let the earthly strain melt into the heavenly chorus, the temporal joy into the eternal bliss!"[693] This is affirmed by Jesus, who said, "I am the resurrection, and the life: he that believeth in me, though he were dead, yet shall he live" (John 11:25).

Matthew Henry explains, "The believing hopes of the soul's redemption from the grave and reception to glory are the great support and joy of the children of God in a dying hour, that God will redeem their souls from the power of the grave, which includes the preserving of the soul from going to the grave with the body. The grave has power over the body by virtue of the curse of sin (Genesis 3:19), and it's cruel in executing that power (Song of Solomon 8:6). It has power to silence and imprison and consume the body, but the soul then moves and acts and converses more freely than ever (Revelation 6:9, 10); it is immaterial and immortal."[694] The soul of the saint will reunite with its body (a glorified body) at the great resurrection when Christ returns. McWherter says of the great resurrection, "It will reunite a redeemed soul with a redeemed body, and while the former is stamped with the image of the Father, it will fashion the latter after the likeness of the Son."[695] The music plays on!

On the resurrection morning,
    Soul and body meet again;
No more sorrow, no more weeping,
    No more pain!

Soul and body reunited,
    Thenceforth nothing shall divide,
Waking up in CHRIST'S own likeness,
    Satisfied.

Oh! the beauty, Oh! the gladness
    Of that Resurrection day,
Which shall not through endless ages
    Pass away!

On that happy Easter morning
    All the graves their dead restore;
Father, sister, child, and mother
    Meet once more.
To that brightest of all meetings
    Bring us, JESUS CHRIST, at last;
To Thy cross, through death and judgment
    Holding fast. ~ Sabine Baring-Gould

The famed evangelist D. L. Moody was absolutely confident that at death the music would play on, for he wrote, "Someday you will read in the papers that D. L. Moody of East Northfield is dead. Don't you believe a word of it! At that moment I shall be more alive than I am now. I shall have gone up higher, that is all—out of this old clay tenement into a house that is immortal, a body that death cannot touch, that sin cannot taint, a body fashioned like unto His glorious body."[696] The quote was adapted and embraced by Billy Graham about his death. I'm confident Moody didn't mind Graham personalizing it, nor will he if we do so. Victor Hugo states, "When I go down to the grave, I can say, like so many others, I have finished my work, but I cannot say I have finished my life. My day's work will begin the next morning. I feel in myself the future life. Heaven lights me with the reflection of an unknown world I cannot see. My soul becomes more luminous when my bodily powers begin to fail. The nearer I approach the end, the plainer I hear around me the immortal symphonies of the world which invites me. The tomb is not a blind alley. It is a thoroughfare. It closes on the twilight. It opens on dawn."[697] The music plays on!

It is most fitting (though somewhat lengthy) to share words upon this subject from the pen of A. W. Tozer. Remarkably he writes, "But Christians die. Every day the bodies of believing men and women are taken out to the cemetery and laid to rest with quiet songs and soft repetitions of Scripture. No matter how we may try to avoid the facts, Christians die as their Lord died before them. Their cold helplessness, their sudden strange silence which no pleadings of anguished love can break, their apparent defeat by the relentless forces of nature—all this stuns the heart and (if the truth were told) arouses uncomfortable fears that this is all, that we have seen our friends for the last time. It is winter when we lay our loved ones down. So it seems to the natural heart. So it must have appeared to some of the Thessalonian Christians. Why otherwise would it have been necessary for Paul to write and exhort them not to sorrow as others who had no hope? One thing the resurrection teaches us is that we must not trust appearances. The leafless tree says by its appearance that there will be no second spring. The body in Joseph's new tomb appears to signify the end of everything for Christ and His disciples. The limp form of a newly dead believer suggests everlasting defeat. Yet how wrong are all these appearances. The tree will bloom again. Christ arose the third day according to the Scriptures, and the Christian will rise at the shout of the Lord and the voice of the archangel."[698] You can't stop the music.

The hour of my departure's come;
I hear the voice that calls me home.
At last, O Lord! let trouble cease
And let Thy servant die in peace.

The race appointed I have run;
The combat's o'er, the prize is won,
And now my witness is on high,
And now my record's in the sky.

Not in mine innocence I trust;
I bow before Thee in the dust,
And through my Savior's blood alone
I look for mercy at Thy throne.

I leave the world without a tear,
Save for the friends I held so dear;
To heal their sorrows, Lord, descend
And to the friendless prove a friend.

I come, I come, at Thy command;
I give my spirit to Thy hand.
Stretch forth Thine everlasting arms
And shield me in the last alarms.

The hour of my departure's come;
I hear the voice that calls me home.
Now, O my God! let trouble cease;
Now let Thy servant die in peace. ~ John Logan (1781)

Upon his deathbed, the great Christian and scientist Sir Michael Faraday was asked by journalists about his speculations for life after death. "Speculations!" said he, "I know nothing about speculations. I'm resting on certainties. 'I know that my redeemer liveth,' and because He lives, I shall live also."[699] The music plays on!

Benjamin Franklin penned the epitaph for his gravestone that is fitting for every saint (perhaps excluding his profession of printer). The epitaph: "The body of Benjamin Franklin, printer, like the cover of an old book, its contents torn out and stripped of its lettering and gilding, lies here....Yet the Work itself shall not be lost; for it will, as he believed, appear once more in a new and more beautiful edition, corrected and amended by the Author."[700] Franklin was confident the music of his life would not be silenced by the dagger of death. The music plays on—just more melodious, jubilant and gratifying!

120
"It Shall Be Well with Them"

"Surely I know that it shall be well with those who fear God, who fear before Him" (Ecclesiastes 8:12 FV). People that fear (reverence, honor, respect God and follow His ways) God nowhere are promised exemption from the trials and troubles of life or even the furnace of affliction or infirmity. But they are promised that regardless what happens, *it shall be well with them*. The word "well" here means "good, beneficial, pleasant, favorable, happy, right."[701] "It is the happiness of all that fear God," writes Matthew Henry, "that in the worst of times it shall be well with them; their happiness in God's favor cannot be prejudiced, nor their communion with God interrupted, by their troubles; they are in a good case, for they are kept in

When the Rain Comes

a good frame under their troubles, and in the end they shall have a blessed deliverance from and an abundant recompence for their troubles."[702]

It shall be well in adversity. "Many are the afflictions of the righteous: but the LORD delivereth him out of them all" (Psalm 34:19).

It shall be well in infirmity. "The Lord will sustain him on his sickbed; You will heal him on the bed where he lies" (Psalm 41:3 HCSB).

It shall be well in bereavement. "He healeth the broken in heart, and bindeth up their wounds" (Psalm 147:3).

It shall be well in death. "To be absent from the body, and to be present with the Lord" (2 Corinthians 5:8).

It shall be well at the resurrection. "But we are citizens of Heaven; our outlook goes beyond this world to the hopeful expectation of the savior who will come from Heaven, the Lord Jesus Christ. He will re-make these wretched bodies of ours to resemble his own glorious body, by that power of his which makes him the master of everything that is" (Philippians 3:20–21 PHILLIPS).

It shall be well at the judgment. "And as we live in God, our love grows more perfect. So we will not be afraid on the day of judgment, but we can face him with confidence because we live like Jesus here in this world." (1 John 4:17 NLT).

It shall be well forever. "Your sun shall no more go down, nor shall your moon withdraw itself, for the Lord shall be your everlasting light, and the days of your mourning shall be ended" (Isaiah 60:20 AMPC). See Revelation 21:4.

Surely, I know. Solomon expresses confidence in the certainty of the promise. Charles Simeon states, "We do not *surmise* it as a thing *possible*. We do not *hope* it as a thing *probable*. We *absolutely know* it as *infallibly certain*. We are not surer of our existence than we are of this truth. Without hesitation therefore we deliver our message. Oh, that the word may sink deep into all our hearts! And that we might from experience unite our testimony to Solomon's."[703] The promises of God (Isaiah 3:10; Psalm 34:9; Psalm 25:13 and Psalm 103:17) and experiences of saints throughout history attest to the certainty that it shall be well for them that fear God in every extremity of life. The confidence in the promise is also aided by a conscience that knows that life is ordered by God's divine providence and will designed for our best good. "'For I know the plans I have for you,' declares the Lord, 'plans to prosper you and not to harm you, plans to give you hope and a future'" (Jeremiah 29:11 NIV).

Through the love of God our Savior,
    All will be well.
Free and changeless is his favor;
    All, all is well.

Precious is the blood that healed us;
Perfect is the grace that sealed us;
Strong the hand stretched forth to shield us;
All must be well.

Though we pass through tribulation,
    All will be well.
Ours is such a full salvation;
    All, all is well.

Happy, still in God confiding,
Fruitful, if in Christ abiding,
Holy, through the Spirit's guiding,
All must be well.

We expect a bright tomorrow;
    All will be well.
Faith can sing through days of sorrow;
    "All, all is well."

On our Father's love relying,
Jesus every need supplying,
In our living, in our dying,
All must be well. ~ Mary Bowley Peters (1847)

121

Homesick for Heaven

It's no wrong when overwhelmed with sickness and suffering to pine for Heaven. A longing for Home is as natural for the child of God as is breathing. After all, our citizenship is not of this present world but in Heaven (Philippians 3:20). It is there where our dearest treasures are stored—the presence of Jesus, family, friends and a new glorified body that is free from sickness, decay and death (Matthew 6:21).

Paul writes, "And we are *eagerly waiting* for him to return as our Savior. He will take our weak mortal bodies and change them into glorious bodies like his own, using the same power with which he will bring everything under his control" (Philippians 3:20–21 NLT).

When the Rain Comes

Again, he says, "So we do not look at what we can see right now, the troubles all around us, but *we look forward to the joys in Heaven* which we have not yet seen. The troubles will soon be over, but the joys to come will last forever" (2 Corinthians 4:18 TLB).

In answer to the question, *Is it wrong to be homesick for Heaven?* Billy Graham said, "No, it isn't wrong. In fact, if we never yearn for Heaven, it may mean we've become too satisfied or too preoccupied with our lives right now!"[704]

Dietrich Bonhoeffer states, "No one has yet believed in God and the kingdom of God, no one has yet heard about the realm of the resurrected and not been homesick from that hour, waiting and looking forward joyfully to being released from bodily existence. Whether we are young or old makes no difference. What are twenty or thirty or fifty years in the sight of God? And which of us knows how near he or she may already be to the goal? That life only really begins when it ends here on earth, that all that is here is only the prologue before the curtain goes up—that is for young and old alike to think about."[705]

Richard Baxter expresses the unreasonableness of not being "homesick" for Heaven: "If there be so certain and glorious a rest for the saints, why is there no more industrious seeking after it? One would think if a man did but once hear of such unspeakable glory to be obtained and believed what he heard to be true, he should be transported with the *forceful passion* of his desire after it and should almost forget to eat and drink and should care for nothing else and speak of and inquire after nothing else but how to get this treasure. And yet people who hear of it daily and profess to believe it as a fundamental article of their faith do as little mind it or labor for it as if they had never heard of any such thing or did not believe one word they hear."[706]

They are never sick in that beautiful land;
No tears there ever dim the sight.

Heaven, sweet Heaven, the Home of the blest,
   That land of the purest delight,
Heaven, sweet Heaven, there I shall abide.
   I'm homesick for Heaven tonight. ~ Johnson Oatman, Jr. (1899)

Henry Ward Beecher says, "One should go to sleep at night as homesick passengers (aboard ship) do, saying, 'Perhaps in the morning we shall see the shore.' To us who are Christians, it is not a solemn, but delightful, thought that perhaps nothing but the opaque, bodily eye prevents us from beholding the gate which is open just before us, and nothing but a dull ear prevents us from hearing the ringing of those bells of joy which welcome us to the heavenly land. That we are so near death is too good to be believed."[707]

> Sure 'tis in vain to seek for bliss,
>   For bliss can ne'er be found,
> Till we arrive where Jesus is
>   And tread on heavenly ground.
>
> There's nothing round the spreading skies
>   Or on this earthy clod,
> Nothing, my soul, that's worth thy joys
>   Or lovely as thy God.
>
> 'Tis Heaven on earth to taste His love,
>   To feel His quickening grace,
> And all the Heaven I hope above
>   Is but to see His face.
>
> Why move my years in slow delay?
>   And why this fear to die?
> Death's but a guide that leads my way
>   To a superior sky.
>
> Dear Sovereign, break these vital strings
>   That bind me to my clay;
> Help me to rise and stretch my wings
>   And mount and soar away. ~ Isaac Watts (1674-1748)

"How can we ever begin to know," writes Billy Graham, "the rejoicing that will take place when the Lord brings all of us home in immortal bodies? The morning stars will sing together, and the angels will shout for glory. Think of having complete fulfillment, knowing that our homecoming brings unspeakable joy to our wonderful Lord! So why do we prefer lingering here? Because we are not only earthbound in body; we are earthbound in our thinking. But when we leave this place, we will never dwell on it again. Our eyes and hearts will be fixed on Christ."[708]

122

An Enlarged Heart through Distress

"Thou hast enlarged me when I was in distress" (Psalm 4:1). This is a figure taken from an army hard pressed by the surrounding enemy escaping into the open plain.[709] David hopelessly was hemmed in by the enemy in a tight spot. But he prayed, and God rescued him—to a wide and open place. Spurgeon paraphrases David: "God has enlarged my heart with joy and comfort when I was like a man imprisoned by grief and sorrow."[710] See Psalm 18:19. What a glorious testimony to God's goodness and mercy to deliver His child either in or through times of crisis.

J. C. Lambert comments, "Our enlargement in distress does not lie only in our new thoughts about God, but in God's new mercies toward us. The Lord has special mercies for His children in distress, as a mother has kisses and fond soothing words for her little child who has hurt himself by a fall. Did you ever consider this, that there are stores of blessing held in reserve within the eternal treasuries, the fullness of which you can only know in the day of trial?"[711]

The saint's faith is enlarged in distress. Answered prayer for rescue or relief increases or expands trust in God.

The saint's hope is enlarged in distress. Being formerly helped, he expects to be so again in times of trouble.

The saint's gratitude is enlarged in distress. The underserved, unmerited mercies (acts of lovingkindness) received of God produces *new* praises and songs of thanksgiving to Him.

The saint's heart also is enlarged in distress sympathetically for others in distress. It was not until my heart was crushed that it was enlarged with deep compassion for the grieving and hurting. Paul admonishes, "Help each other in troubles and problems" (Galatians 6:2 NLV). And who better to help the bruised, broken and bleeding than believers who have walked in their steps. God, through our brokenness, prepares us for the ministry of sympathy and healing. In the dungeon of Potiphar, as Joseph's head was put into an iron collar, "iron entered his soul."[712] We all need the "iron" (sorrows, suffering, sickness) in life to enlarge our character and deepen our compassion for others.[713] George Matheson says, "Your life will be enlarged in proportion to the amount of iron you have endured, for it is in the shadows of your life that you will find the actual fulfillment of your dreams of glory. So do not complain about the shadows of darkness."[714] Joseph's dungeon was the road to his throne.[715]

Hear me when I call, O God of my righteousness. It is because of God's intervention in the past that David implores Him by His mercy to help him in the present distress. Albert Barnes says, "The prayer indicates confidence in the power and the unchangeableness of God and proves that it is right in our prayers to recall the former instances of the divine interposition as an argument or as a ground of hope that God would again interpose."[716] Matthew Henry agrees, saying, "The experience we have had of God's goodness to us in enlarging us when we have been in distress is not only a great encouragement to our faith and hope for the future, but a good plea with God in prayer. 'Thou hast; wilt Thou not? For Thou art God and changest not; Thy work is perfect.'"[717] That is, "Lord, in my former distress (temporal and spiritual) You enlarged me (freed me from its darkness and despair); do so again now in my present crisis."

Whatever the distress, meet it with the same attitude as the psalmist did (faith, hope, and patience) and "thy heart shall be enlarged." You've faced adversities victoriously yesterday by God's grace. You will rise above this present trial likewise! God can do anything but fail you in the hour of need.

123

Dying Grace

On his eightieth birthday, John Quincy Adams was walking slowly along a Boston street. A friend asked the former president, "How is John Quincy Adams today?"

He replied, "Thank you, John Quincy Adams is well, sir, quite well, I thank you. But the house in which he lives at present is becoming dilapidated. It is tottering upon the foundations. Time and the seasons have nearly destroyed it. Its roof is pretty well worn out, its walls are shattered, and it trembles with every wind. The old tenement is becoming almost uninhabitable, and I think John Quincy Adams will have to move out of it soon; but he himself is quite well, sir, quite well." The house of our flesh is perishing, and soon like with John Quincy Adams it will be "Moving Day" to a new home. On that day Christ will give us dying grace to make the "move" peacefully and joyfully.

Grace is Christ's undeserved kindness, love, mercy and favor. Martyn Lloyd-Jones said, "It is grace at the beginning and grace at the end, so that when you and I come to lie upon our deathbeds, the one thing that should comfort and help and strengthen us there is the thing that helped us in the beginning. Not what we have been, not what we have done, *but the grace of God in Jesus Christ our Lord*. The Christian life starts with grace; it must continue with grace; it ends with grace—grace, wondrous grace! By the grace of God, I am what I am—yet not I, but the grace of God which was with me."[718]

The Bible says, "So let us come boldly to the throne of our gracious God. There we will receive his mercy, and we will find *grace to help us when we need it most*" (Hebrews 4:16 NLT). Dying grace, comforting assurances dispensed by Christ to the saint (when dying, not before) are given to make the transition from this life into the next with Him peaceful and tranquil. Saving grace is provided for deliverance from sin's penalty (Ephesians 2:8–9), living grace is provided for life's trials and troubles (Acts 4:33), and dying grace is provided for death and departure to Heaven (2 Corinthians 12:9). As surely as the Lord provides the former two, He also will provide the latter one. D. L. Moody said, "I find that many Christians are in trouble about the future; they think they will not have grace enough to die by. When the dying hour comes, there will be dying grace; but you do not require dying grace to live by."[719] On another occasion Moody was asked, "Do you have dying grace?" to which he replied, "Why no. I have living grace, but when I come to die, I shall have dying grace." Upon falling deathly ill in a meeting in Kansas City, Moody was taken home, where, propped up on pillows, he said to family members gathered around: "The world is receding. Heaven is opening. God is calling me, and I must be away."[720] He experienced dying grace when death visited. In the hour in which dying grace is needed it shall be abundantly provided.

> There's been grace for every trial.
> There's been grace for every mile.
> There's been grace sufficient from His vast supply—
> Grace to make my heart more tender,
> Grace to love and pray for sinners,
> But there'll be new grace when it's my time to die.
>
> Grace not yet discovered,
> Grace not yet uncovered,
> Grace from his bountiful store,
> Grace to cross the river,
> Grace to face forever,
> There'll be new grace I've not needed before. ~ Tom Hayes

"I do not say shudder not at the thought of death," states F. B. Meyer. "Jesus trembled when He took the cup into His hand dropping with bloody sweat. It is human nature to shrink from the grave. *But I can say, 'Fear not.'* When death comes, *you shall have grace to die.*"[721] "I may sometimes tremble on the rock, but blessed be the Lord, the rock never trembles under me."[722]

124

The Prayer of Faith and Healing

With Chuck Swindoll I heartedly agree when he said, "I believe in divine healing. I do not believe in divine healers. I believe in faith healing. I do not believe in faith healers. There is a great difference."[723] I believe in healing at the hands of the Divine Healer for several reasons.

(1. The Bible gives assurance that God heals (James 5:14–16).

(2. One of His compound names declares He is the great healer: *Jehovah-rapha* ("I am the Lord that healeth"—Exodus 15:26).

(3. Numerous documented healings in the Bible affirm His power to heal.[724] Abraham prayed for Abimelech, and Abimelech was healed (Genesis 20:17). God healed a leprous Miriam (Numbers 12:10–15). God heard Hezekiah's request for healing and added fifteen years to his life (Isaiah 38:1–5). Jesus healed Bartimaeus (Mark 10:46–52). He healed Jairus' daughter (Matthew 9:18–26).

James gives instructions to the sick that seek healing. He writes, "Is any among you afflicted? let him pray....Is any sick among you? let him call for the elders of the church; and let them pray over him, anointing him with oil in the name of the Lord: And the prayer of faith shall save [heal] the sick, and the Lord shall raise him up" (James 5:13–15). Let's unpack this passage phrase by phrase for clarity and application.

Let him pray. Christ grants every believer direct access to His throne through prayer. Therefore, the afflicted ought to pray for their own relief or recovery based upon the will of God (James 5:16). This he should do whether or not elders are

> This above everything else: when I am sick, let me take myself to God.
> W. A. Criswell

requested to visit and pray. Chuck Swindoll writes: "In every circumstance— sickness, health, joy, hardship—we must go to God in prayer. Prayer not only reflects an attitude of genuine faith, but it also reveals patient endurance as we turn to God to handle life's struggles in His timing and according to His promises."[725] W. A. Criswell says, "This above everything else: when I am sick, let me take myself to God. Let me take myself to God."[726] In contrast, King Asa (2 Chronicles 16:12–14) with a serious foot disease depended only upon physicians—"yet in his disease he sought not to the LORD, but to the physicians." He died within two years. In healing, God may (and often does) use medicines, physicians, and hospitals, but they are merely the "means" (not cause) for divine healing (the Lord still does the healing). Asa's story, whether he had been healed or not, would have been markedly better had he sought (depended on) the Lord *first* instead of going to the physicians. With God in the equation (even if He chooses not to heal), the saint is a trillion times better off than are the people like Asa.

Let him call. The sickly (extremely ill) that are unable (incapacitated) to get to the "church" for prayer *may* invite the "elders" to come to them (home, hospital, assisted care facility). The act is completely voluntary. "The call is a general call; whether one or many or all the elders respond is not mentioned, although the plural verb indicates James expects several to come."[727] By the way, don't criticize the minister for not visiting you when sick if he is not informed.

When the Rain Comes

For the elders. Although every believer possesses the privilege and power of prayer (and ought to be engaged in such in the hour of sickness, sorrow or suffering, as seen in James 5:16), it is the "elders" that are to be requested for "anointing and prayer." Elders are spiritually mature leaders in the church that have been divinely appointed and qualified by the Holy Spirit to have "the spiritual care of, and to exercise oversight over the church" (the shepherds, the overseers of the flock, 1 Peter 5:1–2).[728]

Let them pray over him. Albert Barnes suggests that elders pray "that relief from pain may be granted, that the mind may be calm and submissive, that the medicines employed may be blessed to a restoration to health [if in accordance with God's divine will], that past sins may be forgiven, that he who is sick may be sanctified by his trials, that he may be restored to health [if in agreement with God's will] or prepared for his 'last change'—all these are subjects of prayer which we feel to be appropriate in such a case, and every sick man should avail himself of the aid of those who 'have an interest at the throne of grace,' that they may be obtained. Prayer is always one important means of obtaining the divine favor, and there is no place where it is more appropriate than by the bedside of sickness."[729]

Anointing him with oil. While prayer is the *primary* function, according to James, it is to be accompanied with the anointing of oil. Frankly, there is diverse opinion over exactly what the anointing denotes. Is it medicinal (Luke 10:34); or symbolic of ceremonial consecration, being set aside for the cause of Christ (Leviticus 8:10–12); or symbolic of the Holy Spirit (typifies the power of the Holy Spirit to heal (Zechariah 4:6); or simply an aid to enhance the sick man's faith (John 9:6)? Each of these opinions are held by some conservatives. Chuck Swindoll argues for the first, citing "oil" was used in biblical times for medicinal purposes, that the word for "anointing" in the text refers to applying or rubbing something into the skin (It literally means to "plaster, spread on, besmear"). Oil soothed the skin. Criswell states, "There is no doubt but that oil was used two thousand years ago as a means of healing. It was medicinal in its purpose."[730] Jamie M. Adams, Billy Graham Evangelistic Association, comments, "There are two Greek words for *anoint*. One means to put oil on the forehead as was done for prophets, priests, and kings. The other word meant to knead or massage into the body. This is the one used in James."[731] Swindoll said, "The idea behind the use of both prayer and anointing is that the church should seek to come to the aid of both physical and spiritual needs of a sick person. The medicinal use of oil provided physical comfort and promoted the healing process. Note that James sees no conflict between prayer and medicine."[732] All evangelicals agree that the anointing with oil bears no "magic" healing power.

With regard to the various takes on the meaning of the anointing of oil, W. A. Criswell, in the sermon *Divine Healing,* said, "Well, what are you going to do about all those things? Let us say just what the Bible says and let us take it just as the Bible says. Do the Scriptures say that the oil, medicinal or otherwise, shall heal him, shall raise him up; or does it say 'the prayer of faith shall raise him up?' What does the Bible say? Well, the Bible is very plain: 'Is any among you sick? let him call for the elders of the church; and let them pray over him, anointing him with oil in the name of the Lord: And *the prayer of faith shall heal the sick*, and the Lord shall raise him up' [James 5:14–15]. You don't have any other choice, in my humble opinion, than to see this word just exactly as it is written."[733] Therefore, what is poignantly clear is that it is the prayer of faith, not the anointing with oil, that is the means of healing.

In Jesus' name. To pray in Jesus name is to pray in accordance with His divine will. It is to pray, "Not my will, but thine be done." John MacArthur remarks, "To pray in Jesus' name is to seek what He seeks, to promote what He desires, to give Him glory. We can rightly ask God for only that which will glorify the Son."[734] Elders therefore are summoned to place praying for the sick under the umbrella of that which is best for Christ, His cause, and them that are sick (the will of God). This is difficult but right praying when the elders (as is natural) want the person recovered and raised up.

And the prayer of faith. Elders at times discern God's will about the specific healing of a sick person. Sometimes it's a yes; sometimes it's a no; and at other times we just don't know. On occasions when it is discerned to be God's purpose to raise the sick up, they engage in the earnest prayer of faith for that to happen. When unsure, they likewise pray but base the bold request upon the contingency of God's will. Obviously, it's not His will to heal everyone. W. A. Criswell comments, "Note that in 2 Corinthians 12:7–10, in which Paul earnestly prays for healing, it does not occur; and in 2 Timothy 4:20, note that Paul's valued friend and helper Trophimus remains sick at Miletus, yet Paul did not heal him." In John 5 we read that although many who were sick surrounded the pool at Bethesda (verse 3), *only* the one man with the infirmity was healed (verses 8–9).

Moses pleaded with God, 'O God, let me live, let me go into the land with these people' (Deuteronomy 3:25). And yet he died. Hezekiah pleaded for additional years, and he lived (Isaiah 38:5). Healing is contingent upon what God counts best for you and His glory. If granted healing, as in the case of Hezekiah, make the best use of it for the Lord and others. If not, like Moses, shine in your faith and commitment to Christ, bearing testimony of the goodness of God even in the dark times and trusting Him for enduring grace.[735] See 2 Corinthians 12:9. Shadrach, Meshach and Abednego, facing the burning furnace, said, 'Our God is able to deliver us' (Daniel 3:17). They didn't say He *would* deliver them. Whether He did or didn't, they trusted Him to do what was best (verse 18).[736] This is the right attitude and approach to embrace regarding sickness and suffering. Faith says we can always trust the judgment of God to do what is expedient regarding our health.

When the Rain Comes

Summary. The incapacitated sick saint is to pray for himself (James 5:13), summon the elders, if desired, to pray (James 5:14), and request the prayers of all the saints (James 5:15). Elders, if summoned, pray in faith specifically for healing and recovery, anointing with oil "in the name of Jesus" (according to His will and plan). The prayer of faith is primary (means of healing); the medicinal oil is secondary (soothes the skin). In cases where it is discerned that healing is not God's will, elders may pray for sustaining grace, comfort, peace, ease of pain and discomfort, and at times dying grace for the heavenly transition. Elders also assist the sick in their *spiritual recovery* from sin through encouraging confession of unforgiven sin upon which healing may depend (James 5:15–16). When healing isn't acquired, it's wrong to blame the "weak" faith of the sick person (as "faith healers" often do). The bottom line of the text seems best put by Max Lucado: "Call out to God for help. Will He do what you want? I cannot say, but this I can say: He will do what is best."[737] See Romans 8:28.

> Yes, ask it for ourselves, if we need healing,
>   Pleading those instances of olden cure;
> But then if He refuse, we still will trust Him,
>   And He will make it happier to endure.
>
> Aye, happier to bear with Him the suffering,
>   Or even death itself, with Him close by,
> For in His presence there is joy forever;
>   And with Him near, it is not death to die.[738]

125

The School of Affliction

Charles Bridges said, "All have been taught in one school. All have known the power of affliction in some of its varied forms of inward conflict or outward trouble. All have found in time of affliction a time of love. All have given proof that the pains bestowed upon them have not been in vain."[739] In agreement John Gill states, "Afflictions are sometimes as a school to the people of God in which they learn much both of their duty and of their privileges, and when they are teaching and instructive, they are for good."[740] See Psalm 119:71 and Psalm 94:12. J. I. Packer says that God may have to deal with us as He dealt with Samson. He writes, "God may have to weaken us and bring us down at the points where we thought we were strong in order that we may become truly strong in real dependence upon Himself. He's done this before, and He may have to do it again with us. If He does, there will be mercy in it."[741]

Comfort for Troubled Hearts

David certainly found affliction to be an instructive school, for he testified, *"It is good for me that I have been afflicted"* (Psalm 119:71). Bridges paraphrases: "I never prized it [the Word of God] before. I could, indeed, scarcely be said to know it. I never understood its comfort until affliction expounded it to me. I never till now saw its suitableness to my case."[742] David's attitude (joy in retrospect) toward his suffering was admirable, for it proved to be of great value and benefit to his walk with the Lord. It enabled greater knowledge and understanding of God's "law." David declared to the Lord with regard to his suffering, "Thou hast dealt well with thy servant, O Lord" (Psalm 119:65). May God give grace sufficient for us to say likewise while in the furnace of affliction or in its aftermath.

Rawlinson says, "Notwithstanding all that he has suffered from the "persecution" of princes (Psalm 119:161) and the "contempt" (Psalm 119:22) and "derision" of the wicked generally (Psalm 119:51), the Psalmist feels that God's dealings with him have, on the whole, been good and gracious."[743] God is a strange Teacher in that He first gives the test, then the lesson.[744] Joseph suffered mistreatment by brothers, false accusations by Potiphar's wife and slavish imprisonment. But afterwards he said to his brothers, "As for you, ye thought evil against me; but God meant it unto good, to bring to pass, as it is this day, to save much people alive" (Genesis 50:20). Sounds very similar to Romans 8:28, doesn't it?[745]

Thou art good, and *doest good* (Psalm 119:68). Spurgeon said, "Even in affliction God is good and does good. This is the confession of experience. God is essential goodness in Himself, and in every attribute of His nature He is good in the fullest sense of the term. His acts are according to His nature."[746] Matthew Henry says, "This is a reason why David reckoned that when by his afflictions he learned God's statutes, and the profit did so much counterbalance the loss, he was really a gainer by them; for God's law, which he got acquaintance with by his affliction, was better to him than all the gold and silver which he lost by his affliction."[747] "So affliction of any kind acts as a wholesome discipline in leading the pious more highly to value the truth and promises of God."[748]

Robert Murray McCheyne said, "Affliction brings out graces that cannot be seen in a time of health. It is the treading of the grapes that brings out the sweet juices of the vine; so it is affliction that draws forth submission, weanedness from the world, and complete rest in God. Use afflictions while you have them."[749] Spurgeon comments, "Those who dive in the sea of affliction bring up rare pearls."[750] David repeats in Psalm 119:68 what, in effect, he already said in Psalm 119:67. Why? Benson suggests this he did "partly to intimate the certainty and importance of this truth (that God is good and does good), and partly because it is a great paradox to worldly men, who generally esteem afflictions to be evils, yea, the worst of evils."[751]

When the Rain Comes

I walked a mile with Pleasure;
    She chatted all the way
But left me none the wiser
    For all she had to say.

I walked a mile with Sorrow,
    And ne'er a word said she,
But, oh! the things I learned from her,
    When Sorrow walked with me. ~ Robert Browning Hamilton

May we look at our adversity, bereavement and infirmity as a theological schoolhouse for godly instruction and edification. The gained spiritual insight affliction affords will more than counterbalance whatever loss and suffering is incurred at its hand. In its aftermath we can say with David, "It was good for me to be have been afflicted." "The furnace of affliction is a good place for you, Christian; it benefits you; it helps you become more like Christ, and it is fitting you for Heaven."[752] J. I. Packer said, "God uses chronic pain and weakness, along with other afflictions, as His chisel for sculpting our lives. Felt weakness deepens dependence on Christ for strength each day. The weaker we feel, the harder we lean; and the harder we lean, the stronger we grow spiritually, even while our bodies waste away. To live with your 'thorn' uncomplainingly—that is, sweet, patient, and free in heart to love and help others, even though every day you feel weak—is true sanctification. It is true healing for the spirit. It is a supreme victory of grace."[753]

Frank E. Peretti remarks, "God does not waste an ounce of our pain or a drop of our tears; suffering doesn't come our way for no reason, and He seems efficient at using what we endure to mold character. If we are malleable, He takes our bumps and bruises and shapes them into something beautiful."[754] Packer says, "He afflicts us to make us lean harder on Him, that His purpose of drawing us into closest fellowship with Himself may be fulfilled."[755] John Piper said, "The strength of patience hangs on our capacity to believe that God is up to something good for us in all our delays and detours."[756]

126

The Joy of the Lord Is My Strength

"Neither be ye sorry; for the joy of the LORD is your strength" (Nehemiah 8:10). Matthew Henry interprets: "The more cheerful we are in our religious exercises, the more we shall abound in them."[757] This divinely imparted joy infuses the believer with enabling and enduring strength to contend with every pressure, problem and pain.

Comfort for Troubled Hearts

The stuff of the joy. It's not worldly in nature; not the hollow laughter, hilarity or cheap emotion of the world.[758] It is a joy conceived in the heart by divine impartation and cultivated by communion with Christ. Matthew Henry states, "Let it not be a carnal sensual joy, but holy and spiritual."[759] Alan Redpath says, "You see, a Christian is one who should always be rejoicing. Not that he goes around shouting, 'Hallelujah, brother!' all the time! Noise is not always an evidence of spirituality. But he should possess rather a calm, quiet serenity in every situation."[760]

The subject of the joy. It is a joy that is imparted to only the redeemed of the Lord, those in relationship and communion with Him (John 15:11 and Galatians 5:22).

The source of the joy. It is a joy that cannot be self-generated but only divinely imparted. The "joy" is one of the nine-fold fruits imparted by the Holy Spirit to the believer (Galatians 5:22–23). See Romans 14:17. The "joy," though present in the believer, may be shallow or lagging. Therefore, Jesus said, "Ask, and ye shall receive, that your joy may be full" (John 16:24). Regrettably, most saints suffer deficiency in the *degree* of Christ's joy when it is abundantly provided upon request.

The support of the joy. "The joy of the LORD is your strength [fortified place, defense, protection, helper]."

(1. It is a strength in that it enables the saint to withstand the calamities, bereavements and infirmities of life (as we see in David, Paul, Daniel, Silas). See Psalm 4:7. "It is a joy that enervates one's powers."[761]

(2. It is a strength ("oils the wheels") to devotion, duty and spiritual disciplines. "Joys are our wings; sorrows are our spurs."[762]

(3. It is a strength to service. The "heart" of a competitor trying to gain a prize will press the body and mind to go through extraordinary exertion.[763] Likewise, it is the supernatural joy of the Lord in the believer that incites him to accomplish tasks and missions for the glory of God when weakened by trials and troubles.

(4. It is a strength for endurance. See John 16:33 and 2 Corinthians 7:4. Redpath says, "Whatever God permits to touch our lives, we may be sure He will bestow power to see us through. Joy can enable us to sing in the night, just as Paul and Silas sang in prison. This does not mean, of course, that the Christian is always happy, for happiness depends on what happens. But it does mean that even in the midst of the heartbreak, deep down in his heart there is a joy that nothing on earth can ever take away."[764]

The scope of the joy. It is not contingent upon the circumstance of life or the condition of body. Since God imparts it, the world cannot stop it.

The secret of the joy. All are familiar with the acrostic for J-O-Y that spells the secret of divine strengthening: Jesus (first), Others (second), Yourself (last). To him that walks in union and communion with Christ, joy will be as natural as breathing when affliction and sorrow rain down. The joy of divine companionship infuses strength to face whatever befalls courageously and triumphantly.

My God, the spring of all my joys,
    The life of my delights,
The glory of my brightest days,
    The comfort of my nights!
In darkest shades, if Thou appear,
    My dawning is begun.
Thou art my soul's bright morning star
    And Thou my rising sun. ~ Isaac Watts

"They go from strength to strength" (Psalm 84:7). Despite the battles that are raging, battle wounds, and battle fatigue, the joy of the Lord is your strength to fight onward. Despite illness, fatigue, grave sorrow, trouble, hardship and/or "caretaker" weariness, the joy of the Lord will be your strength and stay. Tap into its full abundance.

127

An Ocean of Tears

The number of tears that have trickled down the face of man since creation is incalculable. There are the tears of the bereaved. No sorrow opens the fountain of tears like that sorrow of the departure of a loved one through death. There are the tears of the sufferer. Certain sicknesses produce agonizing and lingering tears of pain. There are the tears of a wounded spirit. This injury to the emotions manifests such horrendous pain and misery that it may feel as if we have been torn open and are bleeding from every part of the body. There are the tears of the abused. The sexually exploited and physically maltreated know pain like none other can imagine. There are the tears of the widows. We don't know the countless barrels of tears that flow down the cheeks of women who have lost their husbands.

There are the tears of the impoverished. Inability to provide adequate food, shelter, and clothing to one's children—seeing them destitute—afflicts the heart with indescribable pain. There are the tears of the righteous over the escalation of evil. With the psalmist, the saint says, "Rivers of tears gush from my eyes because people disobey your instructions" (Psalm 119:136 NLT). See Matthew 5:4. There are the tears of the persecuted, rejected, troubled, morally "fallen, and orphans. No eyes are strangers to bitter, painful tears (though hidden to others).

Comfort for Troubled Hearts

Not a tear in the vast ocean of tears that have been shed is unnoticed by God. David said, "The LORD hath heard the voice of my weeping" (Psalm 6:8). God says to all what He said to Hezekiah, "I have seen thy tears" (2 Kings 20:5). The Bible says, "You've [God] kept track of my every toss and turn through the sleepless nights, Each tear entered in your ledger, each ache written in your book" (Psalm 56:8 MSG).

Chuck Swindoll states, "A teardrop on earth summons the King of Heaven. Rather than being ashamed or disappointed, the Lord takes note of our inner friction when hard times are oiled by tears. He turns these situations into moments of tenderness; He never forgets those crises in our lives where tears were shed." The songwriter is correct to say, "Tears are a language that God understands." Charles Dickens was right when he said, "We need never be ashamed of our tears."

But a day is coming when "the voice of weeping shall be no more heard" (Isaiah 65:19). Spurgeon comments about that wondrous day: "The glorified weep no more, for all outward causes of grief are gone. There are no broken friendships nor blighted prospects in Heaven. Poverty, famine, peril, persecution, and slander are unknown there. No pain distresses; no thought of death or bereavement saddens. Sin is shut out, and they are shut in. They dwell within a city which shall never be stormed; they bask in a sun which shall never set; they drink of a river which shall never dry; they pluck fruit from a tree which shall never wither." Heaven is a place where "God will take away all their tears. There will be no more death or sorrow or crying or pain. All the old things have passed away" (Revelation 21:4 NLV). It is an abode where painful sorrow and suffering are eternally banished. Hallelujah!

> God shall wipe away all tears;
> There's no death, no pain, nor fears.
> And they count not time by years
> For there is no night there. ~ John R. Clements (1899)

Barnes comments, "The fullness of this plan will be seen only in Heaven. In anticipation of Heaven, however, the Gospel now does much to alleviate human woes and to wipe away tears from the mourner's eyes. It may be added that nothing but the Gospel will do this. No other religion can furnish such consolation."[765] The Bible says that God presently "healeth the broken in heart, and bindeth up their wounds" (Psalm 147:3). God is always ready to take His handkerchief of love and tenderness and wipe the tears from the face of His child, giving consolation and comfort. This He has done faithfully and compassionately to the extent that an Ocean of Tears can be formed from them. And that which He has done for others, He stands ready to do for you—right now! Just ask Him.

When the Rain Comes

Are you weary; are you heavy-hearted?
Tell it to Jesus; tell it to Jesus.
Are you grieving over joys departed?
Tell it to Jesus alone.

Do the tears flow down your cheeks unbidden?
Tell it to Jesus; tell it to Jesus.
Have you sins that to men's eyes are hidden?
Tell it to Jesus alone.

Do you fear the gath'ring clouds of sorrow?
Tell it to Jesus; tell it to Jesus.
Are you anxious what shall be tomorrow?
Tell it to Jesus alone.

Are you troubled at the thought of dying?
Tell it to Jesus; tell it to Jesus.
For Christ's coming kingdom are you sighing?
Tell it to Jesus alone. ~ Edmund Simon Lorenz (1876)

128

Has God Put on You More Than You Can Bear?

A baby was born with a foot deformity which in time proved to be a grave handicap. The father sought medical remedy from various doctors but without success. In time doctors and surgeons simply gave up on helping the child.

The father personally refused to give up. He acquired books on the subject and studied them. He learned about the bones in the foot and every articulation—the tendons, nerves, and muscles. With that knowledge he constructed a strange looking box with screws and felt washers at various angles. He placed the deformed foot of his child into that weird looking box and tightened the screws. The child wailed in agonizing pain. Every day upon arriving home from work, the father would again tighten the screws despite the child's crying. Day by day, week by week, month by month the father mingled his tears with the child's in tightening the screws.

The day arrived when the father loosened the screws and removed the box from the foot of the child, saying, "Son, stand up." The child stood erect for the first time and eventually, as strength was regained in the foot, walked erect. The deformity was gone. Years later as an adult at the grave of his father, he wept tears of gratitude for that which his father had done.[766]

Comfort for Troubled Hearts

In times when God allows your "foot" to be placed in a box tightened by painful screws (perhaps more than you can bear), remember that such is allowed for divine purposes and your best good. The apostle Paul experienced such "screws" that made things unbearable and look hopeless. He writes, "We want you to know, Christian brothers, of the trouble we had in the countries of Asia. The load was so heavy we did not have the strength to keep going. At times we did not think we could live. We thought we would die. This happened so we would not put our trust in ourselves, but in God Who raises the dead" (2 Corinthians 1:8–9 NLV). Tony Evans said, "In order to take Paul deeper in faith, God put him in a situation that his résumé, abilities and connections could not change. Why? So that Paul would learn to trust God through experiencing Him more fully."[767]

It is wrong to say that God will not put on us more than we can bear. Paul's experience testifies that such may happen, and yours may as well. (By the way, 1 Corinthians 10:13 refers to sinful temptations, particularly sexual immorality and idolatry, not hardships; that is, God will not allow us to be tempted to sin beyond our measure to bear it.) However, it is right to say that God will not put on us more than we can bear in dependence upon Him (Philippians 4:13). All that is allowed to happen to the saint may be borne triumphantly through reliance upon the Lord.

To summarize, it's not that adversities beyond your ability to handle won't come, but that in their coming God will give grace to handle them. However tight the screw is turned in the adversity or trial experienced, God promises to enable you to endure it and that He will bring good in and from it (Romans 8:28). Like the son with the deformed foot you may cry bitterly at each turn of the screw. But in time, you will give the praise of gratitude to your Father for allowing it, as he did.

Is there no other way, O God,
    Except through sorrow, pain and loss
To stamp Christ's likeness on my soul,
    No other way except the cross?

And then a voice stills all my soul,
    That stilled the waves of Galilee,
"Cans't thou not bear the furnace
    If midst the flames I walk with thee?

I bore the cross; I know its weight;
    I drank the cup I hold for thee.
Cans't thou not follow where I lead?
    I'll give thee strength; lean hard on Me. ~ Author unknown

129

Keep Your Chin Up

It's easy in the midst of storms to fall prey to doubt, despondency, fear and distress. After all, all of Hell in such times seem to aim its artillery upon us to blast us from our faith and trust in Almighty God. And the effort would succeed were it not for the saint's unshakable and immoveable confidence in God and His abiding faithfulness to them.

Job under such assault stood firm in the faith even when his wife urged him to curse God and die. See Job 2:9–10. Advice similar to that of Mrs. Job is often voiced to the troubled and distressed. It counsels, "God has abandoned you. Your case is hopeless. Your future is bleak at best. Give up on God and give in to your trouble or adversity. If God loved you, He wouldn't have allowed this to happen." Reject that counsel as Job did. Lean heavily into Christ. Cling to His promises. Doubt Him not in the dark. In the most horrendous of circumstances, say with Job, "Though he slay me, yet will I trust in him: but I will maintain mine own ways before him" (Job 13:15). Spurgeon says, "To trust God in the light is nothing, but trust him in the dark—that is faith."[768]

Inspirer and Hearer of prayer,
  Thou Shepherd and Guardian of Thine,
My all to Thy covenant care
  I sleeping and waking resign.

If Thou art my Shield and my Sun,
  The night is no darkness to me;
And fast as my moments roll on,
  They bring me but nearer to Thee. ~ Augustus Toplady (1774)

W. A. Criswell states, "God wants His people to be a happy people, a walking exclamation mark, not a walking question mark. We are to live on Sunshine Square, facing the heavenly side of the street."[769] Keep your chin up. Manifest Job's faith and trust in God despite the gloom and doom of circumstances. God is still on His throne looking after you despite what the "voices" say—even the voices of doctors or friends. As He sustained Job, so will He keep you.

The year's at the spring,   The lark's on the wing;
And day's at the morn.   The snail's on the thorn;
Morning's at seven;   God's in His heaven—
The hillside's dew-pearl'd.   All's right with the world!
                       ~ Robert Browning (Pippa Passes)

266

130
"Encourage Him"

"Encourage him" (Deuteronomy 1:38). It was to Moses God assigned the task to encourage Joshua. He certainly would need it as he assumed leadership of over three million Israelites, confronted the enemies that awaited in Canaan, and governed. Moses' encouragement would prevent Joshua's discouragement in the face of these enormous challenges. It would be a game changer.

That's God's *modus operandi*. He provides saints who become discouraged in the work of ministry or in adversity encouragement not only from the Holy Spirit (John 15:26) but also from His children. The word *encouragement* is from the same Greek root word used for the Holy Spirit ("the helper" or one who is called alongside another to help). God uses the Holy Spirit to render comfort and help to the hurting, and in a similar way He utilizes saints.

I like to call such saints *balcony people* (those that pull people up, in contrast to *basement people* that pull people down). The role of an encourager (balcony person) to another is "to fill with courage or strength of purpose," "to inspirit, hearten, embolden," "to instill life, energy, courage, vigor," and "to infuse with fresh courage or zeal." Moses was such a balcony person to Joshua. He infused within him confidence and energizing strength to both accept and achieve God's assignment.

God places balcony people like Moses in our lives to give us what Richard DeVos calls a "positive push." There is nothing more powerful than a positive push to someone who is being pushed back! All of us need a positive push, encouragement, from time to time. Even Paul and John Mark did. And Barnabas provided it.

Derek Redmond failed to compete in the 1988 Olympics due to a serious heel injury that occurred minutes prior to its start. It would require five surgeries to repair. Four years later, in the 1992 Barcelona Olympics, he was determined to win a medal (and for certain to finish the race no matter what happened). With only 175 meters to the finish line, Derek pulled his right hamstring muscle, falling to the track. He managed to get up, wave off the medical attendants, and hop on one leg toward the finish line. His father rushed to his assistance. Derek, with his father's arm wrapped around his waist, walked to the finish line; there he crossed it alone to the cheers of 65,000 people.

Derek's dad, Jim, is a picture of a balcony person—a person who throws his arm around you and helps you finish the race. *Who sits in your balcony?* Who gives you a "positive push"? Who is or has been an encourager in ministry, sorrow, suffering, or sickness? Where might you be had he or she not come "alongside" to help?

When the Rain Comes

In whose balcony do you sit? John Maxwell says, "Everyone has the potential to become an encourager. You don't have to be rich. You don't have to be a genius. You don't have to have it all together. All you have to do is care about people and initiate."[770] Paul exhorts: "So encourage each other and build each other up" (1 Thessalonians 5:11 NLT). The writer of Hebrews urges us to "think of ways" to encourage one another (Hebrews 10:24–25 NLT). May I suggest several ideas to spark your "thinking." Encourage and build up others through applauding their accomplishments (regardless of how small) and/or perseverance in trial and in sharing the eternal, unbreakable promises of God. Encourage and build up others by walking with them in the dark paths that incite fear, worry, and hopelessness. And most certainly encourage and build up others by letting them know you are seriously praying for them.

Years ago a man traveling in the northern part of Ireland heard children's voices coming from a small schoolhouse. He entered the building, where he noticed a sad, small boy standing aloof from the other students. "Why does that boy stand there?" asked the man.

"Oh, he is good for nothing," replied the teacher. "There is nothing in him. I can make nothing of him. He is the most stupid boy in the school."

The visitor was taken aback at the sternness and harshness of the teacher toward the child. In placing his hand upon the head of the boy, he said, "One of these days you may be a fine scholar. Don't give up; try, my boy—try." At that moment the boy's soul was lifted and a new purpose formed, and he became a great theological scholar. The boy was Dr. Adam Clarke.[771] Most certainly God assigned that stranger to be an encourager to that small child. Thankfully, he was obedient.

In whose balcony will you sit? What discouraged pastor or missionary; shut-in or invalid; sickly, sorrowing, suffering or downcast saint will you give a "positive push"? Toby Mckeehand wrote, "When the sun won't shine and you don't know why, look into the eyes of the brokenhearted. Watch them come alive as soon as you speak hope."[772] Speaking a fit word at the right time elevates and invigorates the downcast soul. Solomon says, "A word fitly spoken is like apples of gold in pictures of silver" (Proverbs 25:11).

Chuck Swindoll wrote, "Encouragement should take the sting out of life. But be careful not to create other burdens for those you want to encourage. Do what you do with no expectation of being noticed or paid back. Reciprocal expectations are guilt-giving, not encouraging, actions! Also, be sensitive to the timing of your actions; a well-timed expression of encouragement is seldom forgotten."[773] In David's dire distress, Jonathan 'strengthened his grip on God' (1 Samuel 23:16). Onesiphorus "oft refreshed" (encouraged, uplifted) Paul (2 Timothy 1:16). To whom might you be a Jonathan or Onesiphorus?

Press on, my brother, sister,
    And face the deadly foe;
Through Jesus Christ we'll conquer,
    While trav'ling here below.

"Press on; press on,"
    Says Christ, our loving Friend;
"Press on, press on,
    "I'm with thee to the end."

Press on, and let thy failings
    A blessing to thee prove;
No wave of care or sorrow
    Thy trusting soul shall move.

Press on, though raging tempests
    And fiery billows roll;
While crossing life's rough rapids,
    He'll safely guide thy soul.

Press on, 'mid strong temptation;
    Tell Satan he must flee.
In Jesus' name resist him,
    And vict'ry thine shall be.

Press on, forever trusting,
    In faith believing, too;
In spite of doubt or feeling,
    God's Word will take you through.

Press on to what's before us,
    Forgetting all the past;
The light of Heav'n so glorious
    Eternally shall last. ~ Barney E. Warren (1897)

131

Mistrust without a Cause

David's life was much spent in escaping the sword of King Saul. No fewer than twelve times in a mere two chapters (1 Samuel 18 and 19) Saul attempts to kill David. Saul throws a spear at David twice (1 Samuel 18:11). Saul makes him captain of 1,000 men, not out of honor but in hope he would be killed by the enemy as he led the charge into battle (1 Samuel 18:13). Merab is promised to David if he would fight valiantly against the enemy, which again was a ploy to have him killed (1 Samuel 18:17). Michal, Saul's daughter, was given to David to "be a snare to him, and that the hand of the Philistines may be against him" (1 Samuel 18:20–21). Saul orders Jonathan and all his servants to kill David (1 Samuel 19:1). Saul thrusts his spear at David yet again (1 Samuel 19:10). Soldiers are sent by Saul to David's home to kill him (1 Samuel 19:11). Saul sends three groups of servants to Naioth to slay David (1 Samuel 19:19–21). Saul journeys to Naioth to kill David (1 Samuel 19:22). In addition to these efforts by Saul to kill David, numerous others are recorded in 1 Samuel 21–31. In every case David is divinely delivered.

However, despite these multiplied divine deliverances, we read, "And David said in his heart, I shall now perish one day by the hand of Saul" (1 Samuel 27:1). David's reasoning was unjustified. Had God granted him deliverances from the hand of Saul and his soldiers multiple times to allow them to succeed now? Certainly not. God's unrelenting and loving faithfulness to David in the past ought to have been his surety and assurance of His present care and defense.

Spurgeon comments, "*David* should have argued from what God had done for him, that God would be his defender still. But is it not just in the same way that we doubt God's help? Is it not mistrust without a cause? Have we ever had the shadow of a reason to doubt our Father's goodness? Have not His loving kindnesses been marvelous? Has He once failed to justify our trust? Ah, no! our God has not left us at any time. We have had dark nights, but the star of love has shone forth amid the blackness; we have been in stern conflicts, but over our head He has held aloft the shield of our defense. We have gone through many trials, but never to our detriment, always to our advantage; and the conclusion from our past experience is that He who has been with us in six troubles will not forsake us in the seventh. What we have known of our faithful God proves that He will keep us to the end. Let us not, then, reason contrary to evidence. How can we ever be so ungenerous as to doubt our God?"[774]

> As I look back on the road I've travelled,
>   I see so many times He carried me through;
> And if there's one thing that I've learned in my life,
>   My Redeemer is faithful and true.
>
> My Redeemer is faithful and true.
> My Redeemer is faithful and true.
> Everything He has said He will do,
> And every morning His mercies are new.
> My Redeemer is faithful and true. ~ Steven Curtis Chapman

"So then, those who suffer according to God's will should commit themselves *to their faithful Creator* and continue to do good" (1 Peter 4:19 NIV). God's faithfulness to you in the past is evidence that He has not forsaken you in the present adversity. When you have fraudulent thoughts that question God's present care (as David did), cast them aside by remembering His past interventions and deliverances. Whatever the cause for the despondency, be lifted from it without delay by talking spiritual sense into your head, remembering past mercies of the Lord, recalling His promises, praying and placing trust in God for deliverance. Albert Barnes says, "It is the duty of the people of God to look at the bright side of things; to think of the past mercies of God; to survey the blessings which surround us still; to look to the future, in this world and the next, with hope; and to come to God and cast the burden on him."[775] Dickson said, "Experience of God's mercies bygone should fasten resolution to make use of faith hereafter in all troubles. After one trouble, the godly should prepare for another; after one delivery expect another."[776]

> Experience of God's mercies bygone should fasten resolution to make use of faith hereafter in all troubles. After one trouble the godly should prepare for another, after one delivery expect another. ~ Dickson

God can do it again and again and again;
He's the same God today as He always has been.
Yesterday and now, forever, He's always the same.
There's no reason to doubt; God can do it again. ~ Living Sound (1977)

God says, "For I am the LORD, I change not" (Malachi 3:6). Amen and Amen. He still works miracles, deliverances (troubles and trials), healings, liberation (freedom from the bondage of sin and sinful habits) and grants new mercy and grace to endure every hardship (Lamentations 3:22–23). All that God did yesterday He is able to do TODAY. "Trust God to do it again" for others and yourself in the hour of need. Don't hinder God's ableness and willingness to work by your unbelief or 'limitation' (Psalm 78:41). Expect God to meet you at the point of your deepest need.

132

God Gives Songs in the Night

"God my maker, who giveth songs in the night" (Job 35:10).

The source of the song. It's not the saint that creates the song but "God my maker" (Job 35:10). James Hastings wrote, "When, then, our text speaks of God "who giveth songs in the night," it evidently means that it belongs to Him to put songs of praise and joy into the Christian's heart in seasons of sorrow and trial. It belongs to God, and to God alone, to give such songs."[777] Spurgeon comments, "Let but this voice be clear and this body full of health, and I can sing God's praise; silence my tongue, lay me upon the bed of languishing, and how shall I then chant God's high praises, unless He Himself give me the song? No, it is not in man's power to sing when all is adverse, unless an altar coal shall touch his lip. It was a divine song which Habakkuk sang when in the night he said, 'Although the fig tree shall not blossom, neither shall fruit be in the vines; the labor of the olive shall fail, and the fields shall yield no meat; the flock shall be cut off from the fold, and there shall be no herd in the stalls: Yet I will rejoice in the LORD, I will joy in the God of my salvation' (3:17–18). Then, since our Maker gives songs in the night, let us wait upon Him for the music."[778]

The subject of the song. It is composed of various themes, including the richness of God's grace, mercy and compassion; personal redemption through the blood of Christ; eternal life beyond this land of tears and sorrows in the wondrous abode called Heaven; the ever abiding presence of God in the midst of trouble; the second coming of the Lord; the Lord's omnipotence in all and over all; and reunion with the saints in Heaven. Plenteous and various in Heaven are the subjects for songs in the night, assuring the saints there are numerous suited just for their particular circumstance. Often God uses His unbreakable promises and meditation upon Holy Scripture to give birth to these songs. Spurgeon said often in the dark times he would find great delight and cheer in songs about the second coming.[779]

The soul of the song. To whom are songs in the night provided? Not unto all, but unto redeemed souls. Witnesses to such soothing and comforting songs in times of distress are many. Among them are Paul and Silas in the Philippian jail (Acts 16:34); David's forced exile from the palace and Temple of God (2 Samuel 15:30); Hezekiah's news of impending death and then that of its delay (Isaiah 38:20); Paul's imprisonment in a Roman dungeon (Philippians 3:1); and Job in his great loss of family, possessions, and health (Job 19:25–27).

The season of the song. David said, "Yet the LORD will command his lovingkindness in the daytime, and in the night his song shall be with me, and my prayer unto the God of my life" (Psalm 42:8). Night songs are generated in the soul in times of grave calamity, adversity, sickness, sorrow, and suffering to make them bearable and to keep the soul in tune with the source of all comfort and hope as long as the trouble lasts.

The salve of the song. It is the sweet song of Heaven laced with hope, comfort, and peace that soothes the troubled heart by thwarting the terror, fear, despair, and anxiety of the affliction or adversity. Matthew Henry states, "He gives songs in the night; that is, when our condition is ever so dark and sad and melancholy, there is that in God, in His providence and promise, which is sufficient not only to support us, but to fill us with joy and consolation and enable us in everything to give thanks and even to rejoice in tribulation."[780]

The scope of the song. Though the saint is promised a song in the night orchestrated by God, it will not dispel the darkness of the night.[781] That is, the song drives the "darkness" from the heart, not necessarily from the body. God doesn't promise to eradicate our "dark times," but to make them endurable and less disturbing by providing a song in the night.

The purpose of the song. God giveth saints songs in the night to cheer, comfort, and encourage and to instill courage and hope. He giveth suffering saints songs in the night to encourage observers of their affliction. He giveth songs in the night as a testimonial to the world of His faithfulness to His children in adversity.

Spurgeon says, "Your head may be crowned with thorny troubles now, but it will wear a starry crown soon; your hand may be filled with cares—it will hold a harp soon, a harp full of music. Your clothes may be soiled with dust now; they will be pure white in the future. Wait a little longer. Ah! Beloved, how despicable our troubles and trials will seem when we look back on them! Looking at them here today, they seem immense; but when we get to Heaven, our earthly trials will seem to us to have been nothing at all. Let us go on, therefore; and if the night is very dark, remember there is not a night that will not have a morning and that morning is to come soon."[782]

In shady green pastures, so rich and so sweet,
God leads His dear children along;
Where the water's cool flow bathes the weary one's feet,
God leads His dear children along.

Some through the waters, some through the flood,
Some through the fire, but all through the blood,
Some through great sorrow, but God gives a song,
In the night season and all the day long. ~ George A. Young (1903)

God is faithful to provide a song in the night when we are afflicted. However, it's up to us to sing it and thereby be benefitted and sustained. Now is a good time to start.

133

Rest in Hope

My flesh shall rest in hope (Acts 2:26). Biblical hope, unlike secular hope, means certainty, confidence and assurance of something happening. It's not wishful thinking but undoubtable reality. John Bunyan clarifies the difference yet affinity between faith and hope: "Faith says to hope, look for what is promised; hope says to faith, So I do, and will wait for it too."[783] See Romans 8:24–25. John Piper further elucidates, "Christian hope is when God has promised that something is going to happen and you put your trust in that promise. Christian hope is a confidence that something will come to pass because God has promised it will come to pass."[784]

What is the believer's hope?

(1. *It consists of the resurrection of the body*. Paul said, "If in this life only we have hope in Christ, we are of all men most miserable. But now is Christ risen from the dead, and become the firstfruits of them that slept. For since by man came death, by man came also the resurrection of the dead" (1 Corinthians 15:19–21). Jesus is proof of the resurrection. He made a "dead end" into a "thoroughfare" upon being raised from the dead.

Billy Graham says, "There is more evidence that Jesus rose from the dead than there is that Julius Caesar ever lived or that Alexander the Great died at the age of thirty-three."[785] Jesus is the preview of the resurrection. As He rose bodily and recognizable, so shall every believer (Luke 24:39). Paul says, "Just as we have borne the image of the man of dust, we shall also bear the image of the man of heaven" (1 Corinthians 15:49 ESV). Jesus gives promise of the resurrection in John 11:25, "I am the resurrection and the life. He who believes in Me, though he may die, he shall live" (NKJV). Josh McDowell states, "No matter how devastating our struggles, disappointments, and troubles are, they are only temporary. No matter what happens to you, no matter the depth of tragedy or pain you face, no matter how death stalks you and your loved ones, the resurrection promises you a future of immeasurable good."[786]

J. C. Ryle writes, "There is a resurrection after death. Let this never be forgotten. The life that we live here in the flesh is not all. The visible world around us is not the only world with which we have to do. All is not over when the last breath is drawn and men and women are carried to their long home in the grave. The trumpet shall one day sound, and the dead shall be raised incorruptible. All that are in the graves shall hear Christ's voice and come forth—those who have done good to the resurrection of life, and those who have done evil to the resurrection of damnation. This is one of the great foundation truths of the Christian religion. Let us cling to it firmly and never let it go."[787]

In the resurrection morning, when the trump of God shall sound,
    We shall rise. Hallelujah! We shall rise!
Then the saints will come rejoicing, and no tears will e'er be found.
    We shall rise. Hallelujah! We shall rise!

Comfort for Troubled Hearts

I shall see my blessed Savior, who so freely died for me.
  We shall rise. Hallelujah! We shall rise!

~ J. E. Thomas (1904)

The amazing and awesome hope of Easter gives the believer confidence of life beyond death with Christ and all the ransomed host of Heaven.

(2. *It consists of future life in Heaven*. Billy Graham says, "Because Heaven is real, we have hope: hope for the future and hope for our lives right now. No matter what happens to us now, we know it won't last forever, and ahead of us is the joy of Heaven. Paul wrote, 'If only for this life we have hope in Christ, we are to be pitied more than all men' (1 Corinthians 15:19 NIV). But our hope isn't only for this life! In the midst of life's storms, our hope in God's promise of Heaven is 'an anchor for the soul, firm and secure' (Hebrews 6:19 NIV)."[788]

"The glories and blessedness of Heaven," writes Arthur Pink, "are brought before us in the New Testament under a variety of representations. Heaven is called a 'country' (Luke 19:12; Hebrews 11:16); this tells of its vastness. It is called a "city" (Hebrews 11:10; Revelation 21); this intimates the large number of its inhabitants. It is called a "kingdom" (2 Peter 1:11); this suggests its orderliness. It is called "paradise" (Luke 23:43; Revelation 2:7); this emphasizes its delights. It is called the "Father's house," (John 14:2) which bespeaks its permanency."[789]

In Heaven there will be the absence of sickness, sorrow, and suffering that bring tears to our eyes and heart, for "He will wipe every tear from their eyes. There will be no more death or mourning or crying or pain, for the old order of things has passed away" (Revelation 21:4 NIV).

(3. *It consists of Christ's return*. Paul writes, "Looking for that blessed hope, and the glorious appearing of the great God and our Savior Jesus Christ; Who gave himself for us, that he might redeem us from all iniquity, and purify unto himself a peculiar people, zealous of good works" (Titus 2:13–14).

Fear, hopelessness, anxiety, despair and discouragement are dispelled in the hope of Christ's soon return. Confidence for the hope of His return is undergirded by the fact that He initially appeared as promised by Old Testament prophets[790] and His personal promise to return in John 14:3.

A. W. Tozer comments, "Let us be alert to the season in which we are living. It is the season of the Blessed Hope, calling for us to cut our ties with the world and build ourselves on this One who will soon appear. He is our hope—a Blessed Hope enabling us to rise above our times and fix our gaze upon Him."[791] "Lift up your heads; for your redemption draweth nigh" (Luke 21:28).

When the Rain Comes

Marvelous message we bring,
Glorious carol we sing,
Wonderful word of the King,
Jesus is coming again! ~ John Peterson (1957)

(4. *It consists of reunion with loved ones beyond this life*. The Bible says "For this we say to you by the word of the Lord, that we who are alive and remain until the coming of the Lord, will not precede those who have fallen asleep. For the Lord Himself will descend from heaven with a shout, with the voice of the archangel and with the trumpet of God, and the dead in Christ will rise first. Then we who are alive and remain will be caught up together with them in the clouds to meet the Lord in the air, and so we shall always be with the Lord" (1 Thessalonians 4:15–17 NASB1995).

John MacArthur states, "We will be reunited not only with our own families and loved ones, but also with the people of God from all ages. In Heaven we will all be one loving family. The immense size of the family will not matter in the infinite perfection of Heaven. There will be ample opportunity for close relationships with everyone, and our eternity will be spent in just that kind of rich, unending fellowship."[792] To know that we will see loved ones and friends again beyond the veil of this life grants peace and calm in the midst of grave sorrow that is unspeakable. What a glorious Hope we have in Christ Jesus!

There will be a happy meeting in Heaven, I know,
When we see the many loved ones we've known here below,
Gather on the blessed hilltops with hearts all aglow;
That will be a glad reunion day. ~ Adger M. Pace (1940)

J. I. Packer summarizes the believer's hope: "Optimism is a wish without warrant; Christian hope is a certainty, guaranteed by God himself. Optimism reflects ignorance as to whether good things will ever actually come. Christian hope expresses knowledge that every day of his life, and every moment beyond it, the believer can say with truth, on the basis of God's own commitment, that the best is yet to come."[793] Note the words "rest in hope" (Acts 2:26). That means abide in, lean heavily upon and take comfort in the believer's hope (the resurrection, return of Christ, Heaven and reunion with loved ones). It will bring calm in times of calamity, comforting peace in times of sorrow, tranquility in times of grave affliction and adversity, encouragement in times of distress, and courage in the time of death. Without the believer's hope, we are of all people most miserable (1 Corinthians 15:19).

My hope is built on nothing less
Than Jesus' blood and righteousness;
I dare not trust the sweetest frame
But wholly lean on Jesus' name.

On Christ, the solid rock, I stand.
All other ground is sinking sand;
All other ground is sinking sand. ~ Edward Mote (1797–1874)

With the Christian group Third Day, say to the Lord,

My hope is in You;
My hope is in You.
In all my days,
My hope is You.

134

When the Rain Comes to a Nation

"If the foundations be destroyed, what can the righteous do?" (Psalm 11:3). The question posed is one that has been asked by the righteous time and again in the face of sweeping anti-Christian legislation and cultural reform ("deform"). It was asked in 1973 when the Supreme Court issued the landmark decision *(Roe v. Wade)* sanctioning infant murder via abortion. It was asked during the Clinton administration when immorality struck the highest office in the land, signaling that such behavior was acceptable. It was asked during the presidency of Obama when homosexuality was sanctioned as "normal" sexual behavior and the undermining of Christian marriage between a man and woman was made into "law." It is asked today when drug lords have their pushers on nearly every city block enticing and bringing into addiction utterly tens of thousands that eventually will commit theft, physical abuse, or violent acts, including murder. The question is being asked by the righteous today as annually 800,000 women and children are victims of sexual-slave trafficking[794] (those compelled, coerced into sexual slavery commercially). It is being asked when anarchy is allowed to infiltrate cities demolishing homes, stores, businesses, and lives all in the name of social justice. It is being asked more and more as "political correctness" replaces biblical and moral values and Christians are being "persecuted" and "ostracized" for moral convictions. See Psalm 94:3.

What can the righteous do? They must not let despair prevent insistence on allegiance to Almighty God and His holy decrees in Scripture. They must not succumb to the evil tide but resist it with their every tooth and nail. They must, Peter says, be ever ready and courageous to give a defense for the "reason" (hope) for their faith (1 Peter 3:15). They must exemplify the graciousness and holy demeanor of Christ, despite the hostility manifested toward Him, the church, the Bible and themselves (1 Peter 2:23). They must keep their lamps trimmed and burning brightly (Luke 12:35). They must remember that nothing can strip God of His absolute sovereignty or hinder His promise to bring good out of crisis for His people (Romans 8:28). "His eyes behold," etc. (Psalm 11:4). E. R. Conder and W. Clarkson state, "In all this wild confusion, as it seems, nothing is *overlooked*, nothing *unjudged* or *uncontrolled*. God rules as well as reigns. Never for a moment is His hand off the helm (Rom. 8:28; Ps. 76:10)."[795]

What can the righteous do? They must engage in fervent intercessory prayer for divine intervention and awakening for the nation (Isaiah 64:1; 1 Timothy 2:1–4 and 2 Chronicles 7:14). Like David, they must refuse to "flee to the mountains" but be vigilant in battle for the right, depending upon the power and authority of God for ultimate victory. *In the Lord put I my trust.* Spurgeon says, "David here declares the great source of his unflinching courage. He borrows his light from Heaven—from the great central orb of Deity. The God of the believer is never far from him; He is not merely the God of the mountain, but of the dangerous valleys and battle plains."[796] Spurgeon answers the question "What can the righteous do in an unrighteous government?" with a counterquestion: "What can they not do?" when they trust in God that reigns supreme in authority and power praying for His divine intervention and protection (Psalm 11:4–7).[797] Matthew Henry remarks, "That which grieved David in this *circumstance* was not that to flee now would savor of cowardice and ill become a soldier, but that it would savor of unbelief and would ill become a saint who had so often said, '*In the Lord put I my trust.*'"[798]

> Other refuge have I none;
>   Hangs my helpless soul on Thee.
> Leave, ah! leave me not alone;
>   Still support and comfort me.
>
> All my trust on Thee is stayed;
>   All my help from Thee I bring.
> Cover my defenseless head
>   With the shadow of thy wing. ~ Charles Wesley

"When prayer engages God on our side and when faith secures the fulfilment of the promise, what cause can there be for flight, however cruel and mighty our enemies?"[799] Jesus said, "Ye are of God, little children, and have overcome them: because greater is he that is in you, than he that is in the world" (1 John 4:4). J. M.

Comfort for Troubled Hearts

Boice writes, "What can the righteous do? They can go on being righteous. And they can stand against the evil of their society."[800] C. Clemance states, "When wickedness gets the upper hand in these ways, times are hard indeed for good and faithful men. In such times Elijah, Jeremiah, and others lived and wept and moaned and prayed. Many a prophet of the Lord has had to look upon such a state of things, when all day long He stretched out His hands to a disobedient and gainsaying people."[801] The believer can do no less. The righteous must persevere confidently, saying with Edward Mote, "When all around my soul gives way, He then is all my hope and stay." Saints must rest confidently knowing that God will triumph over the present rebellion, moral decay, unbelief, and persecution. The foundation of God's authority and biblical faith is indestructible despite vehement opposition to it.

> What can the righteous do? They can go on being righteous.
> And they can stand against the evil of their society.
> J. M. Boice

What can the righteous do? They can trust the promises of God. W. Forsyth comments, "God's promises are good, for He is love; they are certain, for He is faithful; they are sure of accomplishment, for He is able to do exceedingly abundantly above all we can ask or think. Thus, our hearts are revived. There may be delay, but not denial. There may be silence long, but never refusal. God has His own time and His own way."[802]

My refuge is the God of love.
    Why do my foes insult and cry,
"Fly like a tim'rous, trembling dove;
    To distant woods or mountains fly?"

If government be all destroyed,
    That firm foundation of our peace,
And violence make justice void,
    Where shall the righteous seek redress?

The Lord in Heav'n has fixed His throne;
    His eye surveys the world below.
To him all mortal things are known;
    His eyelids search our spirits through.

If He afflicts His saints so far
    To prove their love and try their grace,
What may the bold transgressors fear?
    His very soul abhors their ways.

When the Rain Comes

On impious wretches he shall rain
 Tempests of brimstone, fire, and death
Such as he kindled on the plain
 Of Sodom with his angry breath.

The righteous Lord loves righteous souls
 Whose thoughts and actions are sincere
And with a gracious eye beholds
 The men that His own image bear. ~ Isaac Watts (1806)

Written for *Tracts for the Times:* "If men come to think it of small consequence whether or not they embrace and hold fast divine truth, they will, by degrees, go on to doubt whether there is any such thing as divine truth at all; and so, beginning with what they were pleased to call Christian liberty, they will end in unbelief. If men should be led to encourage the opinion that God's most holy Bible is to be handled, judged, criticized, praised, or blamed like other books, then, beyond all doubt, however human reason may triumph, divine faith will be undermined and by degrees will be destroyed from its foundation."[803]

In corrupt moral and political times, the righteous are to look to God for wisdom, guidance, and strength and courageously stand their ground against the permeating evil with unwaning confident trust in God, as David did. By the way, "Courage," says Webster, "is that quality of mind which enables men to encounter danger and difficulties with firmness, or without any fear or depression of spirits."

135

Benefits of Praising God in Hard Times

In Psalm 68:4 it says, "Sing to God! Sing praises to His name. Exalt Him who rides on the clouds—His name is Yahweh—and rejoice before Him" (HCSB). Why? Praise is not only a spiritual duty that glorifies God (Hebrews 13:15), but a privilege that brings manifold blessings and benefits to His people. Praise, as evangelism, must be done "in season and out of season" (sunshine and rain), when it's easy and not so easy. See Psalm 34:1.

What are the benefits of praise?

Praise ushers us into God's presence. Psalm 22:3 declares, "But thou art holy, O thou that inhabitest the praises of Israel." Matthew Henry comments, "Thou [God] art pleased to manifest Thy glory and grace and special presence with Thy people in the sanctuary where they attend Thee with their praises."[804] C. S. Lewis writes, "It is in the process of being worshipped that God communicates His presence to men."[805] "True spiritual worship will cause God Almighty," states Joseph L. Garlington, "to come and sit with you, for He is enthroned in the midst of your praises."[806]

Praise boosts the spirit. Praise has the power to lift the spirit of heaviness. Emotional heaviness zaps spiritual vitality, robs joy and peace, crushes faith and diminishes hope (all orchestrated by Satan). God promises the saint a great exchange: "the garment of praise for the spirit of heaviness" (Isaiah 61:3). The "garment of praise" literally means to be "wrapped up in praise." Wrap or envelope your soul in continual praise to God and the depressing and oppressing spirit of heaviness will vanish. See Psalm 42:1–11.

Praise fixes our gaze upon Christ. Praise turns the focus away from the problem, re-centering it upon the Savior who stands ready to meet us at our point of need. The psalmist, David, in times of grave trouble and trial praised God for His great power which refocused his attention away from his difficulty to Him that was able to grant deliverance. The Bible exhorts, "Let us look only to Jesus, the One who began our faith and who makes it perfect. He suffered death on the cross. But he accepted the shame as if it were nothing because of the joy that God put before him. And now he is sitting at the right side of God's throne" (Hebrews 12:2 NCV).

Oh, soul, are you weary and troubled?
   No light in the darkness you see?
There's light for a look at the Savior
   And life more abundant and free.

Turn your eyes upon Jesus;
   Look full in His wonderful face,
And the things of earth will grow strangely dim
   In the light of His glory and grace. ~ Helen Howarth Lemmel (1922)

Praise impacts others. With death perhaps approaching the next morning, Paul and Silas sang praises at midnight in the prison cell, which was heard by the prison keepers. The word "heard" (Acts 16:25) means "to listen carefully to and pay attention; to mark someone's words."[807] The prison guards undoubtedly were greatly impacted by the praises of the two inmates who had experienced unjust flogging and imprisonment. People take note as to how we handle life's storms. Let us therefore in storms be mindful to lift Christ up through praise (John 12:32), as did Paul and Silas. Spurgeon said, "Others who have been in like circumstances shall take comfort if we can say, 'Oh! magnify the Lord with me, and let us exalt His name together; this poor man cried, and the Lord heard him.' Weak hearts will be strengthened, and drooping saints will be revived as they listen to our 'songs of deliverance.' Their doubts and fears will be rebuked as we teach and admonish one another in psalms and hymns and spiritual songs. They too shall 'sing in the ways of the Lord' when they hear us magnify His holy name. Praise is the most heavenly of Christian duties."[808] Augustine urges caution, saying, "Don't let your life give evidence against your tongue. Sing with your voices....sing also with your conduct."

And I'll praise you in this storm,
And I will lift my hands
That you are who you are
No matter where I am,
And every tear I've cried
You hold in your hand;
You never left my side,
And though my heart is torn,
I will praise you in this storm. ~ Casting Crowns (2005)

Praise brings joy. The psalmist's praise filled his "heart and flesh" with joy. He testified, "How lovely are Your dwelling places, O Lord of hosts! My soul longed and even yearned for the courts of the Lord; My heart and my flesh sing for joy to the living God" (Psalm 84:1–2 NASB1995). Again, he says, "My lips will shout for joy when I sing praises to You; And my soul, which You have redeemed" (Psalm 71:23 NASB). Praise is the spout where joy floods out. William Law remarked, "Just as singing is a natural effect of joy in the heart, so it has also a natural power of rendering the heart joyful."[809]

Praise strengthens and enlarges faith. Romans 4:20 says, Abraham "grew strong and was empowered by faith as he gave praise and glory to God" (AMPC). When we praise God for His mighty works, our faith is enlarged and increased at their remembrance. Wesley L. Duewel states, "Faith comes through God's Word and through praise. Faith grows as you praise the Lord."[810]

Praise bolsters security. David's praise of God being a mighty and impenetrable refuge and a present and proven help in trouble (Psalm 46:1) enabled him to say, "Therefore will not we fear, though the earth be removed, and though the mountains be carried into the midst of the sea; Though the waters thereof roar and be troubled, though the mountains shake with the swelling thereof" (Psalm 46:2–3). Praise prompts recollection that there is nothing too hard or difficult to endure, thwart or accomplish with God in the equation. It reminds us that God and God alone is our source of strength and security in life's storms. The praising saint says, "For thou art my hope, O Lord GOD: thou art my trust" (Psalm 71:5). See Jeremiah 32:27.

Praise calms the soul. Praise repels disquietude, anxiety and fear. David's praise through the lyre (a stringed musical instrument similar but different from the harp) calmed King Saul (1 Samuel 16:21–23); the praise of others is medicine for our hurts. Through praise (private or corporate) the Good Shepherd leads His sheep to "calm water" (Psalm 23:2) which refreshes and satisfies their soul (Psalm 23:3). Paul instructs, "Don't fret or worry. Instead of worrying, pray. Let petitions and praises shape your worries into prayers, letting God know your concerns. Before you know it, a sense of God's wholeness, everything coming together for good, will come and settle you down. It's wonderful what happens when Christ displaces worry at the center of your life" (Philippians 4:6–7 THE MSG). Harry Ironside remarked, "We would worry less if we praised more. Thanksgiving is the enemy of discontent and dissatisfaction."[811]

Praise alters perspective. Praise enables us to see our present hardship, sorrow or sickness in light of God's omnipotence, love and sovereignty. Psalm 8:1 (NLT) declares, "O Lord, our Lord, your majestic name fills the earth! Your glory is higher than the heavens." God is in control of our destiny and promises to bring good out of every trial (Romans 8:28). Praise reminds us that God takes notice of our dire circumstances and deepest needs, that He watches over us with love and compassion.

Praise brings victory. Jehoshaphat in the time of battle assigned the singers (choir) as the frontline troops (2 Chronicles 20:21). Why? The singing of praise would marshal the power of God against their foe. And it did. The Bible says that "when they began to sing and praise, the LORD set an ambush against the men of Ammon, Moab, and Mount Seir, who had come against Judah, so that they were routed" (2 Chronicles 20:22 ESV). See Psalm 9:1–4. Imprisoned, Paul and Silas sang praises unto God at midnight, which resulted in their miraculous freedom through an earthquake that shook the prison (Acts 16:25–26). Both accounts (Jehoshaphat and Paul and Silas) teach that prayer and praise are the saint's essential weapon for deliverance and victory in spiritual warfare. God shakes things up for our good when praises and petitions ascend unto His throne.

> I sing the Doxology and dismiss the Devil.
> Mary Slessor

Praise drives Satan back. Praise empowers us to thwart the Devil's efforts to discourage, depress, dissuade and defeat us. When we praise Christ for His mighty work at Calvary, triumphant resurrection, personal salvation, absolute truth, and superior power in and over all things, Satan recoils. William Thasher said, "Satan so hates the genuine praise of Christ that his fiery darts of discouragement are not effective against us when we respond in praise."[812] Paul states, "And the God of peace will crush Satan under your feet shortly. The grace of our Lord Jesus Christ be with you. Amen" (Romans 16:20 NKJV). Mary Slessor, a godly missionary to the Chinese, said, "I sing the Doxology and dismiss the Devil."[813] Amy Carmichael, a missionary in

When the Rain Comes

South India, said, "I believe truly that Satan cannot endure it [praise] and so slips out of the room—more or less—when there is a true song." Martin Luther testifies in *Here I Stand*: "Music is a fair and lovely gift of God which has often wakened and moved me to the joy of preaching....Music drives away the Devil and makes people happy....Next after theology I give to music the highest place and the greatest honor. I would not change what little I know of music for something great. Experience proves that next to the Word of God only music deserves to be extolled as the mistress and governess of the feelings of the human heart. We know that to the Devils music is distasteful and insufferable. My heart bubbles up and overflows in response to music, which has so often refreshed me and delivered me from dire plagues."[814] Jack Taylor wrote, "The liars from the pit of Hell cannot market their wares in an atmosphere of praise and worship."[815] John Piper states, "God has appointed the use of spiritual songs as an effective weapon against his archenemy Satan."[816]

Praise empowers for service. Spurgeon says, "It [praise] is a healthful and invigorating exercise which quickens the pulse of the believer and nerves him for fresh enterprises in his Master's service."[817]

Praise inflames the soul. William Law says, "There is nothing that so clears a way for your prayers, nothing that so disperses dullness of heart, nothing that so purifies the soul from poor and little passions, nothing that so opens Heaven or carries your heart so near it as these songs of praise. They create a sense and delight in God, they awaken holy desires, they teach you how to ask, and they prevail with God to give. They kindle a holy flame; they turn your heart into an altar, your prayers into incense, and carry them as a sweet-smelling savor to the throne of grace."[818]

Praise glorifies God. Psalm 50:23 states, "Whoso offereth praise glorifieth me: and to him that ordereth his conversation aright will I shew the salvation of God." Praise pleases God, honors God, and exalts God. John Piper comments, "The climax of God's happiness is the delight He takes in the echoes of His excellence in the praises of His people."[819]

> When you're up against a struggle that shatters all your dreams
> And your hopes have been cruelly crushed by Satan's manifested schemes
> And you feel the urge within you to submit to earthly fears,
> Don't let the faith you're standing in seem to disappear.
>
> Praise the Lord; He can work through those who praise Him.
> Praise the Lord, for our God inhabits praise.
> Praise the Lord, for the chains that seem to bind you
> Serve only to remind you that they drop powerless behind you
> When you praise Him. ~ Brown Bannister and Mike Hudson (1978)

Comfort for Troubled Hearts

Rick Warren said, "The deepest level of worship is praising God in spite of pain, thanking God during a trial, trusting Him when tempted, surrendering while suffering, and loving Him when He seems distant. At my lowest, God is my hope. At my darkest, God is my light. At my weakest, God is my strength. At my saddest, God is my comforter."[820] Praise may take the form of a shout, song, or Scripture. Paul states it may be engaged in silently from the heart: "I will sing praise with my spirit, but I will also sing praise with my mind" (1 Corinthians 14:15 LEB). Here and now, break out in singing either another's praise song or a "new song" (personal composition) unto the Lord (Psalm 144:9) and experience its rich ministry and medicine to your soul.

136

A Rock Higher Than the Adversity

"From the end of the earth will I cry unto thee, when my heart is overwhelmed: lead me to the rock that is higher than I. For thou hast been a shelter for me, and a strong tower from the enemy. I will abide in thy tabernacle for ever: I will trust in the covert of thy wings. Selah" (Psalm 61:2–4). As David struggled to get through each day, as his heart fainted, he cried out to be led to the "Rock" (place of refuge, retreat and rest in God) higher than himself.

As it was with David, there arrive seasons in which our heart is *overwhelmed (trials and troubles are too great to bear)*. Spurgeon pictures the state of being overwhelmed: "Imagine a vessel at sea, and you can get an idea of the meaning of our text. It has been laboring in a storm; sometimes lifted up to heaven, as though its masts would sweep the stars; then again descending until its keel seemed dragging on the ocean bed; first staggering this way, and then that way, reeling to and fro, now rushing forward and now starting back—like a drunken man, or like a madman who has lost his way. At last a huge sea comes rolling on; its white crest of foam can be seen in the distance, and the sailors give up all for lost; on comes the wave, gathering up all its strength till it dashes against the ship, and down the vessel goes; it is *overwhelmed*. The decks are swept; the masts are gone; the timbers are creaking; the ship descends and is sucked down as in a whirlpool. All is lost. David says, 'That is the case with my heart; it is overwhelmed, drawn into a vortex of trouble, borne down by a tremendous sea of difficulty, crushed and broken. The ribs of my soul seem to have given way; every timber of my vessel is cracked and gone out of its place. My heart is overwhelmed within me.'"[821]

If you identify with David's being *overwhelmed*, you're not alone. Bodily pains and frailty, fears and depressions, abandonment of friends and/or family, and prospect of death *overwhelm* the best of Christians. In such times all is dark and puzzling. All seems helpless and hopeless. God seems distant and prayers useless.

285

When the Rain Comes

It's difficult to see tomorrow because of the trials of today. In these times of crisis and emergency, don't panic or fear, but like David pray passionately, trustingly, and persistently despite its difficulty. David knew from past experiences, the example of others and Holy Scripture that God was dependable and trustworthy to help in the hour of need. Therefore, in exile in a distant land far from home, family and friends, with his heart deeply crushed by what Absalom had done, he cries out to God for comfort, strength and help. See 2 Samuel 15:13–18. "In his weakness he calls out and desires to find a sure place of refuge with his God."[822] Spurgeon comments, "It was a wise resolution, for had he ceased to pray he would have become the victim of despair; there is an end to a man when he makes an end to prayer."[823] Matthew Henry states, "Weeping must quicken praying and not deaden it."[824] Spurgeon again said, "It is hard to pray when the very heart is drowning, yet gracious men plead best at such times. Tribulation brings us to God and brings God to us. It is all over with me, affliction is all over me, yet God is near, near enough to hear my voice, and I will call Him."[825]

> Weeping must quicken praying and not deaden it.
> Matthew Henry

See the specificity of the prayer that David uttered. He said, *Lead me to the rock that is higher than I.* Divine assistance is needed to reach the Rock. Mathew Henry states that David is saying, lead me

(1. "To the rock which is too high for me to get up to unless Thou help me to it. Lord, give me such an assurance and satisfaction of my own safety as I can never attain to but by Thy special grace working such a faith in me;

(2. "To the rock on the top of which I shall be set further out of the reach of my troubles and nearer the serene and quiet region than I can be by any power or wisdom of my own."[826]

Jeremiah Dyke writes, "The tower (Psalm 18:2) and the ROCK were too high for David himself to get into, and therefore he sets to the scaling ladder. "Lead me to the ROCK and into the tower that is higher than I. Hear my cry; attend unto my prayer." So he makes prayer the scaling ladder to get upon that ROCK and into that TOWER that otherwise had been too high for him; he gets that safety and deliverance which otherwise but by prayer unto God had been impossible to have been obtained."[827] Spurgeon comments, "Alas! such is the confusion in which the troubled mind is often cast that we need piloting to this divine shelter. Hence the prayer of the text. O Lord our God, by Thy Holy Spirit, teach us the way of faith, lead us into Thy rest. The wind blows us out to sea; the helm answers not to our puny hand. Thou, Thou alone canst steer us over the bar between yon sunken rocks, safe into the fair haven. How dependent we are upon Thee—we need Thee to bring us to Thee. To be wisely directed and steered into safety and peace is Thy gift, and Thine alone."[828]

Oh! sometimes the shadows are deep,
 And rough seems the path to the goal;
And sorrows, sometimes how they sweep
 Like tempests down over the soul.

Oh, then to the Rock let me fly,
 To the Rock that is higher than I!
Oh, then to the Rock let me fly,
 To the Rock that is higher than I!

Oh! sometimes how long seems the day;
 And sometimes how weary my feet!
But toiling in life's dusty way,
 The Rock's blessed shadow, how sweet!

Then near to the Rock let me keep,
 If blessings or sorrows prevail,
Or climbing the mountain way steep,
 Or walking the shadowy vale. ~ Erastus Johnson (1871)

From the end of the earth will I cry unto thee. Prayer is always present. There is not a place on earth (loneliness, isolation from friends and their ability or willingness to help) or season of life (regardless of its difficulty, sorrow, sickness or trouble) to which God's "help" does not extend in response to prayer. See Psalm 139:8–13. Remember, there is no locale on earth where God is not and does not forever stand ready to give answer to prayer. J. W. Reeve states, "For our encouragement, how very numerous are the instances recorded in the Word of God of definite prayers on the part of God's saints and definite answers on the part of God! No fewer than eighty-eight distinct prayers of men of God and eighty-eight distinct answers from the Lord are recorded in the Old Testament, and no fewer than forty-eight instances of the same kind occur in the New Testament."[829]

Incessantly and earnestly pray with David: "Lord, I am overwhelmed with my present trial and affliction so intensely that I find it difficult in seeing beyond today. The hope of help seems to have disappeared. All is dark and dismal. I am as a drowning man gasping for air and a terrified blind man walking along the edge of a gigantic cliff. I will surely drown and stumble unless you help me. As You did for David in his time of desperation, send Thy Holy Spirit to lead me to that Rock that is higher than I am that I might have rest from my disquietude and obtain a secure standing. Your faithfulness to sustain him in his great distress reassures me of Thy dependability and trustworthiness to lift me up above the billowing waves and boisterous wind that assail my life to a high and lofty place of safety and rest. And for this knowledge and promise, I give unto You my praise and thankfulness. In Jesus name, Amen."

Faith-based praying (Matthew 21:22) will lead you to confidently say with David, 'I will abide in the safety of God's tabernacle forever and trust in the covert of His wings' (Psalm 61:4). G. Campbell Morgan writes, "David had found Jehovah to be at once the Rock, that is foundation; Fortress, that is the place of refuge founded on the rock; and Deliverer, that is the One who guarded the refuge."[830] George Horne says, "Grounded on Him, by faith in His sufferings and exaltation, we may defy all the storms and tempests that can be raised against us by the adversary, while, as from the top of a lofty mountain on the shore, we behold the waves dashing themselves in pieces beneath us."[831] "Walk in your path of integrity with steadfast steps, and show that you are invincibly strong in the strength which confidence in God alone can confer. Thus you will be delivered from anxious care; you will not be troubled with evil tidings; your heart will be fixed, trusting in the Lord."[832]

> I do not stand on shifting sand
> And fear the storm that rages;
> But calm and sure, I stand secure
> Upon the Rock of Ages. ~ Anonymous

The bottom line is that Christ is the saint's asylum (Rock and Refuge) from the overwhelming trials and setbacks of life. Flee to that asylum for protection from despair and defeat and for provision of peace, hope and endurance. Spurgeon summarizes, "Now, as some of you will be exercised with troubles, remember that the Rock is higher than you are; and when your troubles reach you, if you are not high enough to escape them, climb up to the Rock Christ, for there is no trouble that can reach you when you get there."[833] Amen and Amen.

137

Make Use of Thy God

"I will be their God" (Jeremiah 32:38).

The source of the promise. Its giver is not a prophet or disciple, but God Himself assuring its authority and truthfulness.

The sphere of the promise. "I will be their God." Though God is Creator of all people, He is the Father of only those who embrace His only begotten Son, the Lord

Comfort for Troubled Hearts

Jesus Christ. John says, "But to all who did receive Him, who believed in His name, he gave the right to become children of God, who were born, not of blood nor of the will of the flesh nor of the will of man, but of God" (John 1:12–13 ESV). What a delightful and awesome promise to the redeemed, the born-again ones (John 3:3), that God is and will be forever their *personal* God. All that is encompassed in the mighty and glorious name of God belongs to His children. Every time we pray, "Our Father" (Matthew 6:9), we testify to God's exclusivity to the saved.[834]

The scope of the promise. "I will be their God." The height and depth and length and width of the Sovereign declaration is incomprehensible, for it exceeds man's finite mind to fully grasp it. In part, the Bible reveals:

God is thy Preserver

"The LORD shall preserve you from all evil; He shall preserve your soul" (Psalm 121:7 NKJV).

God is thy Deliverer

"Sovereign LORD, my strong deliverer" (Psalm 140:7 NIV).

God is thy Comforter

"Praise be to the God and Father of our Lord Jesus Christ, the Father of compassion and the God of all comfort, who comforts us in all our troubles" (2 Corinthians 1:3–4 NIV).

God is thy Friend

"No longer do I call you servants, for the servant does not know what his master is doing; but I have called you friends" (John 15:15 ESV).

God is thy Defender

"The Lord is your mighty defender" (Deuteronomy 32:4 GNT).

God is thy Redeemer

"Our redeemer, the LORD of hosts is his name, the Holy One of Israel" (Isaiah 47:4).

God is thy Guide

"And the LORD shall guide thee continually" (Isaiah 58:11).

God is thy Ruler

"God rules: there's something to shout over!" (Psalm 97:1 MSG).

God is thy Helper

"Behold, God is mine helper" (Psalm 54:4).

God is thy Forgiver

"I, even I, am he that blotteth out thy transgressions for mine own sake, and will not remember thy sins" (Isaiah 43:25).

When the Rain Comes

God is thy Provider

"But my God shall supply all your need according to his riches in glory by Christ Jesus" (Philippians 4:19).

God is thy Companion

"God has said, 'I will never leave you; I will never abandon you'" (Hebrews 13:5 NCV).

God is thy Strength

"The LORD is my strength and song, and he is become my salvation: he is my God" (Exodus 15:2).

God is thy Shepherd

"The LORD is my shepherd; I shall not want" (Psalm 23:1). "He will feed His flock like a shepherd. He will gather the lambs in His arms and carry them close to His heart." (Isaiah 40:11 NLV).

God is thy Counselor

"With Your counsel You will guide me, and afterward receive me to glory" (Psalm 73:24 NASB).

God is thy Healer

"Heal me, O LORD, and I shall be healed; save me, and I shall be saved" (Jeremiah 17:14).

God is thy Vindicator

"O God, my vindicator! Answer me when I call! When I was distressed, you set me free; now have mercy on me, and hear my prayer" (Psalm 4:2 CJB).

God is thy Rock

"The Lord is my rock, my protection, my Savior. My God is my rock. I can run to him for safety" (Psalm 18:2 NCV).

God is thy Transformer

"A new heart also will I give you, and a new spirit will I put within you: and I will take away the stony heart" (Ezekiel 36:26).

God is thy Buttress

"He gives strength to the weary, and increases the power of the weak" (Isaiah 40:29 NIV).

God is thy Courage and Fortitude

"Fear thou not; for I am with thee: be not dismayed; for I am thy God: I will strengthen thee; yea, I will help thee; yea, I will uphold thee with the right hand of my righteousness" (Isaiah 41:10).

Comfort for Troubled Hearts

God is thy Everlasting God

"Do you not know? Have you not heard? The LORD is the everlasting God, the Creator of the ends of the earth. He will not grow tired or weary, and his understanding no one can fathom" (Isaiah 40:28 NIV).

> Oh! Christian, do but consider what it is to have God to be thine own; consider what it is, compared with anything else.
> C. H. Spurgeon

All that God is in nature (omnipotent, omniscient, immutable, omnipresent) He makes available to His people in saying, "I will be their God." John Gill remarks, "All things are [His children's], nor can they want any good thing; they need fear no enemy; they may depend upon the love of God and be secure of His power; they may expect all blessings here and hereafter (1 Peter 2:9)."[835] "I conceive that God Himself," proclaims Spurgeon, "could say no more than that. I do not think if the Infinite were to stretch His powers and magnify His grace by some stupendous promise which could outdo every other, I do not believe that it could exceed in glory this promise: 'I will be their God.' Oh! Christian, do but consider what it is to have God to be thine own; consider what it is, compared with anything else."[836]

Ponder that truth until it inflames your heart with hope, encouragement and peace. Every believer jubilantly and confidently may say with Paul, "What shall we then say to these things? If God be for us, who can be against us? He that spared not his own Son, but delivered him up for us all, how shall he not with him also freely give us all things?" (Romans 8:31–32).

The satisfaction of the promise. Matthew Henry says, "God's being to us a God is the summary of all happiness; Heaven itself is no more (Hebrews 11:16; Revelation 21:3)."[837] Spurgeon says, "Come, soul, is there not enough here to delight thee? Put this promise to thy lips [and drink]: 'I will be their God.' Oh! here is a very sea of bliss, a very ocean of delight. Come, bathe thy spirit in it. Thou mayest swim, aye, to eternity, and never find a shore; thou may'st dive to the very infinite and never find the bottom, 'I will be their God.' Oh! if this does not make thine eyes sparkle, if this make not thy foot dance for joy and thy heart beat high with bliss, then assuredly thy soul is not in a healthy state."[838]

The security of the promise. God eternally will be the God of His people. He is presently their God in their sojourn on earth and will continue to be in the realms of Heaven. The psalmist declared, "This God is our God forever and ever. He will lead us beyond death" (Psalm 48:14 GWT). The Bible again states, "For God himself has said, 'I will never fail you or abandon you'" (Hebrews 13:5 CJB). And God cannot lie (Titus 1:2).

When the Rain Comes

The strength of the promise. As marvelous and magnificent as the promise is, much of its rich benefit and blessing lies not only in knowing it but in using it. Therefore, readily utilize *thy* God by trusting Him and relying upon Him regardless of the trial or trouble. Sad it is to possess such a promise without using it fully.

Spurgeon says, "Child of God, let me urge thee to make use of thy God. Make use of Him in prayer; I beseech thee, go to Him often, because He is thy God. He is thy God; He has made Himself over to thee, if we may use such an expression (and I think we may). He has become the positive property of all His children so that all He has and all He is, is theirs. O child, wilt thou let thy treasury lie idle when thou needest it? No; go and draw from it by prayer. Fly to Him; tell Him all thy wants. Use Him constantly by faith, at all times. Oh! I beseech thee, if some dark providence has come over thee, use thy God as a **Sun**, for He is a sun. If some strong enemy has come out against thee, use thy God for a **Shield**, for He is a shield to protect thee (Psalm 84:11). If thou hast lost thy way in the mazes of life, use Him for a **Guide**, for the great Jehovah will direct thee. If thou art in storms, use Him, for He is the God Who stills the raging sea and says to the waves, 'Be still' (Mark 4:39). If thou art a poor thing, knowing not which way to turn, use Him for a **Shepherd**, for the Lord is thy Shepherd, and thou shalt not want (Psalm 23:1). Whate'er you are, where'er you are, remember that God is just what you want (and all that you need). I beseech you, then, make use of thy God."[839] Use Him also for a **Healer**, for He is able to restore health and heal broken hearts (Isaiah 38:16–17).

"Fear not," your Maker now proclaims,
    "I am the Lord, your God.
"You're mine; I've called you by your name.
    "I am the Lord, your God.

"I'll help you through the waters;
    "They're not too deep for God.
"The rivers won't sweep o'er you;
    "I am the Lord, your God.

"I'll walk with you through fiery ways;
    "I am the Lord, your God.
"You won't be burned or set ablaze;
    "I am the Lord, your God.

"I've ransomed and redeemed you;
    "I am the holy God.
"You're precious and I love you;
    "I am the Lord, your God.

"Before Me no god e'er was formed;
   "I am the Lord, your God.
"Nor after Me will any come;
   "I am the Lord, your God.

"For I alone can save you;
   "I am Jehovah God.
"This day you are my witness;
   "I am the Lord, your God." ~ Susan H. Peterson (1998)

The surety of the promise. "I will be *their* God." Don't doubt God and His promise to you. "The angels never doubted him, nor the devils either. We alone, out of all the beings that God has fashioned, dishonor Him by unbelief and tarnish His honor by mistrust. Shame upon us for this! Our God does not deserve to be so basely suspected. In our past life we have proved Him to be true and faithful to His Word, and with so many instances of His love and of His kindness as we have received and are daily receiving at His hands, it is base and inexcusable that we suffer a doubt to sojourn within our heart. May we henceforth wage constant war against doubts of our God and with an unstaggering faith believe that what He has promised, He will also perform. 'Lord, I believe; help thou mine unbelief.'"[840]

Make use of "thy God," for He longs to supply all your needs (physically, emotionally and materially) and either alleviate your adversity or grant new grace for enduring it, which He is more than able to do.

138
The Vanity and Variety of Earthly Dependencies

"Now on whom dost thou trust" (Isaiah 36:5). Is your *foundational* trust for help in the hour of adversity, bereavement or sickness in physicians, politicians, preachers, personal prowess or in Sovereign God? Hear the psalmist's answer in Psalm 20:7: "Some trust in chariots, and some in horses: but we will remember the name of the LORD our God." W. G. Lewis summarized the text: "The vanity and the variety of earthly dependences."[841] The Christian is exhorted to "remember the name of the LORD" in times of need; to trust in His power, protection and provision. Albert Barnes remarks, "We will not forget that our reliance is not on armies, but on God, the living God. Whatever instrumentality we may employ, we will remember always that our hope is in God, and that He only can give success."[842]

"Great certainly is the faith," says Luther, "which hath such courage by remembering the name of the Lord."[843] W. S. Plumer writes, "The righteous put nothing with God to form the basis of their joy and trust. He alone is enough. They need neither help, nor guidance, nor wisdom, nor strength, nor righteousness but in Him alone."[844] Thomas Brooks says, "We trust *as* we love and *where* we love. If we love Christ much, surely we will trust Him much."[845]

> We trust as we love, and where we love. If we love Christ much, surely, we will trust Him much.
> Thomas Brooks

It is irrational and sinful for the Christian not to so "remember" and "trust." Joseph Parker says of God's trustworthiness, "He who trusts in the Eternal is eternally safe. He has no need to reckon or compute or arrange as to contingencies and possibilities; he says, 'God is my refuge and strength, therefore will not I fear, though the earth be removed, and though the mountains be carried into the midst of the sea.'"[846] Spurgeon remarks, "Chariots and horses make an imposing show and with their rattling and dust and fine caparisons make so great a figure that vain man is much taken with them; yet the discerning eye of faith sees more in an invisible God than in all these."[847]

However, instinctively some believers instead of first looking to the Lord for help in the time of need look to secondary sources and means (chariots and horses). Like the unbeliever, they believe the more "chariots and horses" (human instrumentation instead of divine dependence) that are utilized, the greater the chance for deliverance, healing or victory. But they are wrong and partake of the bitter consequences of their error. "They [all that trust in 'chariots and horses'] are brought down and fallen [defeat and collapse]: but we [all that rely upon the Lord] are risen, and stand upright [successful, victorious]" (Psalm 20:8). He that depends upon human ingenuity or ability or skill will be sorely disappointed and defeated, while the person that trusts in the Lord will be delighted and delivered. Such is affirmed time and again in Scripture: 2 Chronicles 14:11–12 (Asa); 2 Chronicles 20:12 (Jehoshaphat); 2 Chronicles 32:7–8 (Hezekiah); Psalm 33:17; 34:22; 118:8 (David).

Placing trust in God first and foremost opens the door to Him to supply our needs through miraculous intervention or human agency. Every need is an opportunity for God to intervene and meet. Say with David, "The LORD is my strength and my shield; my heart trusted in him, and I am helped: therefore my heart greatly rejoiceth; and with my song will I praise him" (Psalm 28:7). See 1 John 5:15. God has proved throughout history His worthiness of man's trust. E. M. Bounds says, "Trust always operates in the present tense. Hope looks toward the future. Trust looks to the present. Hope expects. Trust possesses. Trust receives what prayer acquires. So, what prayer needs, at all times, is abiding and abundant trust."[848]

"On whom dost thou trust?" THE CHRISTIAN'S ANSWER: "'I trust," says the Christian, "a triune God—Father, Son, and Holy Spirit." To some this does not look like a real trust. "Why, we cannot see God," says one. "How do we know all about this Trinity? Is this a real trust?" Can you not trust in a thousand things you have never seen or heard? Some have said, "But does God interfere to help His people? Is the trust you place in Him really so recognized by Him that you can distinctly prove that He helps you?" Yes, we can. We can say also, by way of commending our God to others, that we feel we can rest upon Him for the future" (Spurgeon).[849] God is worthy of your trust; therefore, wholly trust Him without doubting His ability, for He "is able, through his mighty power at work within us, to accomplish infinitely more than we might ask or think" (Ephesians 3:20 NLT). Spurgeon exclaims, "Oh, blessed trust! To trust Him whose power will never be exhausted, whose love will never wane, whose kindness will never change, whose faithfulness will never fail, whose wisdom will never be nonplussed, and whose perfect goodness can never know a diminution! Happy art thou, reader, if this trust is thine! So trusting, thou shalt enjoy sweet peace now and glory hereafter, and the foundation of thy trust shall never be removed."[850] Amen and Amen. "Trust in him at all times; ye people, pour out your heart before him: God is a refuge for us" (Psalm 62:8).

To summarize, "Trust in the Lord [entire reliance upon Him] with all thine heart [entire mind]; and lean [depend upon] not unto thine own understanding [don't rely upon personal insights, impressions, impulsiveness or experience] (Proverbs 3:5). See Proverbs 28:26.

> Tis so sweet to trust in Jesus,
>   Just to take Him at His Word,
> Just to rest upon His promise,
>   Just to know, "Thus saith the Lord!"
>
> Jesus, Jesus, how I trust Him!
>   How I've proved Him o'er and o'er!
> Jesus, Jesus, precious Jesus!
>   Oh, for grace to trust Him more!
>
> I'm so glad I learned to trust Him,
>   Precious Jesus, Savior, Friend,
> And I know that He is with me,
>   Will be with me to the end. ~ Louisa M. R. Stead (1882)

What to Do When Afraid

"The LORD is my light and my salvation; whom shall I fear? the LORD is the strength of my life; of whom shall I be afraid?" (Psalm 27:1). David, who wrote the psalm, was no coward, but rather one of the boldest men of history. Recall how he faced Goliath. The trained soldiers of King Saul trembled in fear before this giant, yet David fearlessly fought him in the name of the Lord with only a sling in his hand. On another occasion, David, with the help of three men, slew an entire Philistine army. Indeed, he was a "man's man." Yet this great warrior, this hero of Israel, this mighty man of God states that he had his times in life when he was afraid. And who of us cannot state the same? All can testify that there are those times in life when we are struck with fear and tremble and are afraid. The fear causes anxiety, emotional chaos, sickness, and loss of realistic perspective. In such times, what are we to do? The same as David did—say, "What time I am afraid, I will trust in thee [and] praise his word" (Psalm 56:3–4).

Sooner or later you will face the 'what times I am afraid' in life—times of facing trouble, sickness, sorrow, suffering, and death. In such times, remember six things.

(1. Wholeheartedly trust God, despite what circumstances seem to say. Never allow what appears to be to generate fear of abandonment by God and a spirit of hopelessness. Fear is induced often by a lie parading as truth. A. B. Simpson remarks, "Fear is born of Satan, and if we would only take time to think a moment, we would see that everything Satan says is founded upon a falsehood. He is the father of lies. Even his fears are falsehoods, and his terrors ought to serve as encouragements. When Satan tells you, therefore, that some ill is going to come, you may quietly look in his face and tell him he is a liar. Instead of ill, goodness and mercy shall follow you all the days of your life. And then turn to your blessed Lord and say, 'What time I am afraid, I will trust in thee' (Psalm 56:3). Every fear is distrust, and trust is the remedy for fear."[851]

(2. Perfect love drives away all fear. The Bible states, "Where God's love is, there is no fear, because God's perfect love drives out fear" (1 John 4:18 NCV). Fear has no place in love. "We cannot fear if we understand God's love toward us."[852] Adrian Rogers comments, "When you see God's mighty power on one hand and His mighty love on the other, fear melts away. Rest in that love. Say, 'Lord, no matter what happens to me, I know You love me.'"[853] William Gurnall says, "The chains of love are stronger than the chains of fear."[854] John Piper declares, "The presence of hope in the invincible sovereignty of God drives out fear."[855]

(3. God promises never to abandon you. The Bible states in Hebrews 13:5, "He hath said, I will never leave thee, nor forsake thee." Fear is conquered and replaced

with calm and peace when the heart says, "Yea, though I walk through the valley of the shadow of death, I will fear no evil: for thou art with me; thy rod and thy staff they comfort me" (Psalm 23:4). The presence of Jesus aboard the "ship" gives calm and rest to its passengers when all about it is tumultuous. See 1 John 4:18–20. Clay Smith well stated that "Trust is the dance partner of Hope."[856] The two cannot be divorced. Coupled together Godward, they extinguish fear, replacing it with peace.

(4. Even spiritual giants encounter fear. David did. It's not the encounter with fear that determines the dimension (height and depth) of one's spirituality, but the response to it.

(5. Focus on Christ, not the subject of the fear. G. Campbell Morgan says, "The man who measures things by the circumstances of the hour is filled with fear; the man who sees Jehovah enthroned and governing has no panic."[857] Adrian Rogers states, "Fear caused Timothy to forget (2 Timothy 1:7). Focusing on what you fear takes your eyes off the Lord—His blessings, what He has done in the past, and what He will do in the future."[858] What is put in God's control by faith is always under His control.

> The presence of hope in the invincible sovereignty of God drives out fear.
> John Piper

(6. Tap hold of the power God has given to conquer fear. Paul writes, "For God did not give us a spirit of timidity (of cowardice, of craven and cringing and fawning fear), but [He has given us a spirit] of power and of love and of calm and well-balanced mind and discipline and self-control" (2 Timothy 1:7 AMPC). God gave His *Spirit of Power* to every believer to thwart fear. Use it. See 1 John 4:4.

To thwart fear, Charles Simeon wrote:

"*We must trust in His Word*, which, [since] it is in reality the only proper ground of confidence, must also be the measure of it. We have no authority to trust in God for anything which He has not promised, and we are bound to trust in Him for everything that He has promised. To do the former is presumption; to decline the latter is unbelief.

"*We must trust, also, in His providence*, for everything is ordered by Him, even to 'the falling of a sparrow upon the ground' and we are incapable of ordering anything for ourselves; 'it is not in man that walketh to direct his steps.'

"*We must trust also in His grace*, for we cannot do any good thing without Him. It is from Him that we must obtain power either to do, or even to will, what is acceptable in His sight, and in every stage of our existence must we depend on Him for more grace and receive from Him the grace that shall be sufficient for us."[859]

When the Rain Comes

I fear no foe with Thee at hand to bless;
Ills have no weight and tears no bitterness.
Where is death's sting? Where, grave, thy victory?
I triumph still, if Thou abide with me. ~ Henry Francis Lyte (1847)

> The man who measures things by the circumstances of the hour is filled with fear; the man who sees Jehovah enthroned and governing has no panic.
> G. Campbell Morgan

Believers ask with David, "Whom shall I fear?" It's a question which is its own answer. "The powers of darkness are not to be feared, for the Lord, our light, destroys them; and the damnation of hell is not to be dreaded by us, for the Lord is our salvation."[860] Alexander Maclaren said, "Only he who can say, 'The Lord is the strength of my life' can say, 'Of whom shall I be afraid?'"[861]

140

God's Promises to His Children in Trouble

"Because he hath set his love upon me, therefore will I deliver him: I will set him on high, because he hath known my name. He shall call upon me, and I will answer him: I will be with him in trouble; I will deliver him, and honor him. With long life will I satisfy him, and shew him my salvation" (Psalm 91:14–16). Alexander Maclaren says for the believer to *"set his love upon"* God "implies the binding or knitting of oneself to anything. Now, though love be the true cement by which men are bound to God, as it is the only real bond which binds men to one another, yet the word itself covers a somewhat wider area than is covered by the notion of love. It is not my love only that I am to fasten upon God, but my whole self that I am to bind to Him. God delights in us when we cling to Him."[862] The promises therefore are not for everyone but them that "know Him" intimately and walk with Him obediently and devotedly. Keep in mind the promises are undeserved and unmerited even by the choicest of saints. They are not given by man's desert but by God's delight.

I will deliver him. The first "I will" of God to them that "set his love upon Him" is the promise of rescue in the time of trouble, calamity or difficulty.

I will set him on high. God promises to place the saint in a place that is inaccessible to the enemy. David said, "The name of the LORD is a strong tower: the righteous runneth into it, and is safe" (Proverbs 18:10).

I will answer him. What wondrous joy and peace it is to know that God actually bends His ear toward us when we pray, to hear and fulfill our requests. Sorrow of sorrows it would be if God's ear was deaf to our cry. But, alas, that shall never be!

Comfort for Troubled Hearts

I will be with him in trouble. "Trouble" refers to times of distress, especially distress caused by emotional pain or anxiety. Spurgeon says, "Heirs of Heaven are conscious of a special divine presence in times of severe trial. God is always near in sympathy and in power to help His tried ones."[863] God will be with us in trouble to prevent our sinking under its burden.[864] Charles Simeon wrote, "The people of God are exposed to troubles no less than others. But they are supported under them by the presence of their God. As the Son of man walked with the Hebrew youths in the furnace, so will he with all his afflicted people; nor shall a hair of their head be singed."[865]

> The people of God are exposed to troubles no less than others. But they are supported under them by the presence of their God.
> Charles Simeon

I will deliver him. Once again God affirms His promise to provide a means of escape or rescue to His children in their times of calamity or crisis: "from the snare of the fowler" (Psalm 91:3). Spurgeon comments, "God delivers His people from the snare of the fowler in two senses. From and out of. First, He delivers them *from* the snare—does not let them enter it; and secondly, if they should be caught therein, He delivers them out of it. The first promise is the most precious to some; the second is the best to others."[866]

I will honor him. Matthew Henry says, "Those are truly honorable whom God puts honor upon by taking them into covenant and communion with Himself and designing them for His kingdom and glory."[867] *Honor* bears the meaning of something weighted down as one might be with riches of gold and silver. God has weighted down His children with a great honor that far exceeds the weight and value of silver and gold.

John Gill remarked, "The Lord will honor such that know Him and love Him. All His saints are honored by Him, by taking them into His family and giving them a name better than that of sons and daughters of the greatest potentate, by clothing them with the righteousness of his Son, by adorning them with the graces of his Spirit, by granting them communion and fellowship with Himself, and by bringing them to His kingdom and glory."[868] How can it be that the sovereign God would choose to so honor redeemed sinners such as you and me! See Isaiah 63:9 and 1 Samuel 2:30.

I will satisfy him with long life. God promises to give the saints a full and meaningful life. Matthew Henry says, "They shall live long enough; they shall be continued in this world till they have done the work they were sent into this world for and are ready for Heaven, and that is long enough. Who would wish to live a day longer than God has some work to do, either by him or upon him?"[869] See Deuteronomy 32:46–47.

When the Rain Comes

I will show him my salvation. The promise extends beyond this life and the grave. Matthew Henry remarks, "It is more probable that the word refers to the better country, that is, the heavenly, which the patriarchs desired and sought. He will show him that, bring him to that blessed state, the felicity of which consists so much in seeing that face to face which we here see through a glass darkly; and, in the meantime, He will give him a prospect of it. All these promises, some think, point primarily at Christ, and had their accomplishment in His resurrection and exaltation."[870] What a thought, what a promise just to know one day we will see Jesus face to face and ever be with Him in the glorious abode of Heaven. This He has promised. Hallelujah! See John 14:1–3. "He has Pisgah views of the promised land even here; and as soon as he has finished his appointed course, God will shew him his full salvation, causing him to behold all its glory and enjoy all its blessedness. Then shall be given to him a life which will fully satisfy his most enlarged desires. God will say to him, in the presence of the whole assembled universe, 'Come, thou servant, whom I have decreed to "set on high." See the kingdom that was prepared for thee from eternity; take possession of it as thine own, and inherit it forever.'"[871]

> Christ will not fail me; how precious the word!
>   I am secure with my Savior and Lord.
> His love faileth never, endureth forever,
>   And legions of angels shall over me guard.
>
> He promised to keep me, support and defend me
>   When trials o'ertake and temptations assail;
> He promised to guide me, and I am persuaded
>   His promises never, no, never can fail.
>
> Christ will not fail me! a child of His care;
>   All of my burdens He gladly will share.
> He's ever beside me; no harm can betide me,
>   For when I most need Him, my Savior is there.
> Onward I journey; no need shall I know
>   But that His goodness and power will bestow.
> The while I am clinging, my glad heart is singing,
>   For Christ is beside me wherever I go. ~ William C. Poole (1912)

What comfort, assurance, peace, and hope the "I will's" of God are to His children in times of calamity and trouble. Rest upon them. Rely upon them. All the various troubles and trials Psalm 91 refers to are ineffective against Him that "sets his love upon Him." Salter wrote, "Every promise is built upon four pillars: God's justice or holiness, which will not suffer Him to deceive; His grace or goodness, which will not suffer Him to forget; His truth, which will not suffer Him to change; and His power, which makes Him able to accomplish."[872]

141
Choose to Hope in God

"Blessed is the man that trusteth in the LORD, and whose hope the LORD is" (Jeremiah 17:7). It was said that man can live about forty days without food, about three days without water, about eight minutes without air, but only for one second without hope. Without hope, the fabric of life comes unseamed and life comes crashing down. Gloriously and wondrously God has made available the hope that is needed to sustain man victoriously through the various storms of life, and in death.

Hope's Premise. Hope says that we confidently can expect something to happen because God promised it would come to pass.[873]

Hope's permanence. Spurgeon said, "Hope is one of the last blessings God gives us, and one that abides last with us."[874] Hope will abide with the believer in every circumstance, and then as he fords the chilly Jordan into the promised land it will prop him up.

Hope's periphery. George Müller said, "'Hope thou in God.' Oh, remember this: There is never a time when we may not hope in God. Whatever our necessities, however great our difficulties, and though to all appearance help is impossible, yet our business is to hope in God, and it will be found that it is not in vain. In the Lord's own time help will come."[875]

Hope's Proof. The validation of hope's claim to the believer for an abundant life in the present despite its troubles and illnesses (John 10:10), all things (good and bad) working together for good (Romans 8:28), and eternal life in Heaven (John 3:16) lies solely in the death, burial and resurrection of Jesus Christ (1 Corinthians 15:4). Hope was born at Calvary and validated at the empty tomb. Clay Smith said hope is more about "Who" than "what."[876]

Hope's power. The power of hope is not in the hope itself but in Christ's indisputable power to fulfill His promises with regard to the specific aspect of the hope.

Hope's positivism. Hope is not wishful thinking, but certitude based upon God's unalterable promises. R. C. Sproul says, "Hope is called the anchor of the soul (Hebrews 6:19), because it gives stability to the Christian life. But hope is not simply a 'wish' (I wish that such-and-such would take place); rather, it is that which latches on to the certainty of the promises of the future that God has made."[877] Augustine said, "God is not a deceiver, that He should offer to support us and then, when we lean upon Him, should slip away from us." See Titus 1:2.

Hope's Procurement. Hope is a decision, a personal choice to trust God despite the circumstance or news received. Although divinely generated at conversion to Christ, it requires personal implementation—decision to appropriate it. Recall that David exhorted his own soul, saying, "Hope thou in God" (Psalm 42:5). Sometimes the night is so dark, rain so hard, and storm so severe that we need to remind ourselves to do the same.

Hope's Progression. Hope is strengthened by trust (confidence) in God that He is in absolute control of all that happens, the certainty and validity of His promises, the confirmation of history, and multitudes of personal experiences of His trustworthiness and reliability. With Spurgeon, I say, "Ah! man, I like to see thee have a good long measuring rod, when it is made of hope. Hope is a tall companion; he wades right through the sea and is not drowned; you cannot kill him, do what you may."[878]

Hope's Propulsion. The promises of God fuel the believer's hope. Francis Ridley Havergal wrote, "Every year I live—in fact nearly every day—I seem to see more how all the peace, happiness and power of the Christian life hinges on one thing. That one thing is taking God at His Word, believing He really means exactly what He says, and accepting the very words that reveal His goodness and grace without substituting other words or changing the precise moods and tenses He has seen fit to use."[879] Mark Twain cautions, "Lord, save us all from old age and broken health and a hope tree that has lost the faculty of putting out blossoms."[880] Keep sowing God's promises in the heart so it will keep putting out fresh blossoms of hope.

Hope's Place. G. K. Chesterton said, "Hope means hoping when things are hopeless, or it is no virtue at all. As long as matters are really hopeful, hope is mere flattery or platitude; it is only when everything is hopeless that hope begins to be a strength."[881] Alfred Lord Tennyson wrote, "Hope smiles from the threshold of the year to come, whispering, 'It will be happier.'"[882]

Hope's Pertinacity. Thomas Brooks remarks, "A Christian will part with anything rather than his hope; he knows that hope will keep the heart both from aching and breaking, from fainting and sinking; he knows that hope is a beam of God, a spark of glory, and that nothing shall extinguish it till the soul be filled with glory."[883]

Hope's patience. It's difficult at times to see hope in every circumstance. But that's biblical. Genuine hope is unseen. Paul says, "Hope [object of hope] that is seen is not hope: for what a man seeth, why doth he yet hope for? But if we hope for that we see not, then do we with patience wait for it" (Romans 8:24–25). J. B. Phillips renders the text, "We were saved by this hope, but in our moments of impatience let us remember that hope always means waiting for something that we haven't yet got. But if we hope for something we cannot see, then we must settle down to wait for it in patience." Albert Barnes comments, "'But if we hope'—The effect here stated is one which exists everywhere. Where there is a strong desire for an object and a corresponding expectation of obtaining it—which constitutes true hope—then we can wait for it with patience. Where there is a strong desire without a corresponding expectation of obtaining it, there is impatience."[884] The believer's hope is threaded with patience for that which is hoped to come to pass until it does. Paul, in commending the brethren at Thessalonica, said, "Remembering without ceasing your work of faith, and labor of love, and patience of hope in our Lord Jesus Christ, in the sight of God and our Father" (1 Thessalonians 1:3).

Hope's Practice. Exhibit an enduring (unwavering, steadfast) hope regardless of trials, troubles, illnesses and approaching death. John W. Ritenbaugh says, "Our relationship is with a Being—not a book, not words on the page, but a Person. We can have enduring hope, not only because of what He has done in the past when He died for our sins as our Savior, but because of what He is doing in the present as our High Priest—and what He will do in the future because of His promises and His character."[885] An enduring hope in Christ Jesus enabled the Thessalonian believers to withstand grave suffering and trouble. Regarding them Paul says, "As we pray to our God and Father about you, we think of your faithful work, your loving deeds, and *the enduring hope* you have because of our Lord Jesus Christ" (1 Thessalonians 1:3 NLT).

An enduring hope in Christ Jesus spurred Paul onward in ministry and life despite life's numerous trials and troubles. An enduring hope in Christ Jesus enabled the apostles (except John who died of natural causes) to experience martyrdom without recanting their faith. An enduring hope in Christ Jesus enabled Polycarp to refuse to renounce Christ when threatened with being burned at the stake, saying, "Eighty and six years have I served Him, and He never once wronged me; how then shall I blaspheme my King, Who has saved me?" An enduring hope in Christ Jesus enabled Latimer and Ridley to be burned at the stake for the faith on October 16, 1555. An enduring hope in Christ Jesus enabled the famous pastor Dr. George W. Truett, who agonizingly suffered from an illness an entire year prior to death, to repeat numerous times, "Not my will, but Thine be done."[886] W. A. Criswell states, "In that faith and in that yielded submissiveness, the great pastor died."[887] Clutch tightly to the believer's hope; don't let it die despite the affliction, trial, persecution, fear or pain.

Hope's Promise. "And you will feel secure, because there is hope; you will look around and take your rest in security" (Job 11:18 ESV). Possessor's of the believer's hope attest to peace, tranquility, security, and rest in the midst of the most turbulent storms.

When the Rain Comes

Hope in God, for thou shalt praise Him;
    His salvation thou shalt see.
Thy eternal Rock and Fortress,
    And thy present help, is He.

Hope in God, for well He knoweth
    How to help in time of need.
Those who know His name will trust Him;
    He will answer all who plead.

God of hope and God of comfort,
    He will never faint or fail.
Hope may firmly cast her anchor
    Far above within the veil.

Hope in God! Why shouldest thou doubt Him?
    None He leaveth desolate.
Lift your heart; the morning cometh!
    Live and trust Him; watch and wait.

Hope in God, the Lord Jehovah;
    Look beyond and look above!
Thou shalt see His light and glory;
    Thou shalt prove His faithful love. ~ Julia H. Johnson (1902)

142

It's Not "Good-bye" but "Good-night"

It was the custom of the early saints to bid their dying family members and friends (those that would fall asleep in Jesus) not "good-bye," but "good-night," fully assured of a coming reunion with them in the "morning." An ancient hymn expressed that custom and the believer's hope upon which it was based.

SLEEP on, beloved, sleep on and take thy rest;
Lay down thy head upon thy Savior's breast.
We love thee well, but Jesus loves thee best—
Good-night!

Calm is thy slumber as an infant's sleep,
But thou shalt wake no more to toil and weep;
Thine is a perfect rest, secure and deep—
Good-night!

Comfort for Troubled Hearts

Until the shadow from this earth is cast,
Until He gathers in His sheaves at last,
Until the Lenten gloom is overpast—
Good-night!

Until the Easter glory lights the skies,
Until the dead in Jesus shall arise
And He shall come—but not in lowly guise—
Good-night!

Until, made beautiful by love divine,
Thou, in the likeness of Thy Lord, shalt shine
And He shall bring that golden crown of thine—
Good-night!

Only "Good-night," beloved, not "Farewell"!
A little while, and all His saints shall dwell
In hallowed union, indivisible—
Good-night!

Until we meet again before His throne,
Clothed in the spotless robe He gives His own;
Until we know, even as we are known—
Good-night! ~ Sarah Doudney (1841–1926)

Death is horrifying to people that possess no hope of future life or in being reunited with family and friends in Heaven. Death is to them a forever "good-bye," not a temporary "good-night." Their sorrow far exceeds that of the believer in the death of others because it is a sorrow without hope (1 Thessalonians 4:13). Albert Barnes comments, "Hence, when they buried them, they buried their hopes in the grave, and so far as they had any evidence, they were never to see them again. They looked forward to no glorious resurrection when that body shall rise and when they shall be reunited to part no more. It is no wonder that they weep—for who would not weep when he believes that he parts with his friends forever?"[888]

Jesus Christ, however, gloriously rescues His followers from that horror.[889]

John Stott proclaims, "We will not only survive death, but be raised from it. We are to be given new bodies like His resurrection body, with new and undreamed-of powers. For he is called both the 'firstfruits' of the harvest and 'the firstborn from the dead.' Both metaphors give the same assurance. He was the first to rise; all his people will follow. We will have a body like his. 'Just as we have borne the likeness of the earthly man (Adam), so shall we bear the likeness of the man from Heaven (Christ)' (1 Corinthians 15:49)."[890] It is only in the hope (confident certainty) of the resurrection of the dead, reunion with them that die in the Lord, and the delight of Heaven that sorrow can be mitigated in the hour of death. The hope doesn't remove the sorrow, just drastically diminishes it. We sorrow not as those that possess no hope (1 Thessalonians 4:13–14).

Albert Barnes writes, "It is a sad thing to die without hope—so to die as to have no hope for ourselves, and to leave none to our surviving friends that we are happy. Such is the condition of the whole pagan world, and such the state of those who die in Christian lands who have no evidence that their peace is made with God. As I love my friends, my father, my mother, my wife, my children, I would not have them go forth and weep over my grave as those who have no hope in my death. I would have their sorrow for my departure alleviated by the belief that my soul is happy with my God, even when they commit my cold clay to the dust; and were there no other reason for being a Christian, this would be worth all the effort which it requires to become one. It would demonstrate the unspeakable value of religion that my living friends may go forth to my grave and be comforted in their sorrows with the assurance that my soul is already in glory and that my body will rise again! No eulogium for talents, accomplishments, or learning; no pæans of praise for eloquence, beauty, or martial deeds; no remembrances of wealth and worldly greatness would then so meet the desires which my heart cherishes as to have them enabled, when standing around my open grave, to sing the song which only Christians can sing."[891] Amen, may it even be so with me in my death and yours! May family and friends be able to say, "Good-night," not "Good-bye."

Sheldon Vanauken, a student of the English professor and Christian apologist C. S. Lewis, recounted their last meeting (Vanauken was departing Oxford for the United States) at a pub for lunch in the book *A Severe Mercy*. In that final meeting they voiced thoughts about the nature of life after death. As they departed, Lewis said to Vanauken, "I shan't say good-bye. We'll meet again." Lewis then crossed the busy highway to the other side. Upon looking back to his friend he said loudly over the roar of the traffic, "Besides—Christians never say good-bye."

Christians never say good-bye;
We only move to our home on high. ~ Nelons

143

When You Feel Abandoned by God

Do you feel abandoned by God? If so, you are not alone. C. S. Lewis, in the aftermath of his wife's death, testified that he cried out to God for comfort but no answer came. He asked, "What can this mean? Why is He so present a commander in our time of prosperity and so very absent a help in time of trouble?"[892] Spurgeon, in commenting on Psalm 88:6, testified, "He who now feebly expounds these words knows within himself more than he would care or dare to tell of the abysses of inward anguish. He has sailed round the Cape of Storms and has drifted along by the dreary headlands of despair."[893] Even David, the psalmist, experienced times when God seemed to be afar off. In Psalm 88:14 he cried, "LORD, why castest thou off my soul? why hidest thou thy face from me?"

Feeling abandoned by God, Job said, "O that I knew where I might find him!" (Job 23:3 NET).

> The flesh can bear only a certain number of wounds and no more, but the soul can bleed in ten thousand ways and die over and over again each hour.
> C. H. Spurgeon

Job's Relapse. Job's disheartening and terrible despair, like that of Lewis, Spurgeon and David, prompted the belief that God had deserted him when he needed Him the most. Saints at large, regardless of spirituality or status, in times of grave affliction or adversity are susceptible to the same faulty irrational thought. Charles C. Stewart explains, "Bodily suffering or the pressure of severe and long-continued outward calamities may contribute to enfeeble the mind and lead the soul to conclude that it is forsaken by its God. The dispensations of divine providence appear so complex and difficult that faith is unable to explore them or hope to rise above them. The mind magnifies its distresses and dwells on its own griefs to the exclusion of those grounds of consolation and causes of thankfulness afforded in the many mercies that tend to alleviate their bitterness. In reality God is not more distant from the soul, though He appears to be so."[894]

Spurgeon states, "The mind can descend far lower than the body; for it there are bottomless pits. The flesh can bear only a certain number of wounds and no more, but the soul can bleed in ten thousand ways and die over and over again each hour. It is grievous to the good man to see the Lord whom he loves laying him in the sepulcher of despondency, piling nightshade upon him, putting out all his candles, and heaping over him solid masses of sorrow. Faith tells the despondent heart that God never placed a Joseph in a pit without drawing him up again to fill a throne, that he never caused a horror of great darkness to fall upon an Abraham without revealing His covenant to him, and that He never cast even a Jonah into the deeps without preparing the means to land him safely on dry land. Alas, when under deep depression the mind forgets all this and is only conscious of its unutterable misery, the man sees the lion but not the honey in its carcass; he feels the thorns but he cannot smell the roses which adorn them. It is an unspeakable consolation that our Lord Jesus knows this experience right well, having, with the exception of the sin of it, felt it all and more than all in Gethsemane when He was exceeding sorrowful even unto death."[895]

Job's Resolve. Augustine said, "You have made us for Yourself, O Lord, and our hearts are restless until they find their rest in You." Knowing that ultimate comfort, peace and hope in times of distress are not to be found in doctors, therapists, counselors, or medications, Job pursued the presence and intervention of God. Note that although Job felt abandoned by God, he doesn't quit on God but seeks Him (evidence of genuine faith). Joseph Parker wrote, "Job looks round for God as a man might look round for an old acquaintance, an old but long-gone friend. Memory has a great ministry to discharge in life; old times come back and whisper to us, correct us, or bless us, as the case may be. After listening to all new doctors, the heart says, 'Where is your old friend? where the quarter whence light first dawned? recall yourself; think out the whole case.' So Job would seem now to say, Oh that I knew where I might find Him! I would go round the earth to discover Him; I would fly through all the stars if I could have but one brief interview with Him; I would count no labor hard if I might see Him as I once did."[896] He that knows the darkness and despair of a Job attests to the same. When God seems distant, all that matters is *finding* Him and enjoying the sweet delight of His presence.

"O that I knew where I might find him!" Note, the specific priority of the prayer: "where I might find Him." Spurgeon remarked, "In Job's uttermost extremity he cried after the Lord. His first prayer is not 'Oh, that I might be healed of the disease which now festers in every part of my body!' nor even 'Oh, that I might see my children restored from the jaws of the grave and my property once more brought from the hand of the spoiler!' but the first and uppermost cry is, 'Oh, that I knew where I might find Him who is my God! that I might come even to His seat!'"[897] It is as if Job said, "God, I can bear any adversity or suffering if I am but confident Thou art with me." "God's children run home when the storm comes on. It is the heaven-born instinct of a gracious soul to seek shelter from all ills beneath the wings of Jehovah."[898]

> God reveals Himself to faith. We believe in order
> that we may see, trust in order that we may know.
> W. F. Adeney

Job's Reward. "Mine eye seeth thee" (Job 42:5). Job's quest resulted in finding Him for whom his soul craved. God has promised the same for all that seek Him. He says, "I love those who love me; and those who seek me early and diligently will find me" (Proverbs 8:17 AMP). None that seek God will be disappointed. But how does a mere man go about finding God? "God reveals Himself to faith. We believe in order that we may see, trust in order that we may know."[899] The Bible states, "But without faith it is impossible to please him: for he that cometh to God must believe that he is, and that he is a rewarder of them that diligently seek him" (Hebrews 11:6). By faith, the Christian "trusts Him where he cannot trace Him, looks up to Him in the darkest hour and believes that all is well."[900] J. I. Packer states, "Your faith will not fail while God sustains it; you are not strong enough to fall away while God is resolved to hold you."[901]

Rick Warren counsels, "When you feel abandoned by God yet continue to trust Him in spite of your feelings, you worship Him in the deepest way."[902] John MacArthur says, "Take solace in knowing that sorrowful times—even periods of feeling God has withdrawn His presence—are an integral part of your spiritual experience. God hasn't utterly abandoned you, though you feel He has."[903]

In finding God, the heart will testify, "No sooner did I depart from them than I found the one whom I love with all my heart. I held on to him and now I won't let him go" (Song of Solomon 3:4 CEB). So may it be even with you.

There's a peace in my heart that the world never gave,
　A peace it cannot take away;
Tho' the trials of life may surround like a cloud,
　I've a peace that has come there to stay!

Constantly abiding, Jesus is mine;
　Constantly abiding, rapture divine!
He never leaves me lonely, whispers, oh, so kind:
　"I will never leave thee"; Jesus is mine. ~ Anne S. Murphy (1908)

144

Reflect upon God's Past Provisions and Deliverances

"Remember the former things of old: for I am God, and there is none else; I am God, and there is none like me" (Isaiah 46:9). An often untapped treasure chest of comfort, hope, rest, and peace in the storms of life is found easily and simply by remembering the former goodness of God.

The What of Remembrance. We are to remember and reflect upon past deliverances wrought at God's hand. Recall how He gave comfort in deepest sorrow, peace in persecution, healing in sickness, coping grace in affliction, strength in weakness, provision in the hour of need, calm in crisis, courage in conflict, forgiving mercy in transgression, and restoration in defeat. Remember how God made a way when there was no way, stood by you when others deserted, silenced the fears and dried the tears, restored hope when dreams were dashed, and came through for you just when you needed Him the most. Say hallelujah and give praise for His merciful deliverances!

The Why of Remembrance. Recollection of God's past interventions and deliverances grants confidence and assurance of His readiness to help in present and future times of crisis. The immutability of God affirms it. God says, "For I am the LORD, I change not" (Malachi 3:6). Hebrews 13:8 states: "Jesus Christ the same yesterday, and today, and forever."

W. A. Criswell remarked, "Whether in the yesteryear gone by, or whether in the today, or whether in the tomorrow, He is always the same in His person, in His offices, and in His presence. What a comfort to know that though I may change, He will not. What a comfort to know that though my life fades away, He abides forever. What a solace and what a comfort to know that though my feet may tremble, the Rock on which I stand is never moved. And what a blessedness to realize that the salvation He has offered to me is like Christ Himself, unchanging, abiding forever and forever."[904]

Every special blessing is not only for the hour itself, but for the future as well. It is a pledge; it is as though God were to say, "I'll do this for you now; then you will always know that you are the object of my love."
William E. Sangster

Why remember?

(1. It is a pledge. What God did yesterday for us is an argument for His willingness to do it again for us. It's the argument (rationale, reasoning) that David used in fighting the giant Goliath. He testified to King Saul prior to the encounter, "The LORD that delivered me out of the paw of the lion, and out of the paw of the bear, he will deliver me out of the hand of this Philistine" (1 Samuel 17:37). David was exceedingly calm (virtually fearless) and confident in facing the giant all because of his past victories and deliverances through God's hand. Remembering instills trust in God's faithfulness to be "a very present help in trouble" (Psalm 46:1). William E. Sangster said, "God never gives a blessing just for the hour. Every special blessing is not only for the hour itself, but for the future as well. It is a pledge; it is as though God were to say, 'I'll do this for you now; then you will always know that you are the object of my love.' What a sad thing it is, therefore, that we forget so soon. That is why new dangers can startle you with fear and dismay. You have forgotten the past mercies. You would have been calm and confident in the presence of new trouble had you remembered vividly the old deliverance, had you kept it fresh in mind and been able to say, 'The God who delivered me then didn't deliver me then to desert me now.'"[905] Hengstenberg remarked, "One of God's wonders placed before the eyes gives reality also to all the others."[906]

(2. It is a preventative. Remembering the past mercies of God protects the soul from grave despondency, despair, and fear. Matthew Henry states, "The remembrance of the works of God will be a powerful remedy against distrust of His promise and goodness; for he is God and changes not."[907]

(3. It is a precursor. Recollection of past deliverances of mercy establishes a firm foundation for God's intervention and help today.

(4. It is a praise. To recount times of divine deliverances prompts the heart to testify, "If it had not been the LORD who was on our side...Then the waters had overwhelmed us, the stream had gone over our soul" (Psalm 124:1, 4) and to declare "Bless the LORD, O my soul: and all that is within me, bless his holy name" (Psalm 103:1). Remembering incites worship.

(5. It is a proof. Recounting the past acts of God supplies convincing evidence of His dependability, trustworthiness and love to help presently.

The When of Remembrance. Remember NOW and ALWAYS. With the psalmist declare, "I will remember the works of the LORD. Yes, I will remember the amazing things you did long ago. I will think about all you have done; I will reflect upon your deeds. O God, your deeds are extraordinary" (Psalms 77:11–13 NET).

Spurgeon says, "Fly back, my soul, away from present turmoils to the grandeurs of history, the sublime deeds of Jehovah, the Lord of Hosts; for He is the same and is ready even now to defend His servants as in days gone by. Surely, I will remember Thy wonders of old. Whatever else may glide into oblivion, the marvelous works of the Lord...must not be forgotten. When faith has its seven years of famine, memory, like Joseph in Egypt, opens her granaries."[908] He continues, "Never let us neglect thanksgiving [fueled by remembering], or we may fear that at another time our prayers will remain unanswered."[909]

The Way of Remembrance. Erect your personal "Ebenezer." Israel prayed for God's help in battle and won the day. Samuel, their priest immediately erected a monument to remind them of God's power that enabled the victory. He called it *Ebenezer*, saying, "Hitherto hath the LORD helped us" (1 Samuel 7:12). Its purpose was to constantly cause the people to recall the deliverance wrought at the strong hand of God so that in future conflict they confidently would rely upon Him for victory. It served as a reminder of the faithfulness of God to deliver His people in trouble. Our Ebenezer is not a chiseled stone pillar but a sanctified memory chest that details our numerous deliverances at the hand of God. As often as we thumb through its many pages, our heart will be strengthened and encouraged by those remembrances.

At your Ebenezer reflect and mediate upon how God in past troubles and afflictions delivered you, guided you, "spoke" to you, used others to help you, and manifested Himself to you (Psalm 77:12). Muse upon the how of deliverance until the heart is inflamed with peace, hope and trust (Psalm 39:3). Recount the how of deliverance to others. David said, "I will recount all of your wonderful deeds" (Psalm 9:1 ESV). Voicing to others stories of God's deliverances instills trust in God, which brings calm and hope to them as well as to us.

In storms, don't rely upon or submit to irrational emotions. J. Sidlow Baxter says, "Your emotions are the shallowest part of your nature. Salvation is the deepest work of God. God doesn't do the deepest work in the shallowest part. Forget your emotions....Put your confidence in the unshakable power of God."[910] God in the past incontrovertibly and indisputably kept you safe in the fiercest of storms. Don't doubt Him now. He remains now, as yesterday, your soul's strong and abiding hope, help and refuge.

> Yesterday, today, forever, Jesus is the same,
> All may change, but Jesus never glory to His name!
> Glory to His name! Glory to His name!
> All may change, but Jesus never glory to His name!
>
> Oft on earth He healed the suff'rer by His mighty hand:
> Still our sicknesses and sorrows go at His command;
> Glory to His name! Glory to His name!
> All may change, but Jesus never glory to His name!

~ Albert B. Simpson (1980)

145
The Name That Can Be Trusted

"And they that know thy name will put their trust in thee: for thou, LORD, hast not forsaken them that seek thee" (Psalm 9:10). The Hebrew word for "trust" means to "trust, rely on, put confidence in, i.e., believe in a person or object to the point of reliance upon."[911] Its root word means to "lie face down on the ground."[912] The concept and picture is that of a person who is totally helpless having been cast down with nothing to stand upon (no visible means of support).[913] John Stott said, "Faith is a reasoning trust, a trust which reckons thoughtfully and confidently upon the trustworthiness of God."[914] Alexander Maclaren remarked, "It literally means to 'hang upon' something, and so, beautifully, it tells us what faith is—just hanging upon God."[915]

The Subject of this Trust. Its foundation is not physicians, preachers, possessions, or wealth but the majestic, sovereign God. He alone is the soul's sufficient source of all comfort, hope, peace, and help. See Psalm 20:7. Martin Luther wrote, "It is much easier to learn than to believe that we who have by us the Word of God and receive it are surrounded with divine aid. If we were surrounded by walls of steel and fire, we should feel secure and defy the Devil. But the property of faith is not to be proud of what the eye sees, but to rely on what the Word reveals."[916]

The Secret of this Trust. The condition for this trust is intellectual (Romans 10:17) and experiential (Psalm 116:1–9) knowledge of God. Knowledge of the Lord (His name or perfection, eternal faithfulness and divine attributes) instills confidence and trust in Him for help in the time of trouble or illness. A. J. F. Behrends said, "Faith is trust, a trust without suspicion or fear, trust passing into glad and habitual surrender, so that He in whom we trust becomes our teacher, guide, and master. Such trust, if intelligently exercised, promotes fixedness of conviction and steadiness of moral purpose—it issues in deliberate fidelity and loyalty. And when this trust is challenged by the reason, either the reason in me or the reason in others, the answer forms a bed of truth which takes the name of 'faith,' because it represents the rational basis of trust or conviction. Faith as a system of doctrine simply states what I believe or why I trust."[917] W. S. Plumer states, "To know God's name is to have His excellence revealed in our hearts by His Spirit so that we apprehend His nature and have a spiritual discernment of His beauty and glory."[918] God exclusively reveals Himself as the faithful God to all who diligently seek Him (Psalm 9:10).[919] Albert Barnes said, "It is much to say of anyone that the more he is known the more he will be loved; and in saying this of God, it is but saying that one reason why men do not confide in Him is that they do not understand His real character."[920]

The Seed of this Trust. Matthew Henry comments, "The better God is known, the more He is trusted. Those who know Him to be a God of infinite wisdom will trust Him further than they can see Him (Job 35:14); those who know Him to be a God of almighty power will trust Him when creature confidences fail and they have nothing else to trust to (2 Chronicles 20:12); and those who know Him to be a God of infinite grace and goodness will trust Him though He slay them (Job 13:15). Those who know Him to be a God of inviolable truth and faithfulness will rejoice in His word of promise and rest upon that. Those who know Him to be the everlasting Father will trust Him with their souls as their main care and trust in Him at all times, even to the end."[921] Knowing God better theologically (Bible), experientially (fellowship with Him), and historically (His mighty works in the world and among man) strengthens faith in and dependence upon Him.

The Season of this Trust. Jennings and Lowe translate Psalm 9:9 to read, "The LORD is a stronghold upon occasions (desperation, trouble) when all hope is cut off."[922] W. S. Plumer states, "One of the excellencies of true religion is that it is a source of the greatest consolation when consolation is most needed."[923] David doesn't define the form or season of trouble; therefore, it applies to whatever trouble the saint encounters. We trust God at all times, but in the "night" seasons of duress, trust is manifested and appropriated more consciously, completely and conspicuously.

The Surety of Trust. "For thou, LORD, hast not forsaken them that seek thee." J. M. Boice writes, "David is not without personal experience to back up his words when he says, 'You, LORD, have never forsaken those who seek you' (v. 10). Any Christian who cannot echo those words should be ashamed. Has God not said, 'Never will I leave you; never will I forsake you' (Hebrews 13:5; Deuteronomy 31:6)? Did Jesus not say, 'Surely I am with you always, to the very end of the age' (Matthew 28:20)?"[924] "Men forsake him; He does not forsake them."[925] History and the testimonial of the saints give proof to God's faithfulness to His children in all seasons of life. Spurgeon comments: "A fiery dart of Satan is constantly shot at the people of God. It is the suggestion that God has forsaken us. Of all the arrows of Hell, it is the most sharp, the most poisonous, the most deadly. It is sent against us in time of great trouble. The deep waters are around and almost overflow you; just then, when in the very deepest part of the stream, Satan sends this suggestion into your very soul—thy God hath forsaken thee. We believe in the truth and love of earthly friends. Shall we not believe in God?"[926] Morison says, "In their greatest straits, God's people shall find themselves garrisoned by omnipotent love."[927]

Conder and Clarkson say, "This—that God may safely be trusted—is infinitely worthy of unswerving absolute trust. Those who know Him best trust Him most, and those who have trusted Him most bear witness to His faithfulness. We may say that the truth of the whole Bible is involved in the truth of this verse. For what is the Bible from end to end but an invitation to trust God—with the reasons for so doing?"[928]

> We have to be humble enough to trust Him, determined enough to wait for Him, and confident enough to walk by faith rather than sight.
> David Jeremiah

The Signifying of this Trust. To advocate that you trust God without manifesting total reliance upon Him is hypocritical and ineffective. Francis Chan wrote, "Worry implies that we don't quite trust that God is big enough, powerful enough, or loving enough to take care of what's happening in our lives."[929] L. B. Cowman wrote, "Genuine faith puts its letter in the mailbox and lets go. Distrust, however, holds on to a corner of the envelope and then wonders why the answer never arrives."[930] Genuine trust says, "I will trust Him. Whatever, wherever I am, I can never be thrown away. If I am in sickness, my sickness may serve Him; in perplexity, my perplexity may serve Him; if I am in sorrow, my sorrow may serve Him. My sickness or perplexity or sorrow may be necessary causes of some great end which is quite beyond us. He does nothing in vain."[931] David Jeremiah states, "When you don't understand why pain happens, He does. Though you can't explain why people suffer, He can. When you don't know what's next, He knows the way. There's freedom in saying, 'I don't know, but He does!' There's something liberating about that. We have to be humble enough to trust Him, determined enough to wait for Him, and confident enough to walk by faith rather than sight."[932] Matthew Henry says, "The more God is trusted, the more He is sought unto. If we trust God, we shall seek Him by faithful and fervent prayer."[933]

The Song of this Trust. "Sing praises to the LORD, which dwelleth in Zion" (Psalm 9:11). David declared in Psalm 28:7, "The LORD is my strength and my shield; my heart trusted in him, and I am helped: therefore my heart greatly rejoiceth; and with my song will I praise him." The heart that places confidence in and reliance upon the Lord has a praise song to sing in times of trouble unlike those who embrace false trusts and hopes. Paul and Silas' trust in God begat a song of praise and deliverance unto Him in a cold dungeon cell at midnight.

> Why should I feel discouraged?
>   Why should the shadows come?
> Why should my heart be lonely
>   And long for Heav'n and home,
> When Jesus is my portion?
>   My constant friend is He.
> His eye is on the sparrow,
>   And I know He watches me.
>
> "Let not your heart be troubled,"
>   His tender word I hear,
> And resting on His goodness,
>   I lose my doubts and fears.
> Though by the path He leadeth,
>   But one step I may see,
> His eye is on the sparrow,
>   And I know He watches me.
>
> Whenever I am tempted,
>   Whenever clouds arise,
> When songs give place to sighing,
>   When hope within me dies,
> I draw the closer to Him.
>   From care He sets me free.
> His eye is on the sparrow,
>   And I know He watches me.

When the Rain Comes

I sing because I'm happy;
    I sing because I'm free,
For His eye is on the sparrow,
    And I know He watches me. ~ Civilla D. Martin (1905)

The Satisfaction of this Trust. The Bible says, "May the God of hope fill you with all joy and peace as you trust in him" (Romans 15:13 NIV). Complete trust in God results in a peace that passeth all understanding and unspeakable joy. "Chords that are broken will vibrate once more." Let us therefore declare with the psalmist, "I will say of the LORD, He is my refuge and my fortress: my God; in him will I trust" (Psalm 91:2).

We may trust Him fully all for us to do;
They who trust Him wholly find Him wholly true.

~ Frances Ridley Havergal (1836–1879)

146

The Lord Is My Portion

"The LORD is my portion [all that He is and possesses], saith my soul; therefore will I hope in him" (Lamentations 3:24). The reason for rational hope and contentment in times of sickness or adversity is that Christ is the believers' inheritance ("portion") of absolute sufficiency in every circumstance and condition. Paul underscores the truth, saying, "Our sufficiency is from God" (2 Corinthians 3:5 ESV). And Jesus told Paul concerning his thorn in the flesh, "My grace is sufficient for you, for my power is made perfect in weakness" (2 Corinthians 12:9 ESV).

With David, the believer says, "My flesh and my heart may fail, But God is the strength of my heart and my portion [sufficiency] forever" (Psalm 73:26 NASB). God is our sufficient (2 Corinthians 9:8), sure (Isaiah 55:3), satisfying (Psalm 103:5), suitable (Psalm 73:25), and steadfast (Hebrews 6:19) portion. We desire or want none other. William Guthrie is correct when he writes of Christ, "Less would not satisfy; more could not be desired." With Augustine we pray, "Lord, give me Thyself." He is not a partial or temporary portion but a full and everlasting portion.

Affirm that the Lord is thy portion. Who is he that can truthfully say, "The Lord is my portion"? The soul that saith the Lord is my portion knows Him intimately as Lord and Savior. The soul that saith the Lord is my portion loves Him superlatively. The soul that saith the Lord is my portion trusts Him implicitly when all his world gives sway. The soul that saith the Lord is my portion pines to know Him better. The soul that saith the Lord is my portion seeks to please Him. The soul that saith the

Comfort for Troubled Hearts

Lord is my portion values His presence above all others. The soul that saith the Lord is my portion exhibits continual praise unto Him for all that He has done and is doing. The soul that saith the Lord is my portion counts Him that pearl of great price worthy of all that he possesses to obtain (Matthew 13:45). The soul that saith the Lord is my portion groans with all creation for that day when Christ Jesus will return to take His children home to Heaven. The soul that saith the Lord is my portion is unashamed to proclaim Him as such.

Spurgeon says, "Can you say, 'The Lord is MY portion?' Let it not be a general declaration but a particular affirmation—'The Lord is MY portion.' Yes, with streaming eyes and bursting heart, many a soul here that can now see Jesus hanging on the cross taking away all its guilt can say, though almost choked with tears, 'Yes, blessed be His name, the Lord is my portion.'"[934]

But if that cannot be said by you, make it so now by embracing Him as Lord and Savior (Romans 10:9–13). With Spurgeon I attest, "Better Christ and the old Mamertine dungeon of the Apostle Paul than to be without Christ and live in the palace of Caesar. Christ Jesus, Thou blessed portion of our souls! Thou art altogether lovely; and if we had to begin again, we would begin with Thee." [935]

Jesus, lover of my soul,
   Let me to Thy bosom fly,
While the nearer waters roll,
   While the tempest still is high.

Hide me, O my Savior, hide,
   Till the storm of life is past.
Safe into the haven guide;
   Oh, receive my soul at last.

Other refuge have I none;
   Hangs my helpless soul on Thee.
Leave, oh, leave me not alone;
   Still support and comfort me.

All my trust on Thee is stayed;
   All my help from Thee I bring.
Cover my defenseless head
   With the shadow of Thy wing.

When the Rain Comes

Thou, O Christ, art all I want;

More than all in Thee I find. ~ Charles Wesley (1740)

Appropriate the promise that the Lord is thy portion.

(1. Dwell in it. Rest and reside in the knowledge that Christ Himself is your portion. "Christ is a rich Christ who hath wherewithal to portion such abundance of people as in all ages and generations have been portioned by Him. The apostle calls it the *unsearchable riches* of Christ (Ephesians 3:8). He is a bottomless mine of merit and spirit, a boundless ocean of righteousness and strength, a full fountain of grace and comfort."[936] 'Shall not God with Christ also freely give you all things?' (Romans 8:32).

(2. Delight in it. Embrace Him as your dearest friend. John Piper says, "Therefore, 'delight yourself in the Lord' means delight yourself in seeing His infinite admirableness. Delight in His love, His care, His protection, and His desire to have that kind of intimate personal relationship with you."[937]

(3. Depend on it. Rely upon the Lord's omnipotent power, divine goodness and unchanging love to supply every need and sustain in the darkest of hours. If it be that the Lord is your portion, then depend upon Him to render the care, guidance, relief, or help that is needed.

The soul that saith, "The Lord is my portion" is confident despite unsettling and disturbing news. The soul that saith, "The Lord is my portion" is calm despite the ferocious storm. The soul that saith, "The Lord is my portion" is comforted despite the piercing pain and grief. The soul that saith, "The Lord is my portion" is content despite the persecution, sickness or suffering. The soul that saith, "The Lord is my portion" is cheerful despite being distraught and anguished. The soul that saith, "The Lord is my portion" is courageous despite the great unknown. The soul that saith, "The Lord is my portion" is hopeful despite the dire hopelessness experienced (Habakkuk 3:17–18).

A sailor in the olden days of sailing said, "In fierce storms we have but one resource: we keep the ship in a certain position. We cannot act in any way but this. We fix her head to the wind, and in this way we weather the storm." It is just so with the Christian. In the storms of life he endeavors to put his head in a certain position.[938] "The LORD is my portion, saith my soul; therefore will I hope in him." He that employs this piece of heavenly navigation shall victoriously weather the fiercest of storms.[939]

(4. Demonstrate it. Bear witness to the Lord's being your dependable and trustworthy portion by attitude and action in times of trial and trouble. If the Lord is your portion, then live and die manifesting that hope in His being such to you.[940]

Jesus Christ is made to me
   All I need, all I need,
He alone is all my plea;
   He is all I need.

To my Savior will I cleave,
   All I need, all I need.
He will not His servant leave;
   He is all I need.

Wisdom, righteousness and pow'r,
Holiness forevermore,
My redemption full and sure,
He is all I need.

He's the treasure of my soul,
   All I need, all I need.
He hath cleansed and made me whole;
   He is all I need.

Jesus is my all in all,
   All I need, all I need.
While He keeps I cannot fall;
   He is all I need.

Glory, glory to the Lamb,
   All I need, all I need.
By His Spirit sealed I am;
   He is all I need.

~ Charles Price Jones (1908)

To say "The Lord is my portion" is to profess that He is more than enough to provide all that is needed in living and dying. Chris Tomlin echoes that note in saying, "All of You is more than enough for all of me." And He is.

147

Comfort in Affliction

"This is my comfort in my affliction: for thy word hath quickened me" (Psalm 119:50). David says that in his direst affliction the Bible was his strong and sure consolation. God's Word (the promise ["the word unto thy servant"] to which he referred in the previous verse) was David's *only* healing and soothing medicine of "hope." See Psalm 119:49. Charles Bridges wrote, "One word of God, sealed to the heart, infuses more sensible relief than ten thousand words of man. When therefore the word assures us of the presence of God in affliction, of His continued pity and sympathy in His most severe dispensations and of their certain issue to our everlasting good, must not we say of it, 'This is our comfort in our affliction?'"[941] Paul testified to the "comfort" and "hope" that the Holy Scripture instills: "For whatsoever things were written aforetime were written for our learning, that we through patience and comfort of the scriptures might have hope" (Romans 15:4). "The man whose hope comes from God feels the life-giving power of the Word of the Lord. Comfort in affliction is like a lamp in a dark place. Some are unable to find comfort at such times, but it is not so with believers, for their Savior has said to them, 'I will not leave you comfortless.'"[942] See John 14:18.

When the Rain Comes

> One word of God, sealed to the heart, infuses more sensible relief than ten thousand words of man.
> Charles Bridges

James Buchanan states, "The Bible cannot be known in its excellence nor its truths relished in their sweetness nor its promises duly appreciated and enjoyed, until by adversity all other consolation is lost and all other hopes destroyed. But then, when we carry it with us into the fiery furnace of affliction, like the aromatic plant which must be burned before the precious perfume is felt, it emits a refreshing fragrance and is relished in proportion as our sufferings are great. Glorious peculiarity! Other books may amuse the hours of ease. Other knowledge may suffice to pass the short day of prosperity, but this Book alone is for the hour of sorrow. This knowledge comes to my aid when all other knowledge fails; and, like the sweet stars of Heaven, the truths of God shine most brightly in the darkest night of sorrow!"[943] Buchanan continues, "The Bible breathes the spirit of compassion over all our sorrows; its divine Author sympathizes with us in the lowest depths of our affliction; He ridicules not even the weakness of nature but tenderly binds up the heart when it bleeds—'even as a father that *pitieth* his children, so the Lord *pitieth* them that fear him,' and that divine pity breathes throughout every page of Scripture." [944]

For thy word hath quickened me. God's Word has reviving, renewing and reinvigorating strength for him that is cast down in soul and body. Spurgeon elucidates, "Troubles which weigh us down while we are half dead become mere trifles when we are full of life. Thus, have we often been raised in spirit by quickening grace [through God's Word], and the same thing will happen again, for the Comforter is still with us."[945] He continues, "What energy a text will breathe into a man! There is more in one Divine sentence than in huge folios of human composition. There are tinctures of which one drop is more powerful than large doses of the common dilutions. The Bible is the essence of truth; it is the mind of God, the wisdom of the Eternal. By every word of God men are made to live and are kept in life."[946] W. S. Plumer states, "The Word of God is quick and has a quickening power. It makes men both alive and lively in God's service."[947] See Hebrews 4:12. Not only does it possess quickening power from despair and trouble, but also from the depravity and damnation of sin. Arthur Pink writes, "The writings of men may sometimes stir the emotions, search the conscience, and influence the human will; but in a manner and degree possessed by no other book, the Bible convicts men of their guilt and lost estate."[948]

Charles Bridges is correct in saying, "It is not, however, the Word without the Spirit nor the Spirit generally without the Word, but the Spirit by the Word—first putting life into the Word, and then by the Word quickening the soul. The Word then is only the instrument. The Spirit is the Almighty agent."[949] See John 6:63. Apart from the Holy Spirit's *quickening* the Word, its treasure chest of comfort and solace to *quicken* the heart in times of sorrow and distress remains concealed. As Stephen Charnock wrote "The Word is the chariot of the Spirit, the Spirit the Guider of the Word."[950]

Tony Evans observes that "in revelation, God discloses His truth. Through inspiration, He sees that it is recorded for us. And by the illumination of His Spirit, He enables us to understand and apply it."[951] D. L. Moody said that Holy Spirit-led "study of God's Word brings peace to the heart. In it, we find a light for every darkness, life in death, the promise of our Lord's return, and the assurance of everlasting glory."[952] This knowledge begs that we pray for the Holy Spirit's guidance in searching the Scripture, illumination of the Scripture (truth taught and how it applies) and quickening by the Scripture (help, comfort, strength).

The Bottom Line: Says Spurgeon: "There is no authority that is so powerful over the minds of Christian men as that of the Word of God. [All the truths of Scripture] are invested with divine authority....Dearly beloved, if you want comfort, never rest satisfied with the mere words of men....Be not content unless you get the truth from the mouth of God. Say in your spirit, 'I shall not be comforted, unless God Himself shall comfort me.'"[953] The sure source of comfort and hope for the believer is the memory of and meditation upon Holy Scripture and its divine author. Scripture is enabled by the Holy Spirit to bring consolation. George Horne says, "The promise (God's Word) is our 'comfort in affliction'; a comfort divine, strong, lasting; a comfort that will not, like all others, fail us when we most want it—in the day of sickness and at the hour of death—but will always keep pace with our necessities, increasing in proportion as the pleasures of the world and the flesh decrease in us, and then becoming complete when they are no more. So powerful is the Word of God to revive us when dead, either in sins or in sorrow."[954] Therefore, "Banquet your faith upon God's own Word, and whatever your fears or wants, repair to the Bank of Faith with your Father's note of hand, saying, 'Remember the word unto Thy servant, upon which Thou hast caused me to hope.'"[955] What a consolation when "my affliction" is countered with "God's Word" granting "my comfort."

Thanks for Thy Word, O blessed Redeemer!
Open our eyes its beauty to see.
Grant us Thy grace to study it wisely;
Close every heart to all but Thee.

Thanks for Thy Word of precept and promise,
Lamp to our feet and light to our way;
Points us afar where pleasures immortal
Bloom in Thine own bright realm of day.

Thanks for the Bible, offering so freely
Pardon and peace to all who believe;
Help us, O Lord, its counsel to follow,
Meekly by faith its truth receive. ~ Fanny Crosby (1902)

148

The Courageous "Yet"

"Although the fig tree shall not blossom, neither shall fruit be in the vines; the labor of the olive shall fail, and the fields shall yield no meat; the flock shall be cut off from the fold, and there shall be no herd in the stalls: Yet I will rejoice in the LORD, I will joy in the God of my salvation" (Habakkuk 3:17–18).

The Saint's Confidence in Crisis. Habakkuk pictures the worst scenario possible that might befall a man—complete and utter calamity—to stress that even in such crisis God faithfully and compassionately watches over and cares for His children. It is this confidence that prompts Habakkuk to say that should he lose all—health, possessions, investments and livelihood—he "yet" will rejoice in the Lord and joy in the God of his salvation. Says Adam Clarke, "He knew that God was merciful and gracious. He trusted to His promise, though all appearances were against its fulfillment, for he knew that the word of Jehovah could not fail, and therefore his confidence is unshaken."[956]

The Saint's Composure in Crisis.

(1. Peaceful. Habakkuk's type of strong confidence and trust in the Lord forbids panic, fear or stress, despite the severity of the storm, and envelopes the believer in a calm and serene assurance that everything will work out for their best good (Romans 8:28).

(2. Joyful. Tears of sorrow are accompanied with joy of soul. Habakkuk says, "Yet I will rejoice in the Lord, I will joy in the God of my salvation." This is a divine joy. "There is a great difference between a human and a divine joy. One arises from without, but the other from within; one comes from the creature, the other from the Creator. If our joy depended upon our wealth, it might fail; if upon our friends, it might change; if upon our health, it might be broken. But it depends upon God, and we know that 'He will supply all our need according to His riches in glory, through Jesus Christ.'"[957]

No extremity of adversity should quench the saint's joy. So says Paul in Philippians 4:4: "Rejoice in the Lord alway: and again I say, Rejoice." "Spiritual joy," says Caleb Morris, "is a free, full, and overflowing stream that takes its rise in the very depth of the Divine Essence, in the immutability, perfection, abundance, munificence (kindness, generosity) of the divine nature. While there is a God and that God is happy, there is no necessity that there should be any unhappy Christians."[958] "Happiness is like a thermometer—it registers conditions. Joy is like a thermostat—it controls them!" Rejoicing in God while battling sickness, sorrow or hardship is the fruit of the believer's unshakable faith in God and His promises. The rejoicing in God will be proportionate to the degree in which God and the promises are believed and appropriated.

An elderly lady suffered from a chronic illness that inflicted agonizing pain—but in joy, not complaint. Upon being asked why she was in such good spirits, she replied, "I have a lovely robin that sings outside my window. I love him, because he sings in the rain." The storms silence most birds, but robins keep singing in the rain. Robins picture Habakkuk and every believer; they go on singing in the rain.

(3. Contented. Brownrigg says, "Here is the low degree of the affliction and the high degree of the affection. He will suffer patiently and meekly. He will not only be content with it; he will be well pleased with his condition."[959] Like Habakkuk, the spiritual believer in dire straits does not accuse God of being unfaithful or uncaring, but says with Job, "Though he slay me, yet will I trust in him" (Job 13:15).

The Saint's Comfort in Crisis.

(1. The Lord's Power. "The LORD God is my strength" (Habakkuk 3:19). The Lord says to all His children that are in the midst of calamity, "Don't worry—I am with you. Don't be afraid—I am your God. I will make you strong and help you. I will support you with my right hand that brings victory" (Isaiah 41:10 ERV).

(2. The Lord's Promise. Great consolation is found in His promises to the saint in affliction or adversary. The psalmist says, "Weeping may endure for a night, but joy cometh in the morning" (Psalm 30:5). Albert Barnes comments, "The morning will come—a morning without clouds, a morning when the sources of sorrow will disappear. This often occurs in the present life; it will always occur to the righteous in the life to come. The sorrows of this life are but for a moment, and they will be succeeded by the light and the joy of Heaven. Then, if not before, all the sorrows of the present life, however long they may appear to be, will seem to have been but for a moment; weeping, though it may have made life here but one unbroken night, will be followed by one eternal day without a sigh or a tear."[960] Another comforting promise while in the storm is Romans 8:28: "And we know that all things work together for good to them that love God, to them who are the called according to his purpose." A third promise is that of Psalm 55:22: "Give all your cares to the Lord and He will give you strength. He will never let those who are right with Him be shaken" (NLV). Then Job 5:11 says, "So that He sets on high those who are lowly, And He lifts to safety those who mourn" (AMP).

(3. The Lord's Presence. The saint's greatest consolation in hard times however, is the sweet presence of Christ with them continuously. The Bible says,

When the Rain Comes

"Be strong and of a good courage, fear not, nor be afraid of them: for the LORD thy God, he it is that doth go with thee; he will not fail thee, nor forsake thee" (Deuteronomy 31:6). All things are doable, bearable and tolerable with Christ in the boat with us (Mark 4:35–41). See Psalm 24:3. *The Saint's Conquest in Crisis.* "The LORD God is my strength, and he will make my feet like hinds' feet, and he will make me to walk upon mine high places" (Habakkuk 3:19). Warren Wiersbe said, "Habakkuk knew that he had no strength of his own, but that God could give him the strength he would need to go through the trials that lay ahead. 'He will make me like a deer—I will jump over the mountains.'"[961]

Despite the hardship and pain experienced, the believer will stand surefooted in the faith by the grace and strength of God. See Zechariah 10:12 and Philippians 1:6. J. P. Gledstone said, "We shall never get forward until we see what Habakkuk saw—that God is our strength and that He will uphold us through the trial by which we shall come into the possession of our purer blessings. No experience is so uniform among the people of God as that they enjoyed more of the presence of God in their trouble than at any other time. But there is more than the experience of the nearness of God, more than a vision of His glory and grace. There is deliverance out of our straits."[962] The expression, "make me to walk upon mine high places" spiritually refers to the believer's restoration (freedom) from trouble (deliverance from the valley of trial and trouble).

> Down in the valley with my Savior I would go,
> Where the storms are sweeping and the dark waters flow.
> With his hand to lead me I will never, never fear;
> Dangers cannot fright me if my Lord is near.
>
> Down in the valley or upon the mountain steep,
> Close beside my Savior would my soul ever keep;
> He will lead me safely in the path that He has trod,
> Up to where they gather on the hills of God. ~ Author: W. O. Cushing (1878)

Tragically, aboard a ship to Europe, Horatio Spafford's four daughters perished when it sank. YET, even in that traumatic time, he was able to write (by the grace of God):

> When peace like a river attendeth my way,
> When sorrows like sea billows roll,
> Whatever my lot, Thou hast taught me to say,
> "It is well; it is well with my soul."

May you, along with Habakkuk and Spafford, in the deepest darkness and direst of storms exclaim confidently and courageously, "YET will I trust God."

149

The Believer's Safeguard in Trouble

"If it had not been the LORD who was on our side, now may Israel say; If it had not been the LORD who was on our side" (Psalm 124:1–2).

If it had not been the Lord who was on our side. "It is tantamount to saying, what if the Lord had not been for us?—leaving the answer to the imagination of the reader."[963] The Lord has done great things for the redeemed. He has snatched them (salvation, deliverance) from the hand of the enemy (Satan), giving him a crushing defeat at Calvary by dying for man's sin (substitutionary death—1 John 2:2); thoroughly washed away the defilement and ugliness of their sin (justification), casting it into the 'sea of forgetfulness' (Micah 7:19) to remember it no more, making them "the righteousness of God" (2 Corinthians 5:21); and eternally secured their soul for Himself (His ransom for the sinner paid at Calvary is eternally binding; Satan never again can take his soul "captive"—John 10:28). Further, He sustains them without interruption (protection, provision, pardon); walks with them in holy communion (John 15:4); enables victory over the enemy in life battles (1 John 4:4; 1 Corinthians 15:57 and Romans 8:37); directs their steps that they may not drift into unrighteousness or defeat (Psalm 37:23; Proverbs 3:5–6 and Proverbs 16:9); floods their heart with joy, comfort and contentment in all circumstances (1 Thessalonians 5:18; John 7:38 and Philippians 4:11); lifts up their head when they sin, through mercy and grace (Psalm 3:3); grants comfort and consolation in times of adversity and affliction (2 Corinthians 1:3–5); and prepares them a Home in Heaven (John 14:1–3). And the list continues without end, for His goodness unto those that love Him is perpetual, indescribable, immeasurable and incalculable.

When the storms of life are raging,
Tempests wild on sea and land,
I will seek a place of refuge
In the shadow of God's hand.

He will hide me; He will hide me,
Where no harm can e'er betide me.
He will hide me, safely hide me,
In the shadow of His hand. ~ Mary E. Servoss (1881)

When the Rain Comes

If we had stood alone, if God had not been with us, if unerring wisdom had not guided us, if divine strength had not enabled us, if refuge in the shadow of His hand had not protected us and if holy consolation had not comforted us in the calamity—then had we been overwhelmed! "It was not the stamp of our foot," says E. J. Robinson, "that quieted the earthquake, not the sound of our voice that stilled the tempest, not the might of our arm that slew the lion, not the power of our hand that rent the network. It was not any creature except as sent by God, armed with a portion of His strength, and for the sake of Jesus Christ, that in any degree accomplished our deliverance."[964] Spurgeon says, "The glorious Lord became our ally; He took our part and entered into treaty with us. If Jehovah were not our protector, where should we be? Nothing but His power and wisdom could have guarded us. The Lord was on our side, and *is* still our defender, and will be so from henceforth, even forever. Let us with holy confidence exult in this joyful fact."[965] Amen and amen.

What if God shunned us when trouble struck? What if He did not intervene for us in the time of our desperation and brokenness? What if He turned a deaf ear to our cry for help when we needed Him the most? What if He did not preserve us from death (annihilation)? Embrace the biblical answer: If the Lord had not been on my side, then what we are experiencing would be far worse. "The waters had overwhelmed us" (Psalm 124:4). We would be utterly cast down in despair and hopelessness.

> Embrace the fact that God is on your side, and if God is on your side, He will not only sustain you in the affliction or adversity but make a way through it for you.

Rejoice, believer, for Jehovah (Immanuel) *is on your side.* In the past He was on your side, presently He is on your side, and in the future He will remain on your side granting help and deliverance in the hour of need. In ecstasy we say with Paul, "What shall we then say to these things? If God be for us, who can be against us? He that spared not his own Son, but delivered him up for us all, how shall he not with him also freely give us all things?" (Romans 8:31–32). John Gill comments, "If God is on the side of us, it matters not who is against us; but if He is not on our side, or against us, it signifies nothing who is for us."[966] Embrace the fact that God is on your side, and if God is on your side, He will not only sustain you in the affliction or adversity but will make a way through it for you. See Psalm 118:6.

Be still, my soul! for God is on your side;
    Bear patiently the cross of grief or pain.
Leave to your God to order and provide,
    Who through all changes faithful will remain.

~ Kathrina von Schlegel (1697–1768)

150

Christ, Man's Hope Beyond the Hurt

"Come unto me, all ye that labor and are heavy laden, and I will give you rest" (Matthew 11:28). Though Christ extends this invitation to all, sadly many distance themselves far from it to bear their pain and sorrow "alone." Horatius Bonar wrote, "To grieve, and yet have no comforter; to be wounded, and yet have no healer; to be weary, and yet know no resting place—this is the world's hard lot. Yet it is a self-chosen one. GOD did not choose it for them. They chose it for themselves. GOD invites, nay, pleads earnestly with them to quit it, yet they will not. Oh, that a weary, brokenhearted world would learn these lessons of grace! Oh, that they would taste and see that GOD is good! Let them but come home to Him. He will not mock them with shadows nor feed them with husks. He will satisfy their craving souls; He will turn their midnight into noon; He will give them beauty for ashes, the oil of joy for mourning, the garment of praise for the spirit of heaviness that they may be called trees of righteousness, the planting of the Lord."[967]

Relief from pain and sorrow is available.

Rest (sweet peace), not *from* trouble but *in times* of trouble, is available.

Remedy for the burden of sin—its bondage, misery, and guilt—is available.

Resolution to life's problems and troubles is available.

Rescue from weariness to liveliness is available.

Release from Satan's captivity to Christ's liberty is available.

The only thing necessary to obtain all this is to "come." Just "come"—not to the church, not to a minister or priest, not even to a book like this one, but to Jesus Christ. There is no need to do anything else to find hope and help for your troubled heart but to "come unto me." Thomas Brooks said, "'Come,' saith Christ, 'and I will give you rest. I will not *show* you rest, nor barely *tell* you of rest, but I will *give* you rest. I am faithfulness itself and cannot lie; I will give you rest. I that have the greatest power to give it, the greatest will to give it, the greatest right to give it—come, laden sinners, and I will give you rest.' Rest is the most desirable good, the most suitable good, and to you the greatest good. 'Come,' saith Christ—that is, 'believe in Me, and I will give you rest; I will give you peace with God and peace with conscience; I will turn your storm into an everlasting calm; I will give you such rest that the world can neither give to you nor take from you.'"[968] Augustine remarked, "Lord, Thou madest us for Thyself, and we can find no rest till we find rest in Thee!"[969]

The promise, though certain, calls for response by "coming." How might you come? Come with a repentant (godly sorrow) heart over sin in simple childlike trust, receiving Christ's gift of forgiveness and abundant and eternal life. John Stott testified, "My perceptions of God and of myself, however distorted, convince me that in myself I am completely unfit to spend eternity in His presence. I need to be 'made fit' to share in the saints' inheritance in the light. Without those white robes made clean in the blood of the Lamb, I could never stand before God's throne. 'Hell-deserving sinner' sounds an absurdly antiquated phrase, but I believe it is the sober truth. Without Christ, I am 'perishing' and deserve to perish."[970] This diagnosis and prognosis are true of all men. But the Good News of the Gospel is that all who turn from sin and embrace Christ (though undeserving) will be saved (forgiven, cleansed, made righteous), and become possessors of abundant and eternal life through His precious blood.

The Bible says, "For whosoever shall call upon the name of the Lord shall be saved" (Romans 10:13). C. H. Spurgeon says, "A shelter is nothing if we stand in front of it. The main thought with many a would-be Christian is his own works, feelings and attainments; this is to stand on the windy side of the wall by putting self before Jesus. Our safety lies in getting behind Christ and letting Him stand in the wind's eye. What is a roof to a man who lies in the open or a boat to one who sinks in the sea? Even the Man Christ Jesus, though ordained of God to be a covert from the tempest, can cover none but those who are in Him."[303]

A picture of "salvation" is given in Genesis 21:14–19. Hagar and her son were dying, wandering aimlessly in the desert due to lack of water, when "God opened Hagar's eyes, and she saw a well full of water. She quickly filled her water container and gave the boy a drink" (Genesis 21:19 NLT). The source for hope and healing was right in front of her the whole time!

Lowering the water bucket in faith into the well, she found refreshing and restorative water (she and her son were saved). Perhaps you are like Hagar aimlessly, hopelessly searching "everywhere" for "water" which satisfies the troubled soul, not knowing it was in front of you all along in the Christ of Calvary. As Hagar placed faith in the well for physical "salvation," place faith in Christ Jesus for the same spiritually. "O taste and see that the LORD is good: blessed is the man that trusteth in him" (Psalm 34:8).

Come, every soul by sin oppressed;
   There's mercy with the Lord,
And He will surely give you rest
   By trusting in His Word.
Only trust Him; only trust Him;
   Only trust Him now.
He will save you; He will save you;
   He will save you now. ~ John H. Stockton (1874)

Comfort for Troubled Hearts

May God *open your eyes,* as He did Hagar's, to see that the end of the quest for meaning, happiness, peace, and purpose awaits in a personal relationship with Jesus Christ (John 10:9–10). And when He does, respond immediately. "There are many heads resting on Christ's bosom," said Samuel Rutherford, "but there's room for yours there."[971] Assuredly Hagar never forgot the place or the miraculous way she found "salvation"; neither will you. See Ephesians 1:18 and Acts 26:18.

The cross upon which Jesus died
Is a shelter in which we can hide,
And its grace so free is sufficient for me,
And deep is its fountain as wide as the sea.

There's room at the cross for you;
There's room at the cross for you.
Though millions have come, there's still room for one.
Yes there's room at the cross for you.

Though millions have found Him a friend
And have turned from the sins they have sinned,
The Savior still waits to open the gates
And welcome a sinner before it's too late. ~ Ira F. Stanphill (1946)

Upon entering into a personal relationship with Jesus Christ, you will joyously testify:

In loving-kindness Jesus came,
My soul in mercy to reclaim,
And from the depths of sin and shame
Through grace He lifted me.

From sinking sand, He lifted me;
With tender hand He lifted me.
From shades of night to plains of light,
Oh, praise His name, He lifted me!

Now on a higher plane I dwell,
and with my soul I know 'tis well,
yet how or why I cannot tell
He should have lifted me. ~ Chas. H. Gabriel (1905)

The End Has Come

With its chapters concluded, this book now ends—but not the story of your life (if you are a Christian), for when its present chapter ends (whether by death or Christ's coming), immediately a new one begins in the realms of Glory with Christ and the saints. Hallelujah to the King! Until then, may "the Lord bless you and keep you; The Lord make His face shine upon you, And be gracious to you; The Lord lift up His countenance upon you, And give you peace" (Numbers 6:24–26 NKJV).

It is not death to die,
    To leave this weary road,
And midst the brotherhood on high
    To be at home with God.

It is not death to close
    The eye long dimmed by tears
And wake, in glorious repose,
    To spend eternal years.

It is not death to bear
    The wrench that sets us free
From dungeon chain, to breath the air
    Of boundless liberty.

It is not death to fling
    Aside this sinful dust
And rise, on strong exulting wing,
    To live among the just.

Jesus, Thou Prince of Life,
    Thy chosen cannot die;
Like Thee, they conquer in the strife
    To reign with Thee on high. ~ H. A. César Malan (1832)

Endnotes

1 Criswell, W. A. *Daily Word.* "The Comfort of the Blessed Lord," July 16, 2020. dailyword@wacriswell.com, accessed July 16, 2020.

2 https://biblehub.com/library/brown/the_story_of_the_hymns_and_tunes/ chapter_v_hymns_of_suffering.htm, accessed July 5, 2020.

3 Ryle, J. C. *Holiness: Its Nature, Hindrances, Difficulties, and Roots.* (Peabody, MA: Hendriksen Publishers, 2007), 398.

4 Graham, Billy. *The Secret of Happiness.* (New York: Doubleday, 1955), 95.

5 Spurgeon, C. H. *Morning and Evening.* (London: Passmore & Alabaster), January 21.

6 Truett, George W. *A Quest for Souls.* (New York and London: Harper & Brothers Publishers, 1917), 140.

7 Ibid., 142.

8 Spurgeon, C. H. *Morning and Evening.* (London: Passmore & Alabaster), October 21.

9 Wiersbe, W. W. (1991). *With the Word Bible Commentary.* (Nashville: Thomas Nelson), Rev. 21:1.

10 Jones, G. C. *1000 Illustrations for Preaching and Teaching.* (Nashville, TN: Broadman & Holman Publishers, 1986), 149.

11 Redpath, Alan. *Blessings out of Buffeting.* (Grand Rapids: Fleming H. Revell, 1993), 78.

12 Wiersbe, W. W. *The Bible Exposition Commentary, Vol. 1.* (Wheaton, IL: Victor Books, 1996), 645.

13 Exell, J. S. *The Biblical Illustrator: Second Corinthians.* (New York; Chicago; Toronto: Fleming H. Revell Company), 236.

14 Shandon Baptist Church, Columbia, SC. Sermon, June, 2020.

15 O'Brien, P. T. *The Epistle to the Philippians: A Commentary on the Greek Text.* (Grand Rapids, MI: Eerdmans, 1991), 520.

16 Exell, J. S. *The Biblical Illustrator: Philippians–Colossians, Vol. 1.* (New York; Chicago; Toronto; London; Edinburgh: Fleming H. Revell Company), 347.

17 Cowman, L. B. *Streams in the Desert.* (Grand Rapids: Zondervan, 1997), January 5.

18 Pink, A. W. *Comfort for Christians.* (Lafayette, IN: Sovereign Grace Publishers, 2007), 74.

19 Exell, J. S. *The Biblical Illustrator: Philippians–Colossians, Vol. 1.* (New York; Chicago; Toronto; London; Edinburgh: Fleming H. Revell Company), 352.

20 Wiersbe, Warren. *The Bumps Are What You Climb On.* (Grand Rapids: Baker Books, 2005), 152.

21 http://christian-quotes.ochristian.com/Contentment-Quotes/page-4.shtml, accessed June 14, 2020.

22 Wuest, K. S. *Wuest's Word Studies from the Greek New Testament: For the English Reader,* Vol. 10. (Grand Rapids: Eerdmans, 1997), 193.

23 MacArthur, J., Jr. (Ed.). *The MacArthur Study Bible,* (electronic ed.). (Nashville, TN: Word Pub., 1997), 1916.

24 https://www.christianquotes.info/top-quotes/18-powerful-quotes-trust/ #ixzz5Dj8gaFH7, accessed April 25, 2018.

25 Exell, J. S. *The Biblical Illustrator: Hebrews,* Vol. 2. (London: James Nisbet & Co.), 189.

26 Dixon, A. C. *Through Night to Morning.* (Sermon No. 11), 1913.

[27] https://www.christianquotes.info/quotes-by-topic/quotes-about-endurance/, accessed July 8, 2020.

[28] Olivia Benjamin. *Billy Graham: 70 Greatest Life Lessons.* (Kindle Edition, 33 pages, Published March 16th 2015).

[29] Cowman, L. B. *Streams in the Desert.* (Grand Rapids: Zondervan, 1997), October 8.

[30] https://www.christianquotes.info/top-quotes/16-encouraging-quotes-about-hope/, July 2, 2020.

[31] Packer, J. I. *The J. I. Packer Classic Collection.* (Colorado Springs: NavPress, 2010), 251.

[32] Groopman, Jerome. *The Anatomy of Hope.* (NY: Random House, 2004), xiv.

[33] Ibid., 208.

[34] Hutson, Curtis, (ed.). *Great Preaching on Comfort.* (Murfreesboro, TN: Sword of the Lord Publishers, 1990), 164–165.

[35] Jeremiah, David. *Hope: An Anchor For Life,* (Taken from the Promotion for the Book). https://www.davidjeremiah.org/store/product/hope-an-anchor-for-life-5995, accessed June 22, 2020.

[36] Ibid.

[37] Packer, J. I. *The J. I. Packer Classic Collection.* (Colorado Springs: NavPress, 2010), 251.

[38] *Funeral Sermons and Outlines.* (Grand Rapids: Baker Book House, 1951), 79.

[39] Bridges, Charles. *Proverbs.* (Carlisle, PA: The Banner of Truth Trust, 2008), 192.

[40] Ibid.

[41] http://biblereasons.com/fear-of-death/, accessed February 28, 2017.

[42] Exell, J. S. *The Biblical Illustrator: Proverbs.* (New York; Chicago; Toronto; London; Edinburgh: Fleming H. Revell Company), 385.

[43] Simeon, C. *Horae Homileticae: John XIII to Acts, (Vol. 14).* (London: Holdsworth and Ball, 1833), 23.

[44] Spurgeon, C. H. *Morning and Evening.* (London: Passmore & Alabaster), October 2 (Morning).

[45] Ritzema, E. and E. Vince, (Eds.). *300 Quotations for Preachers from the Puritans.* (Bellingham, WA: Lexham Press, 2013).

[46] Henry, M. *Matthew Henry's Commentary on the Whole Bible: Complete and Unabridged in One Volume.* (Peabody: Hendrickson,1994), 986.

[47] Lawson, G. *Exposition of the Book of Proverbs,* (Vol. 1). (Edinburgh; Glasgow; London: David Brown; W. Oliphant; F. Pillans; M. Ogle; Ogle, Duncan, and Co.; J. Nisbet, 1821), 310.

[48] Cowman, L. B. *Streams in the Desert.* (Grand Rapids: Zondervan, 1997), 217.

[49] Exell, J. S. *The Biblical Illustrator: Revelation.* (London: James Nisbet & Co.), 635.

[50] Ibid.

[51] Ibid.

[52] Swindoll, Chuck. *Insight for Today. A Daily Devotional* (Pain), August 2, 2017.

[53] https://www.whatchristianswanttoknow.com/top-15-christian-quotes-about-pain-and-suffering/#ixzz6SHfaAKFG, accessed July 15, 2020.

[54] Keller, Tim. *Walking with God through Pain and Suffering.* (New York: Riverhead Books, 2015), 5.

[55] https://www.whatchristianswanttoknow.com/top-15-christian-quotes-about-pain-and-suffering/#ixzz6SHefezLa, accessed July 15, 2020.

Endnotes

56 Exell, J. S. *The Biblical Illustrator: Revelation.* (London: James Nisbet & Co.), 632–633.

57 Swindoll, Chuck. *Insight for Today. A Daily Devotional* (Pain), August 2, 2017.

58 Keller, Tim. *Walking with God through Pain and Suffering.* (New York: Riverhead Books, 2015), 30.

59 Morrison, George H. *The Afterglow of God,* "The Problem with Pain." (London: Hodder and Stoughton, 1912).

60 Keller, Tim. *Walking with God through Pain and Suffering.* (New York: Riverhead Books, 2015), 47.

61 Swindoll, Chuck. *Insight for Today. A Daily Devotional* (Pain), August 2, 2017.

62 https://www.whatchristianswanttoknow.com/top-15-christian-quotes-about-pain-and-suffering/#ixzz6SHdyeQiR, accessed July 15, 2020.

63 Smellie, Alexander. In the Hour of Silence. (London: Andrew Melrose, 1899), 86.

64 Exell, J. S. *The Biblical Illustrator: Revelation.* (London: James Nisbet & Co.), 633.

65 Courson, J. *Jon Courson's Application Commentary.* (Nashville, TN: Thomas Nelson, 2003), 941–942.

66 Exell, J. S. *The Biblical Illustrator: Romans,* Vol. 2. (New York; Chicago; Toronto; London; Edinburgh: Fleming H. Revell Company), 153.

67 Fitzmyer, J. A., S. J. *Romans: A New Translation with Introduction and Commentary*, Vol. 33, (New Haven; London: Yale University Press 2008), 522.

68 MacArthur, John. *The MacArthur New Testament Commentary: Romans*, Vol. 1 (Chicago: Moody Press, 1991), 473.

69 Ibid.

70 Criswell, W. A. "God's Providential Care" (Sermon). October 24, 1954.https://wacriswell.com/sermons/1954/god-s-providential-care/, accessed August 22, 2020.

71 Henry, M. *Matthew Henry's Commentary on the Whole Bible: Complete and Unabridged in One Volume.* (Peabody: Hendrickson, 1994), 2214.

72 MacArthur, J., Jr. (Ed.). *The MacArthur Study Bible* (electronic ed.) (Nashville, TN: Word Pub, 1997), 1708.

73 Barnes, Albert. *Notes on the Bible.* (1834), Romans 8:28.

74 Ibid.

75 "Do All Things Work Together for Good?" Billy Graham Evangelistic Association, July 6, 2010. https://billygraham.org/story/do-all-things-work-together-for-good/, accessed July 25, 2020.

76 Ibid.

77 Criswell, W. A. "God's Providential Care" (Sermon). October 24, 1954.https://wacriswell.com/sermons/1954/god-s-providential-care/, accessed August 22, 2020.

78 MacArthur, John. "What Jesus' Death Meant to Him" (August 1, 1971), Gty.org accessed June 14, 2011.

79 Josh McDowell. *The New Evidence That Demands a Verdict.* (Nashville: Thomas Nelson, 1999), 9.

80 Spurgeon, C. H. "The Bible" (sermon, March 18, 1855). http://www.spurgeon.org/sermons/0015.htm, accessed October 6, 2014.

81 Exell, J. S. *The Biblical Illustrator: Romans,* Vol. 1. (New York; Chicago; Toronto; London; Edinburgh: Fleming H. Revell Company), 310.

Endnotes

82 Ibid.

83 Jones, G. C. *1000 Illustrations for Preaching and Teaching.* (Nashville, TN: Broadman & Holman Publishers, 1986), 97.

84 Cowman, L. B. *Streams in the Desert.* (Grand Rapids: Zondervan, 1997), February 14.

85 Exell, J. S. *The Biblical Illustrator: Isaiah,* Vol. 3. (New York; Chicago; Toronto; London; Edinburgh: Fleming H. Revell Company), 18.

86 Ibid., 15.

87 Ibid., 18.

88 Cowman, L. B. *Streams in the Desert.* (Grand Rapids: Zondervan, 1997), January 5.

89 Adapted from Truett, George W. *A Quest for Souls.* (New York and London: Harper & Brothers Publishers, 1917), 271.

90 Exell, J. S. *The Biblical Illustrator: Isaiah,* Vol. 3. (New York; Chicago; Toronto; London; Edinburgh: Fleming H. Revell Company), 15.

91 Ritzema, E. and E. Vince, (Eds.). *300 Quotations for Preachers from the Puritans.* (Bellingham, WA: Lexham Press, 2013).

92 Chambers, Oswald. *Our Utmost for His Highest,* June 25.

93 Simeon, C. *Horae Homileticae: Psalms, LXXIII–CL,* Vol. 6. (London: Samuel Holdsworth, 1836), 186.

94 Dark Night of the Soul Quotes, www.azquotes.com/quotes/topics/dark-night-of-the-soul.htm, accessed May 31, 2018.

95 Lewis, C. S. *The Problem of Pain.* (San Francisco: HarperSanFrancisco, 2001), 91.

96 Spurgeon, C. H. *The Treasury of David,* Psalm 23:1.

97 Dixon, A. C. *Through Night to Morning.* (Sermon No. 1), 1913.

98 Parker, Joseph. *The People's Bible,* Psalm 23:4.

99 The text refers to wisdom but certainly no harm is done in applying it to Heaven for it is accurate in that regard as well.

100 Rice, John R. *The Gospel of John.* (Murfreesboro, TN: Sword of the Lord Publishers, 1976), 276.

101 Cowman, L. B. *Streams in the Desert.* (Grand Rapids: Zondervan, 1997), January 14.

102 Henry, M. *Matthew Henry's Commentary on the Whole Bible: Complete and Unabridged in One Volume.* (Peabody: Hendrickson, 1994), 791.

103 Barnes, Albert. *Notes on the Bible.* (1834), Psalm 35:13.

104 Perowne, J. J. S. *The Book of Psalms; A New Translation, with Introductions and Notes, Explanatory and Critical, 5th Edition, Revised,* Vol. 1. (London; Cambridge: George Bell and Sons; Deighton Bell and Co., 1883), 314.

105 Henry, M. *Matthew Henry's Commentary on the Whole Bible: Complete and Unabridged in One Volume.* (Peabody: Hendrickson, 1994), 2228.

106 Exell, J. S. *The Biblical Illustrator: Romans,* Vol. 2. (New York; Chicago; Toronto; London; Edinburgh: Fleming H. Revell Company), 533.

107 Jamieson, R., A. R. Fausset, & D. Brown. *Commentary Critical and Explanatory on the Whole Bible,* Vol. 2. (Oak Harbor, WA: Logos Research Systems, Inc., 1997), 253.

108 Henry, M. *Matthew Henry's Commentary on the Whole Bible: Complete and Unabridged in One Volume.* (Peabody: Hendrickson, 1994), 552.

[109] Spence-Jones, H. D. M. (Ed.). The Pulpit Commentary: 2 Kings. (London; New York: Funk & Wagnalls Company, 1909), 415.

[110] Ibid., 413.

[111] Spence-Jones, H. D. M. (Ed.). The Pulpit Commentary: Proverbs. (London; New York: Funk & Wagnalls Company, 1909), 335.

[112] Stress management. https://www.mayoclinic.org/healthy-lifestyle/stress-management/in-depth/stress-relief/art-20044456, accessed July 7, 2020.

[113] Fairchild, Mary. "The Healing Power of Laughter," http://christianity.about.com, accessed August 11, 2014.

[114] Ibid.

[115] Ibid.

[116] Stress management. https://www.mayoclinic.org/healthy-lifestyle/stress-management/in-depth/stress-relief/art-20044456, accessed July 7, 2020.

[117] http://www.laughfactory.com/jokes/clean-jokes/2, accessed July 7, 2020.

[118] Reader's Digest. https://www.rd.com/list/funniest-jokes-of-all-time/, accessed July 24, 2020.

[119] https://bestlifeonline.com/funny-clean-jokes/, accessed July 23, 2020.

[120] Ibid.

[121] Reader's Digest. https://www.rd.com/list/funniest-jokes-of-all-time/, accessed July 24, 2020.

[122] Moody, D. L. cited in Funeral Sermons and Outlines. (Grand Rapids, Michigan: Baker Book House, 1951), 76.

[123] Exell, J. S. The Biblical Illustrator: Hebrews, Vol. 1. (London: James Nisbet & Co.), 172.

[124] Ritzema, E. and E. Vince, (Eds.). 300 Quotations for Preachers from the Puritans. (Bellingham, WA: Lexham Press, 2013).

[125] Spurgeon, C. H. Sermon 3125. "Fear of Death," December 17, 1874.

[126] Talmage, T. De Witt. "The Ferry Boat of the Jordan" (sermon), http://biblehub.com/sermons/auth/talmage/the_ferry-boat_of_the_jordan.htm, accessed January 2, 2017.

[127] Malphurs, Aubrey and Keith Willhite. A Contemporary Handbook for Weddings and Funerals and other Occasions. (Grand Rapids, Michigan: Kregal Publications, 2006), 238. (adapted)

[128] Christie, Vance. John and Betty Stam: Missionary Martyrs (History Makers), Kindle Edition. (Kindle Locations 1347–1364). Christian Focus Publications, 2015-02-11.

[129] Spurgeon, C. H. "Precious Deaths" (A Sermon) Delivered Sunday Morning, February 18, 1872, The Metropolitan Tabernacle, Newington.

[130] Ibid.

[131] http://www.biblebaptistliveoak.com/index.cfm?i=11980&mid=1000&id=277637, accessed January 2, 2017.

[132] https://www.whatchristianswanttoknow.com/21-inspirational-christian-quotes-for-difficult-times/#ixzz6TCMcysie, accessed July 25, 2020.

[133] Plumer, W. S. Studies in the Book of Psalms: Being a Critical and Expository Commentary, with Doctrinal and Practical Remarks on the Entire Psalter. (Philadelphia; Edinburgh: J. B. Lippincott Company; A & C Black, 1872), 1042.

[134] Spurgeon, C. H. The Treasury of David, Psalm 119:49.

Endnotes

[135] Henry, M. *Matthew Henry's Commentary on the Whole Bible: Complete and Unabridged in One Volume.* (Peabody: Hendrickson, 1994), 918.

[136] Plumer, W. S. Studies in the Book of Psalms: Being a Critical and Expository Commentary, with Doctrinal and Practical Remarks on the Entire Psalter. (Philadelphia; Edinburgh: J. B. Lippincott Company; A & C Black, 1872), 1043.

[137] Courson, J. *Jon Courson's Application Commentary.* (Nashville, TN: Thomas Nelson, 2003), 1472.

[138] Blackwood, Andrew W. *The Funeral.* (Grand Rapids, Michigan: Baker Book House, 1942), 140.

[139] Moody, D. L. *The Seven "I Will's" of Christ.* www.jesus-is-savior.com/Books, accessed May 22, 2013.

[140] Spurgeon, C. H. *Morning and Evening.* (London: Passmore & Alabaster), April 28 (Morning).

[141] https://faithunlocked.wordpress.com/2014/10/18/quotes-on-gods-promises/, accessed September 6, 2020.

[142] Ibid.

[143] Clarke, Adam. *The Adam Clarke Commentary.* "Commentary on Psalms 41:3." https://www.studylight.org/commentaries/acc/psalms-41.html. 1832.

[144] *Barnes Notes on the Bible*, Psalm 41:3.

[145] *Gill's Exposition of the Entire Bible,* Psalm 41:3.

[146] *Barnes Notes on the Bible*, Psalm 41:3.

[147] Plumer, W. S. Studies in the Book of Psalms: Being a Critical and Expository Commentary, with Doctrinal and Practical Remarks on the Entire Psalter. (Philadelphia; Edinburgh: J. B. Lippincott Company; A & C Black, 1872), 488.

[148] Spurgeon, C. H. *Psalms.* (Wheaton, IL: Crossway Books, 1993), 169.

[149] Ironside, H. A. *Studies on Book One of the Psalms.* (Neptune, NJ: Loizeaux Brothers, 1952), 243.

[150] R. C. Sproul. "The Last Enemy." *Tabletalk Magazine,* April 1, 2000. https://www.ligonier.org/learn/articles/the-last-enemy/, accessed April 25, 2020.

[151] Graham, Billy. *Death and the Life After.* (Nashville: W Publishing Group, 1987), 6.

[152] Sanders, J., Ed. *Memorial Tributes: A Compend of Funeral Addresses.* (New York: B.B. Treat, 1883), 160–161.

[153] R. C. Sproul. "The Last Enemy." *Tabletalk Magazine,* April 1, 2000. https://www.ligonier.org/learn/articles/the-last-enemy/, accessed April 25, 2020.

[154] Ibid.

[155] Ritzema, E. and E. Vince, (Eds.). *300 Quotations for Preachers from the Puritans.* (Bellingham, WA: Lexham Press, 2013).

[156] Graham, Billy. *Till Armageddon.* (Waco, TX: Word, 1981), 199.

[157] Exell, J. S. *The Biblical Illustrator: Romans,* Vol. 2. (New York; Chicago; Toronto; London; Edinburgh: Fleming H. Revell Company), Isaiah 25:8

[158] Ibid.

[159] https://www.whatchristianswanttoknow.com/21-inspirational-christian-quotes-for-difficult-times/#ixzz6TCKjStj1, accessed July 25, 2020.

[160] https://gracequotes.org/quote/we-are-always-in-the-forge-or-on-the-anvil-by-trials-god-is-shaping-us-for-higher-things/, accessed July 8, 2020.

[161] Sangster, W. E. *He Is Able.* (London: Hodder and Stoughton, 1936). Sermon Title: "When Worn With Sickness."

[162] Spurgeon, C. H. *The Metropolitan Tabernacle Pulpit,* Vol. XIX. "For the Troubled" (Sermon: January 12, 1873).

[163] Ibid.

[164] Criswell, W. A. A Purpose in Trials. dailyword@wacriswell.com, October 29.

[165] https://www.whatchristianswanttoknow.com/21-inspirational-christian-quotes-for-difficult-times/#ixzz6T9aXN9QF, accessed July 24, 2020.

[166] Exell, J. S. *The Biblical Illustrator: Romans,* Vol. 2. (New York; Chicago; Toronto; London; Edinburgh: Fleming H. Revell Company), 231.

[167] Ibid., 229.

[168] Ibid., 230.

[169] Ibid.

[170] Ibid., 228.

[171] Ibid., 233.

[172] Spurgeon, C. H. *Psalms.* (Wheaton, IL: Crossway Books, 1993), 143.

[173] Boice, J. M. *Psalms 1–41: An Expositional Commentary.* (Grand Rapids, MI: Baker Books, 2005), 313.

[174] Simeon, C. *Horae Homileticae: Psalms, I–LXXII,* Vol. 5. (London: Samuel Holdsworth, 1836), 283.

[175] https://www.goodreads.com/quotes/368087-there-is-something-you-can-t-fix-can-t-heal-or-can-t, accessed July 17, 2020.

[176] Spurgeon, C. H. *The Treasury of David,* Psalm 91:1.

[177] Pink, A. W. *Comfort for Christians.* (Lafayette, IN: Sovereign Grace Publishers, 2007), 76.

[178] Spurgeon, C. H. *The Treasury of David,* Psalm 116:15 (Samuel Totshell, in "The House of Mourning," 1660.)

[179] Spurgeon, C. H. *The Treasury of David,* Psalm 116:15.

[180] Dixon, A. C. cited in *The Biblical Illustrator,* Psalm 116:15 (Precious death).

[181] Pink, A. W. *Comfort for Christians.* (Lafayette, IN: Sovereign Grace Publishers, 2007), 77.

[182] Brooks, Phillips. *The Spiritual Man and Other Sermons.* (London: R.D. Dickinson, 1891), 286.

[183] Spence-Jones, H. D. M. (Ed.). The Pulpit Commentary: St. John, Vol. 2. (London; New York: Funk & Wagnalls Company, 1909), 359.

[184] Francis W. Dixon. "THE HOME-GOING OF A CHILD OF GOD." Lansdowne Bible School and Postal Fellowship. (Lansdowne Baptist Church, Bournemouth, England, August, 1963).

[185] Wierbse, Warren. *Prayer, Praise & Promises.* (Grand Rapids: Baker Books, 2011), 297.

[186] https://www.brainyquote.com/quotes/authors/m/max_lucado.html, accessed January 9, 2017.

[187] Piper, John. "Nothing Can Separate Us from the Love of Christ" (sermon), September 8, 2002. https://www.desiringgod.org/messages/nothing-can-separate-us-from-the-love-of-christ, accessed June 22, 2020.

Endnotes

[188] Henry, M. *Matthew Henry's Commentary on the Whole Bible: Complete and Unabridged in One Volume.* (Peabody: Hendrickson, 1994), 2215.

[189] Witmer, J. A. In J. F. Walvoord & R. B. Zuck (Eds.). *The Bible Knowledge Commentary: An Exposition of the Scriptures, Romans,* Vol. 2. (Wheaton, IL: Victor Books, 1985), 476.

[190] Ibid.

[191] Ibid.

[192] Spence-Jones, H. D. M. (Ed.). The Pulpit Commentary: Romans. (London; New York: Funk & Wagnalls Company, 1909), 254.

[193] Ibid.

[194] Morgan, G. Campbell. "The Vanquished Enemy," The Westminster Record, 8 (May 30, 1913), 170.

[195] Spurgeon, C. H. "Precious Deaths" (A Sermon) Delivered Sunday Morning, February 18, 1872, The Metropolitan Tabernacle, Newington.

[196] The Spurgeon Center for Biblical Preaching at Midwestern Seminary. "10 Spurgeon Quotes on Dying Well," June 29, 2017. https://www.spurgeon.org/resource-library/blog-entries/10-spurgeon-quotes-on-dying-well/, accessed June 26, 2020.

[197] Wiersbe, W. W. *Wiersbe's Expository Outlines on the New Testament.* (Wheaton, IL: Victor Books, 1992), 466.

[198] Dixon, A. C. *Through Night to Morning.* (Sermon No. 6), 1913.

[199] Barnes, Albert. *Notes on the Bible.* (1834), 1 Corinthians 15:26.

[200] Ibid.

[201] Courson, J. *Jon Courson's Application Commentary.* (Nashville, TN: Thomas Nelson, 2003), 1087–1088.

[202] *Hymns and Lyrics for the Seasons and Saints' Days of the Church.* (London: Joseph Masters, 1847), 112–113.

[203] Langham Partnership Daily Thought, "The Hope of Glory." 11 November 2020.

[204] Hutson, Curtis, (ed.). *Great Preaching on Comfort.* (Murfreesboro, TN: Sword of the Lord Publishers, 1990), 124.

[205] Words inspired from Spurgeon, C. H. "Precious Deaths" (A Sermon) Delivered Sunday Morning, February 18, 1872, The Metropolitan Tabernacle, Newington

[206] Ibid.

[207] Ibid.

[208] Exell, J. S. *The Biblical Illustrator,* Psalm 17:15.

[209] *Funeral Sermons and Outlines.* (Grand Rapids: Baker Book House, 1951), 11.

[210] Ibid.

[211] Simeon, C. *Horae Homileticae: Luke XVII to John XII,* Vol. 13. (London: Samuel Holdsworth, 1836), 528.

[212] Sanders, J., Ed. *Memorial Tributes: A Compend of Funeral Addresses.* (New York: B.B. Treat, 1883), 228.

[213] Spurgeon, C. H. *His Own Funeral Sermon.* (Sermon Number: 2243). Delivered at the Metropolitan Tabernacle, October 19, 1890.

[214] The thoughts were inspired and adapted from the sermon by Dixon, A. C. Hutson, Curtis, (ed.). *Great Preaching on Comfort.* (Murfreesboro, TN: Sword of the Lord Publishers, 1990), 88.

[215] Lincoln, Dick. "The Idols We Worship," sermon March 9, 2015. Shandon Baptist Church, Columbia, SC

[216] Graham, Billy. *Hope for the Troubled Heart.* (Dallas: Word, 1991), 71.

[217] Vincent, M. R. *Word Studies in the New Testament.* (New York: Charles Scribner's Sons, 1887), 2 Cor. 12:9.

[218] Spurgeon, C. H. *Morning and Evening.* (London: Passmore & Alabaster), October 7.

[219] Spurgeon, C. H. *New Park Street Pulpit,* Vol. 1. "The Death of the Christian" (Sermon No. 43, 1855).

[220] Jamieson, R., A. R. Fausset, & D. Brown. *Commentary Critical and Explanatory on the Whole Bible,* Vol. 2. (Oak Harbor, WA: Logos Research Systems, Inc., 1997), 314.

[221] Clarke, Adam. *Commentary on the Bible,* (1831).

[222] Henry, M. *Matthew Henry's Commentary on the Whole Bible: Complete and Unabridged in One Volume.* (Peabody: Hendrickson, 1994), 667.

[223] "Five Insights on Death and Dying from Dietrich Bonhoeffer," April 26, 2018. (The quotation is a paraphrase of the Book of Wisdom 4:14).

[224] Rogers, Adrian. "The God of all Encouragement." https://www.lightsource.com/ministry/love-worth-finding/articles/the-god-of-all-encouragement-12899.html, accessed October 20, 2020.

[225] Barclay, W. (Ed.). *The Letter to the Hebrews,* (electronic ed.). (Philadelphia: The Westminster John Knox Press, 1975), 122–123.

[226] Spurgeon, C. H. *Psalms.* (Wheaton, IL: Crossway Books, 1993), 204.

[227] Spurgeon, C. H. *Morning and Evening.* (London: Passmore & Alabaster), April 20 (Morning).

[228] Barnes, Albert. *Barnes Study Notes on the Bible,* 2 Timothy 4:6.

[229] Ibid.

[230] Ibid.

[231] Ibid.

[232] Barclay, W. (Ed.). *The Letters to the Philippians, Colossians, and Thessalonians,* (electronic ed.). (Philadelphia: The Westminster John Knox Press, 1975), 28.

[233] Packer, J. I. *Finishing Our Course with Joy.* (Wheaton, Ill: Crossway Books, 2014), 21.

[234] https://www.christianquotes.info/quotes-by-topic/quotes-about-death/, accessed June 23, 2020.

[235] Ritzema, E. and E. Vince, (Eds.). *300 Quotations for Preachers from the Puritans.* (Bellingham, WA: Lexham Press, 2013).

[236] Exell, J. S. *The Biblical Illustrator: Second Timothy–Titus, Philemon,* Vol. 1. (New York; Chicago; Toronto; London; Edinburgh: Fleming H. Revell Company), 336.

[237] *Merriam-Webster Dictionary.*

[238] Exell, J. S. *The Biblical Illustrator,* Psalm 17:15.

[239] Plumer, W. S. Studies in the Book of Psalms: Being a Critical and Expository Commentary, with Doctrinal and Practical Remarks on the Entire Psalter. (Philadelphia; Edinburgh: J. B. Lippincott Company; A & C Black, 1872), 232.

[240] Ibid., 228.

[241] Exell, J. S. *The Biblical Illustrator,* Psalm 17:15.

[242] Ibid.

Endnotes

[243] Plumer, W. S. Studies in the Book of Psalms: Being a Critical and Expository Commentary, with Doctrinal and Practical Remarks on the Entire Psalter. (Philadelphia; Edinburgh: J. B. Lippincott Company; A & C Black, 1872), 228–229.

[244] Ritzema, E. and E. Vince, (Eds.). *300 Quotations for Preachers from the Puritans*. (Bellingham, WA: Lexham Press, 2013).

[245] Knight, Walter B. *Knight's Illustrations for Today*. (Chicago: Moody Press, 1975), 88.

[246] *Merriam-Webster Dictionary*.

[247] Spurgeon, C. H. *Metropolitan Tabernacle Pulpit*. "A Last Look-Out" (Sermon No. 989).

[248] "Five Insights on Death and Dying from Dietrich Bonhoeffer," April 26, 2018. (Letters and Papers From Prison). https://www.hourofourdeath.org/five-insights-on-death-and-dying-from-dietrich-bonhoeffer/, accessed June 23, 2020.

[249] *Funeral Sermons and Outlines*. (Grand Rapids: Baker Book House, 1951), 74.

[250] Ibid.

[251] Thiselton, A. C. *The First Epistle to the Corinthians: A Commentary on the Greek Text*. (Grand Rapids, MI: W. B. Eerdmans, 2000), 1297.

[252] McWherter, Leroy. The King of Glory. (Nashville: Southwestern Publishing House, 1884), 245.

[253] Courson, J. *Jon Courson's Application Commentary*. (Nashville, TN: Thomas Nelson, 2003), 1090.

[254] Thiselton, A. C. *The First Epistle to the Corinthians: A Commentary on the Greek Text*. (Grand Rapids, MI: W. B. Eerdmans, 2000), 1297.

[255] T. DeWitt Talmage. The Ferry Boat of the Jordan (sermon), http://biblehub.com/sermons/auth/talmage/the_ferry-boat_of_the_jordan.htm, accessed January 2, 2017.

[256] Spurgeon, C. H. *Morning and Evening*. (London: Passmore & Alabaster), July 2 (Morning).

[257] *Funeral Sermons and Outlines*. (Grand Rapids: Baker Book House, 1951), 11.

[258] Spurgeon, C. H. *Morning and Evening*. (London: Passmore & Alabaster), March 3.

[259] Wiersbe, W. W. *With the Word Bible Commentary*. (Nashville: Thomas Nelson, 1991), Mt. 14:1.

[260] Wiersbe, W. W. *The Bible Exposition Commentary, Vol. 1*. (Wheaton, IL: Victor Books, 1996), 177–178.

[261] Henry, M. *Matthew Henry's Commentary on the Whole Bible: Complete and Unabridged in One Volume*. (Peabody: Hendrickson, 1994), 1830.

[262] *Funeral Sermons and Outlines*. (Grand Rapids: Baker Book House, 1955), 97.

[263] https://quotefancy.com/quote/1592035/Adoniram-Judson-I-am-not-tired-of-my-work-neither-am-I-tired-of-the-world-yet-when-Christ, accessed May 11, 2020.

[264] Exell, J. S. *The Biblical Illustrator: St. Luke*, Vol. 1. (London: James Nisbet & Co.), 225.

[265] Simeon, C. *Horae Homileticae: Mark-Luke,* Vol. 12. (London: Samuel Holdsworth, 1836), 264.

[266] Cowman, L. B. *Streams in the Desert*. (Grand Rapids: Zondervan, 1997), 314–315.

[267] Morgan, R. J. *Nelson's Annual Preacher's Sourcebook,* 2002 Edition. (Nashville: Thomas Nelson Publishers, 2001), 397.

[268] Spurgeon, C. H. *Morning and Evening*. (London: Passmore & Alabaster), July 28 (Morning).

Endnotes

[269] Henry, Matthew. *Matthew Henry's Concise Bible Commentary,* Psalm 56:8.

[270] Maclaren, Alexander. *The Book of Psalms: Book II,* 177.

[271] Plumer, W. S. Studies in the Book of Psalms: Being a Critical and Expository Commentary, with Doctrinal and Practical Remarks on the Entire Psalter. (Philadelphia; Edinburgh: J. B. Lippincott Company; A & C Black, 1872), 544.

[272] Simeon, C. *Horae Homileticae: Psalms, LXXIII–CL,* Vol. 6. (London: Samuel Holdsworth, 1836), 291.

[273] Rogers, Adrian. "The Day Death Died." Love Worth Finding. Oneplace.com, accessed August 8, 2013.

[274] Graham, B. *The Heaven Answer Book.* (Nashville: Thomas Nelson, 2012).

[275] Morgan, R. J. *Nelson's Complete Book of Stories, Illustrations, and Quotes* (electronic ed.). (Nashville: Thomas Nelson Publishers, 2000), 645–646.

[276] Spurgeon, C. H. *Morning and Evening.* (London: Passmore & Alabaster), February 21 (Morning).

[277] "Beware of False Peace." https://www.backtothebible.org/post/beware-of-false-peace, accessed May 20, 2020.

[278] Spurgeon, C. H. "A Blast of the Trumpet Against False Peace," (Sermon No. 301), February 26, 1860.

[279] Lloyd-Jones, D. Martyn. *Assurance: An Exposition of Romans 5,* 14.

[280] Morgan, R. J. *Nelson's Annual Preacher's Sourcebook,* 2002 Edition. (Nashville: Thomas Nelson Publishers, 2001), 397.

[281] Dixon, A. C. *Through Night to Morning.* (Sermon No. 19), 1913. The opportunities cited for Paul while in bonds are adapted in part from this sermon.

[282] Ibid.

[283] Himes, Andrew. *The Sword of the Lord: The Roots of Fundamentalism in an American Family.* (Seattle, Washington: Chiara Press, 2011), 291.

[284] Dixon, A. C. *Through Night to Morning.* (Sermon No. 19), 1913.

[285] Malone, Tom. *Dr. Tom Malone Preaches on Certainties.* (Murfreesboro, TN: Sword of the Lord, 1990), 210. Inspiration and several headings were adapted from this sermon.

[286] Ibid., 214.

[287] Hutson, Curtis, (ed.). *Great Preaching on Comfort.* (Murfreesboro, TN: Sword of the Lord Publishers, 1990), 224.

[288] Malone, Tom. *Dr. Tom Malone Preaches on Certainties.* (Murfreesboro, TN: Sword of the Lord, 1990), 216.

[289] Spurgeon, C. H. *Metropolitan Tabernacle Pulpit,* Volume 34. "The Secret of Power in Prayer" (Sermon No. 2,022, 1888).

[290] Spurgeon, C. H. "The Dumb Become Singers," (Sermon No. 3,332). Delivered at the Metropolitan Tabernacle, Newington.

[291] Ibid.

[292] *King James Bible Dictionary.* www.kingjamesbibledictionary.com, accessed May 26, 2020.

[293] Cowman, L. B. *Streams in the Desert.* (Grand Rapids: Zondervan, 1997), 108.

[294] Spence-Jones, H. D. M. (Ed.). The Pulpit Commentary: Psalms, Vol. 1. (London; New York: Funk & Wagnalls Company, 1909), 280.

[295] https://www.viralbeliever.com/christian-quotes/christian-quotes-about-faithfulness/, accessed May 9, 2018.

[296] Cowman, L. B. *Streams in the Desert.* (Grand Rapids: Zondervan, 1997), 107.

[297] Smellie, Alexander. In the Hour of Silence. (London: Andrew Melrose, 1899), 42.

[298] Graham, Billy. Peace with God. (Waco, TX: Word, 1953), 83.

[299] Spence-Jones, H. D. M. (Ed.). The Pulpit Commentary: Psalms, Vol. 2. (London; New York: Funk & Wagnalls Company, 1909), 381.

[300] Spurgeon, C. H. "Thoughts on the Last Battle." (Sermon, May 13, 1855).

[301] https://www.christianquotes.info/quotes-by-topic/quotes-about-death/, accessed June 23, 2020.

[302] Exell, J. S. *The Biblical Illustrator: 1 Samuel,* Vol. 2. (New York; Chicago; Toronto; London; Edinburgh: Fleming H. Revell Company), 523.

[303] Spence-Jones, H. D. M. (Ed.). The Pulpit Commentary: 1 Samuel. (London; New York: Funk & Wagnalls Company, 1909), 384.

[304] Spurgeon, C. H. "The Deathday Better Than the Birthday." (sermon) Thursday Evening, March 3, 1881, Metropolitan Tabernacle, Newington.

[305] Exell, J. S. *The Biblical Illustrator: Ecclesiastes & The Song of Solomon, Vol. 1.* (New York; Chicago; Toronto; London; Edinburgh: Fleming H. Revell Company), 152.

[306] https://www.christianquotes.info/quotes-by-topic/quotes-about-death/, accessed June 23, 2020.

[307] Spurgeon, C. H. "The Deathday Better Than the Birthday." (sermon) Thursday Evening, March 3, 1881, Metropolitan Tabernacle, Newington.

[308] Knight, Walter B. *Knight's Illustrations for Today.* (Chicago: Moody Press, 1975), 352.

[309] https://www.scrapbook.com/quotes/doc/26631.html, accessed July 2, 2020.

[310] Boice, J. M. Psalms 42–106: *An Expositional Commentary.* (Grand Rapids, MI: Baker Books, 2005), 370.

[311] Ibid.

[312] Chambers, Oswald. *My Utmost for His Highest,* July 4.

[313] Taylor, Hudson. *Hudson Taylor's Spiritual Secret.* (London: China Inland Mission, 1955), 107.

[314] Spurgeon, C. H. *Morning and Evening.* (London: Passmore & Alabaster), May 28 (Evening).

[315] Exell, J. S. *The Biblical Illustrator: The Psalms,* Vol. 4. (New York; Chicago; Toronto; London; Edinburgh: Fleming H. Revell Company), 144.

[316] Spurgeon, C. H. "Good Cheer for the New Year." (Sermon # 728). Delivered January 6, 1867, at the Metropolitan Tabernacle, Newington.

[317] Weber, Frederick Parkes. *Aspects of Death and Correlated Aspects of Life in Art, Epigram, and Poetry.* (New York: Paul B. Hoeber, 1918), 357.

[318] Truett, George W. *A Quest for Souls.* (New York and London: Harper & Brothers Publishers, 1917), 265, 267.

[319] Redpath, Alan, *The Making of a Man of God: Lessons from the Life of David.* (Alan Redpath Library)

[320] Jones, G. C. *1000 Illustrations for Preaching and Teaching.* (Nashville, TN: Broadman & Holman Publishers, 1986), 142.

321 Pithy gems from Adrian Rogers. https://www.gracegems.org/30/short_pithy_gems_ from_adrian_rogers.htm, accessed July 21, 2020.

322 Lloyd-Jones, Martyn. *Spiritual Depression.* (Grand Rapids: Eerdmans Printing Company, 1965), 23.

323 Tan, P. L. *Encyclopedia of 7700 Illustrations: Signs of the Times.* (Garland, TX: Bible Communications, Inc., 1996), 309.

324 MacDonald, W. *Believer's Bible Commentary: Old and New Testaments,* (A. Farstad, ed.). (Nashville: Thomas Nelson, 1995), 1696.

325 MacArthur, John. *Safe in the Arms of God.* (Nashville: Thomas Nelson Publishers, 2003), 127.

326 Exell, J. S. *The Biblical Illustrator: Hebrews*, Vol. 2. (London: James Nisbet & Co.), 613.

327 Spurgeon, C. H. *New Park Street Pulpit,* Vol. 4. "As Thy Days, So Shall Thy Strength Be" (Sermon No. 210, August 22, 1858).

328 Exell, J. S. *The Biblical Illustrator: Hebrews*, Vol. 2. (London: James Nisbet & Co.), 616.

329 bobrogers.me/tag/eternal-life, accessed August 20, 2013.

330 Told by Spurgeon, C. H. Exell, J. S. *The Biblical Illustrator: Leviticus and Numbers,* Vol. 2. (New York; Chicago; Toronto; London; Edinburgh: Fleming H. Revell Company), 259.

331 https://www.brainyquote.com/quotes/blaise_pascal_159845, accessed May 20, 2020.

332 Ironside, H. A. *Proverbs and Song of Solomon.* (Grand Rapids: Kregel, 2006), 117.

333 Tan, P. L. *Encyclopedia of 7700 Illustrations: Signs of the Times.* (Garland, TX: Bible Communications, Inc., 1996), 502.

334 Morgan, R. J. *Nelson's Annual Preacher's Sourcebook,* 2002 Edition. (Nashville: Thomas Nelson Publishers, 2001), 397.

335 Morgan, R. J. *Nelson's Complete Book of Stories, Illustrations, and Quotes* (electronic ed.). (Nashville: Thomas Nelson Publishers, 2000), 767.

336 Brown, Scott Wesley. "When Answers Are Not Enough, There Is Jesus." www. bensonsound.com/lyrics/1095.htm, accessed March 30, 2013.

337 Jackson, Edgar, *Leadership,* Vol. 5, Number 1.

338 Ritzema, E. and E. Vince, (Eds.). *300 Quotations for Preachers from the Puritans.* (Bellingham, WA: Lexham Press, 2013).

339 Morgan, R. J. *Nelson's Annual Preacher's Sourcebook,* 2003 Edition. (Nashville: Thomas Nelson Publishers, 2002), 400.

340 Pink, A. W. *The Sovereignty of God.* (Dallas, TX: Gideon House Books, 2016), Chapter 8.

341 Hastings, James. *The Great Texts of the Bible: Job to Psalm XXIII,* 122.

342 Hunter, William (1811–1877). "The Great Physician Now Is Near" (hymn).

343 Clarke, Adam. *Commentary on the Bible.* (1831), Psalm 46:1.

344 Chambers, Oswald. *My Utmost for His Highest,* October 30.

345 Maclaren, Alexander. *Expositions of Holy Scripture, Vol. 3, The Psalms, Isaiah 1–48.* (Grand Rapids: Eerdmans, 1959), part 2, 61.

346 Wiersbe, W. W. *Wiersbe's Expository Outlines on the New Testament.* (Wheaton, IL: Victor Books, 1992), 837.

347 Ibid.

348 Barnes, Albert. *Notes on the Bible.* (1834).

349 Ibid.

350 Exell, J. S. *The Biblical Illustrator: The Psalms,* Vol. 4. (New York; Chicago; Toronto; London; Edinburgh: Fleming H. Revell Company), 448–449.

351 Buxton. *The Biblical Illustrator,* Electronic Database. "Divine Testing," James 1:12.

352 Criswell, W. A., "Trusting God." Daily Word, November 22, 2017. W. A. Criswell Sermon Library.

353 http://www.gracegems.org/15/pure_gold.htm, accessed November 17, 2017.

354 Wiersbe, W. W. *Be Patient.* (Wheaton, IL: Victor Books, 1996), 94–95.

355 Spurgeon, C. H. Sermon Notes, (James 1:12, "The Tried Man the Blessed Man").

356 https://www.christianquotes.info/top-quotes/20-encouraging-quotes-trials-struggles/#ixzz4yi1xkUxD, accessed November 17, 2017.

357 Ibid.

358 https://www.christianquotes.info/quotes-by-topic/quotes-about-death/, accessed June 23, 2020.

359 Boice, James Montgomery. *Boice Expositional Commentary, Psalms, Volume 2: Psalms 42–106.* (Grand Rapids: Baker, 2005), 715. Database © 2008 WORDsearch Corp.

360 Rogers, Adrian P. "Can God Be Trusted in Your Troubles?" Sermon Notes (Job 13:15), The Adrian Rogers Legacy Collection. Database © 2011 WORDsearch Corp.

361 Wiersbe, W. W. *Be Obedient.* (Wheaton, IL: Victor Books, 1991), 41.

362 Hooper, Walter. (ed.). *The Collected Letters of C. S. Lewis,* Vol. 3. (New York: Harper Collins, 2007).

363 Ironside, H. A. "Commentary on Isaiah 40:4". Ironside's Notes on Selected Books. https://www.studylight.org/commentaries/isn/isaiah-40.html. 1914.

364 *Barnes Notes on the Bible*, Psalm 77:2.

365 Spurgeon, C. H. *Psalms.* (Wheaton, IL: Crossway Books, 1993), 324.

366 Henry, Matthew. *Matthew Henry's Concise Bible Commentary,* Psalm 77:11.

367 Spurgeon, C. H. "Refusing to Be Comforted," (Sermon No. 2578), March 18, 1883.

368 Plumer, W. S. Studies in the Book of Psalms: Being a Critical and Expository Commentary, with Doctrinal and Practical Remarks on the Entire Psalter. (Philadelphia; Edinburgh: J. B. Lippincott Company; A & C Black, 1872), 983.

369 *Barnes Notes on the Bible*, Psalm 112:4.

370 *Ellicott's Commentary for English Readers,* Psalm 112:4.

371 Ker, John. "Changes of Life and Their Comforts In God," Sermon First Series. (Edinburgh: Edmonston and Douglas, 1870).

372 Exell, J. S. *The Biblical Illustrator: St. John*, Vol. 2. (London: James Nisbet & Co.), 656.

373 Vine, W. E., M. F. Unger & W. White, Jr. *Vine's Complete Expository Dictionary of Old and New Testament Words,* Vol. 2. (Nashville, TN: T. Nelson, 1996), 256.

374 Exell, J. S. *The Biblical Illustrator: St. John*, Vol. 2. (London: James Nisbet & Co.), 661.

375 https://www.brainyquote.com/quotes/marcus_tullius_cicero_156345, accessed June 14, 2020.

376 Exell, J. S. *The Biblical Illustrator: Second Corinthians,* Vol. 2. (New York; Chicago; Toronto; London; Edinburgh: Fleming H. Revell Company), 479.

377 Ibid.

378 Ibid., 480.

Endnotes

379 Ryle, J. C. *Holiness: Its Nature, Hindrances, Difficulties, and Roots.* (Peabody, MA: Hendriksen Publishers, 2007), 398.

380 Simeon, C. *Horae Homileticae: Psalms, LXXIII–CL,* Vol. 6. (London: Samuel Holdsworth, 1836), 384.

381 Exell, J. S. *The Biblical Illustrator: St. John*, Vol. 2. (London: James Nisbet & Co.), 663.

382 Plumer, W. S. Studies in the Book of Psalms: Being a Critical and Expository Commentary, with Doctrinal and Practical Remarks on the Entire Psalter. (Philadelphia; Edinburgh: J. B. Lippincott Company; A & C Black, 1872), 628.

383 Bratcher, R. G., & W. D. Reyburn. *A Translator's Handbook on the Book of Psalms.* (New York: United Bible Societies, 1991), 116.

384 McLaren, Alexander. *Week-Day Evening Addresses.* (London: Clay, Sons and Taylor, 1877), 133.

385 McConkey, James. *The Three-Fold Secret of the Holy Spirit.* (Pittsburgh, PA: Silver Publishing Society, 1975), 65–66.

386 Spurgeon, C. H. *Psalms.* (Wheaton, IL: Crossway Books, 1993), 252.

387 Exell, J. S. *The Biblical Illustrator: The Psalms,* Vol. 3. (New York; Chicago; Toronto; London; Edinburgh: Fleming H. Revell Company), 154.

388 Simeon, C. *Horae Homileticae: Psalms, I–LXXII,* Vol. 5. (London: Samuel Holdsworth, 1836), 450.

389 Exell, J. S. *The Biblical Illustrator: Matthew.* (Grand Rapids, MI: Baker Book House), 622.

390 Courson, J. *Jon Courson's Application Commentary.* (Nashville, TN: Thomas Nelson, 2003), 193.

391 http://christian-quotes.ochristian.com/Contentment-Quotes/, accessed June 14, 2020.

392 Hutson, Curtis, (ed.). *Great Preaching on Comfort.* (Murfreesboro, TN: Sword of the Lord Publishers, 1990), 124-125.

393 Smellie, Alexander. In the Hour of Silence. (London: Andrew Melrose, 1899), 17.

394 Spurgeon, C. H. "Five Fears," (Sermon No. 148). Delivered on August 23, 1857.

395 https://www.preceptaustin.org/christ_our_rock, accessed November 7, 2020.

396 Smalley, S. S. *1, 2, 3 John,* Vol. 51. (Dallas: Word, Incorporated, 1984), 259.

397 Courson, J. *Jon Courson's Application Commentary.* (Nashville, TN: Thomas Nelson, 2003), 1630.

398 Jamieson, R., A. R. Fausset, & D. Brown. *Commentary Critical and Explanatory on the Whole Bible,* Vol. 2. (Oak Harbor, WA: Logos Research Systems, Inc., 1997), 1 John 4:18.

399 Barnes, Albert. *Notes on the Bible.* (1834), 1 John 4:18.

400 Spence-Jones, H. D. M. (Ed.). The Pulpit Commentary: 1 John. (London; New York: Funk & Wagnalls Company, 1909), 125.

401 Cowman, L. B. *Streams in the Desert.* (Grand Rapids: Zondervan, 1997), January 29.

402 Packer, J. I. *The J. I. Packer Classic Collection.* (Colorado Springs: NavPress, 2010), 276.

403 Ibid.

404 Hutson, Curtis, (ed.). *Great Preaching on Comfort.* (Murfreesboro, TN: Sword of the Lord Publishers, 1990), 98.

405 Exell, J. S. *The Biblical Illustrator: St. John*, Vol. 2. (London: James Nisbet & Co.), 117.

406 Ibid.

[407] Henry, M. *Matthew Henry's Commentary on the Whole Bible: Complete and Unabridged in One Volume.* (Peabody: Hendrickson, 1994), 1976.

[408] Ibid.

[409] Jones, E. Stanley. *Christ and Human Suffering.* (Abingdon, 1933), 192–193.

[410] https://www.whatchristianswanttoknow.com/top-15-christian-quotes-about-pain-and-suffering/#ixzz6RFzfWy2q, accessed July 4, 2020.

[411] https://gracequotes.org/topic/suffering-faith/, accessed July 4, 2020.

[412] Hutson, Curtis, (ed.). *Great Preaching on Comfort.* (Murfreesboro, TN: Sword of the Lord Publishers, 1990), 100.

[413] Spurgeon, C. H. *Spurgeon's Sermons,* Vol. 17: 1871 (Woodstock, Ontario, Canada: Devoted Publishing, 2017), 200.

[414] https://www.cru.org/train-and-grow/life-and-relationships/hardships/the-significance-of-trials.html, accessed October 20, 2017.

[415] Stated by Dixon, A. C. in the sermon, "Comfort for The Weak" cited in Hutson, Curtis, (ed.). *Great Preaching on Comfort.* (Murfreesboro, TN: Sword of the Lord Publishers, 1990), 87.

[416] Ulmer, Selah. "3 Things You Didn't Know About Spurgeon's Wife," October 17, 2017. https://www.spurgeon.org/resource-library/blog-entries/3-things-you-didnt-know-about-spurgeons-wife/, accessed July 7, 2020.

[417] Spurgeon, C. H. "The Minister in These Times" in *An All-Round Ministry.* (Banner of Truth, 2000), 384, italics in the original.

[418] Cowman, L. B. *Streams in the Desert.* (Grand Rapids: Zondervan, 1997), October 4.

[419] Barnes, Albert. *Notes on the Bible.* (1834), Psalm 119:75.

[420] Spurgeon, C. H. *New Park Street Pulpit,* Vol. 4. "The Christian's Heaviness and Rejoicing" (Sermon No. 222), 461.

[421] Packer, J. I. "Rediscovering Holiness."

[422] Keller, Tim. *Walking with God through Pain and Suffering.* (New York: Riverhead Books, 2015), 58.

[423] Graham, Billy. *Till Armageddon.* (Waco, TX: Word, 1981), 24.

[424] *Matthew Henry's Concise Commentary,* 2 Corinthians 12:9.

[425] Graham, Billy. *Hope for the Troubled Heart.* (Dallas: Word, 1991), 96.

[426] Cowman, L. B. *Streams in the Desert.* (Grand Rapids: Zondervan, 1997), January 3.

[427] Death's Door. https://www.wisconsinshipwrecks.org/learn/DeathsDoor, accessed May 29, 2020.

[428] Ibid.

[429] Spurgeon, C. H. *Morning and Evening.* (London: Passmore & Alabaster), April 20 (Morning).

[430] *Funeral Sermons and Outlines.* (Grand Rapids: Baker Book House, 1951), 7.

[431] Spurgeon, C. H. *Morning and Evening.* (London: Passmore & Alabaster), November 16 (Evening).

[432] *The Sword of the Lord.* "What the Saved Said at Death's Door and What the Lost Said at Death's Door." (Murfreesboro, TN: Sword of the Lord Publishers, August 11, 2006). Additional quotations from other sources.

433 Spurgeon, C. H. "Precious Deaths" (A Sermon) Delivered Sunday Morning, February 18, 1872, The Metropolitan Tabernacle, Newington.

434 Tan, P. L. *Encyclopedia of 7700 Illustrations: Signs of the Times.* (Garland, TX: Bible Communications, Inc., 1996), 312–313.

435 Exell, J. S. *The Biblical Illustrator: Leviticus and Numbers,* Vol. 2. (New York; Chicago; Toronto; London; Edinburgh: Fleming H. Revell Company), 269.

436 Tan, P. L. *Encyclopedia of 7700 Illustrations: Signs of the Times.* (Garland, TX: Bible Communications, Inc., 1996), 314.

437 Adrian Rogers. "Dying Grace" (audio sermon). https://www.lwf.org/sermons/audio/dying-grace-0781, accessed June 21, 2020.

438 Graham, Billy's last column: "By the Time You Read This, I Will Be in Heaven." https://www.fayobserver.com/news/20180221/billy-grahams-last-column-by-time-you-read-this-i-will-be-in-Heaven, accessed March 22, 2020.

439 From Christianty.com, "Famous Last Words," accessed March 21, 2020.

440 Ibid.

441 Ibid.

442 MacArthur, John. "The Solution to a Troubled Heart." http://www.gty.org, accessed May 22, 2013.

443 https://www.gracegems.org/Books2/dh08.htm, accessed April 4, 2020.

444 Ibid.

445 Ibid.

446 Ibid.

447 Ibid.

448 Ibid.

449 Fouse, Michael. Baptist Press, November 16, 2005. https://www.baptistpress.com/resource-library/news/in-his-final-days-adrian-rogers-told-those-gathered-around-him-i-am-at-perfect-peace/, accessed October 22, 2020.

450 https://gracequotes.org/topic/suffering-faith/, accessed July 4, 2020.

451 Graham, Billy. *The Journey.* (Nashville: W Publishing Group, 2006), 221.

452 *Expositor's Bible Commentary,* Psalm 56:8. The author adapted.

453 Martindale, Wayne, and Jerry Root, (ed.). *The Quotable Lewis.* (Grand Rapids, Michigan: Tyndale House, 1989), 156.

454 Spurgeon, C. H. "No Tears in Heaven," August 6, 1865. http://www.biblebb.com, accessed April 1, 2013.

455 https://wacriswell.com/sermons/1970/taking-hold-of-god-s-ableness/, accessed July 4, 2020.

456 Ibid.

457 Phillips, John. *Exploring the Gospel of John.* (Grand Rapids: Kregal Publications, 1989), 263. [The author paraphrased John Phillips words, entire paragraph].

458 http://www.christianquotes.info/quotes-by-topic/quotes-about-Heaven/?listpage=9&instance=2, accessed January 2, 2017.

459 *Funeral Sermons and Outlines.* (Grand Rapids: Baker Book House, 1955), 96.

460 Exell, J. S. *The Biblical Illustrator: Isaiah,* Vol. 3. (New York; Chicago; Toronto; London; Edinburgh: Fleming H. Revell Company), 477.

[461] Spurgeon, C. H. *Faith's Checkbook,* March 14.

[462] Swindoll, Charles. David: A Man of Passion & Destiny. (Dallas: Word Publishing, 1997), 243.

[463] Ibid., 247.

[464] Cowman, L. B. *Streams in the Desert.* (Grand Rapids: Zondervan, 1997), October 4.

[465] Ibid., September 30.

[466] W. A. Criswell. "The Beginning and the End of Sorrows." www.wacriswell.com, accessed April 2, 2013.

[467] Smellie, Alexander. In the Hour of Silence. (London: Andrew Melrose, 1899).

[468] Packer, J. I. *The J. I. Packer Classic Collection.* (Colorado Springs: NavPress, 2010), 86.

[469] Spurgeon, C. H. *Morning and Evening.* (London: Passmore & Alabaster), August 17 (Evening).

[470] Ibid., 123.

[471] Barnes, Albert. *Notes on the Bible.* (1834), James 5:16.

[472] Hutson, Curtis. *Great Preaching on Prayer.* (Murfreesboro, TN: Sword of the Lord Publishers, 1988), 117.

[473] From Ryle, J. C., "A Call to Prayer." https://www.goodreads.com/quotes/8443868-there-is-a-way-by-which-any-person-however-sinful, accessed June 26, 2020.

[474] Barnes, Albert. *Notes on the Bible.* (1834), James 5:16.

[475] Henry, M. *Matthew Henry's Commentary on the Whole Bible: Complete and Unabridged in One Volume.* (Peabody: Hendrickson, 1994), 2420.

[476] J. C. Ryle. "A Call to Prayer." www.gracegems.org, accessed May 9, 2017.

[477] Ibid., 113.

[478] Gothard, Bill. 19.

[479] Ibid, *The Power of Crying Out,* 19.

[480] Cowman, L. B. *Streams in the Desert.* (Grand Rapids: Zondervan, 1997), April 24.

[481] Tennyson, Alfred. "Idylls of the King."

[482] Barnes, Albert. *Notes on the Bible.* (1834), James 5:16.

[483] Christian Prayer Quotations. www.christian-prayer-quotes.christian-attorney.net/, accessed November 30, 2011.

[484] Hutson, Curtis, (ed.). *Great Preaching on Comfort.* (Murfreesboro, TN: Sword of the Lord Publishers, 1990), 122.

[485] Jeremiah, David. Blog. "4 Questions Answered on the Importance of Prayer." https://davidjeremiah.blog/4-questions-answered-on-the-importance-of-prayer/, accessed July 24, 2020.

[486] Spurgeon, C. H. *Morning and Evening.* (London: Passmore & Alabaster), May 19 (Morning).

[487] Courson, J. *Jon Courson's Application Commentary.* (Nashville, TN: Thomas Nelson, 2003), 1153–1154.

[488] Packer, J. I. *The J. I. Packer Classic Collection.* (Colorado Springs: NavPress, 2010), 223.

[489] Cowman, L. B. *Streams in the Desert.* (Grand Rapids: Zondervan, 1997), July 27.

[490] Ibid., December 30.

[491] Dixon, A. C. *Through Night to Morning.* (Sermon No. 18), 1913.

[492] Packer, J. I. *The J. I. Packer Classic Collection.* (Colorado Springs: NavPress, 2010), 267.

[493] http://www.matthewhenry.org/resources-for-public-prayer/prayer/Heaven-desired/ #.XrvLXahKhPY, accessed May 13, 2020.

[494] Truett, George W. *A Quest for Souls.* (New York and London: Harper & Brothers Publishers, 1917).

[495] Charles Spurgeon's Prayers. https://www.spurgeongems.org/spurgeon-prayers/#1, accessed May 13, 2020. Adapted.

[496] Psalm 55 (NLT), adapted.

[497] A prayer entitled "Peril" by a Puritan.

[498] Prayer written by the author, Frank Shivers.

[499] *The Nazarene,* Vols. 7–9, 1922.

[500] Matthew 14:30.

[501] A prayer written by the author, Frank Shivers.

[502] Jerome, c. 342–420.

[503] Columba, c. 521–597.

[504] 1 Clement c. 96.

[505] Luke 22:42, prayer of Jesus in the garden.

[506] A prayer of Augustine. http://dailychristianquote.com/dcqlonely.html, accessed April 20, 2013.

[507] Syrian Clementine Liturgy.

[508] Basil of Caesarea, 329–379.

[509] St. Ambrose of Milan, c. 339–397.

[510] Prayer written by the author, Frank Shivers.

[511] Martin Luther, 1483–1546.

[512] Prayer written by the author, Frank Shivers.

[513] Ibid.

[514] Charles Albert Tindley (1905).

[515] Henry, M. *Matthew Henry's Commentary on the Whole Bible: Complete and Unabridged in One Volume.* (Peabody: Hendrickson, 1994), 961.

[516] https://www.brainyquote.com/quotes/martin_luther_151409, accessed July 7, 2020.

[517] Maclaren, Alexander. *Expositions of Holy Scripture, Vol. 3, The Psalms, Isaiah 1–48.* (Grand Rapids: Eerdmans, 1959), part 2, 61.

[518] Hutson, Curtis, (ed.). *Great Preaching on Comfort.* (Murfreesboro, TN: Sword of the Lord Publishers, 1990), 161–162.

[519] *The Herald and Presbyter.* "Two" (Vol. 93, January 18, 1922), 5.

[520] *Barnes Notes on the Bible*, Psalm 86:7.

[521] Ibid.

[522] Spence-Jones, H. D. M. (Ed.). The Pulpit Commentary: Psalms, Vol. 2. (London; New York: Funk & Wagnalls Company, 1909), 221.

[523] Hutson, Curtis, (ed.). *Great Preaching on Comfort.* (Murfreesboro, TN: Sword of the Lord Publishers, 1990), 161–164.

[524] Dilday, R. H., Jr., & J. H. Kennedy. In Paschall, H. F. & H. H. Hobbs (Eds.). *The Teacher's Bible Commentary,* Psalms. (Nashville: Broadman and Holman Publishers, 1972), 328.

[525] Boice, J. M. Psalms 42–106: *An Expositional Commentary.* (Grand Rapids, MI: Baker Books, 2005), 703.

[526] Ibid.

[527] Bradbury, 82.

[528] Craigie, P. C. *Psalms 1–50,* Vol. 19. (Dallas: Word, Incorporated, 1983), 309.

[529] Spence-Jones, H. D. M. (Ed.). The Pulpit Commentary: Psalms, Vol. 1. (London; New York: Funk & Wagnalls Company, 1909), 306.

[530] Simeon, C. *Horae Homileticae: Psalms, I–LXXII,* Vol. 5. (London: Samuel Holdsworth, 1836), 312.

[531] Spurgeon, C. H. *The Treasury of David,* Psalm 142:4.

[532] Ibid.

[533] Henry, M. *Matthew Henry's Commentary on the Whole Bible: Complete and Unabridged in One Volume.* (Peabody: Hendrickson, 1994), 945.

[534] Ironside, H. A. *Studies on Book One of the Psalms.* (Neptune, NJ: Loizeaux Brothers, 1952), 29.

[535] Ibid.

[536] Ibid.

[537] Spurgeon, C. H. "The Peculiar Sleep of the Beloved," (Sermon). March 4, 1855.

[538] Ibid.

[539] Graham, Billy. *Day by Day.* (Minneapolis, MN: World Wide, 1965), January 13.

[540] Plumer, W. S. Studies in the Book of Psalms: Being a Critical and Expository Commentary, with Doctrinal and Practical Remarks on the Entire Psalter. (Philadelphia; Edinburgh: J. B. Lippincott Company; A & C Black, 1872), 57.

[541] Smith, Clay. "Hope: Hope 101," (Psalm 25:1–7). Sermon preached October 7, 2018, Alice Drive Baptist Church, Sumter, SC.

[542] Craigie, P. C. *Psalms 1–50,* Vol. 19. (Dallas: Word, Incorporated, 1983), 74.

[543] Plumer, W. S. Studies in the Book of Psalms: Being a Critical and Expository Commentary, with Doctrinal and Practical Remarks on the Entire Psalter. (Philadelphia; Edinburgh: J. B. Lippincott Company; A & C Black, 1872), 57.

[544] Exell, J. S. *The Biblical Illustrator: The Psalms,* Vol. 1. (New York; Chicago; Toronto; London; Edinburgh: Fleming H. Revell Company), 55.

[545] *Benson Commentary,* John 11:3.

[546] Wiersbe, W. W. With the Word Commentary. (Nashville: Thomas Nelson, 1991), Mt. 14:1.

[547] *Benson Commentary,* John 11:45.

[548] Exell, J. S. *The Biblical Illustrator: St. John*, Vol. 2. (London: James Nisbet & Co.), 243.

[549] https://quotes.pub/q/cast-not-away-your-confidence-because-god-defers-his-perform-602076, accessed July 13, 2020.

[550] Spurgeon, C. H. "A Happy Christian," (sermon).

[551] Chambers, Oswald. *My Utmost for His Highest,* October 11.

[552] Cowman, L. B. *Streams in the Desert.* (Grand Rapids: Zondervan, 1997), July 25.

[553] Ford, Herschel. *Simple Sermons for Funeral Services.* (Grand Rapids, MI: Zondervan Publishing House, 1968), 30.

[554] MacArthur, John. *Safe in the Arms of God.* (Nashville: Thomas Nelson Publishers, 2003), 133–134.

Endnotes

555 Spence-Jones, H. D. M. (Ed.). The Pulpit Commentary: 2 Samuel. (London; New York: Funk & Wagnalls Company, 1909), 316.

556 Exell, J. S. *The Biblical Illustrator: 2 Samuel.* (New York; Chicago; Toronto; London; Edinburgh: Fleming H. Revell Company), 196.

557 Criswell, W. A. & Paige Patterson. *Heaven.* (Wheaton, Ill: Tyndale House Publications, Inc., 1991), 34.

558 Ibid., 42.

559 Brown, Elizabeth. *Surviving the Loss of a Child.* (Grand Rapids, MI: Revell, 2010), 65.

560 *Company of Heaven: Daily Links with the Household of God.* (London: Longmans, Green & Co., 1901), 356.

561 Exell, J. S. *The Biblical Illustrator: 2 Kings,* Vol. 2. (New York; Chicago; Toronto; London; Edinburgh: Fleming H. Revell Company), 57.

562 Ibid.

563 Miller, J. R. "Afterward You Will Understand," (sermon, 1909), http://www.gracegems.org/Miller/afterward_you_will_understand.htm, accessed August 15, 2013.

564 Spence-Jones, H. D. M. (Ed.). The Pulpit Commentary: 2 Kings. (London; New York: Funk & Wagnalls Company, 1909), 76.

565 Ibid., 77.

566 Conwell, Russell H. *One Thousand Thoughts for Funeral Sermons.* (Kessinger Publishing, reprint edition, 2004), 60.

567 Smellie, Alexander. In the Hour of Silence. (London: Andrew Melrose, 1899), 274.

568 Maclaren, Alexander. *Exposition on the Holy Scripture,* Proverbs 18:10, 213.

569 Ibid., 215.

570 Exell, J. S. *The Biblical Illustrator: Leviticus and Numbers,* Vol. 2. (New York; Chicago; Toronto; London; Edinburgh: Fleming H. Revell Company), 259.

571 Graham, Billy. *Hope for the Troubled Heart.* (Dallas: Word, 1991), 209.

572 Truett, George W. *A Quest for Souls.* (New York and London: Harper & Brothers Publishers, 1917), 250.

573 Henry, M. *Matthew Henry's Commentary on the Whole Bible: Complete and Unabridged in One Volume.* (Peabody: Hendrickson, 1994), 940.

574 Alexander, J. A. *The Psalms Translated and Explained.* (Edinburgh: Andrew Elliot; James Thin, 1864), 464.

575 Exell, J. S. *The Biblical Illustrator: The Psalms,* Vol. 4. (New York; Chicago; Toronto; London; Edinburgh: Fleming H. Revell Company), 449.

576 Ibid., 453.

577 Spence-Jones, H. D. M. (Ed.). The Pulpit Commentary: Psalms, Vol. 3. (London; New York: Funk & Wagnalls Company, 1909), 185.

578 Henry, Matthew. *Matthew Henry's Concise Bible Commentary,* Psalm 121:2.

579 Spence-Jones, H. D. M. (Ed.). The Pulpit Commentary: Psalms, Vol. 3. (London; New York: Funk & Wagnalls Company, 1909), 187.

580 Exell, J. S. *The Biblical Illustrator: The Psalms,* Vol. 5. (New York; Chicago; Toronto; London; Edinburgh: Fleming H. Revell Company), 160.

581 Unknown.

[582] Exell, J. S. *The Biblical Illustrator: The Psalms,* Vol. 2. (New York; Chicago; Toronto; London; Edinburgh: Fleming H. Revell Company), 44.

[583] Swanson, J. *Dictionary of Biblical Languages with Semantic Domains: Hebrew* (Old Testament). (electronic ed.). (Oak Harbor: Logos Research Systems, Inc., 1997).

[584] Barnes, Albert. *Notes on the Bible.* (1834), Psalm 62:5.

[585] Spurgeon, C. H. *Morning and Evening.* (London: Passmore & Alabaster), August 30 (Morning).

[586] Brown, F., S. R. Driver, & C. A. Briggs. *Enhanced Brown-Driver-Briggs Hebrew and English Lexicon.* (Oxford: Clarendon Press, 1977), 54.

[587] Spurgeon, C. H. *Morning and Evening.* (London: Passmore & Alabaster), August 30 (Morning).

[588] Ibid., December 22 (Morning).

[589] *Promises and Prayers for a Christian Friend.* (Brentwood, TN: Freeman-Smith, 2012), 51.

[590] Swindoll, Chuck. *Abraham.* (Carol Stream, Illinois: Tyndale House Publishers, Inc., 2014), 8.

[591] Exell, J. S. *The Biblical Illustrator: The Psalms,* Vol. 2. (New York; Chicago; Toronto; London; Edinburgh: Fleming H. Revell Company), 46.

[592] https://viralbeliever.com/christian-quotes-about-peace/, accessed July 23, 2020.

[593] McConkey, James. *The Three-Fold Secret of the Holy Spirit.* (Pittsburgh, PA: Silver Publishing Society, 1975), 14–15.

[594] MacDonald, W. *Believer's Bible Commentary: Old and New Testaments,* (A. Farstad, ed.). (Nashville: Thomas Nelson, 1995), 956.

[595] Graham, Billy. *Day by Day.* (Minneapolis, MN: World Wide, 1965), December 31.

[596] https://viralbeliever.com/christian-quotes-about-peace/, accessed July 23, 2020.

[597] Exell, J. S. *The Biblical Illustrator: Isaiah,* Vol. 1. (New York; Chicago; Toronto; London; Edinburgh: Fleming H. Revell Company), 474.

[598] Morgan, R. J. *Nelson's Annual Preacher's Sourcebook,* 2003 Edition. (Nashville: Thomas Nelson Publishers, 2002), 396.

[599] https://www.christianquotes.info/quotes-by-topic/quotes-about-death/, accessed June 23, 2020.

[600] Jones, G. C. *1000 Illustrations for Preaching and Teaching.* (Nashville, TN: Broadman & Holman Publishers, 1986), 103.

[601] The Spurgeon Center for Biblical Preaching at Midwestern Seminary. "10 Spurgeon Quotes on Dying Well," June 29, 2017. https://www.spurgeon.org/resource-library/blog-entries/10-spurgeon-quotes-on-dying-well/, accessed June 26, 2020.

[602] Spence-Jones, H. D. M. (Ed.). The Pulpit Commentary: Jeremiah, Vol. 1. (London; New York: Funk & Wagnalls Company, 1909), 217.

[603] Newman, B. M., Jr., & P. C. Stine. *A Handbook on Jeremiah.* (New York: United Bible Societies, 2003), 250.

[604] Simeon, C. *Horae Homileticae: Jeremiah to Daniel,* Vol. 9. (London: Samuel Holdsworth, 1836), 86–87.

[605] African-American Spiritual.

[606] https://www.azquotes.com/quote/703860, accessed July 14, 2020.

607 Spurgeon, C. H. *Morning and Evening.* (London: Passmore & Alabaster), May 31 (Evening).

608 Henry, M. *Matthew Henry's Commentary on the Whole Bible: Complete and Unabridged in One Volume.* (Peabody: Hendrickson, 1994), 2291.

609 MacDonald, W. *Believer's Bible Commentary: Old and New Testaments,* (A. Farstad, ed.). (Nashville: Thomas Nelson, 1995), 1866.

610 Spurgeon, C. H. *Metropolitan Tabernacle Pulpit,* Volume 22. "Strengthening Words from the Savior's Lips" (sermon preached April 2, 1876).

611 Jamieson, R., A. R. Fausset, & D. Brown. *Commentary Critical and Explanatory on the Whole Bible,* Vol. 2. (Oak Harbor, WA: Logos Research Systems, Inc., 1997), 319–320.

612 Spurgeon, C. H. *Metropolitan Tabernacle Pulpit,* Volume 22. "Strengthening Words from the Savior's Lips" (sermon preached April 2, 1876).

613 Dixon, A. C. *Through Night to Morning.* (Sermon No. 12), 1913.

614 Warren, Rick. https://www.brainyquote.com/quotes/rick_warren_456861, accessed June 21, 2020.

615 Exell, J. S. *The Biblical Illustrator: Second Corinthians,* Vol. 2. (New York; Chicago; Toronto; London; Edinburgh: Fleming H. Revell Company), 488.

616 Ibid., 487.

617 Ibid.

618 Courson, J. *Jon Courson's Application Commentary.* (Nashville, TN: Thomas Nelson, 2003), 1153.

619 Henry, M. *Matthew Henry's Commentary on the Whole Bible: Complete and Unabridged in One Volume.* (Peabody: Hendrickson, 1994), 1176.

620 Exell, J. S. *The Biblical Illustrator: Isaiah,* Vol. 3. (Grand Rapids: Baker Book House), 21.

621 Ibid.

622 Spurgeon, C. H. "Five Fears," (Sermon No. 148). Delivered on August 23, 1857.

623 Cowman, L. B. *Streams in the Desert.* (Grand Rapids: Zondervan, 1997), October 6.

624 Wiersbe, W. W. *Be Comforted,* "Be" Commentary Series. (Wheaton, IL: Victor Books, 1996, 126.

625 Ibid.

626 Spurgeon, C. H cited in *The Biblical Illustrator,* Isaiah Vol. III, 15.

627 *Promises and Prayers for a Dedicated Teacher.* (Brentwood, TN: Freeman-Smith, 2010), 129.

628 Ibid., 26.

629 Alcorn, Randy. *God's Promise of Happiness.* (Carol Streams, ILL: Tyndale House Publishers, 2015), 83.

630 Spurgeon, C. H. *Morning and Evening.* (London: Passmore & Alabaster), October 21 (Evening).

631 Exell, J. S. *The Biblical Illustrator: Deuteronomy,* Vol. 2. (New York; Chicago; Toronto; London; Edinburgh: Fleming H. Revell Company), 607.

632 *The Vance Havner Quote Book.*

633 Rogers, Adrian. "Outrageous Hope, Extravagant Joy." https://www.bellevue.org/wp-content/uploads/Week-8-Lecture-notes.pdf, accessed June 21, 2020.

634 Cowman, C. Bible.org, "Consolation," 70. accessed April 6, 2013.

635 *Funeral Sermons and Outlines.* (Grand Rapids: Baker Book House, 1951), 8.

636 Robertson, Frederick W. *Sermons,* Fifth Series, "Tears of Jesus." (London: Kegan, Paul, Trench, Trubner and Company, 1900).

637 Ibid.

638 Smellie, Alexander. In the Hour of Silence. (London: Andrew Melrose, 1899), 304.

639 Tan, P. L. *Encyclopedia of 7700 Illustrations: Signs of the Times.* (Garland, TX: Bible Communications, Inc., 1996), 305.

640 Lucado, Max. *Waiting for Christ's Return.* (Nashville: Word, 2000), Chapter 4.

641 Grace Quotes. https://gracequotes.org/quote/worry-is-the-sin-of-distrusting-the-promise-and-pr/, accessed January 11, 2018.

642 Ibid.

643 www.brainyquote.com/quotes/keywords/anxiety.html, accessed September 4, 2017.

644 Rogers, Adrian. "Two Days That Will Steal Your Joy" (devotional). http://www.lwf.org, accessed July 25, 2014.

645 Cowman, L. B. *Streams in the Desert.* (Grand Rapids: Zondervan, 1997), October 7.

646 Graham, Billy. *The Holy Spirit.* (Nashville: Thomas Nelson, 1978), 255.

647 Graham, Billy. *The Billy Graham Christian Worker's Handbook.* (Charlotte, NC: BGEA, 1984), 49.

648 Dixon, Francis. "The Conquest of Worry." (Words of Life Ministries Bible Studies, Series 13, Study 6).

649 Müller, George. "Signs of the Times," *Christianity Today,* v. 35, n. 1.

650 Graham, Billy. *Alone with the Savior.* (Charlotte, NC: BGEA, 2010), 40.

651 Dixon, A. C. *Through Night to Morning.* (Sermon No. 1), 1913.

652 Ibid.

653 Funk & Wells, ed., *The Homiletic Review* Vol. XXIV (New York, London & Canada: Funk & Wagnalls Company, 1892), 148.

654 Dixon, A. C. *Through Night to Morning.* (Sermon No. 1), 1913.

655 Smith, Hannah Whitall. "The God of All Comfort." https://biblehub.com/library/smith/the_god_of_all_comfort/chapter_11_things_that_cannot.htm, accessed July 5, 2020.

656 Dixon, Francis. "The Guarantee of God's Keeping Power." (Words of Life Ministries: Series 29, Study 3).

657 Dixon, Francis. "The Guarantee of God's Keeping Power." (Words of Life Ministries: Series 29, Study 3).

658 http://villagehymns.com/music/unsinkable/, accessed July 6, 2020.

659 https://www.brainyquote.com/quotes/ving_rhames_440264, accessed July 6, 2020.

660 Courson, J. *Jon Courson's Application Commentary.* (Nashville, TN: Thomas Nelson, 2003), 1100.

661 Ibid.

662 Barclay, W. (Ed.). *The Letters to the Corinthians,* (electronic ed.). (Philadelphia: The Westminster John Knox Press, 1975), 174.

663 Simeon, C. *Horae Homileticae: 1 and 2 Corinthians,* Vol. 16. (London: Samuel Holdsworth, 1836), 404.

664 Exell, J. S. *The Biblical Illustrator: Second Corinthians,* Vol. 2. (New York; Chicago; Toronto; London; Edinburgh: Fleming H. Revell Company), 21.

665 Plumer, W. S. Studies in the Book of Psalms: Being a Critical and Expository Commentary, with Doctrinal and Practical Remarks on the Entire Psalter. (Philadelphia; Edinburgh: J. B. Lippincott Company; A & C Black, 1872), 400.

666 Spurgeon, C. H. *Landlord and Tenants.*

667 Spurgeon, C. H. *Morning and Evening.* (London: Passmore & Alabaster), January 29 (Morning).

668 http://saintsquotes.net/Selection%20-%20Heaven%20-%20II.html, accessed June 25, 2020.

669 http://saintsquotes.net/Selection%20-%20Heaven.html, accessed June 25, 2020.

670 Ritzema, E. and E. Vince, (Eds.). *300 Quotations for Preachers from the Puritans.* (Bellingham, WA: Lexham Press, 2013).

671 Spence-Jones, H. D. M. (Ed.). The Pulpit Commentary: 2 Corinthians. (London; New York: Funk & Wagnalls Company, 1909), 112–113.

672 Lewis, C. S. *Mere Christianity.* (1952; Harper Collins, 2001), 135, 136–137.

673 Jones, G. C. *1000 Illustrations for Preaching and Teaching.* (Nashville, TN: Broadman & Holman Publishers, 1986), 152.

674 Pink, Arthur W. The Wisdom of Arthur W. Pink, Vol. I. (Zeeland, Michigan: Reformed Church Publications, 2009), 329.

675 Barnes, Albert. *Notes on the Bible.* (1834), Isaiah 40:31.

676 Ibid.

677 Exell, J. S. *The Biblical Illustrator: Isaiah,* Vol. 2. (New York; Chicago; Toronto; London; Edinburgh: Fleming H. Revell Company), 231..

678 Eagle Facts. www.rockland-eaglesrest.org › eagle-facts, accessed July 23, 2020.

679 Barnes, Albert. *Notes on the Bible.* (1834), Isaiah 40:31.

680 Alexander, J. A. *The Psalms Translated and Explained.* (Edinburgh: Andrew Elliot; James Thin, 1864), 416.

681 Barry, J. D., D. Mangum, D. R. Brown, M. S. Heiser, M. Custis, E. Ritzema,...D. Bomar. *Faithlife Study Bible.* (Bellingham, WA: Lexham Press, 2012, 2016), Is. 42:3.

682 Smellie, Alexander. In the Hour of Silence. (London: Andrew Melrose, 1899), 92.

683 Ibid.

684 Joseph Parker cited in Exell, J. S. *The Biblical Illustrator: Isaiah,* Vol. 2. (New York; Chicago; Toronto; London; Edinburgh: Fleming H. Revell Company), 304.

685 PastForward: The Truth about Suicide, healpastlives.com/pastlf/quote/qusuicid.htm, accessed November 23, 2011.

686 https://www.insight.org/resources/article-library/individual/still-living-grieving-after-a-suicide, accessed July 10, 2020.

687 *Promises and Prayers for a Dedicated Teacher.* (Brentwood, TN: Freeman-Smith, 2010), 134.

688 Earliest known version cited in Mother Goose's Melody published in 1803, which has the modern version with a different last line: "Could not set Humpty Dumpty up again." en.wikipedia.org/wiki/Humpty_Dumpty, accessed May 30, 2011.

689 Bonhoeffer, Dietrich. Ethics. (New York: Touchstone, 1995), 168, accessed on Google Books http://books.google.com/books?id=djM15pn4yOsC&printsec=frontcover (accessed May 22, 2013).

[690] Spurgeon, C. H. *Morning and Evening.* (London: Passmore & Alabaster), December 4 (Evening).

[691] Quotes About Suicide Prevention. www.yourlifeyourvoice.org/DiscoverIt/Pages/Quotes.aspx, accessed November 23, 2011.

[692] *The Alliance Tozer Devotional,* "Two Forms of Death." https://www.cmalliance.org/devotions/tozer?id=1146, accessed May 28, 2020.

[693] Spurgeon, C. H. *Morning and Evening.* (London: Passmore & Alabaster), April 8.

[694] Henry, M. *Matthew Henry's Commentary on the Whole Bible: Complete and Unabridged in One Volume.* (Peabody: Hendrickson, 1994), 814.

[695] McWherter, Leroy. The King of Glory. (Nashville: Southwestern Publishing House, 1884), 240.

[696] Moody, William R. *The Autobiography of Dwight L. Moody.* (New York, Chicago and Toronto: Fleming H. Revell Company, 1900), First page of book.

[697] Knight, Walter B. *Knight's Illustrations for Today.* (Chicago: Moody Press, 1975), 93–94.

[698] "Tozer on the Resurrection." https://awtozer.com/2019/09/24/tozer-on-the-resurrection/, accessed May 28, 2020.

[699] Tan, P. L. *Encyclopedia of 7700 Illustrations: Signs of the Times.* (Garland, TX: Bible Communications, Inc., 1996), 311.

[700] Ibid., 312.

[701] Bowling, A. Harris, R. L., G. L. Archer Jr., & B. K. Waltke (eds.). *Theological Wordbook of the Old Testament,* 793 טוב, (electronic ed.). (Chicago: Moody Press, 1999), 345.

[702] Henry, M. *Matthew Henry's Commentary on the Whole Bible: Complete and Unabridged in One Volume.* (Peabody: Hendrickson, 1994), 1047.

[703] Simeon, C. *Horae Homileticae: Proverbs to Isaiah XXVI,* Vol. 7. (London: Samuel Holdsworth, 1836), 381.

[704] Graham, B. *The Heaven Answer Book.* (Nashville: Thomas Nelson, 2012).

[705] "Five Insights on Death and Dying from Dietrich Bonhoeffer," April 26, 2018. (Letters and Papers From Prison). https://www.hourofourdeath.org/five-insights-on-death-and-dying-from-dietrich-bonhoeffer/, accessed June 23, 2020.

[706] Baxter, Richard. *The Saint's Everlasting Rest.* (London: William Tegg and Company, 1852), 97.

[707] Beecher, Henry Ward. *Life Thoughts: Gathered from the Extemporaneous Discourses of Henry Ward Beecher.* (New York: Sheldon and Company, 1869), 176.

[708] Graham, Billy. *Where I Am: Heaven, Eternity, and Our Life Beyond.* (Nashville: Thomas Nelson, 2015).

[709] Spurgeon, C. H. *Psalms.* (Wheaton, IL: Crossway Books, 1993), 11.

[710] Ibid., 12.

[711] Exell, J. S. *The Biblical Illustrator: The Psalms,* Vol. 1. (New York; Chicago; Toronto; London; Edinburgh: Fleming H. Revell Company), 62.

[712] Matheson, George cited in *Streams in the Desert,* September 8.

[713] Ibid.

[714] Ibid.

[715] Ibid.

[716] Barnes, Albert. *Notes on the Bible.* (1834), Psalm 4:1.

Endnotes

[717] Henry, M. *Matthew Henry's Commentary on the Whole Bible: Complete and Unabridged in One Volume.* (Peabody: Hendrickson, 1994), 748.

[718] https://www.christianquotes.info/quotes-by-topic/quotes-about-death/, June 23, 2020.

[719] Moody, D. L. *Sovereign Grace.* (Grand Rapids: Fleming H. Revell, 1891).

[720] Truett, George W. *A Quest for Souls.* (New York and London: Harper & Brothers Publishers, 1917), 333.

[721] F. B. Meyer, C. H. Spurgeon, Albert Barnes, and Others. *Funeral Sermons and Outlines.* (Grand Rapids: Baker Book House, 1955), 44–45.

[722] Sanders, J., Ed. *Memorial Tributes: A Compend of Funeral Addresses.* (New York: B.B. Treat, 1883), 124.

[723] Swindoll, Chuck. "JAMES: Hands-On Christianity, Suffering, Sickness, Sin—and Healing." https://insightforliving.swncdn.com/pdf/broadcast/2017.01.11-notes.pdf, accessed July 20, 2020.

[724] Criswell, W. A. "Divine Healing," (Sermon). James 5:14–15. July 25, 1965. https://wacriswell.com/sermons/1965/divine-healing-2/, accessed July 20, 2020.

[725] Swindoll, Charles R. *Insights on James, 1 and 2 Peter.* (Zondervan, 2010), 123.

[726] Criswell, W. A. "Divine Healing," (Sermon). James 5:14–15. July 25, 1965. https://wacriswell.com/sermons/1965/divine-healing-2/, accessed July 20, 2020.

[727] Davids, P. H. *The Epistle of James: A Commentary on the Greek Text.* (Grand Rapids, MI: Eerdmans, 1982), 193.

[728] Vine, W. E., M. F. Unger & W. White, Jr. *Vine's Complete Expository Dictionary of Old and New Testament Words,* Vol. 2. (Nashville, TN: T. Nelson, 1996), 195.

[729] Barnes, Albert. *Notes on the Bible.* (1834), James 5:14.

[730] Criswell, W. A. "Divine Healing," (Sermon). James 5:14–15. July 25, 1965. https://wacriswell.com/sermons/1965/divine-healing-2/, accessed July 20, 2020.

[731] Adams, Jamie M. "Praying for Healing," (Article). https://www.nelsonprice.com/praying-for-healing/, accessed July 21, 2020.

[732] Swindoll, Chuck. *Swindoll's Living Insights New Testament Commentary: James, 1 & 2 Peter,* James 5:14–15.

[733] Criswell, W. A. "Divine Healing," (Sermon). James 5:14–15. July 25, 1965. https://wacriswell.com/sermons/1965/divine-healing-2/, accessed July 20, 2020.

[734] MacArthur, John. *The Keys to Spiritual Growth.* (Wheaton, Illinois: Crossway Books, 1991), 123.

[735] Criswell, W. A. "Divine Healing," (Sermon). James 5:14–15. July 25, 1965. https://wacriswell.com/sermons/1965/divine-healing-2/, accessed July 20, 2020.

[736] Adams, Jamie M. "Praying for Healing," (Article). https://www.nelsonprice.com/praying-for-healing/, accessed July 21, 2020.

[737] Max Lucado. Tweet. Aug 4, 2016.

[738] Hutson, Curtis, (ed.). *Great Preaching on Comfort.* (Murfreesboro, TN: Sword of the Lord Publishers, 1990), 124.

[739] Bridges, C. *Exposition of Psalm 119: As Illustrative of the Character and Exercises of Christian Experience,* Seventeenth Edition. (New York: Robert Carter & Brothers, 1861), Psalm 119:67.

[740] *Gill's Exposition of the Entire Bible,* Psalm 119:71.

741 Packer, J. I. *The J. I. Packer Classic Collection.* (Colorado Springs: NavPress, 2010), 37.

742 Bridges, C. *Exposition of Psalm 119: As Illustrative of the Character and Exercises of Christian Experience,* Seventeenth Edition. (New York: Robert Carter & Brothers, 1861), 110.

743 Spence-Jones, H. D. M. (Ed.). The Pulpit Commentary: Psalms, Vol. 3. (London; New York: Funk & Wagnalls Company, 1909), 107.

744 Rogers, Adrian. "Do All Things Work Together for Good?" Graham, Billy Evangelistic Association, July 6, 2010. https://billygraham.org/story/do-all-things-work-together-for-good/, accessed July 25, 2020.

745 Ibid.

746 Spurgeon, C. H. *The Treasury of David,* Psalm 119:68.

747 Henry, M. *Matthew Henry's Commentary on the Whole Bible: Complete and Unabridged in One Volume.* (Peabody: Hendrickson, 1994), 920.

748 Jamieson, R., A. R. Fausset, & D. Brown. *Commentary Critical and Explanatory on the Whole Bible,* Vol. 2. (Oak Harbor, WA: Logos Research Systems, Inc., 1997), Psalm 119:71–72.

749 https://www.christianquotes.info/quotes-by-topic/quotes-about-affliction/, accessed July 7, 2020.

750 Ibid.

751 *Benson Commentary,* Psalm 119:71.

752 Quote by Spurgeon, C. H. https://www.christianquotes.info/quotes-by-topic/quotes-about-affliction/, accessed July 7, 2020.

753 Packer, J. I. *God's Plans for You.* (Nashville: Crossway, 2001).

754 Peretti, Frank E. *The Wounded Spirit.* (Nashville: Thomas Nelson, 2000).

755 Packer, J. I. *The J. I. Packer Classic Collection.* (Colorado Springs: NavPress, 2010), 285.

756 Cited in Kluck, Ted & Ronnie Martin. *Finding God in the Dark.* (Minneapolis: Minnesota: Bethany House Publishers, 2013), 45.

757 Henry, M. *Matthew Henry's Commentary on the Whole Bible: Complete and Unabridged in One Volume.* (Peabody: Hendrickson, 1994), 635.

758 Redpath, Alan. *Victorious Christian Service.* (Old Tappan, NJ: Fleming H. Revell Company, 1958), 141.

759 Henry, M. *Matthew Henry's Commentary on the Whole Bible: Complete and Unabridged in One Volume.* (Peabody: Hendrickson, 1994), 635.

760 Redpath, Alan. *Victorious Christian Service.* (Old Tappan, NJ: Fleming H. Revell Company, 1958), 141.

761 Exell, J. S. *The Biblical Illustrator: First Chronicles, Second Chronicles, Ezra, Nehemiah, and Esther,* Vol. 4. (New York; Chicago; Toronto; London; Edinburgh: Fleming H. Revell Company), 114.

762 Ibid.

763 Ibid.

764 Redpath, Alan. *Victorious Christian Service.* (Old Tappan, NJ: Fleming H. Revell Company, 1958), 145–146.

765 Barnes, Albert. *Notes on the Bible.* (1834), Isaiah 25:8.

Endnotes

766 Criswell, W. A. "The Trials of Faith," (Sermon preached July 28th, 1974). Criswell, W. A. Sermon Library. https://wacriswell.com/sermons/1974/the-trials-of-faith/, accessed September 6, 2020.

767 Tony Evans. "Has God Put More on You Than You Can Bear?" (Blog). https://tonyevans. org/has-god-put-more-on-you-than-you-can-bear/, accessed September 6, 2020.

768 https://sermonquotes.com/c-h-spurgeon/12427-to-trust-god-in-the-light-is-nothing-but-to-trust-him-in-the-dark-that-is-faith-ch-spurgeon.html, accessed September 14, 2020.

769 Criswell, W. A. *Daily Word.* "A Defeated Christian." W. A. Criswell Sermon Library. dailyword@wacriswell.com, accessed September 12, 2020.

770 https://www.azquotes.com/quotes/topics/encouragers.html, accessed September 17, 2020.

771 Exell, J. S. *The Biblical Illustrator: Deuteronomy,* Vol. 2. (New York; Chicago; Toronto; London; Edinburgh: Fleming H. Revell Company), 15–16.

772 TobyMac, "Speak Life," (song), 2012.

773 Swindoll, Chuck. "Encouragement Takes the Sting Out of Life," April 17, 2014. https:// insight.org/resources/article-library/individual/encouragement-takes-the-sting-out-of-life, accessed September 19, 2020.

774 Spurgeon, C. H. *Morning and Evening.* (London: Passmore & Alabaster), October 17 (Morning).

775 *Barnes Notes on the Bible*, Psalm 42:5.

776 Plumer, W. S. Studies in the Book of Psalms: Being a Critical and Expository Commentary, with Doctrinal and Practical Remarks on the Entire Psalter. (Philadelphia; Edinburgh: J. B. Lippincott Company; A & C Black, 1872), 405.

777 Hastings, James. *The Great Texts of the Bible: Job to Psalm XXIII,* 121.

778 Spurgeon, C. H. *Morning and Evening.* (London: Passmore & Alabaster), October 19 (Evening).

779 Spurgeon, C. H. *Metropolitan Tabernacle Pulpit,* Volume 44. "Songs in the Night," (sermon). Intended for Reading February 27, 1898.

780 Henry, M. *Matthew Henry's Commentary on the Whole Bible: Complete and Unabridged in One Volume.* (Peabody: Hendrickson, 1994), 726.

781 Spence-Jones, H. D. M. (Ed.). The Pulpit Commentary: Job. (London; New York: Funk & Wagnalls Company, 1909), 574.

782 Spurgeon, C. H. *Metropolitan Tabernacle Pulpit,* Volume 44. "Songs in the Night," (sermon). Intended for Reading February 27, 1898.

783 Bunyan, John. *Israel's Hope Encouraged.* (Bellingham, WA: Logos Bible Software) 1:578.

784 Piper, John. "What Is So Important About Christian Hope?" March 7, 2008. https:// www.desiringgod.org/interviews/what-is-so-important-about-christian-hope, accessed October 20, 2020.

785 https://www.communicatejesus.com/40-quotes-life-changing-power-resurrection/ accessed October 25, 2020.

786 Ibid.

787 Ibid.

788 Graham, Billy. "In His Own Words: The Hope of Heaven." March 21, 2017. https:// billygrahamlibrary.org/in-his-own-words-the-hope-of-heaven/, accessed October 20, 2020.

789 Pink, A. W. *Exposition of the Gospel of John.* (Swengel, PA: Bible Truth Depot, 1923–1945), 757.

790 Criswell, W. A. & Paige Patterson. *Heaven.* (Wheaton, Ill: Tyndale House Publications, Inc., 1991), 162.

791 Tozer, A.W. "Preparing for Jesus' Return: Daily Live the Blessed Hope."

792 John MacArthur. "Will We Recognize and Be Reunited with Our Loved Ones in Heaven?," https://www.gty.org/library/questions/QA100/will-we-recognize-and-be-reunited-with-our-loved-ones-in-heaven, accessed October 25, 2020.

793 https://www.communicatejesus.com/40-quotes-life-changing-power-resurrection/, accessed October 25, 2020.

794 https://www.soroptimist.org/trafficking/faq.html, accessed April 17, 2018.

795 Spence-Jones, H. D. M. (Ed.). The Pulpit Commentary: Psalms, Vol. 1. (London; New York: Funk & Wagnalls Company, 1909), 72.

796 Spurgeon, C. H. *Psalms.* (Wheaton, IL: Crossway Books, 1993), 32.

797 Ibid.

798 Henry, M. *Matthew Henry's Commentary on the Whole Bible: Complete and Unabridged in One Volume.* (Peabody: Hendrickson, 1994), 758.

799 Spurgeon, C. H. *Psalms.* (Wheaton, IL: Crossway Books, 1993), 32.

800 Boice, J. M. *Psalms 1–41: An Expositional Commentary.* (Grand Rapids, MI: Baker Books, 2005), 93.

801 Spence-Jones, H. D. M. (Ed.). The Pulpit Commentary: Psalms, Vol. 1. (London; New York: Funk & Wagnalls Company, 1909), 79.

802 Ibid., 80.

803 Contributors to the "Tracts for the Times," cited in *The Biblical Illustrator,* Psalm 11:3–4.

804 Henry, M. *Matthew Henry's Commentary on the Whole Bible: Complete and Unabridged in One Volume.* (Peabody: Hendrickson, 1994), 771.

805 https://sites.google.com/site/worshipbasic101/about-praise-worship, accessed October 31, 2020.

806 Ibid.

807 Louw, J. P., & E. A. Nida. *Greek-English Lexicon of the New Testament: Based on Semantic Domains* (electronic ed. of the 2nd edition., Vol. 1). (New York: United Bible Societies, 1996), 283.

808 Spurgeon, C. H. *Morning and Evening.* (London: Passmore & Alabaster), October 30 (Morning).

809 Law, William. *A Serious Call to a Holy and Devout Life.* (Hendrickson Publishers, 2009).

810 https://www.christianquotes.info/top-quotes/20-glorious-quotes-about-praise/, accessed October 30, 2020.

811 Ibid.

812 Ibid.

813 Eastman, Dick. *The Hour That Changes the World.* (Grand Rapids: Chosen, 2002), 94.

814 Luther, Martin. *Here I Stand.* (Nashville: Abingdon Press, 2013), 266.

815 Jeremiah, David. *My Heart's Desire.* (Nashville: Integrity Publishers, 2002), 124.

816 Piper, John. "Ambushing Satan with Song." January 20, 1985. https://www.desiringgod.org/messages/ambushing-satan-with-song, accessed November 1, 2020.

Endnotes

[817] Spurgeon, C. H. *Morning and Evening.* (London: Passmore & Alabaster), October 30 (Morning).

[818] Law, William. *A Serious Call to a Holy and Devout Life.* (Hendrickson Publishers, 2009).

[819] https://www.christianquotes.info/top-quotes/20-glorious-quotes-about-praise/, accessed October 30, 2020.

[820] https://www.azquotes.com/author/15314-Rick_Warren/tag/worship, accessed October 31, 2020.

[821] Spurgeon, C. H. "The High Rock" (Sermon # 2728). New Park Street Chapel, 1859. https://www.spurgeongems.org/vols46-48/chs2728.pdf, accessed September 29, 2018.

[822] Harman, A. *Psalms: A Mentor Commentary,* Vol. 1–2. (Ross-shire, Great Britain: Mentor, 2011), 452.

[823] Spurgeon, C. H. *Psalms.* (Wheaton, IL: Crossway Books, 1993), 247.

[824] Henry, M. *Matthew Henry's Commentary on the Whole Bible: Complete and Unabridged in One Volume.* (Peabody: Hendrickson, 1994), 829.

[825] Spurgeon, C. H. *Psalms.* (Wheaton, IL: Crossway Books, 1993), 247–248.

[826] Henry, M. *Matthew Henry's Commentary on the Whole Bible: Complete and Unabridged in One Volume.* (Peabody: Hendrickson, 1994), 829.

[827] https://www.preceptaustin.org/christ_our_rock, accessed November 7, 2020.

[828] Spurgeon, C. H. *Morning and Evening.* (London: Passmore & Alabaster), September 22 (Evening).

[829] Exell, J. S. *The Biblical Illustrator:* Psalm 61:2.

[830] https://www.preceptaustin.org/christ_our_rock, accessed November 7, 2020.

[831] Horne, G. *A Commentary on the Book of Psalms.* (New York: Robert Carter & Brothers, 1856), 213–214.

[832] Spurgeon, C. H. *Morning and Evening.* (London: Passmore & Alabaster), September 1 (Evening).

[833] Spurgeon, C. H. "The High Rock" (Sermon # 2728). New Park Street Chapel, 1859. https://www.spurgeongems.org/vols46-48/chs2728.pdf, accessed September 29, 2018.

[834] "The Fatherhood of God." Daily Devotional. www.Ligonier.org, accessed November 9, 2020.

[835] Gill, John. *Exposition of the Entire Bible by John Gill,* [1746–63], Jeremiah 31:33.

[836] Spurgeon, C. H. *New Park Street Pulpit,* Vol. 2. "God in the Covenant" (Sermon, August 3, 1856).

[837] Henry, M. *Matthew Henry's Commentary on the Whole Bible: Complete and Unabridged in One Volume.* (Peabody: Hendrickson, 1994), 1291.

[838] Spurgeon, C. H. *New Park Street Pulpit,* Vol. 2. "God in the Covenant" (Sermon, August 3, 1856).

[839] Ibid.

[840] Spurgeon, C. H. *Morning and Evening.* (London: Passmore & Alabaster), November 9 (Evening).

[841] Exell, J. S. *The Biblical Illustrator:* Psalm 20:7.

[842] *Barnes Notes on the Bible,* Psalm 20:7.

Endnotes

[843] Perowne, J. J. S. *The Book of Psalms; A New Translation, with Introductions and Notes, Explanatory and Critical, 5th Edition, Revised,* Vol. 1. (London; Cambridge: George Bell and Sons; Deighton Bell and Co., 1883), 239.

[844] Plumer, W. S. Studies in the Book of Psalms: Being a Critical and Expository Commentary, with Doctrinal and Practical Remarks on the Entire Psalter. (Philadelphia; Edinburgh: J. B. Lippincott Company; A & C Black, 1872), 273.

[845] https://www.christianquotes.info/top-quotes/18-powerful-quotes-trust/#axzz5Dj7VIZNh, accessed April 25, 2018.

[846] Parker, Joseph. *The People's Bible,* Psalm 20:7.

[847] Spurgeon, C. H. *Psalms.* (Wheaton, IL: Crossway Books, 1993), 73.

[848] https://www.christianquotes.info/top-quotes/18-powerful-quotes-trust/#ixzz5Dj8gaFH7, accessed April 25, 2018.

[849] Exell, J. S. *The Biblical Illustrator: Isaiah,* Vol. 2. (New York; Chicago; Toronto; London; Edinburgh: Fleming H. Revell Company), 99.

[850] Spurgeon, C. H. *Morning and Evening.* (London: Passmore & Alabaster), October 7 (Evening).

[851] *Barnes Notes on the Bible*, Psalm 27:1.

[852] Derickson, G. W. *First, Second, and Third John,* (House, H. W., W. H. Harris III, & A. W. Pitts, [eds.]) (Bellingham, WA: Lexham Press, 2012), 467.

[853] Rogers, Adrian. "Facing Your Fear." May 14, 2013. https://www.lwf.org/articles/facing-your-fear, accessed November 12, 2020.

[854] https://www.christianquotes.info/top-quotes/22-powerful-quotes-overcoming-fear/, accessed November 12, 2020.

[855] Ibid.

[856] Smith, Clay. "Hope: Hope 101," (Psalm 25:1–7). Sermon preached October 7, 2018, Alice Drive Baptist Church, Sumter, SC.

[857] "Christian Quotes on Fear," dailychristianquote.com/dcqfear.html, accessed December 1, 2011.

[858] Rogers, Adrian. "Facing Your Fear." May 14, 2013. https://www.lwf.org/articles/facing-your-fear, accessed November 12, 2020.

[859] Simeon, C. *Horae Homileticae: Psalms, LXXIII–CL,* Vol. 6. (London: Samuel Holdsworth, 1836), 270.

[860] Spurgeon, C. H. *Morning and Evening.* (London: Passmore & Alabaster), June 16 (Evening).

[861] https://www.christianquotes.info/top-quotes/22-powerful-quotes-overcoming-fear/, accessed November 12, 2020.

[862] Maclaren, Alexander. *Maclaren's Expositions,* "The Answer to Trust," Psalm 91:14.

[863] Spurgeon, C. H. *The Treasury of David,* Psalm 91:15.

[864] Poole, Matthew. *Matthew Poole's Commentary,* Psalm 91:15.

[865] Simeon, C. *Horae Homileticae: Psalms, LXXIII–CL,* Vol. 6. (London: Samuel Holdsworth, 1836), 143.

[866] Spurgeon, C. H. *Morning and Evening.* (London: Passmore & Alabaster), January 24 (Morning).

Endnotes

[867] Henry, M. *Matthew Henry's Commentary on the Whole Bible: Complete and Unabridged in One Volume.* (Peabody: Hendrickson, 1994), 877.

[868] *Gill's Exposition of the Entire Bible,* Psalm 91:15.

[869] Henry, M. *Matthew Henry's Commentary on the Whole Bible: Complete and Unabridged in One Volume.* (Peabody: Hendrickson, 1994), 878.

[870] Ibid.

[871] Simeon, C. *Horae Homileticae: Psalms, LXXIII–CL,* Vol. 6. (London: Samuel Holdsworth, 1836), 143.

[872] Hamilton, William W. *Sermons on the Books of The Bible:* Vol. 3, 212.

[873] Piper, John. "What Is So Important About Christian Hope?" March 7, 2008. https://www.desiringgod.org/interviews/what-is-so-important-about-christian-hope, accessed October 20, 2020.

[874] Spurgeon, C. H. "The High Rock" (Sermon # 2728). New Park Street Chapel, 1859. https://www.spurgeongems.org/vols46-48/chs2728.pdf, accessed September 29, 2018.

[875] Cowman, L. B. *Streams in the Desert.* (Grand Rapids: Zondervan, 1997), February 7.

[876] Smith, Clay. "Hope: Hope 101," (Psalm 25:1–7). Sermon preached October 7, 2018, Alice Drive Baptist Church, Sumter, SC.

[877] https://www.christianquotes.info/top-quotes/16-encouraging-quotes-about-hope/, accessed November 13, 2020.

[878] Spurgeon, C. H. "The High Rock" (Sermon # 2728). New Park Street Chapel, 1859. https://www.spurgeongems.org/vols46-48/chs2728.pdf, accessed September 29, 2018.

[879] Cowman, L. B. *Streams in the Desert.* (Grand Rapids: Zondervan, 1997), March 24.

[880] https://www.brainyquote.com/topics/hope-quotes_3, accessed November 13, 2020.

[881] http://victoryminded.com/53-christian-quotes-on-hope-including-bible-verses/, accessed November 13, 2020.

[882] https://www.brainyquote.com/topics/hope-quotes_5, accessed November 13, 2020.

[883] http://victoryminded.com/53-christian-quotes-on-hope-including-bible-verses/, accessed November 13, 2020.

[884] Barnes, Albert. *Notes on the Bible.* (1834), Romans 8:25.

[885] *Forerunner Commentary,* 1 Thessalonians 1:2-3.

[886] Criswell, W. A. "Comfort in Affliction." dailyword@wacriswell.com. Excerpt from the sermon, Divine Healing.

[887] Ibid.

[888] Barnes, Albert. *Notes on the Bible.* (1834), 1 Thessalonians 4:13.

[889] Langham Partnership Daily Thought, 17 November 2020. dailythought@langham.org, accessed November 17, 2020.

[890] Ibid.

[891] Barnes, Albert. *Notes on the Bible.* (1834), 1 Thessalonians 4:13.

[892] https://www.gty.org/library/questions/QA155/i-feel-abandoned-in-my-trial-why-does-god-seem-so-distant-when-i-need-him-most, accessed November 18, 2020.

[893] Spurgeon, C. H. *The Treasury of David,* Psalm 88:6.

[894] Exell, J. S. *The Biblical Illustrator: Job.* (New York; Chicago; Toronto; London; Edinburgh: Fleming H. Revell Company), 417.

[895] Spurgeon, C. H. *The Treasury of David,* Psalm 88:6.

Endnotes

896 Exell, J. S. *The Biblical Illustrator: Job.* (New York; Chicago; Toronto; London; Edinburgh: Fleming H. Revell Company), 419.

897 Spurgeon, C. H. *Morning and Evening.* (London: Passmore & Alabaster), November 19 (Evening).

898 Ibid.

899 Spence-Jones, H. D. M. (Ed.). The Pulpit Commentary: Job. (London; New York: Funk & Wagnalls Company, 1909), 403.

900 Spurgeon, C. H. "A Happy Christian," (sermon).

901 Packer, J. I. *Knowing God.* (Downers Grove, Ill: IVP Books, 1973), 80.

902 Quotefancy.com, accessed November 20, 2020.

903 https://www.gty.org/library/questions/QA155/i-feel-abandoned-in-my-trial-why-does-god-seem-so-distant-when-i-need-him-most, accessed November 18, 2020.

904 Criswell, W. A. "The Unchanging Christ." The Daily Word, November 24, 2018.

905 Hutson, Curtis. *Great Preaching on Thanksgiving.* (Murfreesboro: Sword of the Lord Publishers, 1987), 36.

906 Plumer, W. S. Studies in the Book of Psalms: Being a Critical and Expository Commentary, with Doctrinal and Practical Remarks on the Entire Psalter. (Philadelphia; Edinburgh: J. B. Lippincott Company; A & C Black, 1872), 729.

907 Henry, Matthew. *Matthew Henry's Concise Bible Commentary,* Psalm 77:11.

908 Spurgeon, C. H. *Psalms.* (Wheaton, IL: Crossway Books, 1993), 326.

909 Spurgeon, C. H. *The Treasury of David,* Psalm 75:1.

910 Love Worth Finding. "He Has Called You by Name and You Are His." June 15,2012. https://www.crosswalk.com/devotionals/loveworthfinding/love-worth-finding-june-15-2012.html, accessed November 21, 2020.

911 Swanson, J. *Dictionary of Biblical Languages with Semantic Domains: Hebrew* (Old Testament). (electronic ed.). (Oak Harbor: Logos Research Systems, Inc., 1997.

912 Rogers, Adrian. "Is Trusting God a Challenge for You?" Love Worth Finding, February 24. https://www.oneplace.com/ministries/love-worth-finding/read/devotionals/love-worth-finding/is-trusting-god-a-challenge-for-you-love-worth-finding-february-24-11822393.html, accessed November 29, 2020.

913 Ibid.

914 https://www.wisesayings.com/trusting-god-quotes/#ixzz6f7XOxU00, accessed November 28, 2020.

915 *Maclaren's Expositions,* "Mountains Around Mount Zion," Psalm 125.

916 Plumer, W. S. Studies in the Book of Psalms: Being a Critical and Expository Commentary, with Doctrinal and Practical Remarks on the Entire Psalter. (Philadelphia; Edinburgh: J. B. Lippincott Company; A & C Black, 1872), 1109.

917 Exell, J. S. *The Biblical Illustrator:* Psalm 9:10.

918 Plumer, W. S. Studies in the Book of Psalms: Being a Critical and Expository Commentary, with Doctrinal and Practical Remarks on the Entire Psalter. (Philadelphia; Edinburgh: J. B. Lippincott Company; A & C Black, 1872), 138.

919 Spence-Jones, H. D. M. (Ed.). The Pulpit Commentary: Psalms, Vol. 1. (London; New York: Funk & Wagnalls Company, 1909), 64.

920 Barnes, Albert. *Notes on the Bible.* (1834), Psalm 9:10.

[921] Henry, M. *Matthew Henry's Commentary on the Whole Bible: Complete and Unabridged in One Volume.* (Peabody: Hendrickson, 1994), 756.

[922] Jennings, A. C. & W. H. Lowe. *The Psalms, with Introductions and Critical Notes, Second Edition,* Vol. 1. (London: Macmillan and Co., 1884), 35.

[923] Plumer, W. S. Studies in the Book of Psalms: Being a Critical and Expository Commentary, with Doctrinal and Practical Remarks on the Entire Psalter. (Philadelphia; Edinburgh: J. B. Lippincott Company; A & C Black, 1872), 138.

[924] Boice, J. M. *Psalms 1–41: An Expositional Commentary.* (Grand Rapids, MI: Baker Books, 2005), 79.

[925] Spence-Jones, H. D. M. (Ed.). The Pulpit Commentary: Psalms, Vol. 1. (London; New York: Funk & Wagnalls Company, 1909), 64.

[926] Spurgeon, C. H. *New Park Street Pulpit,* Vol. 6. "Dilemma and Deliverance" (Sermon No. 287, December 4, 1859)

[927] Plumer, W. S. Studies in the Book of Psalms: Being a Critical and Expository Commentary, with Doctrinal and Practical Remarks on the Entire Psalter. (Philadelphia; Edinburgh: J. B. Lippincott Company; A & C Black, 1872), 138.

[928] Spence-Jones, H. D. M. (Ed.). The Pulpit Commentary: Psalms, Vol. 1. (London; New York: Funk & Wagnalls Company, 1909), 59.

[929] https://www.wisesayings.com/trusting-god-quotes/#ixzz6f7Xx9wf, accessed November 28, 2020.

[930] Cowman, L. B. *Streams in the Desert.* (Grand Rapids: Zondervan, 1997), April 24.

[931] Newman, John Henry. https://www.christianquotes.info/top-quotes/18-powerful-quotes-trust/, accessed November 28, 2020.

[932] Jeremiah, David. "Trusting God When Your Prayers Aren't Answered." DavidJeremiah.blog, accessed November 28, 2020.

[933] Henry, M. *Matthew Henry's Commentary on the Whole Bible: Complete and Unabridged in One Volume.* (Peabody: Hendrickson, 1994), 756.

[934] Spurgeon, C. H. *Metropolitan Tabernacle Pulpit,* Vol. 8. "Choice Portions," (sermon delivered May 25, 1862).

[935] Ibid.

[936] Exell, J. S. *The Biblical Illustrator: The Lamentations of Jeremiah.* (London: James Nisbet & Co.), 55.

[937] Interview with John Piper. "How Do I Delight Myself in the Lord?," July 9, 2013. https://www.desiringgod.org/interviews/how-do-i-delight-myself-in-the-lord, accessed November 30, 2020.

[938] Exell, J. S. *The Biblical Illustrator: The Lamentations of Jeremiah.* (London: James Nisbet & Co.), 60.

[939] Ibid.

[940] Ibid., 52.

[941] Bridges, C. *Exposition of Psalm 119: As Illustrative of the Character and Exercises of Christian Experience,* Seventeenth Edition. (New York: Robert Carter & Brothers, 1861), 82.

[942] Spurgeon, C. H. *The Treasury of David,* Psalm 119:50.

[943] Buchanan, James. *Comfort in Affliction.* (Edinburgh: Johnstone & Hunter, 1751), 9.

[944] Ibid.

945 Spurgeon, C. H. *The Treasury of David,* Psalm 119:50.

946 Exell, J. S. *The Biblical Illustrator: The Psalms,* Vol. 5. (New York; Chicago; Toronto; London; Edinburgh: Fleming H. Revell Company), 56.

947 Plumer, W. S. Studies in the Book of Psalms: Being a Critical and Expository Commentary, with Doctrinal and Practical Remarks on the Entire Psalter. (Philadelphia; Edinburgh: J. B. Lippincott Company; A & C Black, 1872), 1043.

948 Pink, Arthur W. "The Power of God's Word to Convict Men of Sin: The Divine Inspiration of the Bible." http://biblehub.com/library/pink/the_divine_inspiration_of_ the_bible/i_the_ power_of_gods.htm, accessed July 16, 2018.

949 Bridges, Charles, *Exposition on Psalm 119,* Psalm 119:50.

950 "The Bible and Illumination." October 17, 2014. https://preceptaustin.wordpress.com/ category/the-names-of-god/, accessed December 1, 2020.

951 Ibid.

952 Ekstrand, D.W. "The Power of God's Word." http://www.thetransformedsoul.com/ additional-studies/spiritual-life-studies/the-power-of-god-s-word, accessed December 1, 2020.

953 Spurgeon, C. H. "God's People, or Not God's People," (Sermon # 2295). Intended for reading February 12, 1893, at the Metropolitan Tabernacle.

954 Horne, G. *A Commentary on the Book of Psalms.* (New York: Robert Carter & Brothers, 1856), 437–438.

955 Spurgeon, C. H. *Morning and Evening.* (London: Passmore & Alabaster), April 28 (Morning).

956 Clarke, Adam. *Commentary on the Bible,* (1831), Habakkuk 3:17–18.

957 Exell, J. S. *The Biblical Illustrator: The Minor Prophets,* Vol. 8. (New York; Chicago; Toronto; London; Edinburgh: Fleming H. Revell Company), 57.

958 Ibid., 56.

959 Ibid.

960 Barnes, Albert. *Notes on the Bible.* (1834), Psalm 30:5.

961 Wiersbe, W. W. *Wiersbe's Expository Outlines on the Old Testament.* (Wheaton, IL: Victor Books, 1993), Hab. 3.

962 Exell, J. S. *The Biblical Illustrator: The Minor Prophets,* Vol. 8. (New York; Chicago; Toronto; London; Edinburgh: Fleming H. Revell Company), 55–56.

963 Alexander, J. A. *The Psalms Translated and Explained.* (Edinburgh: Andrew Elliot; James Thin, 1864), 512.

964 Exell, J. S. *The Biblical Illustrator: The Psalms,* Vol. 5. (New York; Chicago; Toronto; London; Edinburgh: Fleming H. Revell Company), 182.

965 Spurgeon, C. H. *The Treasury of David,* Psalm 124:1.

966 Gill, John. *Exposition of the Entire Bible by John Gill,* [1746–63], Psalm 124:1.

967 Bonar, Horatius. *Why God's Children Suffer.* (Chicago: Moody Press, 1845), Preface.

968 Exell, J. S. *The Biblical Illustrator: Matthew.* (Grand Rapids, MI: Baker Book House), 224.

969 Ibid.

970 Stott, John and Timothy Dudley-Smith. *Daily Thought,* October 27, 2020. (Inter-Varsity Press, 1995). Accessed October 27, 2020.

971 Exell, J. S. *The Biblical Illustrator: Matthew.* (Grand Rapids, MI: Baker Book House), 224.

www.ingramcontent.com/pod-product-compliance
Lightning Source LLC
Chambersburg PA
CBHW031232090426

42742CB00007B/161